Modernization, Cultural Change, and Democracy
The Human Development Sequence

This book demonstrates that people's basic values and beliefs are changing, in ways that affect their political, sexual, economic, and religious behavior. These changes are roughly predictable: to a large extent, they can be explained by the revised version of modernization theory presented here. Drawing on a massive body of evidence from societies containing 85 percent of the world's population, the authors demonstrate that modernization is a process of human development, in which economic development gives rise to cultural changes that make individual autonomy, gender equality, and democracy increasingly likely. The authors present a model of social change that predicts how value systems are likely to evolve in coming decades. They demonstrate that mass values play a crucial role in the emergence and flourishing of democratic institutions.

Ronald Inglehart is a professor of political science and program director at the Institute for Social Research at the University of Michigan. He helped found the Eurobarometer surveys and is the president of the World Values Survey Association. His most recent books are *Modernization and Postmodernization: Cultural, Economic and Political Change in 43 Societies* (1997), *Rising Tide: Gender Equality in Global Perspective* (with Pippa Norris, Cambridge University Press, 2003), and *Sacred and Secular: Religion and Politics Worldwide* (with Pippa Norris, Cambridge University Press, 2004). The author of almost 200 publications, Inglehart has been a visiting professor or scholar in France, Germany, the Netherlands, Switzerland, Japan, South Korea, Taiwan, Brazil, and Nigeria, and he has served as a consultant to the U.S. State Department and the European Union.

Christian Welzel is associate professor of political science and program coordinator at International University Bremen and is a member of the Executive Committee of the World Values Survey Association. He was a senior research Fellow at the Social Science Research Center Berlin and visiting professor at the University of Potsdam. He is a two-time recipient of a grant from the Institute for Social Research, and he has published numerous articles in the *European Journal of Political Research*, *Comparative Politics*, *Comparative Sociology*, *International Journal of Comparative Sociology*, and *Political Culture and Democracy*, among others. He has also published extensively in German.

Modernization, Cultural Change, and Democracy

The Human Development Sequence

RONALD INGLEHART
University of Michigan

CHRISTIAN WELZEL
International University Bremen

CAMBRIDGE
UNIVERSITY PRESS

CAMBRIDGE UNIVERSITY PRESS
Cambridge, New York, Melbourne, Madrid, Cape Town, Singapore, São Paulo

Cambridge University Press
40 West 20th Street, New York, NY 10011-4211, USA

www.cambridge.org
Information on this title: www.cambridge.org/9780521846950

First published 2005
Reprinted 2006 (twice)

Printed in the United States of America

A catalog record for this publication is available from the British Library.

Library of Congress Cataloging in Publication Data

Inglehart, Ronald.
    Modernization, cultural change, and democracy : the human development sequence /
Ronald Inglehart and Christian Welzel.
        p.   cm.
    ISBN 0-521-84695-1 (hardback) – ISBN 0-521-60971-2 (pbk.)
    1. Social change.   2. Social values.   3. Democratization.   4. Democracy.
I. Welzel, Christian, 1964–.   II. Title.
    HM681.I54   2005
    303.4 – dc22   2004024333

ISBN-13   978-0-521-84695-0 hardback
ISBN-10   0-521-84695-1 hardback

ISBN-13   978-0-521-60971-5 paperback
ISBN-10   0-521-60971-2 paperback

Contents

Acknowledgments   page vii

Foreword by Hans-Dieter Klingemann   ix

Introduction   1

PART I   THE FORCES SHAPING VALUE CHANGE

1   A Revised Theory of Modernization   15
2   Value Change and the Persistence of Cultural Traditions   48
3   Exploring the Unknown: Predicting Mass Responses   77
4   Intergenerational Value Change   94
5   Value Changes over Time   115
6   Individualism, Self-Expression Values, and Civic Virtues   135

PART II   THE CONSEQUENCES OF VALUE CHANGE

7   The Causal Link between Democratic Values and
    Democratic Institutions: Theoretical Discussion   149
8   The Causal Link between Democratic Values and
    Democratic Institutions: Empirical Analyses   173
9   Social Forces, Collective Action, and International Events   210
10 Individual-Level Values and System-Level Democracy:
    The Problem of Cross-Level Analysis   231
11 Components of a Prodemocratic Civic Culture   245
12 Gender Equality, Emancipative Values, and Democracy   272
13 The Implications of Human Development   285
    Conclusion: An Emancipative Theory of Democracy   299

Bibliography   301
Index   323

This book is dedicated to our wives, Caroline and Marita,
and our children, Elizabeth, Janika Michelle,
Felipa Fé, Marita, Rachel and Ronald

Acknowledgments

We would like to express our thanks to many friends and colleagues. This book analyzes a unique database that has been generated through the World Values Surveys (WVS) and the European Values Surveys (EVS). We owe a large debt of gratitude to the following WVS and EVS participants for creating and sharing this rich and complex dataset: Anthony M. Abela, Q. K. Ahmad, Rasa Alishauskene, Helmut Anheier, Jose Arocena, Wil A. Arts, Soo Young Auh, Taghi Azadarmaki, Ljiljana Bacevic, Olga Balakireva, Josip Baloban, Miguel Basanez, Elena Bashkirova, Abdallah Bedaida, Jorge Benitez, Jaak Billiet, Alan Black, Ammar Boukhedir, Rahma Bourquia, Fares al Braizat, Pavel Campeanu, Augustin Canzani, Marita Carballo, Henrique Carlos de O. de Castro, Pi-Chao Chen, Pradeep Chhibber, Mark F. Chingono, Hei-yuan Chiu, Margit Cleveland, Andrew P. Davidson, Jaime Diez Medrano, Juan Diez Nicolas, Herman De Dijn, Karel Dobbelaere, Peter J. D. Drenth, Javier Elzo, Yilmaz Esmer, P. Estgen, T. Fahey, Nadjematul Faizah, Georgy Fotev, James Georgas, C. Geppaart, Renzo Gubert, Linda Luz Guerrero, Peter Gundelach, Jacques Hagenaars, Loek Halman, Mustafa Hamarneh, Sang-Jin Han, Stephen Harding, Mari Harris, Bernadette C. Hayes, Camilo Herrera, Virginia Hodgkinson, Nadra Muhammed Hosen, Kenji Iijima, Ljubov Ishimova, Wolfgang Jagodzinski, Aleksandra Jasinska-Kania, Fridrik Jonsson, Stanislovas Juknevicius, Jan Kerkhofs S.J., Johann Kinghorn, Hans-Dieter Klingemann, Hennie Kotze, Zuzana Kusá, Marta Lagos, Bernard Lategan, Abdel-Hamid Abdel-Latif, M. Legrand, Carlos Lemoine, Noah Lewin-Epstein, Ola Listhaug, Jin-yun Liu, Brina Malnar, Mahar Mangahas, Mario Marinov, Carlos Matheus, Robert Mattes, Rafael Mendizabal, Felipe Miranda, Mansoor Moaddel, José Molina, Alejandro Moreno, Gaspar K. Munishi, Neil Nevitte, Elone Nwabuzor, F. A. Orizo, Dragomir Pantic, Juhani Pehkonen, Paul Perry, Thorleif Pettersson, Pham Minh Hac, Pham Thanh Nghi, Gevork Pogosian, Bi Puranen, Ladislav Rabusic, Angel Rivera-Ortiz, Catalina Romero, David Rotman, Rajab Sattarov, Sandeep Shastri, Shen Mingming, Renata Siemienska, John Sudarsky, Tan Ern Ser, Farooq Tanwir, Jean-François Tchernia, Kareem Tejumola, Larissa Titarenko, Miklos Tomka, Alfredo Torres, Niko Tos, Jorge Vala, Andrei

Vardomatskii, Malina Voicu, Alan Webster, Friedrich Welsch, Seiko Yamazaki, Ephraim Yuchtman-Yaar, Josefina Zaiter, Brigita Zepa, and Paul Zulehner. Most of these surveys were supported by sources within the given country, but assistance for surveys where such funding was not available, and for central coordination, was provided by the National Science Foundation, the Bank of Sweden Tercentenary Foundation, the Swedish Agency for International Development, the Volkswagen Foundation, and the BBVA Foundation. For more information about the World Values Survey, see the WVS Web site, http://www.worldvaluessurvey.org, and Ronald Inglehart et al. (eds.), _Human Values and Beliefs: A Cross-Cultural Sourcebook Based on the 1999–2001 Values Surveys_ (Mexico City: Siglo XXI, 2004). The European surveys used here were gathered by the European Values Survey group. For detailed EVS findings, see Loek Halman, _The European Values Study: A Sourcebook Based on the 1999/2000 European Values Study Surveys_ (Tilburg: EVS, Tilburg University Press, 2001). For more information, see the EVS Web site, http://evs.kub.nl.

Moreover, we are grateful to many colleagues who provided valuable comments, including Johan Akerblom, Dirk Berg-Schlosser, Klaus Boehnke, Russell J. Dalton, Franziska Deutsch, Barry Hughes, Gerald Inglehart, William Inglehart, Max Kaase, Markus Klein, Hanspeter Kriesi, Seymour Martin Lipset, Kenneth Newton, Pippa Norris, Guillermo O'Donnell, Daphna Oyserman, Bi Puranen, Dieter Rucht, Manfred G. Schmidt, Carsten Schneider, Dietlind Stolle, Charles L. Taylor, Eric Uslaner, Stefan Walgrave, and Ulrich Widmaier. We owe special thanks to the former department "Institutions and Social Change" at the Social Science Research Center, Berlin (WZB). Under the direction of Hans-Dieter Klingemann, this department produced a number of outstanding studies of the social foundations of democracy. In this context, we profited from valuable comments and critique by Dieter Fuchs, Hans-Dieter Klingemann, Edeltraud Roller, Kai-Uwe Schnapp, and Bernhard Wessels.

The support of Cambridge University Press has been invaluable, particularly the advice and enthusiasm of our editor, Lewis Bateman, as well as the comments of the anonymous reviewers. Much of the analysis for this book was carried out at the Social Science Research Center, Berlin; we are grateful for the center's support. Lastly, this book would not have been possible without the encouragement and stimulation provided by many colleagues and students at the International University Bremen (IUB) and the Department of Political Science and the Institute for Social Research at the University of Michigan.

Ronald Inglehart and Christian Welzel
Ann Arbor, Michigan, and Bremen, Germany

Foreword

This book makes a major contribution to our understanding of social and political change. It tests the impact of culture on political and social life, analyzing the broadest empirical base ever assembled for this purpose. It interprets the evidence in a bold new theoretical framework – a revised version of modernization theory. Analyzing a massive body of data from the perspective of human development theory, the authors produce something that has been declared dead: grand theory.

They demonstrate that fundamental changes are occurring in the belief systems of publics around the world. They show how these changes are shaped by an interaction between the forces of socioeconomic development and persisting cultural traditions. And using data from representative national surveys in eighty societies, the authors demonstrate that changing mass values are producing growing pressures for the establishment and strengthening of democracy.

Earlier versions of modernization theory did not foresee the massively strong linkage that the authors find between rising self-expression values and the emergence and flourishing of democratic institutions. Building on previous work by Welzel, the authors convincingly argue that socioeconomic modernization, rising liberty aspirations, and the quest for democratic institutions all reflect the common underlying process of human development, the theme of which is the broadening of human choice.

This book succeeds in integrating a vast amount of empirical evidence into a coherent theoretical framework, enriching our understanding of how democracy emerges and survives. Its findings have major substantive importance. The authors claim that socioeconomic development and the rise of the knowledge society have roughly predictable consequences. They then develop a model that enables them to make a number of explicit predictions about what will be observed in the future, in the realm of cultural change and democratization.

This is a bold undertaking. Successful predictions are rare in the social sciences. But these predictions build on a foundation that has led to a number of previous predictions being proved accurate. In 1971 Inglehart predicted that intergenerational change would lead to the spread of postmaterialist values. At

the time, materialists outnumbered postmaterialists heavily – by about four to
one – in the six Western societies from which he had data. Today, postmaterialists have become as numerous as materialists in all six of these societies. I
am pleased to have worked with Inglehart as part of the Political Action Study
group that, having analyzed patterns of political behavior and social change
in the 1970s, predicted the spread of what was then called "unconventional
political behavior," including such actions as petitions, boycotts, and demonstrations (Barnes and Kaase et al., 1979). Three decades later, participation in
these forms of behavior has roughly doubled in the eight countries included in
the Political Action Study. At this point, it is impossible to say how accurate
the predictions presented in this book will prove to be – but I would not readily
discount them.

The book is a landmark in the study of political culture and democratization.
It will polarize opinion, provoking both strong acclaim and fierce critique, for
this work presents powerful evidence contradicting several major schools of
thought in the social sciences. It will be debated and cited now and in years to
come.

Hans-Dieter Klingemann
August 2004
Fondation National des Sciences Politiques
Institut d'Etudes Politiques de Paris

Introduction

This book presents a revised version of modernization theory that integrates socioeconomic development, cultural change, and democratization under the overarching theme of human development. Although the classic view of modernization developed by Marx, Weber, and others was wrong on many points, the central insight – that socioeconomic development brings major social, cultural, and political changes – is basically correct. This insight is confirmed by a massive body of new evidence analyzed in this book, including survey data from eighty-one societies containing 85 percent of the world's population, collected from 1981 to 2001, that demonstrates that the basic values and beliefs of the publics of advanced societies differ dramatically from those found in less-developed societies – and that these values are changing in a predictable direction as socioeconomic development takes place. Changing values, in turn, have important consequences for the way societies are governed, promoting gender equality, democratic freedom, and good governance.

Early versions of modernization theory were too simple. Socioeconomic development has a powerful impact on what people want and do, as Karl Marx argued, but a society's cultural heritage continues to shape its prevailing beliefs and motivations, as Max Weber argued. Moreover, sociocultural change is not linear. Industrialization brings rationalization, secularization, and bureaucratization, but the rise of the knowledge society brings another set of changes that move in a new direction, placing increasing emphasis on individual autonomy, self-expression, and free choice. Emerging self-expression values transform modernization into a process of human development, giving rise to a new type of humanistic society that is increasingly people-centered.

The first phase of modernization mobilized the masses, making modern democracy possible – along with fascism and communism. The postindustrial phase of modernization produces increasingly powerful mass demands for democracy, the form of government that provides the broadest latitude for individuals to choose how to live their lives.

This book demonstrates that coherent changes are taking place in political, religious, social, and sexual norms throughout postindustrial societies.

It presents a model of social change that predicts how the value systems of given societies will evolve in coming decades. And it demonstrates that mass values play a crucial role in the emergence and flourishing of democratic institutions. Modernization is evolving into a process of human development, in which socioeconomic development brings cultural changes that make individual autonomy, gender equality, and democracy increasingly likely, giving rise to a new type of society that promotes human emancipation on many fronts.

Democracy is not simply the result of clever elite bargaining and constitutional engineering. It depends on deep-rooted orientations among the people themselves. These orientations motivate them to demand freedom and responsive government – and to act to ensure that the governing elites remain responsive to them. Genuine democracy is not simply a machine that, once set up, functions by itself. It depends on the people.

This book presents a unified theory of modernization, cultural change, and democratization. Building on recent work by Welzel, we interpret contemporary social change as a process of human development, which is producing increasingly humanistic societies that place growing emphasis on human freedom and self-expression. A massive body of cross-national data demonstrates that (1) socioeconomic modernization, (2) a cultural shift toward rising emphasis on self-expression values, and (3) democratization are all components of a single underlying process: human development. The underlying theme of this process is the broadening of human choice. Socioeconomic modernization reduces the external constraints on human choice by increasing people's material, cognitive, and social resources. This brings growing mass emphasis on self-expression values, which in turn lead to growing public demands for civil and political liberties, gender equality, and responsive government, helping to establish and sustain the institutions best suited to maximize human choice – in a word, democracy.

The core of the human development sequence is the expansion of human choice and autonomy. As this aspect of modernization becomes more prominent, it brings cultural changes that make democracy the logical institutional outcome. In previous accounts of modernization, the central role played by cultural change has been either overlooked or underestimated.

To a large extent, culture is transmitted from one generation to the next. But people's basic values reflect not only what they are taught but also their firsthand experiences. During the past half century, socioeconomic development has been changing people's formative conditions profoundly and with unprecedented speed. Economic growth, rising levels of education and information, and diversifying human interactions increase people's material, cognitive, and social resources, making them materially, intellectually, and socially more independent. Rising levels of existential security and autonomy change people's firsthand life experiences fundamentally, leading them to emphasize goals that were previously given lower priority, including the pursuit of freedom. Cultural emphasis shifts from collective discipline to individual liberty, from group conformity to human diversity, and from state authority to individual autonomy,

TABLE 1.1. *The Process of Human Development*

	Human Development		
	Socioeconomic Dimension	Cultural Dimension	Institutional Dimension
Processes advancing human development	Modernization	Value change	Democratization
Components of human development	Socioeconomic resources	Self-expression values	Civil and political liberties
Contributions to human development	Enhancing people's *capabilities* to act according to their choices	Increasing people's *priority* to act according to their choices	Broadening people's *entitlements* to act according to their choices
Underlying theme	The broadening of human choice (an increasingly humanistic society)		

Source: Adapted from Welzel (2002: 46).

giving rise to a syndrome that we call self-expression values. These values bring increasing emphasis on the civil and political liberties that constitute democracy, which provides broader latitude for people to pursue freedom of expression and self-realization. Rising self-expression values transform modernization into a process of human development, generating a society that is increasingly people-centered. This reflects a humanistic transformation of modernity.

In short, socioeconomic modernization brings the objective capabilities that enable people to base their lives on autonomous choices. Rising emphasis on self-expression values leads people to demand and defend freedom of choice. And democratic institutions establish the rights that entitle people to exert free choice in their activities. These three processes all focus on the growth of autonomous human choice. Because autonomous choice is a specifically human ability, we characterize the processes that develop this potential as "human" development (Table 1.1).

As we will demonstrate, a humanistic culture that emphasizes self-expression values radiates into all major domains of life, helping to reshape sexual norms, gender roles, family values, religiosity, work motivations, people's relation to nature and the environment, and their communal activities and political participation. Growing emphasis on human autonomy is evident in all these domains, transforming the fabric of contemporary societies. People in postindustrial societies are coming to demand freer choice in all aspects of life. Gender roles, religious orientations, consumer patterns, working habits, and voting behavior all become increasingly matters of individual choice. Massive contemporary changes – from growing gender equality and changing norms concerning sexual orientation, to growing concern for genuine, effective democracy – reflect growing emphasis on human autonomy. These changes are not a patchwork of loosely related phenomena but a coherent pattern that integrates seemingly isolated events into a common whole. As it coalesces, this process of human development broadens human choice and autonomy in all domains of life.

Nevertheless, despite globalization the world is not becoming homogeneous, and the imprint of cultural traditions is not disappearing. Quite the contrary, high levels of human development reflect a relatively recent trend that so far has been concentrated in postindustrial societies and only emerges in developing societies insofar as they experience sustained economic growth. Most low-income societies and many post-Soviet societies show relatively little impact from the trend toward greater human autonomy and choice. The value systems of these societies continue to impose strong constraints on human self-expression. The diversity of basic cultural values helps to explain the huge differences that exist in how institutions perform in societies around the world. The degree to which given publics give high priority to self-expression largely shapes the extent to which societies provide democratic rights, the degree to which women are represented in positions of power, and the extent to which elites govern responsively and according to the rule of law. Going beyond elitist and institutional explanations of democracy, we demonstrate that democracy, gender equality, and responsive government are elements of a broader human development syndrome. This book explores how the shifting balance between modernization and tradition shapes human values, and how these values affect political institutions, generating a human development sequence in which modernization gives rise to self-expression values, which are favorable to democratic institutions.

This sequence can also operate in the reverse direction, with threats to survival leading to increased emphasis on survival values, which in turn are conducive to authoritarian institutions. Operating in either direction, the sequence has a common theme: the broadening or narrowing of human autonomy and choice. Operating in one direction, it brings human development and increasingly humanistic societies. Operating in the reverse direction, it brings retrogression toward authoritarian and xenophobic societies.

This book has two major parts. The first part, "The Forces Shaping Value Change," explores the major dimensions of cross-national variation in basic values, charts how values are changing, and examines how modernization and tradition interact to shape these changes. The second part, "The Consequences of Value Change," examines the impact of one major dimension of cross-cultural variation – self-expression values – on democracy. We find strikingly strong linkages between these values and democracy, regardless of how it is measured. In fact, self-expression values prove to be more strongly linked with democracy than any other factor, including variables that figure prominently in the literature on democratization, such as interpersonal trust, associational membership, and per capita GDP. Economic prosperity is strongly linked with the emergence and survival of democratic institutions, but it operates primarily through its tendency to give rise to self-expression values. Controlling for self-expression values, the impact of economic development and other structural factors, such as ethnic fractionalization, diminishes sharply. This finding is far from obvious and suggests that future research on democracy and democratization needs to give more attention to the role of mass values.

Extensive analysis of the causal linkage between self-expression values and democracy indicates that the causal arrow flows mainly from culture to institutions rather than the other way around, an issue that has been highly controversial in recent research. These findings contradict the claim that democracy can easily be established in any society, regardless of its underlying culture: it has been claimed that if one provides well-designed formal institutions, a democratic political culture is of secondary importance. Contrary to this claim, the empirical evidence presented here indicates that democratization requires more than just imposing the right constitution. This conclusion is also supported by extensive historical experience, from that of Weimar Germany, to the Soviet successor states, to contemporary Iraq.

A Brief Overview of the Book

Chapter 1 presents a new and unified version of modernization theory. Although previous versions of modernization theory were deficient in several important respects, a massive body of evidence indicates that its most central premise was correct: socioeconomic development brings major changes in society, culture, and politics. Four waves of survey data from more than eighty societies demonstrate that socioeconomic development tends to transform people's basic values and beliefs – and it does so in a roughly predictable fashion. Nevertheless, earlier versions of modernization theory need to be revised in at least three major aspects.

First, although socioeconomic development tends to bring predictable changes in people's worldviews, cultural traditions – such as whether a society has been historically shaped by Protestantism, Confucianism, or communism – continue to show a lasting imprint on a society's worldview. History matters, and a society's prevailing value orientations reflect an interaction between the driving forces of modernization and the retarding influence of tradition.

Second, modernization is not linear. It does not move indefinitely in the same direction but reaches inflection points at which the prevailing direction of change, changes. Thus, modernization goes through different phases, each of which brings distinctive changes in people's worldviews. The Industrial Revolution was linked with a shift from traditional to secular-rational values, bringing the secularization of authority. In the postindustrial phase of modernization, another cultural change becomes dominant – a shift from survival values to self-expression values, which brings increasing emancipation *from* authority. Rising self-expression values transform modernization into a process of human development that increases human freedom and choice.

Third, the inherently emancipative nature of self-expression values makes democracy increasingly likely to emerge; indeed, beyond a certain point it becomes increasingly difficult to *avoid* democratization. Thus, modernization brings cultural changes that lead to the emergence and flourishing of democratic institutions. The growth of human autonomy is the theme underlying the processes of modernization, rising self-expression values, and democratization. These processes give rise to increasingly humanistic societies, that is, societies with a people-centered orientation.

Chapter 2 analyzes the most important dimensions of cross-cultural variation, producing a two-dimensional global map that reflects differences in scores of diverse norms and values. Cross-cultural variation proves to be surprisingly coherent, and a wide range of attitudes (reflecting people's beliefs and values in such different life domains as the family, work, religion, environment, politics, and sexual behavior) reflects just two major dimensions: one that taps the polarization between *traditional values* and *secular-rational values*; and a second dimension that taps the polarization between *survival values* and *self-expression values*. More than eighty societies containing 85 percent of the world's population are plotted on these two dimensions. To a remarkable degree, these societies cluster into relatively homogeneous cultural zones, reflecting their historical heritage – and these cultural zones persist robustly over time. Despite the lasting imprint of a society's cultural heritage, socioeconomic development tends to shift a society's position on these two value dimensions in a predictable fashion: as the work force shifts from the agrarian sector to the industrial sector, people's worldviews tend to shift from an emphasis on traditional values to an emphasis on secular-rational values. Subsequently, as the work force shifts from the industrial sector to the service sector, a second major shift in values occurs, from emphasis on survival values to emphasis on self-expression values.

Chapter 3 undertakes something that is considered the decisive test of theories in the natural sciences, but which social scientists have tended to resist: *prediction*. In the *Logic of Scientific Discovery*, Popper (1992 [1959]) argues that in order to be empirically validated, theories must be able to make reasonably accurate predictions of future events. Nevertheless, social scientists rarely test their theories against genuine predictions. Because modernization theory purports to provide a systematic interpretation of how socioeconomic development reshapes societies, we use this theory to make and test predictions about cultural change.

First, we use data from the first three waves of surveys to "predict" future responses, using regression analyses of existing data to devise predictive formulas that utilize indicators of a society's socioeconomic development together with variables that tap its historical cultural heritage. We use these formulas to "predict" the responses found in the Fourth Wave, carried out in 1999–2001. These, of course, are not genuine predictions but postdictions that explain findings in data already gathered. But a comparison of the predicted and observed values demonstrates that most predictions are in the right ball park (even for societies that were not surveyed in the first three waves) and that a model based on our revised version of modernization theory generates forecasts that are far more accurate than random predictions. We then use our model to predict how the publics of 120 societies will respond to key questions that will be asked in the 2005–6 World Values Survey – predicting the values and beliefs not only of publics that were covered in past surveys but also the responses that we expect to find from the publics of scores of societies that have *not* been surveyed previously. This book's Internet Appendix (which can be downloaded from http://www.worldvaluessurvey.org/publications/humandevelopment.html) presents the predicted values that we expect to find in the next wave of the Values Surveys, enabling researchers to test these predictions when the data become available in 2007.

Chapters 4 and 5 analyze human values in a longitudinal perspective, examining changes observed across the four waves of the Values Surveys that have been carried out so far. We find that rich postindustrial societies show large intergenerational differences, with the younger cohorts generally placing much stronger emphasis on secular-rational values and self-expression values than do the older cohorts. By contrast, low-income societies that have not experienced substantial economic growth during the past five decades do not display intergenerational differences; younger and older cohorts are about equally likely to display traditional or modern values. This result suggests that these intergenerational differences reflect historical changes rather than anything inherent in the human life cycle. This interpretation is reinforced by the fact that, when we follow a given birth cohort's value orientations over time, the cohort does *not* become more traditional or survival-oriented as it ages, as the life-cycle interpretation implies. Instead, the generational differences are an enduring attribute of given cohorts, which seem to reflect the different formative conditions they experienced as succeeding cohorts grew up under increasingly favorable conditions. The intergenerational differences found in postindustrial societies seem to reflect the long-term socioeconomic changes resulting from the economic miracles that occurred during the decades after World War II.

Chapter 5 examines the changes over time that have taken place in specific components of the two value dimensions. For example, one important aspect of the rise of self-expression values has been the spread of elite-challenging forms of civic mass action: people are becoming increasingly likely to sign petitions and take part in demonstrations and boycotts. Another major change concerns family values and sexual norms. Traditionally, the family represents the basic reproductive unit of any society. Consequently, traditional cultures tend to condemn harshly any behavior that seems to threaten reproduction and child-rearing within the family, such as homosexuality, divorce, and abortion. But in postindustrial societies with advanced welfare institutions, a strong family is no longer necessary for survival. These rigid norms gradually lose their function, and more room is given to individual self-expression. This does not happen overnight. Changing norms concerning abortion and homosexuality have given rise to heated political debate in developed societies today, but acceptance of divorce, homosexuality, and abortion is spreading massively throughout rich postindustrial societies – but *not* in low-income societies, where existential insecurity remains widespread.

Chapter 6 explores the psychological traits of self-expression values, showing their close linkages to widely used individualism and autonomy scales developed by social psychologists. These scales are based on various theories and various data sources, using various methods. But as we demonstrate, individualism, autonomy, and self-expression values all tap the same underlying dimension: they reflect a common underlying orientation toward human emancipation. This exercise in triangulation not only confirms the validity of the self-expression values dimension. It also illuminates the antidiscriminatory nature of self-expression values, indicating that the spread of these values will make publics more *humanistic* but not more egocentric.

Having analyzed the forces shaping human values, the second half of this book examines the societal impact of changing value orientations. We focus on self-expression values, the value orientations that are most central to human development and the emergence of democracy. Our other major dimension of cross-cultural variation – traditional versus secular-rational values – is examined in another recent book (Norris and Inglehart, 2004), so we give it relatively little attention here. Instead, we address one of the most debated questions in the social sciences: the causal linkage between values and institutions. In political science, this debate has centered on the question, Is a prodemocratic political culture among the public a *precondition* for the success of democratic institutions at the system level? Or are prodemocratic mass values simply a *consequence* of living under democratic institutions?

Chapter 7 discusses the causal link between democratic values and democratic institutions within the framework of human development, focusing on the conditions that determine how much freedom people have in shaping their lives. Liberal democracy is vital in this regard because it guarantees civil and political rights that entitle people to make autonomous choices in their private and public activities: it institutionalizes freedom of action. Human choice is at the heart of liberal democracy, and mass demand for democracy reflects the priority that people give to autonomous choice. Although the desire for freedom is a universal human aspiration, it does not take top priority when people grow up with the feeling that survival is uncertain. But when survival seems secure, increasing emphasis on self-expression values makes the emergence of democracy increasingly likely where it does not yet exist and makes democracy increasingly *effective* where it already exists. Conversely, adopting democratic institutions does not automatically make self-expression values people's top priority. These values emerge when socioeconomic development diminishes material, cognitive, and social constraints on human choice, nourishing a subjective sense of existential security. This can occur under *either* democratic or authoritarian institutions, depending on whether they attain high levels of socioeconomic development. Rising emphasis on self-expression does not reflect the prior existence of democracy; quite the opposite, it can emerge under either democratic or authoritarian institutions, and when it does, it generates mass demands for democracy. Accordingly, Chapter 7 argues that the causal arrow in the relationship between liberal democracy and self-expression values runs from cultural change to democracy rather than the reverse.

Chapter 8 tests these propositions about the causal linkage between mass values and democratic institutions, analyzing a large body of empirical evidence in order to determine whether self-expression values give rise to democratic institutions, or whether democratic institutions cause self-expression values to emerge. We do this in a four-step strategy, using several different analytical approaches and various ways of measuring our key variables, to analyze the causes of liberal democracy.

First, we use the Freedom House civil and political rights scores as indicators of liberal democracy. Taking advantage of the fact that the Third Wave of democratization brought a massive expansion of democracy, we analyze whether the level of liberal democracy that a given country had before the Third Wave had a stronger impact on its subsequent level of self-expression values; or whether these levels of self-expression values had a stronger impact on levels of democracy after the Third Wave. The results strongly support the latter interpretation.

Second, we test the congruency thesis, analyzing the extent to which *discrepancies* between a given country's level of mass demand for democracy and its level of democracy seems to shape subsequent *changes* in levels of democracy. The results show that large shifts toward more democratic institutions were most likely to occur in societies where mass demands for freedom exceeded the institutional supply of freedom. Conversely, although most societies moved toward higher levels of democracy during this era, a few moved in the opposite direction – and they tended to be societies in which the previous supply of freedom was relatively high, in comparison with the level of mass demands for freedom. Regime changes toward and away from democracy largely reflect the preexisting discrepancies between genuine mass demands for freedom and the society's actual level of democracy.

Third, we build on the recent literature concerning "illiberal democracies," "electoral democracies," "deficient democracies," and "low-quality democracies," which argues that many of the new democracies of the Third Wave are democratic in name only. Civil and political rights do not necessarily exist in actual practice; they can be rendered ineffective by corrupt elite behavior that violates the rule of law. We use indicators of law-abiding elite behavior (i.e., "elite integrity") to measure how effective democracy really is; this enables us to test the impact of self-expression values on subsequent levels of *effective* democracy, controlling for other variables that are prominent in the democratization literature. Self-expression values show a robust and strongly positive impact on effective democracy even when we control for other factors – and even when we control for a society's prior experience with democracy.

Fourth, we examine discrepancies between formal and effective democracy, as they are produced by variations in elite integrity. The analyses demonstrate that self-expression values operate as a social force that closes the gap between formal and effective democracy: if self-expression values are weak, there may be large discrepancies between formal and effective democracy, with a society's level of effective democracy falling far short of its level of formal democracy; but if self-expression values are strongly anchored in a society, its level of effective democracy will be close to its level of formal democracy. Self-expression values help close the gap between nominal and real democracy by generating pressures for elite integrity. Thus, a fundamental aspect of elite behavior – elite integrity – is not independent from mass-level attributes. It reflects them.

These analyses use four different ways of measuring and analyzing democracy, but they all point to the same conclusion: self-expression values have a massive impact on a society's *subsequent* democratic performance but are themselves only modestly influenced by a society's *prior* level of democracy.

Chapters 9 and 10 deal with significant theoretical and methodological problems in the study of democratization and value change. Chapter 9 relates our findings to alternative theories, which emphasize other causal factors behind the emergence and strengthening of democracy than the emancipative social forces linked with rising self-expression values. Most theories that ignore or reject the impact of broader societal forces on democratization emphasize the role of international context and collective actors. Both perspectives are partly right, but they do not invalidate the role of motivational social forces, such as mass self-expression values. In fact, the interplay between international context, collective actors, and social forces is important. Changes in international context have sometimes been necessary in order to unblock the impact of social forces rooted in mass self-expression values. But the international context cannot create these values – they were generated by the public's firsthand existential experiences. Where these values are absent, favorable international conditions do not help to instill effective democratic institutions. Furthermore, democratization always proceeds through collective action. But there must be motivational forces that direct actions toward specific outcomes. Mass self-expression values are such a force, as they channel collective actions toward democratic outcomes, when external conditions permit it.

Chapter 10 deals with a fundamental methodological question that is still widely misunderstood. Even today, many social scientists assume that phenomena must operate in the same way at the individual level as at the system level – and that unless they do, any linkage between them is somehow "spurious." In this book's context, the question is, How can mass values and beliefs, which exist only within individuals, have an impact on democracy, which exists only at the societal level? We show that individual-level attitudes, such as self-expression values, have central tendencies that are genuine societal-level characteristics that can affect other societal-level characteristics, such as democracy, in ways that are not – and cannot be – reflected at the individual level (where democracy does not exist). As we will show, whether such linkages are "spurious" or real can only be analyzed at the level where the linkage exists:

the societal level. In order to examine relationships between the political system and political culture, one must aggregate individual-level values to the national level.

Most of the research on political culture is based on the assumption that certain mass attitudes, such as support for democracy or civic trust, are crucial to democracy at the societal level. But these studies then move on to analyze the determination of these attitudes at the individual level, leaving the assumption that they have societal-level consequences as an unexamined leap of faith. We do not. Having data from eighty societies containing most of the world's population, we can carry out statistically significant tests of the actual linkages between specific mass values and attitudes, and societal-level phenomena such as democracy. Some of the findings are surprising. Many of the mass attitudes that figure prominently in the research on political culture show surprisingly weak empirical linkages with democracy, whereas others that have been neglected show remarkably strong linkages.

Chapter 11 surveys the variables that the political culture literature considers crucial to democracy, in order to examine which of these attitudes *are* actually relevant to democracy, testing their societal-level impact on subsequent levels of democracy. These indicators include communitarian values, such as confidence in public institutions, membership in associations, and norm abidingness. The results are clear: emphasis on self-expression values is more important for democracy than communitarian factors and the other variables tested. And surprising as it may seem, self-expression values play an even more crucial role in strengthening democracy than does overt support for democracy itself – which is often inflated by social desirability effects and instrumentally motivated support. Self-expression values, by contrast, are measured in ways that make no explicit reference to democracy and thus are not inflated by lip service to a term that today has overtones of social desirability almost everywhere. These values reflect an intrinsic commitment to autonomous human choice, the core element of democracy. These findings support the interpretation that democratization is above all a process of human emancipation that empowers people. Its essence is the institutionalization of free choice, and this process is largely driven by the social forces linked with human self-expression.

Chapter 12 addresses another consequence of the emancipative forces linked with self-expression values: their tendency to promote gender equality. Today, the trend toward increasing gender equality is pervasive in postindustrial societies. This trend is historically recent, reflecting the fact that democracy is an evolving concept. Gender empowerment has become an increasingly widely accepted attribute of democracy and, as we demonstrate, rising mass emphasis on self-expression is one of the most powerful social forces behind this trend. Thus, rising gender equality is another major aspect of the process of human development. The welfare state, the emerging knowledge society, and democratic traditions are also relevant to gender equality, but primarily insofar as they are linked with the emancipative thrust of self-expression values. Increasing gender equality is a vital component of the rise of humanistic societies.

Chapter 13 examines the normative implications and historical context of our unified version of modernization theory. We argue that self-expression values are not *egocentric* but *humanistic*: they emphasize not only autonomy for oneself but for *others* as well, motivating movements for the rights of children, women, gays and lesbians, handicapped people, and ethnic minorities and such universal goals as environmental protection and ecological sustainability. This wide range of antidiscriminatory social movements reflects a broad trend that places increasing emphasis on humanistic norms.

The Conclusion summarizes our findings in an "Emancipative Theory of Democracy," arguing that the rise of emancipative social forces linked with self-expression values constitutes the most important single factor pressing for democracy. Consolidating and sustaining democracy is not simply a matter of designing the right constitution or of having elites who are committed to democratic norms. It reflects rising mass emphasis on human autonomy.

Our findings warn against the naive belief that designing the right institutional arrangements and installing elites who are committed to democracy is all one needs to establish democracy. Effective democracy involves far more than institutional design and committed elites; it reflects the broader liberating forces inherent in human development. Much of the recent literature on democratization has ignored democracy's most central theme: human emancipation.

This book integrates a massive body of empirical evidence into a unified version of modernization theory. As it reaches high levels of development, rising self-expression values transform modernization into a process of human development, giving rise to increasingly humanistic societies. The emergence and flourishing of democratic institutions is one component of this broader process.

PART I

THE FORCES SHAPING VALUE CHANGE

I

A Revised Theory of Modernization

The Controversy over Modernization Theory

People in different societies see the world differently and have strikingly different values. In some countries, 95 percent of the people say that God is very important in their lives; in others, as few as 3 percent say so. In some societies, 90 percent of the people believe that if jobs are scarce, men have more right to a job than women; in others, only 8 percent think so. These cross-national differences are robust and enduring. But as this book demonstrates, these and many other important values are gradually changing in developed countries throughout the world.

These changes are roughly predictable, for they are closely linked with socioeconomic development. They are occurring in virtually all modern societies, and they have important consequences. Changing values are reshaping religious beliefs, job motivations, fertility rates, gender roles, and sexual norms and are bringing growing mass demands for democratic institutions and more responsive elite behavior. As we will demonstrate, socioeconomic development brings roughly predictable cultural changes – and beyond a certain point, these changes make democracy increasingly likely to emerge where it does not yet exist, and to become stronger and more direct where it already exists.

Modernization theory is based on the idea of human progress (Carneiro, 2003). Historically, this idea is relatively new. As long as humans did not exert significant control over their natural environment, and agrarian economies were trapped in a steady-state equilibrium where almost no perceptible change took place from one generation to the next, the idea of human progress seemed unrealistic (Jones, 1985; McNeill, 1990). The situation began to change only with the occurrence of sustained economic growth (North, 1981; W. Bernstein, 2004).

Economic growth began to outpace population growth in a sustained way when the Commercial Revolution gave rise to preindustrial capitalism in the urban areas of late medieval Western Europe (Hall, 1989; Lal, 1998; Landes, 1998). As this happened, the philosophies of humanism and enlightenment emerged. The idea that technological innovations based on systematic research would enable humans to overcome the limitations nature imposes on them gained credibility, contesting the established view that human freedom and fulfillment can come only in the afterlife. Science began to provide a source of insight that competed with divine revelation, challenging the intellectual monopoly of the church, which fiercely defended feudal society as an unchangeable eternal order (Landes, 1998). The idea of human progress was born and with it modernization theory began to emerge.

Modernization theory originated in the Enlightenment era, with the belief that technological progress will give humanity increasing control over nature. Antoine de Condorcet (1979 [1795]) was among the first to explicitly link economic development and cultural change, arguing that technological progress and economic development will inevitably bring changes in people's moral values. The idea of human progress had a massive impact on social philosophers, but from its origins to the present, it has been opposed by notions of social decay that saw humanity heading toward a dark age. Edmund Burke (1999 [1790]) formulated such an antimodern view in his *Reflections on the Revolution in France*. In a similar vein, Thomas R. Malthus (1970 [1798]) developed a scientific theory of demographic disasters that is echoed in contemporary theories of growth limits and ecological risks (Meadows et al., 1972; U. Beck, 1992).

The most influential version of modernization theory was propounded by Karl Marx (1973 [1858]). The Marxist version provided a penetrating critique of the harsh exploitation that characterized early industrial society and proposed a utopian solution that allegedly would bring peace and an end to exploitation. Many of Marx's predictions were flagrantly wrong. Today, virtually no one believes that a proletarian revolution is about to take place that will abolish private property and bring an end to history. But the insight that technological changes and socioeconomic development have predictable cultural and political consequences remains valid. When Marx and Engels published *The Communist Manifesto* in 1848, industrialization was limited to a handful of countries, and the working class was small, powerless, and ruthlessly exploited. Marx and Engels argued that industrialization was the wave of the future and that industrial workers would become increasingly numerous and seize power. Although Marx failed to foresee the rise of the service class and the knowledge society, which aborted the numerical preponderance of workers he predicted, industrial workers have become a major political force in most societies, and today most of the world's population lives in countries that are either industrialized or industrializing (Rowen, 1996; Barro, 1997; Estes, 1998; Hughes, 1999).

Adam Smith (1976 [1776]) and Karl Marx (1973 [1858]) propagated competing versions of modernization, with Smith promoting capitalism and Marx advocating communism. But apart from their sharply contradictory views about the best pathway into modernity, both thinkers saw technological innovation and its socioeconomic consequences as the basis of human progress, with pervasive implications for culture and political institutions. Marx was most explicit on this point, arguing that socioeconomic development determines subsequent cultural changes in people's value orientations: a society's prevailing value orientations and moral standards form the "ideological superstructure" that reflects a society's "socioeconomic basis," and ideology necessarily changes as the socioeconomic basis changes. Consequently, the abolition of private property will bring the end of history – a classless society in which people no longer define their identity along the divisive lines of class distinctions but see themselves and others throughout the world as equals. This egalitarian classless society will make humanistic values dominant.

Competing versions of modernization theory enjoyed a new resurgence after World War II when the capitalist and communist superpowers espoused opposing ideologies as guidelines concerning the best route to modernity. Although they competed fiercely, both ideologies were committed to economic growth, social progress, and modernization, and they both brought broader mass participation in politics (Moore, 1966). Furthermore, because both sides believed that the developing nations of the Third World would seek modernization through either the communist path or the capitalist path, the two superpowers struggled to win them over. But industrialization and economic growth turned out to be far more difficult than anticipated (Randall and Theobald, 1998). Rather than modernizing, most of the new nations remained poor and ruled by corrupt regimes. Although these regimes gave lip service to capitalist, communist, or "nonaligned" visions of modernization, in reality most of them were run by rent-seeking elites who created "rogue states" to enrich themselves, doing little to modernize their countries (Rueschemeyer, Stephens, and Stephens, 1992).

In the postwar United States, a version of modernization theory emerged that viewed underdevelopment as a direct consequence of a country's internal characteristics, especially its traditional economies, traditional psychological and cultural traits, and traditional institutions (Lerner, 1958; Almond and Coleman, 1960; Pye and Verba, 1963; Almond and Powell, 1966; Weiner, 1966; Binder et al., 1971; Inkeles and Smith, 1974). From this perspective, traditional values not only were mutable but could – and should – be replaced by modern values, enabling these societies to follow the (virtually inevitable) path of capitalist development. The causal agents in this developmental process were seen as the rich, developed nations that stimulate the modernization of "backward" nations through economic, cultural, and military assistance.

These arguments were criticized as blaming the victim, because modernization theorists assumed that underdeveloped societies needed to adopt "modern" values and institutions to become developed societies (e.g., Bradshaw and Wallace, 1996). Modernization theory was not only criticized; it was pronounced dead (Wallerstein, 1976). Neo-Marxist and world-systems theorists argued that rich countries exploit poor countries, locking them in positions of powerlessness and structural dependence (e.g., Frank, 1966; Wallerstein, 1974; Chirot, 1977, 1994; Chase-Dunn, 1989). Underdevelopment, Frank claimed, is *developed*. This school of thought conveys the message to poor countries that poverty has nothing to do with internal problems: it is the fault of global capitalism. In the 1970s and 1980s, modernization theory seemed discredited (O'Donnell, 1973), and dependency theory came into vogue (Cardoso and Faletto, 1979). Adherents of dependency theory claimed that the Third World nations could only escape from global exploitation if they withdrew from the world market and adopted import-substitution policies.

In recent years, it became apparent that import-substitution strategies have been less successful. Rather than being the most successful, countries that were least involved in global capitalism actually showed the *least* economic growth (Firebaugh, 1992, 1996). Export-oriented strategies were more effective in bringing sustained economic growth and even, eventually, democracy (Barro, 1997; Randall and Theobald, 1998). The pendulum swung back: dependency theory fell out of favor, while the Western capitalist version of modernization regained credibility (Pye, 1990). The rapid development of East Asia and the subsequent democratization of Taiwan and South Korea seemed to confirm its basic claims: producing low-cost goods for the world market initiates economic growth; reinvesting the returns into human capital qualifies the work force to produce high-tech goods, whose export brings even higher returns and enlarges the educated urban middle classes; and once the middle class becomes large enough, its pressure for liberal democracy can no longer be resisted (L. Diamond, 1993a; Lipset, Seong, and Torres, 1993). World-systems theory came under heavy criticism. Evans (1995) argues that the structure of the global division of labor offers opportunities, enabling developing nations to transform themselves and change their positions in the global economy. The involvement of multinational corporations in underdeveloped nations does not seem to be as harmful as world-systems theorists claim. In fact, foreign investment seems to stimulate growth (Firebaugh, 1992) and to improve national welfare, benefiting the masses and not just the elites (Firebaugh and Beck, 1994). Hein (1992), Dollar (1992), and Firebaugh (1996) have demonstrated that nations that traded most and had the most investment from capitalist countries showed *higher*, not lower, subsequent rates of economic growth than other countries.

But it is clear that any simplistic version of modernization theory has serious shortcomings. Modernization theory needs to be revised for a number of reasons. One of the most obvious is the fact that, although the classic modernization theorists in both West and East thought that religion and ethnic traditions would die out, they have proved to be surprisingly resilient throughout the world. Indeed, with the close of the Cold War, Huntington (1996) has argued that future political conflicts will be based primarily on enduring cultural cleavages, largely reflecting a society's religious tradition.

The Persistence of Traditional Cultures

Huntington (1996), Putnam (1993), and Fukuyama (1995) argue that cultural traditions are remarkably enduring and shape the political and economic behavior of their societies today.[1] But modernization theorists from Marx and Weber to Bell and Toffler have argued that the rise of industrial society is linked with coherent cultural shifts away from traditional value systems.[2] Surprising as it may seem, *both* claims are true, as this book will demonstrate.

In recent years, research and theory on socioeconomic development have given rise to two contending schools of thought. One side emphasizes the *convergence* of values as a result of modernization – the overwhelming force that drives cultural change. This school predicts the decline of traditional values and their replacement with modern ones (e.g., Meyer, Boli, Thomas, and Ramirez, 1997; Stevenson, 1997). Another school of thought emphasizes the *persistence* of traditional values despite economic and political changes and assumes that values are relatively independent of economic conditions (e.g., DiMaggio, 1994). Consequently, it predicts that convergence around some set of "modern" values is unlikely; traditional values will continue to exert an independent influence on the cultural changes caused by socioeconomic development.

The central claim of modernization theory is that socioeconomic development is linked with coherent and, to some extent, predictable changes in culture as well as political life (Deutsch, 1963; Pye and Verba, 1963; Stinchcomb, 1965; Huntington, 1968). As we shall see, evidence from around the world indicates that socioeconomic development *does* tend to propel various societies in a roughly predictable direction. Socioeconomic development starts from technological innovations that increase labor productivity; it then brings occupational specialization, rising educational levels, and rising income levels; it diversifies human interaction, shifting the emphasis from authority relations toward bargaining relations; in the long run this brings cultural changes, such as changing gender roles, changing attitudes toward authority, changing sexual norms, declining fertility rates, broader political participation, and more critical and less easily led publics.

But cultural change is path dependent. The fact that a society was historically Protestant or Orthodox or Islamic or Confucian manifests itself in coherent cultural zones with distinctive value systems that persist even when one controls for the effects of socioeconomic development. These cultural zones are robust. Although the value systems of different countries are moving in the same direction under the impact of powerful modernizing forces, their value systems have not been converging, as simplistic notions of cultural globalization suggest (Meyer et al., 1997; Stevenson, 1997).

This may seem paradoxical, but it is not. If the world's societies were all moving in the same direction at the same rate of speed, the distances between

---

[1] For the autonomous influences of culture, see, among others, Gibson, Duch, and Tedin, 1992; Putnam 1993; DiMaggio, 1994; Gibson and Duch, 1994; Miller, Hesli, and Reisinger, 1994; Gibson, 1997; Fleron and Ahl, 1998; Dalton, 1999, 2000; Crothers and Lockhard, 2000; Fukuyama, 2000; Inglehart and Baker, 2000; Lipset and Lenz, 2000.

[2] For the impact of economic development on culture, see, among others, Abramson, 1989; Inglehart, 1990, 1997; L. Diamond, 1993c; Putnam, 1993; Dalton, 1994; Reisinger, Miller, Hesli, and Máher, 1994; Gasiorowski and Power, 1998; Rohrschneider, 1999; Inglehart and Baker, 2000.

them would remain as great as ever, and they would never converge. The reality is not that simple, of course, but this illustrates an important principle: postindustrial societies *are* changing rapidly and are moving in a common direction, but the cultural differences between them were empirically as great in 2001 as they were in 1981.[3] Although socioeconomic development tends to produce systematic changes in what people believe and want out of life, the influence of cultural traditions does not disappear. Belief systems have a remarkable durability and resilience. While values can and do change, they continue to reflect a society's historical heritage. Cultural change is path-dependent.

Nevertheless, it seems clear that socioeconomic development brings predictable long-term changes. One indication of this is the fact that the worldviews and behavior of the people living in developed societies differ immensely from those of peoples in developing ones. Another indication is the fact that the value systems of developed societies are changing in a consistent and roughly predictable direction. These changes do not reflect a homogenizing trend – they cannot be attributed, for example, to the impact of a global communications network that is said to be transmitting a common set of new values throughout the world. If this were the case, the same value changes would occur in all societies that are exposed to global communications. But this is not what has been happening, as we will demonstrate. For these value changes are *not* taking place in societies that have been experiencing sharply declining standards of living, such as the Soviet successor states, even though these societies are integrated into the global communications network. These changes occur only when the people of a given society have experienced high levels of economic prosperity for long periods of time. Socioeconomic development brings predictable cultural and political changes, and economic collapse tends to bring changes in the opposite direction.

These changes are probabilistic. They are not deterministic laws, like the Scientific Socialism that Karl Marx propounded. Moreover, cultural change is not linear, continuously moving in one direction as economic development takes place, until one reaches the end of history. Instead, industrialization brings a shift from traditional to secular-rational values; with the rise of postindustrial society, however, cultural change starts to move in another direction. The shift from traditional to secular-rational values becomes slower and stagnates, while another change becomes more powerful – the shift from survival to self-expression values, through which people place increasing emphasis on human choice, autonomy, and creativity. This change was moving slowly during the transition from preindustrial to industrial societies, but it becomes the dominant trend when industrial society gives way to postindustrial society. Modernization theorists foresaw value changes linked with the process of socioeconomic development, but they focused on the rise of secular-rational values, not anticipating a later wave of change – the rise of self-expression values. The classic modernization theorists, quite understandably, did not foresee the emancipative

---

[3] Empirical evidence supporting this claim is presented in Chapter 2.

impulse that emerges in the later stages of modernization. This impulse is incompatible with the technocratic authoritarianism that many modernization theorists (and such writers as George Orwell) thought would be the outcome of political modernization. In contrast with these expectations, self-expression values make democracy the most likely outcome of political development.

Moore (1966) correctly pointed out that the industrial phase of modernization does not necessarily lead to democracy but follows different paths that allow for authoritarian, fascist, and communist versions of mobilizing the masses into politics. But in the postindustrial phase of modernization, rising self-expression values provide a social force that questions authority and operates in favor of genuinely mass responsive democracy, not only electoral democracy, as we will demonstrate.

Progress is not inevitable. The value changes linked with the various stages of modernization are reversible. Socioeconomic development brings massive and roughly predictable cultural changes, but if economic collapse occurs, cultural changes will tend to move in the opposite direction. Nevertheless, development has been the dominant trend of recent centuries: most countries are considerably more prosperous today than they were two hundred years ago. A powerful logic links high levels of socioeconomic development; cultural changes that emphasize human autonomy, creativity, and self-expression; and democratization. Through this process, democracy itself evolves to become increasingly responsive. With rising self-expression values, even long-established democracies become more responsive to mass preferences, and politics becomes less and less a game restricted to elites who pay attention to the masses in elections only.

Different societies follow different trajectories even when subject to the same forces of modernization, because specific factors, such as the cultural heritage of a given society, also shape how this society develops. Weber (1958 [1904]) argued that traditional religious values have an enduring influence, and scholars from various disciplines have observed that distinctive cultural traits endure over long periods of time and continue to shape a society's political and economic performance. For example, Putnam (1993) shows that the regions of Italy where democratic institutions function most successfully today are those in which civil society was relatively well developed in the nineteenth century and even earlier. According to Fukuyama (1995), societies with a cultural heritage of "low-trust" are at a competitive disadvantage in global markets because they are less able to develop large and complex social institutions. Hamilton (1994) argues that, although capitalism has become an almost universal way of life, civilizational factors continue to structure the organization of economies and societies. "What we witness with the development of a global economy is not increasing uniformity, in the form of a universalization of Western culture, but rather the continuation of civilizational diversity through the active reinvention and reincorporation of non-Western civilizational patterns" (Hamilton, 1994: 184). Thus, there are striking cross-cultural variations in the organization of capitalist production and associated managerial ideologies (DiMaggio, 1994; Guillén, 1994).

The impression that we are moving toward a uniform "McWorld" is largely an illusion. As Watson and his colleagues (1998) demonstrate, the seemingly identical McDonald's restaurants that have spread throughout the world actually have different social meanings and fulfill different social functions in different cultural zones. Although the physical settings look alike, eating in a McDonald's restaurant in Japan is a different social experience from eating in one in the United States or China. The globalization of communications is obvious. But precisely because its manifestations are so evident, their effects tend to be overestimated. One can tell at a glance that young people around the world are wearing jeans, communicating on the internet, and drinking Coca-Cola. The persistence of underlying value differences is much less obvious but equally important.

The fact that a society was historically shaped by a Protestant or Confucian or Islamic cultural heritage leaves an enduring impact, setting that society on a trajectory that continues to influence subsequent development – even if the direct influence of religious institutions is modest today. Thus, although few people attend church in Protestant Europe today, the societies that were historically shaped by Protestantism continue to manifest a distinctive set of values and beliefs. The same is true of historically Roman Catholic societies and historically Islamic or Orthodox or Confucian societies. The secularization thesis is only half true. In the industrialization phase, the role of religion does become less important, and even in postindustrial societies the ability of established religious authorities to dictate to the masses is rapidly crumbling away. But spiritual concerns, broadly defined, are not disappearing – they are becoming more widespread. Thus, while support for the old hierarchical churches is eroding in postindustrial societies, spiritual life is being transformed into forms that are increasingly compatible with individual self-expression.

The Causal Primacy of Socioeconomic Development

The urge to survive is common to all creatures, and normally survival is precarious. This reflects a basic ecological principle: the population of any organism tends to rise to meet the available food supply; it is then held constant by starvation, disease, or predators. Throughout most of history, the survival of all organisms, including humanity, was precarious (Birch and Cobb, 1981).

Humans developed cultures that helped soften the competition for survival. Virtually all traditional societies had cultural norms that repressed aspirations for social mobility. They justified acceptance of the existing social order by the poor. Moreover, cultural norms limiting reproduction softened the ruthless competition for survival brought by overpopulation.

Apart from disasters and wars, no other phenomenon affects people's daily lives more massively and brings changes that are more immediately felt than socioeconomic development (Nolan and Lenski, 1999; Carneiro, 2003). Socioeconomic development changes a society's basis of material subsistence and its social fabric (Sen, 1999). It directly affects people's sense of existential security, determining whether physical survival is uncertain or can be taken for granted. Economic threats concern people's most basic needs and are immediately felt. Its relevance to survival itself places socioeconomic development at the root of key causal chains in the development of societies (Jones, 1985).

Thus, the values and beliefs found in developed societies differ strikingly from those found in developing societies. Some of the most profoundly important cross-cultural differences involve religion, and the importance people attach to religion varies immensely. In agrarian societies, religion tends to be central to people's lives; in industrial societies, it tends to become a relatively peripheral concern. Another major dimension of cross-cultural variation involves gender roles, self-expression, and quality-of-life concerns, and here too the variation is enormous. In some low-income societies, fully 99 percent of the people say that men make better political leaders than women; in rich postindustrial societies, only a small minority agrees with this proposition.

Value orientations set standards for desirable and undesirable goals. This goal-setting function makes value orientations a powerful motivational regulator of human behavior (Rokeach, 1960, 1968, 1973). Cultural anthropologists (Durham, 1991; Barkow, Cosmides, and Tooby, 1992) argue that the function of different value orientations lies in their "cultural fitness": values change is an evolutionary process in which those values that are best suited to cope with life under given existential conditions have a selective advantage over values that are less suited to these conditions. This selection reflects an evolutionary principle, making those values most likely to survive and spread that are most effective in coping with given conditions. This evolutionary principle has two implications. First, prevailing value orientations reflect prevailing existential conditions. Second, if existential conditions change, value orientations are likely to change correspondingly – but only after a significant time lag that is needed to react to the impact of existential changes and to experiment with new life strategies that fit the new conditions better.

Moreover, new life strategies are more likely to be adopted by the young than by the old, who find it more difficult to abandon deeply inculcated habits and worldviews. But once a new life-style has emerged, succeeding generations have a choice between different role models and will adopt those that best fit their existential experiences.

Socioeconomic development is crucial because it impacts powerfully on people's existential conditions and their chances of survival. This is particularly true in societies of scarcity. Survival is such a basic human goal that when it is uncertain, one's entire life strategy is shaped by the struggle to survive. Whether people grow up in a society with an annual per capita income of $300 or $30,000 has more direct impact on their daily lives than whether they grow up in a country that has free elections or not. Throughout history, survival has been precarious and human choice has been restricted for most people. In recent decades, the publics of postindustrial societies have experienced unprecedented levels of existential security: real income levels are many times higher than they ever were before World War II, and welfare states have emerged that provide comprehensive safety nets for most people. Life expectancies have risen to unprecedented levels: in 1900, even in the United States – then the world's richest country – life expectancy was only forty-nine; a century later, it was seventy-eight. Today, most people in rich countries have grown up taking it for granted that they will not starve. These developments have changed people's lives fundamentally. Contemporary events such as the crisis of the welfare state, volatile stock markets, and the risk of unemployment are important but not life-threatening.

Socioeconomic development diminishes objective constraints on human autonomy, creativity, and choice in three ways. First, reduction of poverty diminishes material constraints on human choice and nourishes a sense of existential security. Second, socioeconomic development tends to increase people's levels of formal education and to give them greater access to information through the mass media (Lerner, 1958; Inkeles and Smith, 1974; Inkeles, 1983). In the same vein, the requirements of the emerging knowledge society mobilize people's cognitive abilities (Bell, 1973; Inglehart, 1990). Thus, the second major effect of socioeconomic development is that it diminishes cognitive and informational constraints on human choice, fueling a sense of intellectual independence.

The third important consequence of socioeconomic development is the fact that it increases occupational specialization and social complexity, diversifying human interactions. Growing diversity of human interactions liberates people: it frees them from ascriptive communal ties and closed social circles, bringing them to interact with others on a bargaining basis. These tendencies were recognized by early sociologists who identified a shift from "mechanical solidarity" to "organic solidarity" (Durkheim, 1988 [1893]) and from "community" to "association" (Tönnies, 1955 [1887]). In the same vein, Simmel (1984 [1908]) emphasized the individualizing and liberating effect when people begin to develop ties that bridge social circles (see also Granovetter, 1973). Diversification of human interaction frees people from prefixed social roles and social ties, making them autonomous in defining their social roles themselves and in shaping their social ties to other people. As U. Beck (2002) puts it, there is a shift from "communities of necessity" to "elective affinities" to others. Socialization and socializing become a matter of choice: people are free to connect and disconnect with whomever they want; and rigidly fixed roles for such categories as gender and class are eroding, giving people more room to express themselves as individuals. In short, the third effect of socioeconomic development is to diminish social constraints on human choice, nurturing a sense of social autonomy.

By reducing economic insecurity, by cognitive mobilization, and by diversifying human exchanges, socioeconomic development diminishes objective constraints on human choice. People become materially more secure, intellectually more autonomous, and socially more independent. Thus, people experience a greater sense of human autonomy. Table 1.1 summarizes this emancipative effect of socioeconomic development.

TABLE 1.1. *The Emancipative Effects of Socioeconomic Development*

Socioeconomic Development		
⇓	⇓	⇓
Economic growth and the welfare state increase people's economic resources.	Rising levels of education, expanding mass communication, and increasingly knowledge-intensive work widen people's intellectual resources.	Growing social complexity and diversification of human interactions broaden people's social resources.
⇓	⇓	⇓
People become materially more secure.	People become cognitively more autonomous.	People become socially more independent.
⇓	⇓	⇓
	Diminishing constraints on human choice	
	⇓	
	Growing emphasis on human autonomy	

Two Dimensions of Cultural Change

The impact of socioeconomic development on cultural change operates in two phases. Industrialization gives rise to one major process of cultural change: bringing bureaucratization and secularization. The rise of postindustrial society leads to a second major process of cultural change: instead of rationalization, centralization, and bureaucratization, the new trend is toward increasing emphasis on individual autonomy and self-expression values. Both cultural changes reshape people's authority orientations, but they do it in different ways. The industrial stage of modernization brings the *secularization* of authority, whereas the postindustrial stage brings *emancipation* from authority.

Industrializing societies focused on maximizing material output, at any cost, as the best way of maximizing human well-being. This strategy has been dramatically successful in alleviating starvation and raising life expectancies, but it produces diminishing returns in postindustrial societies. Postindustrial modernization brings a fundamental shift in economic strategies, from maximizing material standards of living to maximizing well-being through life-style changes. The "quality of experience" replaces the quantity of commodities as the prime criterion for making a good living (Florida, 2002). The rise of self-expression values has changed the political agenda of postindustrial societies, challenging the emphasis on economic growth at any price by an increasing concern for environmental protection. It has also brought a shift from political cleavages based on social class conflict toward cleavages based on cultural issues and quality-of-life concerns.

Thus, socioeconomic development produces not one but two major dimensions of cross-cultural variation, one linked with industrialization and the other linked with the rise of postindustrial society. Both dimensions reflect changes in people's authority orientations. Rising secular-rational values bring a secularization *of* authority, which shifts from being legitimized by traditional religious beliefs to being legitimized by secular-rational ones. But these secular beliefs are no less dogmatic than religious ones. Secular beliefs and doctrines do not necessarily challenge unlimited political authority; they usually legitimize it, as did fascist and communist ideologies. By contrast, rising self-expression values bring an emancipation *from* authority: people increasingly tend to reject external authority that encroaches on individual rights. Authority becomes internalized within people themselves.

Industrialization and Rising Secular-Rational Values

Sustained economic growth starts with industrialization as productivity begins to outpace population growth (Landes, 1998; W. Bernstein, 2004). In agrarian societies, humanity was at the mercy of inscrutable and uncontrollable natural forces. Because their causes were dimly understood, people tended to attribute events to anthropomorphic gods. The vast majority of the population made its living from agriculture and depended on things that came from heaven, like the sun and rain. One prayed for good weather, for relief from disease, or from plagues of insects.

In industrial society, production moved indoors into a man-made environment. One did not wait for the sun to rise and the seasons to change; when it got dark, one turned on the lights, and when it got cold, one turned on the heating. One did not pray for good crops because production came from machines that were built by human ingenuity. With the discovery of germs and antibiotics, even disease ceased to be seen as a divine visitation; it became a problem within technological control. As technology gave people increasing control over their environment, God became less central.

The shift from preindustrial to industrial society brought profound changes in people's daily experiences and prevailing worldviews (Bell, 1973; Spier, 1996; Inglehart, 1997). Preindustrial life, Bell (1976: 147) argues, was a "game against nature" in which "one's sense of the world is conditioned by the vicissitudes of the elements – the seasons, the storms, the fertility of the soil, the amount of water, the depth of the mine seams, the droughts and the floods." Industrialization brought less dependence on nature, which had been seen as ruled by inscrutable forces or anthropomorphic spirits. Life now became a "game against fabricated nature" (Bell, 1973: 147), a technical, mechanical, rationalized, bureaucratic world directed toward creating and dominating the environment. As technological control of the environment increased, the role ascribed to religion and God dwindled. Praying to God for a good harvest was no longer necessary when one could depend on fertilizer and insecticides. Materialistic ideologies arose, offering secular interpretations of history and secular utopias to be attained by human engineering operating through rationally organized bureaucratic organizations. But these ideologies were as dogmatic as religion, reflecting the rigidly disciplined and standardized way in which industrial societies organize the work force and life in general (Whyte, 1956; Florida, 2002). Accordingly, the rise of secular-rational values does not bring a decline of authority: it only shifts the basis of authority from traditional religious sources to secular-rational sources. Rational science and its belief in technological progress becomes the new source of authority in a highly mechanical world.

One reason for the decline of traditional religious beliefs in industrial societies is that an increasing sense of technological control over nature diminishes the need for reliance on supernatural powers. In the uncertain world of subsistence societies, the belief that an infallible higher power will ensure that things ultimately turn out well filled a major psychological need. One of the key functions of religion was to provide a sense of certainty in an insecure environment. Physical as well as economic insecurity intensifies this need: the old saying that "there are no atheists in foxholes" reflects the fact that wartime dangers increase the need for faith in a higher power. But as industrial production outpaces population growth and as scientific progress prolongs life expectancy, there is a dwindling need for the reassurance that religion traditionally provided.

In the preindustrial world, humans have little control over nature. They seek to compensate for their lack of physical control by appealing to the metaphysical powers that seem to control the world: worship is seen as a way to influence one's fate, and it is easier to accept one's helplessness if one knows the outcome is in the hands of an omnipotent being whose benevolence can be won by following rigid and predictable rules of conduct. These are important functions of religion in a world where humans have little or no control over their environment. Industrialization vastly increases humans' direct physical control over the environment in which they live and work. This process undermines the traditional function of religion to provide reassurance in an uncertain world.

But industrialization does not increase people's sense of individual autonomy because of the disciplined and regimented way in which industrial societies are organized. In industrial societies, people – and especially factory workers – are embedded in uniform social classes with rigid social controls and conformity pressures. Life in industrial society is as standardized as its uniform mass products. The disciplined organization of uniform masses in industrial societies, which marches armies of workers from their barracks to the assembly line and back, creates a need for rigid codes of conduct. Although it tends to replace religious dogmas with secular ones, industrialization does not emancipate people from authority. The industrial standardization of life discourages self-expression values.

Postindustrialization and Rising Self-Expression Values

The emergence of postindustrial society brings another wave of cultural change, moving in a different direction. In the United States, Canada, Western Europe, and a growing share of East Asia, the majority of the labor force no longer works in factories. Instead of living in a mechanical environment, ever more people now spend their productive hours dealing with people, symbols, and information. Human efforts are no longer so much focused on producing material objects as on communicating with other people and processing information; the crucial products are innovation, knowledge, and ideas. Human creativity becomes the most important production factor (Florida, 2002). In the nineteenth-century United States, 80 percent of the work force was still engaged in agriculture; today, only 2 percent is. By the early twentieth century, industrial production dominated American society; today, the United States has become a knowledge society that spends far more on computers alone than on all industrial equipment combined. One of the most crucial aspects of this shift in economic activities is the fact that people experience far more individual autonomy in doing their jobs than industrial workers did. Routine tasks increasingly are taken over by computers and robots. Instead of being cogs in a huge machine, workers in the knowledge sector exercise individual judgment and choice. Even in the periphery of menial services, people have more flexibility in performing their tasks than did assembly-line workers in the industrial age.

The postindustrial age diminishes objective constraints on human choice in three major ways. First, postindustrial societies attain unprecedentedly high levels of prosperity and have welfare states that make food, clothing, shelter, housing, education, and health service available to almost everyone. Even in the United States, with a relatively limited welfare state, more than one-quarter of the national product is redistributed through the state for public welfare. Despite recent retrenchment of welfare benefits, never before in history have the masses experienced levels of existential security comparable with those that have emerged in postindustrial societies. Physical survival, a minimum living standard, and an average life expectancy of nearly eighty years can be taken for granted by most people living in these societies. This unprecedentedly high degree of existential security enables people to focus increasingly on goals beyond immediate survival.

Second, although mass literacy became widespread with industrialization, postindustrialization launches a massive process of cognitive mobilization. Modern service activities increasingly involve cognitive skills. Researchers, engineers, teachers, writers, lawyers, accountants, counselors, and analysts all belong to the "creative class" (Florida, 2002), whose members work with knowledge, perform analytical tasks, and use information technology. They have a high degree of autonomy in doing their work, even if they work within organizational hierarchies. Moreover, the need for cognitive skills increases the demand for higher education, and educational levels have risen dramatically in all postindustrial societies. Education makes people intellectually more independent because they no longer depend on other people's interpretations of the world. Increasingly, one's formal education and job experience help develop the potential for autonomous decision making (Bell, 1973, 1976). The prevalence of rigid manual routines in the typical factory required (and allowed) very little autonomous judgment. Service and knowledge workers deal with people and concepts, operating in a world where innovation and the freedom to exercise individual judgment are essential. Creativity, imagination, and intellectual independence become central. In addition, the evolution of mass media and modern information technology gives people easy access to knowledge, increasing their informational autonomy. Thus, rising levels of education, increasing cognitive and informational requirements in economic activities, and increasing proliferation of knowledge via mass media make people intellectually more independent, diminishing cognitive constraints on human choice.

Third, postindustrial society has a socially liberating effect. For service-based economies reverse the disciplined, standardized ways in which industrial societies organize people's daily activities. In the industrial age, the mass-production system subjected the labor force to rigid centralized control, and workers were embedded in closely knit groups with strong conformity pressures. By contrast, postindustrialization destandardizes economic activities and social life. The flexible organization of service-based economies and the autonomy they give workers radiate into all domains of life: human interaction is increasingly freed from the bonding ties of closely knit groups, enabling people to make and break social ties readily. The welfare state supports this individualization trend (U. Beck, 2002). Formerly, children's survival largely depended on whether their parents provided for them, and children took care of their parents when they reached old age. Although the role of the family is still important, the life-or-death nature of this relationship has been eroded by the welfare state. Maintaining family relations is nowadays a matter of choice, not of necessity. One-parent families and childless old people are far more viable under contemporary conditions than they once were. What Durkheim (1988 [1893]), Tönnies (1955 [1887]), and Simmel (1984 [1908]) once anticipated is becoming more and more a reality: social ties shift from "communities of necessity" to "elective affinities" (U. Beck, 2002). This makes people personally more independent, diminishing social constraints on human choice.

Postindustrialization brings even more favorable existential conditions than industrialization, making people economically more secure, intellectually more autonomous, and socially more independent than ever. This emancipative process gives people a fundamental sense of human autonomy, leading them to give a higher priority to freedom of choice and making them less inclined to accept authority and dogmatic truths. The shift from traditional to secular-rational values linked with industrialization brings a secularization *of* authority. But the shift from survival to self-expression values linked with postindustrialization brings emancipation *from* authority.

Industrialization gives humans increasing control of their environment, diminishing their deference to supernatural power and encouraging the rise of secular-rational values. But industrialization does not nourish a sense of human autonomy or lead people to question absolute authority, which persists in secular ideologies. By contrast, postindustrialization gives people a sense of human autonomy that leads them to question authority, dogmatism, and hierarchies, whether religious or secular. And because survival comes to be taken for granted, people become increasingly critical of the risks of technology and

TABLE I.2. *Differences between the Impact of the Industrial and Postindustrial Phases of Modernization on Human Values*

Industrialization		Postindustrialization	
⇓	⇓	⇓	⇓
Intensifying exploitation of natural resources	Regimented organization of human activities	Continuing exploitation of nature increases ecological risks	Individualized organization of human activities
⇓	⇓	⇓	⇓
Sense of technological control over natural forces	Weak sense of individual autonomy in society	Revival of spiritual concerns about the protection of Creation	Sense of individual autonomy in society
⇓	⇓	⇓	⇓
Massively growing emphasis on secular-rational values	Slowly growing emphasis on self-expression values	Slowly growing emphasis on secular-rational values	Massively growing emphasis on self-expression values

appreciative of nature. Spiritual concerns about humanity's place in the universe regain prominence. This does not bring a return to dogmatic religiosity, but it does bring the emergence of new forms of spirituality and nonmaterial concerns.

Table I.2 contrasts the ways in which the industrial phase and the postindustrial phase of modernization bring cultural changes. Economic growth and growing material prosperity are common to both phases of modernization, which tends to increase people's sense of existential security. Existential security is conducive to both secular-rational values and self-expression values. Accordingly, both sets of values tend to rise throughout both phases of modernization. But apart from their common tendency to increase existential security, the two phases of modernization differ in how far they promote individual autonomy, which makes them promote the two sets of values to varying degrees.

In the industrial phase, a growing sense of human control over nature is linked with a mechanical worldview, making the need for religion to appease supernatural powers seem superfluous. The mechanical worldview strengthens the tendency to secular-rational values that emerges from growing existential security. But industrial societies continue to organize human activities in a hierarchical and regimented fashion: economic constraints begin to recede, but social constraints continue to exist. Thus, the emerging sense of existential security does not fully translate into a broader sense of human autonomy during industrialization. Strong constraints on people's sense of autonomy slow down the rise of self-expression values. Hence, industrialization brings a pronounced shift toward secular-rational values but only a modest shift toward self-expression values.

In the postindustrial phase, economic scarcity continues to recede, strengthening people's sense of existential security even more. In addition, the destandardization of economic activities and social life that occurs in the postindustrial age diminishes social constraints in unprecedented ways. In this phase, people's sense of existential security *does* translate into a broader sense of human autonomy. As this happens, the secular dogmas that arose in the industrial age erode with the spread of self-expression values. Thus, at the same time as postindustrial society accelerates the emergence of self-expression values, it slows down the trend toward secular-rational values.

Individualized Forms of Spirituality

With the rise of the knowledge society, the mechanical world of the factory shapes the daily lives of fewer and fewer people. One's life experience deals more with people and ideas than with material things. The computer becomes the dominant tool, and computers verge on magic, creating an almost limitless number of virtual realities. In the knowledge society, productivity depends less on material constraints than on ideas and imagination. This creates a climate of intellectual creativity and stimulation in which spiritual concerns again become more central. Although the authority of the established churches continues to decline, during the past twenty years the publics of postindustrial societies have become increasingly likely to spend time thinking about the meaning and purpose of life. Whether one views these concerns as religious depends on one's definition of religion, but it is clear that the materialistic secularism of industrial society is fading. There is a shift from institutionally fixed forms of dogmatic religion to individually flexible forms of spiritual religion. Even one's religious ideas become a matter of choice, creativity, and self-expression.

A sense of insecurity has never been the only factor motivating religion. The desire to understand where we come from and where we are going and why we are here is inherent in humanity, and philosophers and theologians have been concerned with these questions throughout history. But throughout most of history existential insecurity dominated the lives of most people, and the great theological questions were of central concern to only a small minority. The vast majority of the population needed reassurance and a sense of predictability in a world where humans had little control over their environment – and this was the dominant factor underlying the grip of traditional religion on mass publics.

Although the traditional churches (like most bureaucratic organizations from labor unions to political parties) continue to lose members in postindustrial societies, we find no evidence that spiritual concerns, broadly understood, are losing ground. Quite the contrary, comparing the results of the 1981 Values Surveys with the results from 1989–91, 1995–97, and 1999–2001, we find that people in postindustrial societies are spending more time thinking about the meaning and purpose of life than they used to. Religion does not vanish. What we observe is a transformation of religion's function, from institutionalized forms of dogmatic religiosity that provide absolute codes of conduct in an insecure world to individualized spiritual concerns that serve the need for meaning and purpose in societies where virtually no one starves to death.

Religious thought seems to have become superfluous as industrial society demonstrates seemingly unlimited human control over nature and secular ideologies promise a scientifically certain route to utopia. But the publics of postindustrial societies manifest a growing awareness of the risks and limitations of science and technology, and initially religious questions about the relationship of human civilization and natural life again become central. This is most obvious in the debates about the ethical dimensions of genetic engineering, biotechnology, and other new technologies (Gaskell and Bauer, 2001).

Growing individual autonomy undermines the need for dogmatic guidelines and rigid authority, whether religious or secular. Spiritual concerns regain salience. This revival is linked with an increased awareness of the risks of civilization (Giddens, 1990, 1991; U. Beck, 1992). A growing number of people have the time, the information, and the education to understand that modernization has given humanity so much power over its environment that it can destroy life on this planet. This insight propagates respect for life and the limitations of human ingenuity. This has led to the blossoming of new forms of spirituality, many of which focus on a new balance between humans and nature. Postindustrialization makes modernity increasingly "self-reflexive," as Giddens puts it (1991). Postindustrialization replaces the lost ground of institutionalized dogmatic religiosity with individualized spiritual concerns. Whether or not we define this as religion, its function has changed – from providing absolute rules of conduct to providing a sense of the meaning of life.

Humanistic Risks and Egocentric Threats

Uncertainty is part of the human condition, and risks persist in postindustrial society, as U. Beck (1992) has convincingly pointed out, and the risk perceptions on which the ecological movement focuses represent a new form of concerns. But the risk perceptions of postindustrial society are fundamentally different from the survival concerns of the preindustrial and industrial phases of development. In these earlier phases, hunger and economic scarcity present an immediate threat to individual survival that is a direct firsthand experience. It does not require specialized knowledge or intellectual insight to perceive them: hunger is immediately felt.

The risks of postindustrial society, by contrast, are abstract. They are not based on firsthand experience but require cognitive insights. Even full-time specialists disagree about how rapidly global warming is occurring and what its consequences will be. The risks of new technologies, such as genetic engineering, are long-term risks to humanity, not immediate risks to the individual. These risks are not immediately felt but have to be understood, which requires high levels of information and a grasp of complex argumentation. Thus, the related risk perceptions are socially constructed. This makes it possible for much of the population to ignore these risks or view them as hypothetical. No immediate threat forces people to take into consideration the risks of global warming or genetic cloning in their daily activities. But precisely this relief from immediate threats also enables people to focus on problems that are not of an immediate concern to themselves. High levels of existential security and autonomy allow people to widen their horizons, allowing for a higher degree of risk awareness. This risk awareness is the product of cognitive insights among people who – as individuals – are relatively safe and free to devote energy to concerns that do not immediately threaten them. As individual safety and autonomy reduce egocentrism, they increase homocentrism (Maslow, 1988 [1954]).

The best-documented aspect of this process is the shift from materialist to postmaterialist priorities – a shift from giving top priority to economic and physical security, to self-expression and the quality of life. This shift from materialist to postmaterialist values has been measured annually from 1970 to the present, in surveys carried out in a number of Western societies (evidence of this shift is presented in Chapter 4). Postmaterialists are economically more secure than materialists, but much more sensitive to environmental risks. Individual security increases empathy, making people more aware of long-term risks. The rise of self-expression values fuels *humanistic* risk perceptions. These risk perceptions are fundamentally different from the *egocentric* threat perceptions that underlie survival values.

Value Change as a Cultural Process

People have always needed to eat, and they always will. Rising emphasis on self-expression values does not put an end to material desires. But prevailing economic orientations are gradually being reshaped. People who work in the knowledge sector continue to seek high salaries, but they place equal or greater emphasis on doing stimulating work and being able to follow their own time schedules (Florida, 2002). Consumption is becoming progressively less determined by the need for sustenance and the practical use of the goods consumed. People still eat, but a growing component of food's value is determined by its nonmaterial aspects. People pay a premium to eat exotic cuisines that provide an interesting experience or that symbolize a distinctive life-style. The publics of postindustrial societies place growing emphasis on "political consumerism," such as boycotting goods whose production violates ecological or ethical standards. Consumption is less and less a matter of sustenance and more and more a question of life-style – and choice.

People's worldviews and value orientations reflect their basic life experiences. Value orientations are functional: they provide guidelines that allow people to master life under given existential conditions (Durham, 1991; Mark, 2002). Cultural norms tend to be internalized at an early age and reinforced by nonrational sanctions. The power of these sanctions does not lie in their rationality; it lies in their emotionality, so that violations of norms cause feelings of guilt and shame, which is a much more reliable regulator of human behavior than sheer legal sanctions (Lal, 1998).

People's aversion to divorce does not simply reflect rational cost calculations. Instead, traditional value systems tend to make divorce so deeply anchored in people's emotions that it becomes a question of good and evil. Norms that can constrain people's behavior, even when it is in their rational interest to do something else, are norms that are taught as absolute rules and inculcated so that their consciences torture them if they are violated. Such societal norms have considerable momentum. The mere fact that the function of a given cultural pattern has weakened or disappeared does not mean that the norm itself disappears.

But if the original reason behind a given norm vanishes, it does open the way for that norm to weaken gradually. People begin to experiment with new ideas and norms, creating new life-styles. New generations then face a confrontation between old and new norms and life-styles, which offer them alternative role models among which they can choose. Insofar as the new worldview fits the new generations' firsthand formative experiences, they tend to adopt it. Thus, new values, life-styles, and role models can replace older ones in a gradual process of generational replacement.

Norms linked to the maintenance of the two-parent heterosexual family clearly are weakening for a variety of reasons, ranging from the rise of the welfare state to the drastic decline of infant mortality rates, meaning that a couple no longer needs to produce four or five children in order to replace the population. In these realms, one would expect experimentation to take place; gradually, new forms of behavior would emerge that deviate from traditional norms, and the groups most likely to accept these new forms of behavior are the young more than the old, the relatively secure more than the insecure, the educated more than the uneducated, and those having diverse human interactions more than those embedded in closely tied networks.

Value Change in History

Modernization is not linear, and cultural change does not move in a straight line from industrialization to the End of History. It changes direction in response to major changes in existential conditions. Thus, early industrialization did not bring a pronounced shift toward self-expression values. Indeed, it seems likely that the emphasis on individual autonomy underlying self-expression values was more widespread in some preindustrial societies than in industrial society. Industrialization is linked with increasing emphasis on economic accumulation and economic growth – and the mass-production assembly line requires conformity and discipline, rather than individual creativity and self-expression. The standardized nature of work in the Fordist industrial era required routine and strict discipline, in the factory or in private and public bureaucracies (Whyte, 1956). Moreover, the prime virtue by which the labor movement gained power was solidarity, based on group conformity. Preindustrial free-farmer and free-trading societies allowed for more individual autonomy than industrial societies, and the concept of human rights was born in the preindustrial English, American, and French Revolutions led by merchants and free farmers.

Unlike industrial workers, free farmers and merchants in preindustrial capitalist economies experienced a considerable degree of free choice in their daily
activities, which is crucial for the emergence of self-expression values.
This was not the first time in history that cultural change has changed direction. Emphasis on survival versus self-expression values may have shifted
even earlier. Ember and Ember (1996) argue, for example, that the subsistence pattern of hunting, herding, and fishing societies was much less routinized
and allowed for more individual initiative than was found in agrarian empires
whose "labor-repressive regimes" reduced human autonomy to its minimum
(Wittfogel, 1957; J. Diamond, 1997). Accordingly, both McNeill (1990) and
Nolan and Lenski (1999) speculate that hunting and gathering societies emphasize emancipative values more heavily than agrarian empires, which emphasize
collective discipline, group conformity, and divine authority as necessities for
survival. The political implications are obvious; it is noteworthy that hunting and gathering societies tend to be relatively liberal, egalitarian, and democratic, whereas despotic government has been the hallmark of agrarian empires
(McNeill, 1990; J. Diamond, 1997; Ember, Ember, and Russett, 1997; Nolan
and Lenski, 1999).

Interestingly, not all agrarian societies evolved into labor-repressive despotic
empires. This pattern was typical of the "hydraulic states" (Wittfogel, 1957)
in the civilization belt from Egypt to ancient China, in which collective irriga-
tion work necessary to tame large rivers required centralized authority and a
concentration of power. By contrast, rainfall agriculture, which became particularly productive in Western Europe in the late medieval age, evolved into a
system of family farms with property rights and broadly based market access,
giving people more autonomy in their daily activities (Jones, 1985; Hall, 1989;
Landes, 1998).[4] Not accidentally, the philosophy of humanism, the idea of human rights, and early modern versions of limited democracy[5] emerged in these

---

[4] As Jones (1985) and Lal (1998) argue, rainfall agriculture tends to result in a labor-to-land ratio
that is more conducive to human development than river delta agriculture. River delta agriculture
in the Fertile Crescent and in China had higher soil productivity than that found in Northwestern Europe, but Northwestern European rainfall agriculture reached higher labor productivity.
High labor productivity means that labor is valuable, which increases the economic value of the
individual. And as the economic value of the individual developed in the late medieval Commercial Revolution, the ethical value of the individual rose – with the philosophy of humanism.
Although rainfall agriculture was more conducive to human development, river delta agriculture
was more conducive to empire building – and large, powerful agrarian empires were generally
able to overcome smaller societies based on rainfall agriculture (McNeill, 1990). Rare exceptions
existed in classical Greece and late medieval Western Europe – precisely the settings that gave
rise to an emancipative ethos and limited versions of democracy based on civil and political
liberties.

[5] By democracy we mean government that is bound by a social contract (often manifested in a
constitution) that protects the citizens' individual autonomy by granting them civil rights and
gives citizens a say in politics by granting political rights. By "limited" democracy, we mean that
the citizenry that is entitled with civil and political rights is limited by property requirements or
other additional qualifications. What is meant by democracy has evolved over time. An obvious
example is female suffrage. By today's standards, Athens under Pericles would not be counted
as a democracy because it excluded a majority of the adult population (women, slaves, and

areas (Moore, 1966; Huntington, 1968; Dahl, 1973; Jones, 1985; Downing, 1992).

Traditional societies socialize people into closely knit groups held together by bonding ties that drive people to cooperate for the sake of group survival. These norms limited in-group violence, forced people into discipline and hierarchy, and repressed aspirations for social mobility. One way of discouraging internal violence was by encouraging the poor to accept one's God-given place in society (thereby earning salvation in the next world). But other norms emphasized sharing and charity by the well-off, stigmatizing individual accumulation as greed.

In the fourteenth and fifteenth centuries, new technology such as watermills increased the agricultural surplus and initiated a Commercial Revolution in Western Europe (Lal, 1998). The rise of an increasingly commercialized agriculture and the dense trading network that began to interweave Western Europe gave rise to rural and urban middle classes that began to develop property rights, and production began to outpace population growth (Tilly, 1997). The rise of preindustrial capitalism in the fourteenth and fifteenth centuries made societies receptive to Protestantism, especially the Calvinist version; because it encouraged accumulating and reinvesting capital into productive purposes, Calvinism was conducive to the flourishing of commercial societies (Landes, 1998). Thus, the traditional stigma against economic accumulation dwindled, and a mercantile worldview began to manifest itself. Even if economic scarcity did not vanish, farmers and traders in Western Europe experienced more individual autonomy in their daily activities than the peasants and merchants in the labor-repressive regimes of Eastern Europe and the Oriental civilizations from the Middle East to China.

The emancipative civic ethos that established limited versions of democracy through the liberal revolutions in preindustrial commercial societies did not continue in linear fashion through industrialization, which tended to bring universal suffrage for the working class but not necessarily democracy (Rueschemeyer et al., 1992). For universal suffrage often culminated in fascist and communist regimes. Industrial democracy was most likely to emerge in societies that had established limited versions of democracy in preindustrial times (Huntington, 1968; Dahl, 1973).

This situation changed with the rise of postindustrial society. Postindustrial societies bring much higher levels of existential security and individual

foreigners) from full citizenship. However, the idea that the authority of government is bound by the civil and political rights of a citizenry that includes at least a considerable part of the public, usually freeholders and free traders, was already present. This marks a fundamental difference from all other forms of government. Historically, limited versions of democracy occurred in the "protodemocracies" of the Sumerian city-states; the republics of northern India in the sixth century BC; classical Athens; the Roman Republic; and Iceland, Switzerland, northern Italy, the Lowlands, England, and Scandinavia in the medieval age (McNeill, 1990; Downing, 1992; Midlarski, 1997; Lal, 1998; Finer, 1999).

autonomy, which are conducive to the spread of self-expression values. Accordingly, in postindustrial societies, democracy becomes increasingly likely to prevail over communist, fascist, and other authoritarian regimes.

Cognition and Experience as Sources of Value Change

Classic modernization theory needs to be modified in another respect: we need to correct its one-sided emphasis on cognitive factors in shaping cultural change. Weber attributed the rise of a secular, rational worldview to the spread of scientific knowledge. Scientific discoveries had made traditional religious explanations obsolete; as awareness of scientific interpretations spread, religion was inexorably giving way to rationality. God was dead, and science had killed him – or, at least, it was doing so. Similarly, such modernization theorists as Lerner (1958), Inkeles and Smith (1974), and Inkeles (1983) argued that education drives the modernization process: within any given country, the most educated tend to have modern worldviews, and as educational levels rise, traditional religious worldviews inevitably give way to secular-rational ones.

This emphasis on cognitive forces captures an important part of the story but only part. Experiential factors, such as whether people feel that survival is secure or insecure, are at least equally important in shaping people's worldviews. Higher levels of formal education tend to be linked with the presence of secular-rational values and self-expression values. But higher education is not just an indicator of the extent to which one has absorbed scientific knowledge, rationality, and humanistic ideals. It is, at least equally, an indicator of the extent to which one has experienced relatively secure conditions during one's formative years, when formal education takes place. Throughout the world, children from economically secure families are most likely to obtain higher education.

A high level of education is an indicator that an individual grew up with a sufficiently high level of existential security to take survival for granted – and therefore gives top priority to autonomy, individual choice, and self-expression. In virtually every society that has been surveyed, people with a university education place stronger emphasis on self-expression than the public in general. This reflects the fact that the highly educated tend to be recruited from the more privileged strata and have grown up under relatively favorable existential conditions, experiencing more security and autonomy than other citizens of their society. But not only a person's own security and autonomy make a modern worldview more likely. A society's general social climate also helps shape people's sense of security and autonomy. Thus, although there is a universal tendency for higher education to encourage people to place more emphasis on self-expression values, there is much more difference in the degree of emphasis on self-expression values *between* the highly educated people of different nations than between the highly educated and the general public within the same nations (see Figure 9.1).

Thus, we can distinguish between education as an indicator of the extent to which people have experienced a sense of security and education as an indicator of the extent to which people have become familiar with scientific thought and humanistic ideals. Because the highly educated in all countries are relatively familiar with scientific thought and humanistic ideals, cross-national value differences among the highly educated do not reflect differential exposure to scientific thought, so much as they reflect differences in a society's prevailing sense of existential security and human autonomy.

The cognitive component of education is, for all practical purposes, irreversible, whereas one's sense of security and autonomy is not. The feeling that the world is secure or insecure is an early-established and relatively stable aspect of one's outlook. But these feelings can be eroded by short-term period effects and, even more so, by catastrophic events such as the collapse of one's entire society and economy. Such catastrophic events are rare, but an entire group of societies experienced them during the period covered by the Values Surveys. In 1989–91 communism collapsed throughout Central and Eastern Europe. In the Soviet successor states, this event brought drastic decreases in standards of living, stagnant or falling life expectancies, and the traumatic experience of the collapse of the social and political systems and also the belief systems under which these people had lived for many decades. Scientific *knowledge* did not disappear – it continued to grow – and educational levels remained as high as ever in these societies. But the prevailing sense of existential security and individual control over one's life fell sharply. If the emergence of modern values were solely determined by cognitive forces, then self-expression values would have continued to spread. But insofar as these values are shaped by feelings of security or insecurity and a sense of autonomy or heteronomy, we would expect to witness stagnation or a regression toward traditional values and survival values in the ex-Soviet societies. As we will see, this is exactly what happened.

Although the past decade has been a period of slow economic growth, the rich democracies have not experienced anything like the catastrophic changes felt in the ex-Soviet world. Moreover, the relative stagnation since 1990 has been offset by the momentum of intergenerational population replacement, which continues to push the rich democracies toward increasingly modern values. Cultural modernization has continued there, as one would expect. The cognitive interpretation implies that cultural modernization is an irreversible process as knowledge continues to increase. Our interpretation implies that it is reversible, and under the conditions that have prevailed since 1989, we would expect it to be reversing itself in recent years in most ex-Soviet societies. The empirical evidence indicates that it has. A society's prevailing sense of existential security is more important than cognitive factors.

In conclusion, cultural change is determined not simply by cognition and rational choice but by people's exposure to different existential conditions (Mark, 2002). Yet cultural change is not illogical. Quite the contrary, there is an evolutionary logic behind it, driving people to adopt those values that fit given existential conditions.

Cultural Change and Its Institutional Manifestations

Major changes in cultural values at the individual level are reflected in changes at the societal level, but there is rarely a one-to-one relationship between underlying cultural change and its societal-level manifestations. For example, starting in the mid-1960s, birthrates declined throughout postindustrial societies. By 1990 fertility rates were below the population replacement level in almost all postindustrial societies. Cultural change played a significant role in this shift (see Inglehart and Norris, 2003).

From 1960 to 1990 divorce rates rose sharply in almost all postindustrial societies except one: the Republic of Ireland, where divorce remained illegal until 1995. In Italy and Spain, divorce had become legal in the 1970s, and legalization was followed by a surge of divorces. One might attribute this sudden increase in divorce rates to the legal changes that preceded them. This interpretation is true but superficial, focusing only on the immediate cause. If one probes deeper, the first question that arises is, *Why* did divorce suddenly become legal in these countries? Divorce had been illegal for centuries because it violated deeply held religious norms. This remained true in the Republic of Ireland, where a majority of the public voted against legalizing divorce as recently as 1987. But, as our data indicate, these norms have gradually been weakening over time. Public support for legalizing divorce became increasingly widespread and articulate in Italy and Spain, until the laws themselves were changed in the 1970s. By 1995 even the Irish finally accepted divorce in a national referendum. One consequence was a sudden surge of divorces immediately after the laws were changed. Although the behavioral change was sudden and lumpy, it reflected a long process of incremental value change.

The rise of the pro-environmentalist Green Party in West Germany provides another illustration of the disparity between the incremental pace of cultural change and the abrupt emergence of its institutional manifestation. In 1983 the Greens suddenly achieved prominence when they won enough votes to enter the West German parliament for the first time, bringing a fundamental change in German politics. But this abrupt breakthrough reflected a gradual intergenerational rise of mass support for environmentalist policies. Institutional barriers, such as the fact that a party must win at least 5 percent of the vote to gain seats in the German parliament, made the party's breakthrough to prominence sudden and dramatic. But its rise reflected long-term processes of incremental change. If one focuses only on the immediate causes, a society's electoral rules seem to be the decisive factor: the Greens had little visibility until they surmounted the 5 percent threshold; and in societies without proportional representation, such as the United States and Great Britain, ecology parties may never play an important role. But even in these countries, a rising concern for environmental protection has transformed the agendas of existing parties. In most societies, the Green activists are mainly postmaterialists, and it seems unlikely that Green parties or environmentalist movements would have emerged without the

intergenerational cultural changes that gave rise to a postindustrial worldview
that reflects an increased awareness of ecological risks. Starting from obscurity
in the early 1980s, the Green parties have come a long way. At this writing,
environmentalist parties were part of the governing coalitions in Germany and
seven other European countries.

Similarly, in 2001 the Netherlands experienced a sudden surge in same-sex
marriages, starting from a zero base. The immediate cause of this shift was the
fact that the Dutch parliament had just legalized same-sex marriages – which
had been not merely illegal but virtually unthinkable for centuries. The root
cause of this societal-level change was the fact that a gradual shift had taken
place in the Dutch public's attitudes toward homosexuality. In this case, the
societal change is so recent that the four waves of the Values Surveys provide
detailed information about the cultural changes that preceded the societal-level
change. It is by no means coincidental that the Netherlands was the first country in the world to legalize same-sex marriages: the Values Surveys demonstrate
that the Dutch public has consistently been more tolerant of homosexuality
than any other public in the world. But even in the Netherlands, prevailing
attitudes were still unfavorable to homosexuality until recently. In the 1981
Values Survey, 22 percent of the Dutch public said that homosexuality was
never justifiable, selecting point 1 on a 10-point scale on which "1" meant that
homosexuality was never justifiable, and point 10 indicated that homosexuality
was always justifiable. At that time, 40 percent of the Dutch selected points 1
through 5, indicating relative disapproval. Disapproval of homosexuality was
still widespread in the Netherlands in 1981, although the Dutch were more favorable than any other public. In most countries, disapproval of homosexuality
was expressed by overwhelming majorities, ranging from 75 to 99 percent of
the public.

These attitudes have changed markedly since 1981 throughout postindustrial societies, as part of a broad intergenerational value shift toward more tolerant values. Throughout postindustrial societies, the younger birth cohorts are
much more tolerant of homosexuality than are their elders. In the Netherlands,
for example, in 1981 fully 52 percent of those older than sixty-five years felt
that homosexuality can never be justified, placing themselves at point 1 on
the scale. Among those who were eighteen to twenty-four years old, only 11
percent took this position. By 1999 only 7 percent of the Dutch public was
still at point 1, registering absolute disapproval, and only 22 percent at points
1 through 5. Disapproval had fallen to less than half its 1981 level. A year
later, in 2000, the Dutch parliament legalized same-sex marriages. In 2002 the
German constitutional court legalized same-sex marriages, followed by Canada
in 2003 and Spain in 2004. Not surprisingly, the Dutch public had the most
favorable attitudes toward homosexuality of any country in the world, and
the Germans, Spanish, and Canadians also ranked among the most favorable,
as Table 1.3 shows. In only nine countries did less than half of the public
disapprove of homosexuality, and all four of these countries fell into that
group.

TABLE 1.3. *Disapproval of Homosexuality in the Ten Most
Permissive Societies (percentage at points 1 to 5 on a 10-point scale)*

Country	Disapproval (%)
Netherlands	22
Sweden	26
Iceland	32
Denmark	41
Switzerland	43
Germany[a]	45
Spain	47
Canada	49
Luxembourg	49
Czech Republic	51
Norway	52

Note: These are the only societies (among 77) in which less than 53 percent
of the population disapproved of homosexuality in the latest available survey,
as indicated by selecting points 1–5. In the United States in 2000, 60 percent
disapproved of homosexuality – but it ranked among the 18 most tolerant
societies. In 24 societies, fully 95 percent or more of the public disapproved.

[a] German data are based on the combined results from the surveys in the
eastern and western regions of Germany in 1997 and 1999.

Cumulative Changes and Sudden Breakthroughs

It is commonly assumed that only change measures can explain social change.
This assumption seems convincing until one examines it more closely. In many
cases, especially those involving cross-level linkages such as the impact of cultural change on its institutional manifestation, a society's absolute *level* on a
given variable is a much stronger predictor of institutional change than recent
changes on that variable. To illustrate, let us assume that in 2000, 78 percent
of the Dutch public was at least moderately tolerant of homosexuality (some-
where to the right of point "5," the midpoint of the scale). At the same time,
only 8 percent of the Nigerian public was equally tolerant. But the amount of
change observed in Nigeria from 1995 to 2000 was actually greater than that in
the Netherlands: in 1995, only 4 percent of the Nigerian public was on the right
half of the scale, a figure that doubled in 2000, rising to 8 percent. During the
same period, tolerance of homosexuality in the Netherlands only rose slightly,
from 76 to 78 percent.

These figures are hypothetical but close to reality, and they illustrate an
important point: both in absolute and relative terms, the amount of attitudinal change observed in Nigeria from 1995 to 2000 was larger than in the
Netherlands; but the Netherlands was much likelier to manifest institutional
change. Unlike Nigeria, the Netherlands had passed the threshold at which
a majority of the public was tolerant of homosexuality. Accordingly, institutional change occurred in the Netherlands, in the form of legislation legalizing

same-sex marriages. This change is very unlikely to take place in Nigeria in the foreseeable future. The crucial difference lies in the fact that the Dutch public has a much higher *level* of tolerance than the Nigerian public: the absolute "stock" of tolerance is far more important than the short-term fluctuations or "flows" of tolerance.

The Dutch public's relatively high level of tolerance represents a stock that had been built up gradually, through a process of intergenerational value change that took place during the past fifty to sixty years. If one attempted to use standard time series methods to analyze this relationship, one would conclude that the attitudinal changes that took place in the Dutch public from 1940 to 1995 had no impact whatever on same-sex marriages and that the short-term attitudinal changes from 1995 to 2000 were *negatively* correlated with subsequent changes in the rate of same-sex marriages. The relatively high level of tolerance observed among the Dutch public in recent surveys is robust, shows large intergenerational differences, and has been growing gradually – and this relatively high level provides a far better predictor of institutional breakthroughs than do short-term fluctuations, which are relatively small and can fluctuate in either direction, so they may even have the wrong sign when change occurs.

A similar pattern applies to the relationship between cultural change and democratization. As we will demonstrate, there was a gradual intergenerational shift toward growing emphasis on autonomy and self-expression among the publics of Poland, Hungary, Czechoslovakia, East Germany, and other Central European countries during the decades before 1989. But another crucial factor occurred in 1988, when Gorbachev announced that Soviet troops would no longer be used to prop up unpopular communist regimes in Eastern Europe. Within a year communist regimes began collapsing throughout the region. Mass demands for liberalization had built up gradually over many years in these countries; but this cumulating factor could not manifest itself in an institutional breakthrough until the blocking factor – in this case, the Red Army – was removed. When cultural change leads to institutional change, the overcoming of thresholds or blocking factors is the rule, rather than the exception.

There is rarely a one-to-one correspondence between changes at the individual level and the system level. Accordingly, a society's *level* of economic development is a much better predictor of democratization than its economic growth rate. In fact, economic growth rates at any given point in time are misleading as a predictor of democracy – and they may even have the wrong sign (Doorenspleet, 2004). They tend to be highest in low-income countries such as China that are in the early phase of industrialization but have not yet reached a level of development where democracy becomes likely. If high growth continues, we expect that China will eventually make the transition to democracy – *not* because it has high growth rates at that time but because it has reached a high *level* of development.

We reject both economic and cultural determinism. It is clear that given elites, leaders, institutions, and situation-specific factors play crucial roles. The immediate cause of institutional change can virtually always be found at the elite level, almost by definition, because the people who negotiate political changes are *defined* as elites (even if they did not fall into that category a year earlier). But underlying cultural changes also play a major role in the emergence of important institutional changes, from changing legislation concerning gays and lesbians to the massive shift toward democracy that took place from 1985 to 1995.

If one believed that cultural changes alone determined institutional change, one would assume that there must have been a sudden surge of support for democracy among East European publics in 1989, and a massive surge of approval for homosexuality in the Netherlands in 1999. This was not true in either case: instead, a slow but steady intergenerational value change took place during the decades preceding both of these institutional breakthroughs. The precise timing of when the institutional breakthrough occurred was determined by elite-level factors. But gradual underlying value changes were the root cause of the fact that East Germany suddenly democratized in 1989–90, and that same-sex marriage finally became legal in the Netherlands in 2000.

Intergenerational cultural changes have been gradually transforming the value systems of people in many countries, bringing a shift from survival values to self-expression values. As this book demonstrates, the extent to which a given public placed high priority on self-expression values when a window of opportunity opened in 1988 (when Gorbachev announced that the Soviet army would no longer prop up communist regimes in Central and Eastern Europe) was crucial in determining how far toward democracy their society would subsequently move – and how well democratic institutions flourished once they were adopted.

Consequences of Cultural Change

The shift from industrial to postindustrial values is eroding many of the key institutions of industrial society. In the political realm, the rise of postindustrial values brings declining respect for authority and growing emphasis on participation and self-expression. These trends are conducive to democratization in authoritarian societies and to a more elite-challenging, issue-oriented, and direct form of democracy in already-democratic societies. In any case, rising self-expression values push for more genuine democracy. Self-expression values are inherently emancipative and people-centered, giving rise to a new type of humanistic society that promotes human freedom and autonomy on numerous fronts.

Respect for authority is eroding, and the long-term trend toward increased mass participation has taken on a new character. In large-scale agrarian societies, political participation was limited to a narrow minority. In industrializing societies, the masses were mobilized by disciplined, elite-led political parties. This was a major advance for democratization, and it resulted in unprecedented numbers of people taking part in politics by voting; however, mass participation continued to be guided by elites, in keeping with the Iron Law of Oligarchy (Michels, 1962 [1912]).

In postindustrial society the emphasis is shifting from voting to more spontaneous, issue-specific, and elite-challenging forms of civic action. New forms of political self-expression extend the boundary of politics from the narrow domain of elite-led electoral campaigns into increasingly autonomous forms of public self-expression. The traditional representative form of elite-centered democracy transforms into a people-centered form of democracy (Cain, Dalton, and Scarrow, 2003). Contrary to often-repeated claims that social capital and mass participation are eroding, the publics of postindustrial societies are intervening in politics more actively today than ever before; however, they are changing the ways in which they participate.

Elite-led forms of participation are dwindling. Mass loyalties to long-established hierarchical political parties are weakening. No longer content to be disciplined troops, the public has become increasingly autonomous and elite-challenging. Consequently, though voter turnout is stagnant or declining (Dalton and Wattenberg, 2000), people are participating in politics in more active and issue-specific ways (Dalton, 2001; Norris, 2002). In many countries, demonstrations against American military intervention in Iraq in 2002–3 were the largest in history. Increasingly, people are using the public sphere as a stage for expressing commitments to alternative life-styles (Cain et al., 2003). As the leaders of political machines are losing their ability to mobilize voter turnout, the publics of postindustrial societies are engaging in new, largely self-organizing and self-expressive forms of participation (Welzel, Inglehart, and Deutsch, 2004). People engage in these activities even if they think it is unlikely to change official decisions. Political self-expression becomes a value in itself and not just a way to attain specific goals.

Antimodern Reactions to Modernity

Rapid changes linked with postindustrialization stimulate defensive reactions among marginalized parts of the population. Postindustrialization brings increasing individual freedom and growing opportunities for self-actualization for large parts of society, but substantial minorities – particularly the less educated and the unemployed – still feel existential threats. In terms of relative deprivation, they may be even worse off than poor people in poor societies. Education is the most important form of capital in the knowledge society, which puts the less educated in a worse position than they had in the industrial age.

In the industrial age, disciplined mass organizations were a tremendous asset to the lower classes because they enabled them to translate their sheer numbers into political power. They could exert pressure to redistribute wealth from the rich to the poor, bringing an increasing degree of income equality (Esping-Andersen, 1990). The individualizing tendency of postindustrial societies has partly reversed this trend. The working class has declined in numbers and lost the cohesion that gave it political power; labor unions are weakening. In addition, the working classes in postindustrial societies are under increasing economic pressure from globalization and immigration; the high-cost labor force of rich countries is now competing with that of low-income countries. The equalizing trend in income distribution has been reversed since the 1980s (Goesling, 2001). This nourishes threat perceptions and defensive reactions, providing a social base for new dogmas, including right-wing populism and new forms of religious fundamentalism. Contrary to widespread belief, religious fundamentalists have not become more numerous in Western societies, but they *have* become more active and more salient (Norris and Inglehart, 2004). Formerly a relatively quiescent segment of the public, in recent years they have come to believe (accurately) that some of their most basic norms are rapidly eroding, which has galvanized those with traditional religious beliefs into heightened political activism, opposing such things as abortion and same-sex marriage. Consequently, the postindustrial phase of modernization is not conflict-free. On the whole, postindustrialization brings individualization, more autonomy, and more freedom of choice, but it also brings new conflicts. It stimulates anti-modernist reactions among marginalized parts of the population, feeding the ranks of right-wing parties (U. Beck, 2002).

Existential Security, Individual Autonomy, and the Knowledge Society

Socioeconomic development brings rising levels of existential security, which is its most basic contribution to human development. This process relieves people from material constraints on their life choices. This contributes to rising self-expression values because it allows people to move beyond sheer survival and focus on other goals. But providing existential security is not the only way through which socioeconomic development is conducive to self-expression values. The growing experience of autonomy linked with the rise of the knowledge society, and its social complexities, cross-cutting networks and diverse human interactions, is also important.

Some oil-exporting countries, such as Bahrain and the United Arab Emirates, are rich and have maximized their population's existential security through extensive transfer programs. As Barro (1997), M. Ross (2001), and others have demonstrated, however, these societies have not evolved the occupational diversification, social complexity, and knowledge-intensity that characterize the creative economies of postindustrial societies. The availability of vast natural resources made it unnecessary to make major investments in human capital, or to establish a knowledge society. Instead, they established rent-seeking economies based on the revenues of state monopolies in oil exports. Rentier economies can become very rich, but they do not show the massive individualization trend that occurs in postindustrial economies. Although their populations enjoy high levels of existential security, the publics of rich oil-exporting countries do not show an emphasis on self-expression values comparable with that found in postindustrial societies. Existential security gives rise to self-expression values if it is coupled with individualization and the experience of autonomy. This experience arises from the destandardization and diversification of economic activities, social roles, and human interactions typical of postindustrial economies. The experience of existential security evolves into a broader sense of human autonomy in postindustrial economies far more than in rentier economies or in industrial economies.[6]

Conclusion

This book presents a massive body of evidence supporting the central insight of modernization theory: socioeconomic development brings systematic changes in political, social, and cultural life. But it is clear that earlier versions of modernization theory need revision. We propose the following modifications:

1. Although socioeconomic development tends to transform societies in a predictable direction, the process is not deterministic. Many other factors besides socioeconomic development are involved, so our predictions are probabilistic: other things being equal, socioeconomic development tends to make people more secular, tolerant, and trusting and to place more emphasis on self-expression, participation, and the quality of life. But socioeconomic factors are not the only significant influences.

2. Religion and other aspects of a society's traditional cultural heritage are not dying out and will not disappear with modernization. Contrary to Marxist expectations, a society's historical cultural heritage continues to shape the values and behavior of its people. Although the publics of industrializing societies are becoming richer and more educated, we are not moving toward a uniform global culture: cultural convergence is not taking place. A society's cultural heritage is remarkably enduring.

3. Cultural modernization is not irreversible. It results from socioeconomic development and protracted economic collapse can reverse it, as was happening during the 1990s in most of the Soviet successor states.

4. The process of cultural change is not linear. The prevailing direction of change has shifted repeatedly in history. Industrialization gives rise to one major process of cultural change, bringing bureaucratization and secularization. But the rise of postindustrial societies leads to *another* major process of cultural change that moves in a different direction: instead of rationalization, centralization, and bureaucratization, the new trend is toward increasing emphasis on individual autonomy and self-expression values. Thus, economic development produces not one but two major dimensions of cross-cultural variation, one linked with industrialization and the other linked with the rise of postindustrial society.

[6] Landes (1998) discusses a historical example of this contrast in comparing the Spanish and Dutch colonial empires. The Spanish empire established a rent-seeking economy based on the exploitation of Latin American silver mines. The Dutch empire was based on an innovative commercial economy. Accordingly, the sense of individual autonomy, liberty, and freedom of expression was far more pronounced in Dutch society than it was in Spanish society in colonial times.

5. An ethnocentric early version of modernization interpreted the process as Westernization. It is not. Historically, the process of industrialization began in the West, but during the past few decades East Asia has led the world in many aspects of modernization. Similarly, these changes do not constitute Americanization. The United States is not leading the world in cultural change; it is a deviant case, exhibiting much more traditional and religious values than other rich societies. The United States is not the model for the cultural changes that are taking place, and industrializing societies in general are *not* becoming like the United States, as a popular version of modernization theory assumed.

6. Most important, emerging self-expression values transform modernization into a process of human development, giving rise to a new type of humanistic society that promotes human emancipation on many fronts, from equal rights for homosexuals, handicapped people, and women to the rights of people in general. This process reflects a humanistic transformation of modernization.

Throughout history, cultural change has repeatedly changed course. In postindustrial societies in recent decades, rising emphasis on self-expression values has become the key cultural manifestation of modernization. Human choice and emancipation have become the leading themes in all domains of life from politics to child care to gender relations to work motivations to religious orientations and civic engagement. Self-expression values and rising emphasis on freedom of choice emerge as increasingly favorable existential conditions allow the universal desire for autonomy to take priority. Rising emphasis on human choice has immensely important consequences, generating pressures for female empowerment, more responsive elites, effective civil and political liberties, and democratic institutions.

In the postindustrial stage, socioeconomic development, rising self-expression, and effective democracy work together, providing the means, values, and rights that make people increasingly able, willing, and entitled to shape their lives according to their autonomous choices – relatively free from external constraints. This process constitutes "human" development because it emphasizes the most distinctively human ability: the ability to make decisions and actions based on autonomous choices. The process of human development leads to the emergence of increasingly strong societal demands for democracy. Culture alone does not determine the outcome: these changes are probabilistic. World events, wars, depressions, institutional changes, elite decisions, and even specific leaders can influence what happens; but cultural change is a major factor in the emergence and survival of democracy, and one that has generally been underestimated.

2

Value Change and the Persistence of Cultural Traditions

Modernization theorists from Karl Marx to Daniel Bell have argued that socioeconomic development brings pervasive cultural changes. But cultural theorists from Max Weber to Samuel Huntington have claimed that cultural values have an enduring and autonomous influence on society. Paradoxically as it may seem, both schools are right. This chapter presents empirical evidence of massive cultural change *and* the persistence of distinctive cultural traditions.

We analyze evidence of cultural change from the Values Surveys, the largest investigation ever made of attitudes, values, and beliefs around the world. These surveys have carried out four waves of representative national surveys, in 1981–3, 1989–91, 1995–97, and 1999–2001. They cover eighty-one societies on all six inhabited continents, containing more than 85 percent of the world's population.[1]

Our thesis holds that socioeconomic development is linked with a broad syndrome of distinctive value orientations. Does such a syndrome exist? The Values Surveys contain hundreds of items, and not all of them tap important aspects of cross-cultural variation. In order to test the thesis that socioeconomic development brings systematic changes in basic values, we first need to identify a limited number of key dimensions that tap important values and then determine whether they are linked with socioeconomic development. Our theoretical framework implies that we should find *two* such dimensions, one linked with industrialization and the other with the rise of postindustrial society.

In previous research, Inglehart (1997) analyzed aggregated national-level data from the forty-three societies included in the 1989–91 Values Survey, finding large and coherent cross-cultural differences. Each of the two most

---

[1] To avoid prolixity, our figures and tables refer to the 1981, 1989–91, 1995–97, and 1999–2001 rounds of the Values Surveys as the 1980, 1990, 1995, and 2000 data, respectively. For variable specifications of the analyses throughout this book, see the Internet Appendix at http://www.worldvaluessurvey.org/publications/humandevelopment.html.

TABLE 2.1. *Two Dimensions of Cross-Cultural Variation: Aggregate-Level Analysis*

	Factor Loadings
Traditional values emphasize the following (Secular-rational values emphasize the opposite):[a]	
God is very important in respondent's life.	.91
It is more important for a child to learn obedience and religious faith than independence and determination. (Autonomy index)	.88
Abortion is never justifiable.	.82
Respondent has strong sense of national pride.	.81
Respondent favors more respect for authority.	.73
Survival values emphasize the following (Self-expression values emphasize the opposite):[b]	
Respondent gives priority to economic and physical security over self-expression and quality of life. (4-item Materialist/ Postmaterialist Values Index)	.87
Respondent describes self as not very happy.	.81
Homosexuality is never justifiable.	.77
Respondent has not and would not sign a petition.	.74
You have to be very careful about trusting people.	.46

Note: The original polarities vary; the above statements show how each item relates to the given factor (factors = 2, varimax rotation, listwise deletion).
[a] This first factor explains 46 percent of total cross-national variation; secular = positive pole.
[b] This second factor explains 25 percent of total cross-national variation; self-expression = positive pole.
Source: World Values Survey data from more than 200 surveys carried out in four waves in 78 societies.

important dimensions that emerge from this analysis taps scores of variables and demonstrates that the worldviews of peoples in rich societies differ systematically from those prevailing in low-income societies, across a wide range of political, social, and religious norms and beliefs. These two dimensions reflect cross-national polarization between *traditional* versus *secular-rational* values and *survival* versus *self-expression* values. These two dimensions make it possible to locate each society on a global map of cross-cultural variation (Inglehart, 1997: 81–98; Inglehart and Baker, 2000).

We build on these findings by constructing comparable measures of cross-cultural variation that can be used with all four waves of the Values Surveys, at both the individual level and the national level. Starting with the variables identified in analysis of the 1989–91 surveys, we selected variables that not only tapped these two dimensions but had been utilized in the same format in all four waves of the Values Surveys. Inglehart (1997) used factor scores based on twenty-two variables, but we reduced this number to ten items to minimize problems of missing data (when one variable is missing, one loses an entire nation from the analysis). The ten items are shown in Table 2.1. Full documentation of how the variables in our analyses are measured can be obtained from the Internet Appendix on the website of the World Values Surveys Association.[2]

Table 2.1 shows how these ten items tap the traditional versus secular-rational dimension and the survival versus self-expression dimension, using a factor analysis of the Values Surveys data aggregated to the national level by taking the mean score for each nation. The items in each dimension are highly correlated with each other; together, the two dimensions explain 71 percent of the total cross-national variation in these ten variables. This reflects the fact that cross-cultural variation is surprisingly coherent. This coherence exists *although* we deliberately selected items that cover a wide range of topics. With the first dimension, for example, we could have selected five items referring to religion and obtained an even more tightly correlated cluster, but our goal was to measure broad dimensions of cross-cultural variation that tap a variety of important values and beliefs.

The factor scores generated by the ten items used in this analysis are highly correlated with the factor scores based on twenty-two items (Inglehart, 1997: 334–35, 388). The traditional versus secular-rational dimension based on five items that is used here is almost perfectly correlated ($r = .95$) with the factor scores from the comparable dimension based on eleven variables; and the survival versus self-expression dimension based on five variables is almost perfectly correlated ($r = .96$) with the survival versus self-expression dimension based on eleven variables. These dimensions are robust and reflect a much broader pool of items. The ten indicators used here (five to tap each dimension) were chosen for technical reasons: in order to be able to compare findings across time, we used indicators that had been included in all four waves of the Values Surveys. These ten indicators reflect only a handful of the many beliefs and values that these two dimensions tap, and they are not necessarily the most sensitive indicators of these dimensions. They do a good job of tapping two

---

[2] The Internet Appendix lists all variables used in this analysis, with specific information on operationalization, scaling, and data sources. We call attention to one point in particular: to avoid dropping an entire society from our analysis when one of these variables is not available, the nation-level aggregate dataset (but not the individual-level dataset) sometimes uses results from another survey in the same country. For example, the materialist-postmaterialist battery was not included in the 1981 surveys in the United States and Australia; but this battery *was* included in the 1980 National Election Surveys in both countries, and the results from those surveys are used in these cases. Similarly, the question concerning homosexuality was not asked in the 1995 survey in Bangladesh, but it was asked in the 2000 survey in that country, and we used that value for Bangladesh 1995 in the aggregate dataset. This reduces the amount of change over time on the survival/self-expression values indicated for Bangladesh, but the alternative would be to omit Bangladesh 1995 altogether from the aggregate dataset. Because we did have data for the other four high-loading variables on that dimension, Bangladesh's score for 1995 is probably in the right ball park. In a few cases, when a given variable was not available from another survey from the same country, we ranked all societies on the variable most closely correlated with the missing variable and assigned the mean score of the two adjacent countries in this ranking. This extreme measure was used less than 1 percent of the time. In 96 percent of the cases, the correct variable was available from the given country at the given time; in the great majority of the remaining cases, it was available from another survey in the same country.

TABLE 2.2. *Two Dimensions of Cross-Cultural Variation: Individual-Level Analysis*

	Factor Loadings
Traditional values emphasize the following	
(Secular-rational values emphasize the opposite):[a]	
God is very important in respondent's life.	.70
It is more important for a child to learn obedience and religious	
faith than independence and determination. (Autonomy index)	.61
Abortion is never justifiable.	.61
Respondent has strong sense of national pride.	.60
Respondent favors more respect for authority.	.51
Survival values emphasize the following	
(Self-expression values emphasize the opposite):[b]	
Respondent gives priority to economic and physical security	
over self expression and quality of life. (4-item	
Materialist/Postmaterialist Values Index)	.59
Respondent describes self as not very happy.	.59
Homosexuality is never justifiable.	.58
Respondent has not and would not sign a petition	.54
You have to be very careful about trusting people.	.44

Note: The original polarities vary; the above statements show how each item relates to the given factor. Total N = 165,594; smallest N for any of the above variables is 146,789.
[a] First factor explains 26 percent of total individual variation; secular = positive pole.
[b] Second factor explains 13 percent of total individual variation; self-expression = positive pole.
Source: World Values Survey data from 125 surveys carried out in three waves in 65 societies.

extremely important dimensions of cross-cultural variation, but we should bear in mind that these specific items are only indicators of much broader underlying dimensions of cross-cultural variation. We get essentially the same results when we base our analysis on twenty or thirty variables, but when we do so, we lose many cases because of missing data.[3]

The goal of measuring these values optimally is constrained by the fact that, in order to examine changes over time (as we do in Chapter 5), we are restricted to using only those items that were included in all four waves. In fact, one can measure these values even more accurately if one uses as indicators the optimal variables, regardless of whether they were included in all four waves. We do so in Part II of this book, which does not make comparisons over time, but focuses on analyzing the linkages of these values to democratic institutions.

Table 2.2 shows the results from a factor analysis of the same variables using the individual-level data. Instead of about 200 nation-level cases, we now have more than 250,000 individual-level cases. As one would expect, the factor loadings here are considerably lower than at the national level, where

---

[3] We also get basically similar results from extracting the two value dimensions by an alternative procedure (oblimin rotation), although the factors are no longer uncorrelated; see Internet Appendix (note 2).

much of the random measurement error normally found in survey data cancels out. Nevertheless, these items produce two clearly defined dimensions with a basic structure very similar to that found at the national level (see our discussion of level of analysis problems in Chapter 9).

Each factor taps a broad dimension of cross-cultural variation involving dozens of additional variables. Table 2.3 shows twenty-four additional variables in the Values Surveys that are closely correlated with the traditional versus secular-rational values dimension (the median correlation is .61). This dimension reflects the contrast between societies in which religion is very important and those in which it is not, but deference to the authority of God, fatherland, and family are all closely linked with each other. The importance of the family is a major theme: in traditional societies, a main goal in most people's lives is to make their parents proud; and one must always love and respect one's parents regardless of how they behave; conversely, parents must do their best for their children, even at the cost of their own well-being; and people idealize large families (and actually have them: high scores on this dimension correlate strongly with high fertility rates). Although the people of traditional societies have high levels of national pride, favor more respect for authority, take protectionist attitudes toward foreign trade, and feel that environmental problems can be solved without international agreements, they accept national authority passively: they rarely discuss politics. In preindustrial societies the family is crucial to survival. Accordingly, societies at the traditional pole of this dimension reject divorce and take a pro-life stance on abortion, euthanasia, and suicide. They emphasize social conformity rather than individualistic striving, support deference to authority, and have high levels of national pride and a nationalistic outlook. Societies with secular-rational values have the opposite preferences on all of these topics.

The survival versus self-expression dimension taps a syndrome of tolerance, trust, emphasis on subjective well-being, civic activism, and self-expression that emerges in postindustrial societies with high levels of existential security and individual autonomy. At the opposite pole, people in societies shaped by existential insecurity and rigid intellectual and social constraints on human autonomy tend to emphasize economic and physical security above all; they feel threatened by foreigners, ethnic diversity, and cultural change – which leads to intolerance of gays and other outgroups, insistence on traditional gender roles, and an authoritarian political outlook.

A central component of this dimension involves the polarization between materialist and postmaterialist values. These values tap an intergenerational shift from emphasis on economic and physical security, toward increasing emphasis on self-expression, subjective well-being, and the quality of life (Inglehart 1977, 1990, 1997). This cultural shift is found throughout postindustrial society; it emerges among birth cohorts that have grown up under conditions in which one can take survival for granted. These values are linked with the emergence of growing emphasis on environmental protection, the women's movement, and rising demands for participation in decision making in economic and

TABLE 2.3. *Correlates of Traditional versus Secular-Rational Values*

	Correlation with Traditional/Secular-Rational Values[a]
Traditional values emphasize the following (Secular-rational values emphasize the opposite):	
Religion is very important in respondent's life.	.89
Respondent believes in Heaven.	.88
One of respondent's main goals in life has been to make his or her parents proud.	.81
Respondent believes in Hell.	.76
Respondent attends church regularly.	.75
Respondent has a great deal of confidence in the country's churches.	.72
Respondent gets comfort and strength from religion.	.71
Respondent describes self as "a religious person."	.66
Euthanasia is never justifiable.	.65
Work is very important in respondent's life.	.63
There should be stricter limits on selling foreign goods here.	.61
Suicide is never justifiable.	.60
Parents' duty is to do their best for their children even at the expense of their own well-being.	.57
Respondent seldom or never discusses politics.	.57
Respondent places self on right side of a left-right scale.	.57
Divorce is never justifiable.	.56
There are absolutely clear guidelines about good and evil.	.56
Expressing one's own preferences clearly is more important than understanding others' preferences.	.56
My country's environmental problems can be solved without any international agreements to handle them.	.53
If a woman earns more money than her husband, it's almost certain to cause problems.	.49
One must always love and respect one's parents regardless of their behavior.	.45
Family is very important in respondent's life.	.43
Respondent relatively favorable to having the army rule the country.	.41
Respondent favors having a relatively large number of children.	.40

[a] The number shows how strongly each variable is correlated with the traditional/secular-rational values index. The original polarities vary; the statements show how each item relates to the traditional/secular-rational values index.

Source: Nation-level data from 65 societies surveyed in the 1990 and 1996 World Values Surveys.

political life. During the past thirty years, these values have become increasingly widespread in almost all postindustrial societies, as is demonstrated in Chapter 4.

Table 2.4 shows the wide range of values that are linked with the survival versus self-expression dimension. Societies that emphasize survival values have relatively low levels of subjective well-being, report relatively poor health, and are low on interpersonal trust, relatively intolerant of outgroups, and low on support for gender equality. They emphasize materialist values, have relatively high levels of faith in science and technology, and are relatively low on environmental activism and relatively favorable to authoritarian government. Societies that rank high on self-expression values tend to have the opposite preferences on all of these topics. Overall, self-expression values reflect an emancipative and humanistic ethos, emphasizing human autonomy and choice.

When survival is uncertain, cultural diversity seems threatening. When there isn't enough to go around, foreigners are perceived as dangerous outsiders who may take away one's sustenance. People cling to traditional gender roles and sexual norms, emphasizing absolute rules and old familiar norms, in an attempt to maximize predictability in an uncertain world. Conversely, when survival begins to be taken for granted, ethnic and cultural diversity become increasingly acceptable – indeed, beyond a certain point, diversity is not only tolerated but becomes *positively* valued because it is interesting and stimulating. In postindustrial societies, people seek out foreign restaurants to taste new kinds of cuisine; they pay large sums of money and travel long distances to experience exotic cultures. Changing gender roles and sexual norms no longer seem threatening.

The past few decades have witnessed one of the most dramatic cultural changes that has occurred since the dawn of recorded history, the shift toward gender equality, enabling women to choose from among a much wider range of life trajectories than ever before. Polarization over new gender roles is a major component of the survival versus self-expression dimension: one of its highest-loading issues involves whether men make better political leaders than women. In the world as a whole, a majority still accepts the idea that men make better political leaders than women; however, this view is rejected by growing majorities in postindustrial societies and is overwhelmingly rejected by the younger generation within these societies. Equal rights for women, gays and lesbians, foreigners, and other outgroups tend to be rejected in societies where survival seems uncertain but are increasingly accepted in societies that emphasize self-expression values.

Thus, each of the two major phases of modernization – industrialization and the emergence of postindustrial society – gives rise to a major dimension of cross-cultural variation.

Cross-cultural variation is highly constrained. As the first dimension's loadings indicate (see Tables 2.1 and 2.2), if the people of a given society place strong emphasis on religion, one can predict that society's relative position

TABLE 2.4. *Correlates of Survival versus Self-Expression Values*

	Correlation with Survival/ Self-Expression Values[a]
Survival values emphasize the following (Self-expression values emphasize the opposite): Men make better political leaders than women.	.86
Respondent is dissatisfied with financial situation of his or her household.	.83
A woman has to have children in order to be fulfilled.	.83
Respondent rejects foreigners, homosexuals, and people with AIDS as neighbors.	.81
Respondent favors more emphasis on the development of technology.	.78
Respondent has not recycled things to protect the environment.	.78
Respondent has not attended a meeting or signed a petition to protect the environment.	.75
When seeking a job, a good income and safe job are more important than a feeling of accomplishment and working with people you like.	.74
Respondent is relatively favorable to state ownership of business and industry.	.74
A child needs a home with both a father and a mother to grow up happily.	.73
Respondent does not describe own health as very good.	.73
One must always love and respect one's parents regardless of their behavior.	.71
When jobs are scarce, men have more right to a job than women.	.69
Prostitution is never justifiable.	.69
Government should take more responsibility to ensure that everyone is provided for.	.68
Respondent does not have much free choice or control over his or her life.	.67
A university education is more important for a boy than for a girl.	.67
Respondent does not favor less emphasis on money and material possessions.	.66
Respondent rejects people with criminal records as neighbors.	.66
Respondent rejects heavy drinkers as neighbors.	.65
Hard work is one of the most important things to teach a child.	.64
Imagination is *not* one of the most important things to teach a child.	.62

(continued)

TABLE 2.4 *(continued)*

	Correlation with Survival/ Self-Expression Values[a]
Tolerance and respect for others are *not* the most important things to teach a child.	.62
Scientific discoveries will help, rather than harm, humanity.	.60
Leisure is not very important in life.	.60
Friends are not very important in life.	.58
Having a strong leader who does not have to bother with parliament and elections would be a good form of government.	.56
Respondent has not and would not take part in a boycott.	.56
Government ownership of business and industry should be increased.	.55
Democracy is not necessarily the best form of government.	.45
Respondent opposes sending economic aid to poorer countries.	.42

[a] The number shows how strongly each variable is correlated with the survival/self-expression values index. The original polarities vary; the statements show how each item relates to the traditional/secular-rational values index.

Source: Nation-level data from 65 societies surveyed in the 1990 and 1996 World Values Surveys.

on many other variables, from attitudes toward abortion, feelings of national pride, and the desirability of more respect for authority to attitudes toward child-rearing. The second dimension reflects another wide-ranging but strongly correlated cluster of variables involving materialist values (such as maintaining order and fighting inflation) versus postmaterialist values (such as freedom and self-expression), subjective well-being, interpersonal trust, political activism, and tolerance of outgroups (measured by acceptance or rejection of homosexuality, a sensitive indicator of tolerance toward outgroups in general).

Self-expression values emphasize tolerance of diversity and rising demands for participation in decision making in economic and political life. The shift from survival values to self-expression values is linked with a rising sense of existential security and human autonomy, which produces a humanistic culture of tolerance and trust, where people place a relatively high value on individual freedom and self-expression and have activist political orientations.

Socioeconomic Development and Cultural Change

We have identified two major dimensions of cross-cultural variation. Are they linked with socioeconomic development, as we hypothesize? Figure 2.1 shows a global cultural map based on the two dimensions generated by the factor

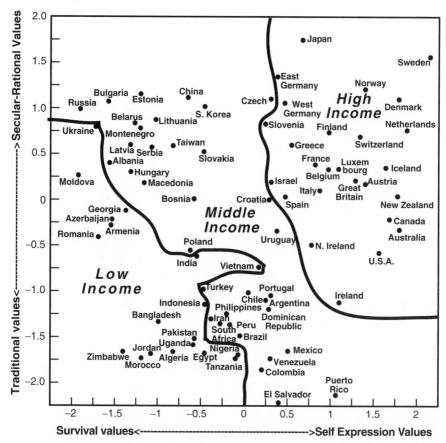

FIGURE 2.1. Economic levels and locations of 80 societies on cultural map. Cultural locations reflect each society's factor scores on two major dimensions of cross-cultural variation. Economic zones are from World Bank, *World Development Indicators, 2002.*

analysis just discussed. The vertical axis reflects the polarization between traditional and secular-rational values: societies that emphasize traditional values fall near the bottom of the map, whereas those with secular-rational values fall near the top. The horizontal axis reflects the polarization between survival values and self-expression values: societies that emphasize survival values fall near the left-hand side of the map, whereas those with self-expression values fall near the right. As this map demonstrates, socioeconomic development is strongly linked with a society's basic cultural values. The value systems of richer countries differ dramatically and systematically from those of poorer countries. *All* of the "high-income" societies (as defined by the World Bank) rank relatively high on both dimensions, falling into a zone toward the upper right-hand corner. Conversely, *all* of the "low-income" societies fall into a zone on the lower left of Figure 2.1. The middle-income societies fall into an intermediate cultural-economic zone. One rarely finds such a consistent pattern in social science data: there are no exceptions to this pattern among the eighty societies for which we have data. Socioeconomic development tends to propel societies in a common direction, regardless of their cultural heritage.

Per capita GDP is only one indicator of a society's level of socioeconomic development. As Marx argued, the rise of the industrial working class was a key event in modern history. Furthermore, the changing nature of the labor force defines three distinct stages of socioeconomic development: agrarian society, industrial society, and postindustrial society (Bell 1973, 1976). Thus, one could draw still another set of boundaries around the societies in Figure 2.1: societies with a high percentage of the labor force in agriculture are located near the bottom of the map, societies with a high percentage of industrial workers near the top, and societies with a high percentage in the service sector near the right-hand side of the map.

The traditional versus secular-rational dimension is associated with the transition from agrarian to industrial society, showing a strong *positive* correlation with the percentage of the work force in the industrial sector ($r = .61$) and a *negative* correlation with the percentage in the agricultural sector ($r = -.49$); it is only weakly linked with the percentage in the service sector ($r = .19$). The shift from an agrarian mode of production to industrial production is linked with a shift from traditional values toward increasing rationalization and secularization.

The survival versus self-expression dimension is linked with the rise of a *service* economy. It shows an $r = .73$ correlation with the size of the work force in the service sector (and a $-.46$ correlation with the agricultural sector), but is only weakly (and negatively) related to the size of the industrial sector ($r = -.21$). The traditional versus secular-rational values dimension and the survival versus self-expression values dimension reflect industrialization and the rise of postindustrial society, respectively. This reflects a two-stage process of cultural modernization. In the first phase of modernization, the industrial sector grows at the expense of the agricultural sector. This process can be measured by subtracting the percentage of the work force in agriculture from the percentage in industry. This process of industrialization is linked with the rationalization of authority, reflected in rising secular-rational values. In the second phase of modernization, the service sector grows at the expense of the industrial sector. This process can be measured by subtracting the percentage of the work force in industry from the percentage in services. This postindustrial economic transformation is linked with another change of authority orientations, the emancipation *from* authority, reflected in rising self-expression values.

Figures 2.2 and 2.3 demonstrate these points. Figure 2.2a shows that, as the proportion of the work force in the industrial sector exceeds the work force in agriculture, a society's belief system tends to shift from traditional to secular-rational values. Cross-national variation in the transition from an agrarian to an industrial society explains 32 percent of the variation in secularization. But this process has no significant impact on the survival versus self-expression values dimension: industrialization does not promote the rise of self-expression values,

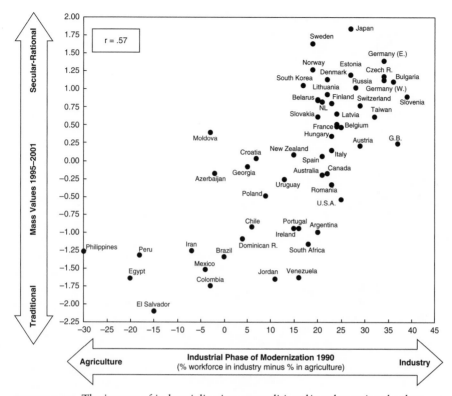

FIGURE 2.2a. The impact of industrialization on traditional/secular-rational values.

as Figure 2.2b illustrates. This is one reason why industrialization brought universal suffrage but did not necessarily bring democracy. Universal suffrage can be, and often is, adopted by authoritarian states such as communist China or the Soviet Union, which regularly produced much higher rates of voter turnout than liberal democracies ever attained. The mass values that emphasize individual autonomy and emancipation are not yet widespread in most early industrial societies, which historically were almost as likely to adopt fascist or communist systems as they were to adopt democratic institutions. The value systems of industrial societies emphasize the rationalization of authority, rather than emancipation *from* authority. The fact that industrialization does not support an emancipative ethos explains why there is no strong specific link between industrialization and democracy. All industrial societies produce mobilized publics, introducing universal suffrage and various other elite-directed forms of participation. But industrialization was about as likely to produce authoritarian forms of mass participation as democratic forms.[4]

---

[4] As Moore (1966) argues, industrialization led to democracy only in societies that had already placed limitations on state authority in preindustrial times. As Tilly (1997) argues, this was most likely to occur in societies that lacked labor-repressive regimes (such as those in Eastern Europe

The Forces Shaping Value Change

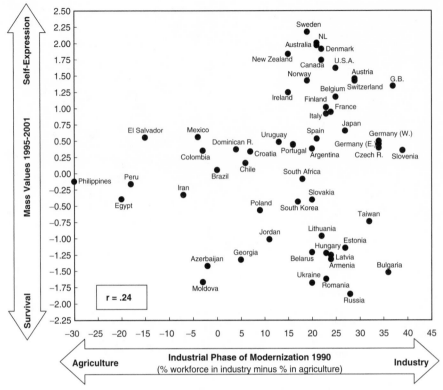

FIGURE 2.2b. The impact of industrialization on survival/self-expression values.

Figure 2.3a demonstrates that, as the percentage of the work force in the service sector grows and the size of the industrial sector shrinks, a society's belief system tends to shift from survival to self-expression values: this process explains 67 percent of the variation in self-expression values. But the rise of postindustrial society has no impact on the traditional versus secular-rational values dimension, as Figure 2.3b demonstrates. Postindustrialization brings emancipation from *both* traditional and secular authority, giving rise to an emancipative ethos. This is why liberal democracy becomes the prevailing political system in postindustrial societies, as we will see.[5]

and Oriental empires) and followed a "capital-intensive mode" of national integration. The degree of existential autonomy that people experienced in preindustrial freeholder economies in much of Western Europe and the British settler colonies established an emancipative ethos strong enough to defeat attempts to impose unlimited political authority.

[5] In societies like the United States, Switzerland, and the Netherlands, which had a commercial freeholder economy in preindustrial times, the rise of postindustrial society strengthened their traditional emancipative ethos. For societies that had labor-repressive agrarian regimes in preindustrial times, the rise of postindustrial society marks the advent of an emancipative ethos.

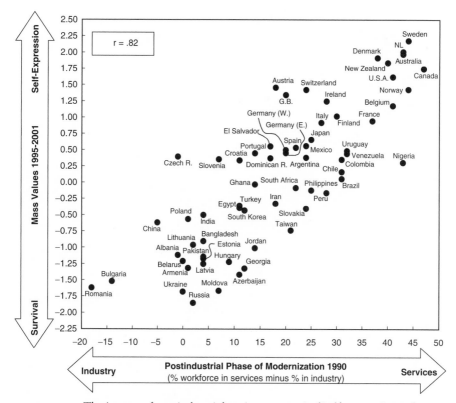

FIGURE 2.3a. The impact of postindustrial society on survival/self-expression values.

The linkage between the rise of the service sector and the strength of self-expression values is replicated at the individual level. Within any given society, those with higher incomes, higher education, and jobs in the service sector tend to emphasize self-expression values more strongly than the rest of their compatriots, falling higher and to the right of them on this map. Thus, as our revised version of modernization theory implies, socioeconomic development is linked with changing values at both the national level and the individual level.

The Global Cultural Map

Figure 2.4 shows the location of eighty societies surveyed on our two main dimensions of cross-cultural variation. The vertical axis on our global cultural map reflects the polarization between traditional authority and secular-rational authority linked with the process of industrialization. The horizontal axis reflects the polarization between survival values and self-expression values linked with the rise of postindustrial society. The boundaries around groups of countries in this figure are drawn using Huntington's (1996) cultural zones as a

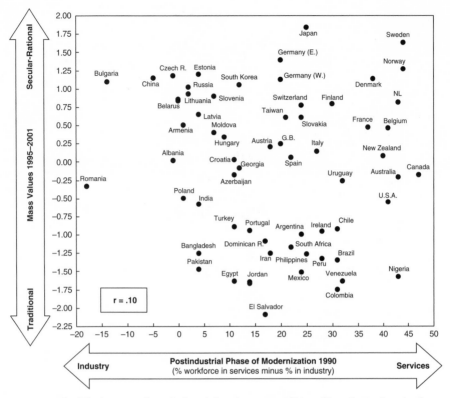

FIGURE 2.3b. The impact of postindustrial society on traditional/secular-rational values.

guide[6] (we test the explanatory power of this classification later). This cultural map resembles an earlier one by Inglehart (1997: 334–37) based on the 1989–91 Values Surveys. Although Figure 2.4 is based on a factor analysis that uses less than half as many variables as were used by Inglehart (1997) – and is based on almost twice as many countries – the locations of the respective societies on this map are strikingly similar to those on the cultural maps produced earlier. The similarity between this map and the earlier ones reflects the fact that these two key dimensions of cross-cultural variation are very robust. Using factor analyses based on a much smaller pool of items, the same broad cultural zones appear, in essentially the same locations, even when we add dozens of societies that were not previously included.

Mapping the location of sixty-six societies surveyed in the 1995–97 wave of the Values Surveys produces a picture very similar to the one based on the

---

[6] An alternative but atheoretical strategy would be to use one of the many available clustering techniques to identify the groups of nations and draw boundaries. We prefer to use the theoretical classifications proposed by Huntington and then to test for their explanatory power. Nevertheless, clustering techniques produce results that are roughly similar to those shown here.

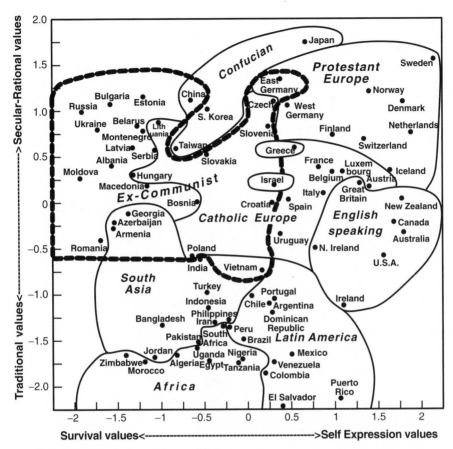

FIGURE 2.4. Cultural map of the world about 2000.

1989–91 surveys (see Inglehart and Baker, 2000, to examine this map). The 1995–97 surveys include a number of additional countries that were not surveyed in 1989–91, adding six Latin American countries and two additional English-speaking countries, all of which fall into the respective cultural zones that appeared on the 1990 map.

The fourth wave of the Values Surveys gave high priority to obtaining better coverage of the Islamic and African cultural zones, which had previously been largely neglected because of difficulties in funding, infrastructure, and access. Thus, the 1999–2001 wave added Algeria, Morocco, Egypt, Jordan, Iran, Indonesia, Tanzania, Uganda, and Zimbabwe as well as Vietnam, Greece, and Luxembourg to the pool of societies surveyed. Nevertheless, the overall pattern shown in Figure 2.4 is remarkably similar to that obtained in previous surveys, although we have added a number of societies with dramatically different socioeconomic and cultural characteristics from the societies surveyed in earlier waves of the Values Surveys.

Previous versions of the cultural map and the more complete current version all show consistent cultural clusters. Although these clusters represent a society's entire historical heritage, including factors that are unique to a given country, the clusters are remarkably coherent. They indicate a systematic pattern that exists *despite* the singularities of each society. Two systematic historical factors are particularly important in grouping societies into coherent clusters: the societies' religious tradition and their colonial histories. Thus, the historically Protestant societies tend to rank higher on the survival/self-expression dimension than the historically Roman Catholic societies. Conversely, all of the former communist societies rank relatively low on the survival/self-expression dimension. The historically Orthodox societies form a coherent cluster within the broader ex-communist zone – except for Greece, an Orthodox society that did *not* experience communist rule and ranks much higher on self-expression values than the other Orthodox societies. The Islamic societies fall into two clusters: a larger group containing the main-line Islamic societies (Indonesia, Iran, Bangladesh, Pakistan, Turkey, Morocco, Algeria, Jordan, and Egypt) constitutes a relatively compact group in the southwest quadrant of the map, whereas the Islamic societies that experienced communist rule (Azerbaijan and Albania) are much more secular than the other Islamic societies. Differences in per capita GDP and occupational structure have important influences on prevailing worldviews, but historical cultural influences persist.

Religious traditions have an enduring impact on the contemporary value systems of these societies, as Weber, Huntington, and others have argued. But a society's culture reflects its entire historical heritage. A central historical event of the twentieth century was the rise and fall of a communist empire that once ruled a third of the world's population. Communism has left a clear imprint on the value systems of those who lived under it. All of the societies that experienced communist rule fall into a large cluster in the upper-left quadrant of the map. East Germany remains culturally close to West Germany despite four decades of communist rule, but its value system has been drawn toward the communist zone. And although China is a member of the Confucian zone, it also falls within a broad communist-influenced zone.

The influence of colonial ties is apparent in the existence of a Latin American cultural zone. The Philippines could also be placed in this zone, reflecting the fact that despite their geographical remoteness, the Philippines and Latin America share the imprint of Hispanic colonial rule and the Roman Catholic Church. Former colonial ties also help account for the existence of an English-speaking zone containing Britain and the other English-speaking societies. All seven of the English-speaking societies included in this study show relatively similar cultural characteristics. The impact of colonization seems especially strong when reinforced by massive immigration from the colonial society. Thus, Spain, Portugal, Italy, Uruguay, Chile, and Argentina are all relatively near each other on the border between Catholic Europe and Latin America: the populations of Uruguay, Chile, and Argentina are largely descended from immigrants from Spain and Italy. Reinforcing these findings, Rice and Feldman (1997) find strong correlations between the values of various ethnic groups in the United States and the values prevailing in their countries of origin – two or three generations after their families migrated to the United States.

These maps indicate that the United States is not a prototype of cultural modernization for other societies to follow, as some postwar modernization writers assumed. In fact, the United States is a deviant case, having a much more traditional value system than any other postindustrial society except Ireland. On the traditional/secular dimension, the United States ranks far below other rich societies, with levels of religiosity and national pride comparable with those found in some developing societies. The phenomenon of American exceptionalism has been discussed by Lipset (1990, 1996), W. Baker (2005), and others; our results support their argument. The United States does rank among the most advanced societies on the survival/self-expression dimension, but even here, it does not lead the world. The Swedes, the Dutch, and the Australians are closer to the cutting edge of cultural change than the Americans. Clearly, modernization is not Americanization.

How Real Are the Cultural Zones?

The location of each society on the global cultural map is objective, determined by a factor analysis of survey data from each country. The *boundaries* drawn around these societies are subjective, using Huntington's (1996) division of the world into several cultural zones. How "real" are these zones? These boundaries could have been drawn in a number of different ways, because these societies have been influenced by many factors. Thus, some of the boundaries overlap others – for example, the ex-communist zone overlaps the Protestant, Catholic, Confucian, Orthodox, and Islamic cultural zones. Similarly, Britain is located at the intersection of the English-speaking zone and Protestant Europe; empirically, it is close to all six of the other English-speaking societies, and our map includes Britain in that zone. But with only slight modification, we could have drawn these borders to put Britain in Protestant Europe, for it is also culturally close to those societies. Reality is complex. Britain is both a historically Protestant European country *and* an English-speaking country, and its empirical position reflects both aspects of reality. Similarly, we have drawn a boundary around the Latin American societies that Huntington postulated to be a distinct cultural zone: all ten of them do indeed show relatively similar values in global perspective. But with only minor changes, we could have drawn this border to define a Hispanic cultural zone that includes Spain and Portugal, which empirically are *also* relatively close to the Latin American societies. We could also draw a still broader boundary that included Latin America, Catholic Europe, and the Philippines and Ireland in a broad Roman Catholic cultural zone. All of these zones are both conceptually and empirically justifiable.

The two-dimensional cultural maps are based on similarity of basic values, but they *also* reflect the relative distances between these societies on many other dimensions, such as religion, colonial influences, the impact of communist rule, the structure of the work force, and level of economic development. It is remarkable that the influence of so many different historical factors can be summed up by a parsimonious two-dimensional map. But because these various factors do not always coincide neatly, there are some anomalies. For example, East Germany and Japan fall rather near each other. This is appropriate in the sense that both societies are highly secular, relatively wealthy, and have high proportions of industrial workers; but it also seems surprising because Japan was shaped by a Confucian heritage, whereas East Germany was shaped by Protestantism (though, interestingly, when the Japanese first drew up a Western-style constitution, they chose the Prussian constitution as their model). Despite such anomalies, societies with a common cultural heritage generally *do* fall into common clusters. But their positions simultaneously reflect their level of socioeconomic development, their occupational structure, their religious heritage, and past imperial ties, such as a Hispanic or British colonial heritage or the imprint of the Soviet empire. This two-dimensional space reflects a multidimensional reality, and the remarkable degree of socioeconomic and cultural coherence that we find reflects the fact that a society's culture is shaped by its entire historical heritage.

Modernization theory implies that as societies develop economically, their cultures will tend to shift in a predictable direction, and our findings fit this prediction. Socioeconomic differences *are* linked with large and pervasive cultural differences, as we saw in Figure 2.1. Nevertheless, we find clear evidence of the influence of long-established cultural zones. Using the data from the 1995–97 surveys for each society, we created dummy variables to reflect whether a given society is predominantly English-speaking or not, or ex-communist or not, and so on, for each of the clusters outlined on the cultural maps. Empirical analysis of these variables shows that the cultural locations of given societies are far from random. Eight of the nine zones outlined on the cultural maps show statistically significant relationships with at least one of the two major dimensions of cross-cultural variation (the sole exception is the Catholic Europe cluster: it is fairly coherent but has a neutral position on both dimensions). For example, the dummy variable for Protestant Europe shows a .46 correlation with the traditional/secular-rational dimension and a .41 correlation with the survival/self-expression dimension (both correlations are significant at the .0001 level). Similarly, the ex-communist dummy variable correlates at .43 with the traditional/secular-rational dimension and at −.74 with the survival/self-expression dimension.

Do these cultural clusters simply reflect socioeconomic differences? For example, do the societies of Protestant Europe have similar values merely because they are rich? The answer is no. As our analyses show, whether a society has a Catholic or Protestant or Confucian or Orthodox or communist heritage makes an independent contribution to its position on the global cultural map. Nevertheless, the influence of socioeconomic development is pervasive. Per capita GDP shows a significant impact on traditional/secular-rational values, for five of eight cultural zones (using a dummy variable for each cultural zone in a separate regression).[7] Moreover, per capita GDP shows a significant impact on survival/self-expression values against controls for each of eight cultural zones. The percentage of the labor force in the industrial sector influences traditional/secular-rational values even more consistently than does per capita GDP, showing a significant impact in seven of the eight regression analyses. The percentage of the labor force in the *service* sector has a significant impact in six of the eight regressions on survival/self-expression values (Inglehart and Baker, 2000).

Still, the impact of a society's historical-cultural heritage persists when we control for per capita GDP and the structure of the labor force in multiple regression analyses. Thus, the ex-communist dummy variable shows a strong and statistically significant impact on traditional/secular-rational values, controlling for socioeconomic development. The secularizing effect of communism is even greater than that of the size of the industrial sector and almost as great as that of per capita GDP. The ex-communist dummy variable also has a significant negative impact on survival/self-expression values. The Protestant Europe dummy variable and the English-speaking variables both have significant impacts on the traditional/secular-rational dimension. But, although the English-speaking societies are clustered near the right-hand pole of the survival/self-expression dimension, this tendency disappears when we control for the fact that they are relatively wealthy and have a high proportion of the work force in the service sector. But each of eight cultural dummy variables shows a statistically significant impact on at least one of the two value dimensions.

When we combine the clusters shown in Figure 2.4 into broader cultural zones with large sample sizes, we generate variables having even greater explanatory power. As the figure demonstrates, the Catholic societies of Eastern Europe constitute a distinct subcluster of the Catholic world – midway between the West European Catholic societies and the Orthodox societies. The Latin American cluster is also adjacent to the two Catholic groups; and two other historically Catholic societies, the Philippines and Ireland, are nearby, so we could combine all of these groups to form a broad Roman Catholic superzone. Similarly, Protestant Europe and all of the English-speaking zone except Ireland could be merged into a broad historically Protestant zone. Each of these two new zones covers a vast geographic, historical, and economic range, but they reflect the impact of common religious-historical influences – and each of them is relatively coherent in global perspective.

So far we have examined how entire societies fit into broad cultural zones shaped by their historical religious heritage. But some societies contain large numbers of both Catholics *and* Protestants (or Hindus and Muslims, or

---

[7] Dummy variables were created to indicate a society's membership in a given cultural zone (coded 1) or nonbelongingness to it (coded 0), including an ex-communist zone, a Protestant European zone, an English-speaking zone, a Latin American zone, an African zone, a South Asian zone, a Christian-Orthodox zone, and a Confucian zone. See Figure 2.4 for the particular societies included in these zones.

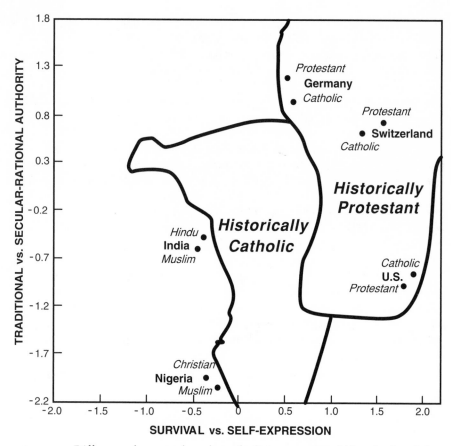

FIGURE 2.5. Differences between the values of religious groups within mixed societies. *Source:* 1999–2001 Values Surveys.

Christians and Muslims). Where do these subgroups fit into the picture? Breaking down the national-level results according to these individual-level characteristics gives insight into how the impact of religious traditions is transmitted today. There are two main possibilities: given religious institutions are *now* instilling distinctively Protestant or Catholic or Islamic values in their respective followers within each society; or given religious traditions have historically shaped the national culture of given societies, but today their impact is transmitted mainly through nationwide institutions to the population as a whole, including those who have little or no contact with religious institutions. If the former were true, we might expect to find the German Catholics falling into the Catholic cultural zone, with their Protestant compatriots located far away from them, near the northeast corner of the map. If the latter interpretation holds true, we would expect to find only modest differences between Catholics and Protestants within a given society.

As Figure 2.5 indicates, the empirical evidence clearly supports the latter interpretation. Although historically Catholic or Protestant or Islamic societies show very distinctive values, the differences between Catholics and Protestants or Muslims *within* given societies are relatively small. In Germany, for example, the basic values of German Catholics are much more similar to those of German Protestants than they are to those of Catholics in other countries. The German Catholics are much more German than Catholic. The same is true in the United States, Switzerland, the Netherlands, and other religiously mixed societies: Catholics tend to be slightly more traditional than their Protestant compatriots, but they do not fall into the historically Catholic cultural zone or anywhere near it. Rather surprisingly, this also holds true of the differences between Hindus and Muslims in India and Christians and Muslims in Nigeria: the basic values of Nigerian Muslims are closer to those of their Christian compatriots than they are to those of Indian Muslims. On questions that directly evoked Islamic or Christian identity, this would almost certainly not hold true; but on these two basic value dimensions, the cross-national differences dwarf the within-nation differences. Similar patterns exist for other variables as well: educational, generational, occupational, and ethnic differences on these two value dimensions are much smaller *within* than *between* societies. Nations, and the cultural zones in which they are embedded, have a major impact on people's belief systems in producing distinct national mass belief systems (for a more detailed discussion of this point, see Chapter 9).

Protestant or Catholic societies display distinctive values today mainly because of the historical impact their respective churches have had on societies as a whole, rather than through the contemporary influence of the church on given individuals. For this reason we classify Germany, Switzerland, and the Netherlands as historically Protestant societies: historically, Protestantism shaped these countries, even though today (as a result of immigration, relatively low Protestant birthrates, and relatively high Protestant rates of secularization) they may have more practicing Catholics than Protestants.

These findings suggest that, once established, the cross-cultural differences linked with religion have become part of a national culture that is transmitted by the educational institutions and mass media of given societies to the people of that nation as a whole. Despite widespread talk of the globalization of culture, the nation remains a key unit of shared experience, with its educational and cultural institutions shaping the values of almost everyone in that society.

Figure 2.6 provides another illustration of this principle, comparing the values of the upper-, middle-, and lower-income groups within each of the societies shown in Figure 2.5. High levels of economic development are linked with greater emphasis on secular values and self-expression values, which is why the rich countries tend to be located in the upper right-hand sector of the global cultural map. Consequently, we would expect the economically more secure strata within each society to fall closer to the upper right-hand corner of the map than the less secure strata, but the question is, How much? Do the rich all fall into the upper right-hand corner, regardless of nationality – or does a nation's central tendency bind even the exceptionally rich and poor in this nation's cultural orbit? As Figure 2.6 demonstrates, the national setting remains an important influence on people's values. Within rich societies, the

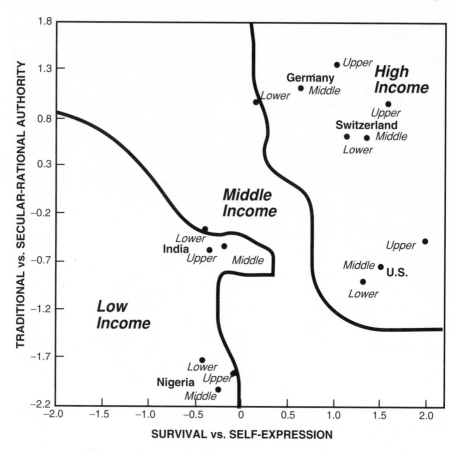

FIGURE 2.6. Differences between the values of income groups (in tertiles) within five societies. *Source:* 1999–2001 Values Surveys.

richer citizens are consistently more likely to emphasize secular-rational values and self-expression values than the poor, but the values of rich Germans (defined as the top third of the income distribution) are more similar to those of poor Germans (the bottom third of the income distribution) than they are to those of rich Swiss or Americans. Although within rich countries the richer and more educated members of society tend to have more-secular values than the less wealthy, this is not necessarily the case in low-income countries: as Figure 2.6 indicates, in India and Nigeria the rich tend to have slightly more-traditional values than the poor. But the main point illustrated by this figure is that, within a given country, the rich and poor strata tend to have values that are more similar to each other than to citizens of other countries – rich or poor. Even in the age of the internet, one's nationality remains a powerful predictor of one's values.

The persistence of distinctive value systems seems to reflect the fact that culture is path dependent. Protestant religious institutions helped shape the

Protestant ethic, relatively high levels of interpersonal trust, and a relatively high degree of social pluralism – all of which probably contributed to the fact that industrialization occurred earlier in Protestant countries than in the rest of the world. Subsequently, the fact that Protestant societies were (and still are) relatively prosperous has shaped them in distinctive ways. Although they have experienced rapid social and cultural change, historically Protestant and Catholic (and Confucian, Islamic, Orthodox, and other) societies remain distinctive. Identifying the specific mechanisms through which these path-dependent developments occurred would require detailed historical analyses that we will not attempt here. But survey evidence from societies around the world demonstrates that these cultures *have* remained distinctive.

To illustrate how coherent these clusters are, let us examine one of the key variables in the literature on cross-cultural differences, interpersonal trust (a component of the survival/self-expression dimension). Almond and Verba (1963), Coleman (1990), Putnam (1993), and Fukuyama (1995) argue that interpersonal trust is essential for building the associations on which democracy depends, and the complex social organizations on which large-scale economic enterprises are based. As Figure 2.7 demonstrates, virtually all historically Protestant societies rank higher on interpersonal trust than virtually all historically Catholic societies. This holds true even when we control for levels of economic development: as the literature implies, interpersonal trust is significantly correlated with the society's level of per capita GDP (r = .60), but even rich Catholic societies rank lower than equally prosperous historically Protestant societies. A heritage of communist rule also seems to have an impact on this variable, with the post-Soviet societies ranking particularly low. Thus, the only historically Protestant societies that rank relatively low on trust are the two that experienced communist rule – Estonia and Latvia. Of the twenty societies in which more than 35 percent of the public believe that most people can be trusted, fourteen are historically Protestant, three are Confucian-influenced, one is predominantly Hindu, another is Islamic, and only one (Spain) is historically Catholic. Not only Protestant countries but also Confucian-influenced societies tend to rank high on interpersonal trust. And, although they tend to have much lower income levels than the historically Catholic societies, on average the Islamic countries rank higher on trust than the Catholic societies. Of the ten lowest-ranking societies in Figure 2.7, six are historically Catholic, and *none* is historically Protestant.

Within given societies, Catholics rank about as high on interpersonal trust as do Protestants. It is not a matter of individual personality but the shared historical experience of given *nations* that is crucial. As Putnam (1993) has argued, horizontal, locally controlled organizations are conducive to interpersonal trust; rule by large, hierarchical, centralized bureaucracies seems to corrode interpersonal trust. Historically, the Roman Catholic Church was the prototype of the hierarchical, centrally controlled institution; Protestant churches were relatively decentralized and more open to local control. The contrast between local control and domination by a remote hierarchy seems to have important

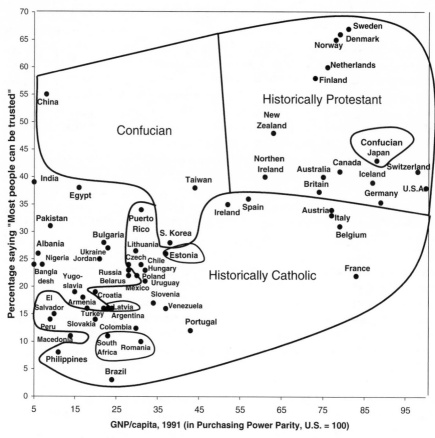

FIGURE 2.7. Cultural heritage and interpersonal trust, controlling for level of economic development.

long-term consequences for interpersonal trust. Societies that emphasize *vertical* ties based on strong hierarchies tend to do so at the expense of the *horizontal* ties that create generalized interpersonal trust. Clearly, these cross-cultural differences do not reflect the contemporary influence of the respective churches. The Catholic Church has changed a great deal in recent decades. And in many countries, especially Protestant ones, church attendance has dwindled to the point where only a small minority of the population attends church regularly. The majority has little or no contact with the church today, but the impact of living in a society that was historically shaped by once-powerful Catholic or Protestant institutions persists today, shaping everyone – Protestant, Catholic, or other – who is socialized into that nation's culture.

Generating Cultural Zone Factors

One can produce a much more parsimonious analysis if one summarizes the impact of cultural zones in a single variable rather than using eight or nine separate dummy variables. We did so as follows: using the data from all available surveys from a given cultural zone obtained in the first three waves of the Values Surveys (carried out from 1981 to 1997), we calculated the extent to which the societies of a given zone deviated from the mean score that would be predicted for that group by a combination of per capita GDP (using the World Bank's purchasing power parity [PPP] estimates), the percentage of the work force in the industrial sector (for the traditional/secular-rational values factor) or the service sector (for the survival/self-expression values factor), and the number of years experienced under communist rule. We used multiple classification analysis to calculate these adjusted scores. These scores measure the extent to which the societies in a given cultural zone show distinctive values, *controlling* for their economic wealth, social structure, and years under communist rule.

As mentioned, the 1999–2001 wave of the Values Surveys gave high priority to obtaining better coverage of Islamic societies than had been attained in the first three waves. The only predominantly Islamic societies that had been surveyed previously were Turkey, Albania, and Azerbaijan – all of which were shaped by regimes that devoted intense efforts to minimize the influence of Islam – plus Bangladesh and Pakistan, which were included in the 1995–97 survey but not in any previous waves. Consequently, our Islamic database was slim and overrepresented the most secular Islamic societies. To compensate for this, in calculating the Islamic cultural zone factor, we took advantage of the fact that both Nigeria and India contain large Islamic populations (about half of the population in the Nigerian case). We broke down Nigeria and India into separate Islamic and non-Islamic samples and treated the two Islamic samples as if they were separate countries, including their mean scores as part of the sample used to calculate the Islamic zone factor on both dimensions. This gave us seven Islamic countries from which to generate the Islamic cultural zone constants that were used as a component of the model that predicted the 1999–2001 positions of all Islamic countries – most of which had never before been surveyed. Table 2.5 shows the cultural zone factors calculated for each cultural region. As this table indicates, historically Protestant European societies fall about half a standard deviation higher on both dimensions than other societies, even controlling for the fact that they are relatively rich and did not experience communist rule. English-speaking societies rank higher on self-expression values than their economic levels would predict, but they have more-traditional values than their other characteristics would predict.

Using these cultural zone shift factors in regression analyses provides additional support for concluding not only that a society's value system is systematically influenced by socioeconomic development but also that cultural zones and an ex-communist heritage exert a persistent and pervasive influence on contemporary values and beliefs. Tables 2.6 and 2.7 show the results of OLS regression analyses of cross-national differences in traditional/secular-rational values (Table 2.6) and survival/self-expression values (Table 2.7), as measured in sixty-four societies. For both dimensions, we find that per capita GDP (measured in purchasing power parities) and the structure of the work force play major roles. The process of industrialization (measured by the percentage of the

TABLE 2.5. *Cultural Zone Deviation Factors on Two Dimensions*

Cultural Zone	Number of Surveys[a]	Factor for Traditional/ Secular Values[b]	Factor for Survival/ Self-Expression Values[c]
Protestant Europe	35	.59	.54
English-speaking	20	−.72	.58
Catholic Europe	44	−.19	.05
Confucian	13	1.25	−.49
Orthodox	30	.40	−.50
Latin America	22	−.49	−.03
South Asia	10	−.44	−.29
Islamic	22	−.53	−.71
Sub-Saharan Africa	11	−.95	−.45

[a] In all four waves.
[b] Based on waves 1–3 surveys, adjusted for GDP per capita, percentage in industrial sector, years of communist rule.
[c] Based on waves 1–3, adjusted for GDP per capita, percentage in service sector, years of communist rule.

TABLE 2.6. *Predicting Traditional versus Secular-Rational Values in 1999–2001*

Independent Variables	Dependent Variable: Traditional/ Secular-Rational Values, 1999–2001[a]				
	Model 1	Model 2	Model 3	Model 4	Model 5
Real GDP per capita, 1995 (in $1,000 U.S.)	.38** (.05)	.33** (.04)	.65** (.08)	.50** (.06)	–
Percentage employed in industrial sector, 1990	–	.54** (.06)	.17* (.02)	.04 (.004)	–
Years under communist rule	–	–	.62** (.02)	.45** (.017)	–
Cultural zone factor (based on first 3 waves)	–	–	–	.50** (.91)	.77** (1.42)
Adjusted R-squared	.14	.45	.63	.80	.59
Number of countries	64	64	64	64	64

[a] Standardized regression coefficients, with the unstandardized coefficients in parentheses. Significance levels: * p ≤ .05; ** p ≤ .01. Formula for predicting a society's score on the traditional/secular-rational values dimension: Loading = −1.046 + 0.063 * GDP/capita + 0.0037 * LaborIndus + .017 * ExComm + .91 * CultZone.
Source: 1999–2001 Values Surveys.

work force in the industrial sector) has a major impact on traditional/secular-rational values, while *post*industrialization (measured as the percentage of the work force in the service sector) has a major impact on survival/self-expression values.

TABLE 2.7. *Predicting Survival versus Self-Expression Values in 1999–2001*

Independent Variables[a]	Dependent Variable: Survival/ Self-Expression Values, 1999–2001[b]				
	Model 1	Model 2	Model 3	Model 4	Model 5
GDP per capita at PPP, 1995 (in $1,000 U.S.)	.78** (.10)	.70** (.09)	.52** (.07)	.24** (.03)	–
Percentage employed in service sector, 1990	–	.13* (.01)	.16* (.01)	.12* (.009)	–
Years of communist rule	–	–	−.39** (−.015)	−.45** (−.018)	–
Cultural zone factor (based on first 3 waves)	–	–	–	.43** (1.06)	.73** (1.84)
Adjusted R-squared	.60	.61	.74	.84	.52
Number of countries	64	64	64	64	64

[a] PPP = purchasing power parity.
[b] Standardized regression coefficients, with the unstandardized coefficients in parentheses. Significance levels: * p ≤ .05; ** p ≤ .01. Formula for predicting a society's score on the survival/self-expression values dimension: Loading = −.215 + 0.031 * GDP/capita + 0.0093 *LaborServ − 0.0175 *ExComm + 1.06 *CultZone.
Source: 1999–2001 Values Surveys.

The people of poorer societies, in which the agrarian sector exceeds the industrial sector, tend to hold traditional values, whereas the people of richer societies, in which the industrial sector is larger than the agrarian sector, tend to hold secular-rational values. But a given society's historical heritage also has an important influence on the contemporary values and behavior of its people, even when we control for economic prosperity and occupational structure.[8] As Table 2.6 indicates, a society's cultural zone location also shows a significant relationship with traditional/secular-rational values. This reflects such things as the fact that Confucian societies have, for centuries, been characterized by a relatively secular worldview. They remain so today. Communist regimes made major efforts to eradicate traditional religious values, and they had some success. But historically Roman Catholic societies proved relatively resistant to secularization, even controlling for the effects of socioeconomic development and communist rule.

Modernization theory holds that the process of socioeconomic development and the rise of the industrial sector are conducive to a secular-rational

---

[8] By controlling for socioeconomic development, we may be underestimating the impact of a society's historical heritage. For it is possible that Protestantism, Confucianism, or communism helped *shape* the society's contemporary level of socioeconomic development. For example, Weber attributes a crucial role to Protestantism in launching economic growth in Europe, and it is a historical fact that – in its early phase, though clearly not today – industrialization was overwhelmingly concentrated in predominantly Protestant societies and among the Protestant segment of mixed societies.

worldview. As Table 2.6 demonstrates, when we control for a society's cultural heritage, the impact of per capita GDP is significant at the .001 level, while the impact of industrialization becomes insignificant when we include the number of years a country spent under communist rule (Model 3). Model 4 explains most of the cross-national variation in traditional/secular-rational values with four variables: per capita GDP, size of the industrial work force, the number of years under communism, and the cultural zone shift factor. As Models 3 and 5 demonstrate, both the number of years spent under communist rule and the cultural zone shift factor make a substantial contribution to the percentage of variance explained. And adding both cultural indicators to the regression increases the percentage of explained variance from 45 to 80 percent. A society's historical heritage makes a big difference.

The socioeconomic modernization indicators (GDP per capita and postindustrial work force) in Model 1 of Table 2.7 explain 61 percent of the cross-national variation in survival/self-expression values. Again, the influence of tradition factors is also significant, adding 23 percent to the total explained variance in survival/self-expression values. Both modernization and a society's cultural tradition shape both secular-rational values and self-expression values, but historical factors have a greater relative impact on secular-rational values, whereas modernization factors have a greater relative impact on self-expression values.

Summary

The extent to which both secular-rational values and self-expression values are present can be explained by a combination of retarding and driving forces, with tradition and modernization influencing both processes of cultural change. But the balance between these forces differs greatly. A society's cultural tradition has much stronger impact on traditional/secular-rational values than on survival/self-expression values, whereas self-expression values are much more strongly shaped by the forces of modernization than by those of tradition. In this broader historical perspective, one must go beyond Weber: it is not the rationalization of authority but the emancipation *from* authority that becomes the dominant trend of modernization, transforming modernization into a process of human development that promotes human emancipation on all fronts. This humanistic transformation of modernity has important societal-level consequences. As we will see in the second half of this book, human development strengthens civil society, political liberties, good governance, and gender equality – and makes democracy increasingly likely, where it does not yet exist, and increasingly responsive, where it already exists. Self-expression values play a major role in this process.

3

Exploring the Unknown

Predicting Mass Responses

In the previous chapter, we claimed that cultural change is predictable, insofar as it is shaped by the factors in our cultural modernization model. But cultural change is also affected by other factors such as war, nation-specific events, and a society's political parties and leaders, so any predictions based on modernization theory alone will not be precisely accurate. Nevertheless, in this chapter we predict the locations on the two main cultural dimensions of all countries that are reasonably likely to be included in the next wave of the Values Surveys, in 2005–6. Using a simple predictive model based on our revised version of modernization theory, we first "predict" and test the positions that 80 societies should have on our two major dimensions of cross-cultural variation in the most recent wave of surveys (carried out in 1999–2001). We then use this same model to predict the basic values that we expect to find among the publics of more than 120 countries that are likely to be surveyed in the next wave of surveys, in 2005–6. More than 40 of these countries have not been included in previous waves of the Values Surveys, and some of them have never been explored in *any* survey of which we are aware.

Prediction is an important challenge for social scientists. Social science rarely makes genuine blind predictions and then tests its theories against them. It generally advances hypotheses and tests them against data already on hand. Hypotheses that are not supported can be dropped or reformulated in light of the actual data; and independent variables can be added or transformed in order to better fit the hypotheses. Although social scientists rarely publish predictions of findings expected from data not yet available, the exceptions have been important. Economic forecasts have played a valuable role in formulating counter-cyclical policy. And predictive political economy models of U.S. presidential elections have an impressive track record; although their forecasts are imperfect, the fact that their predictions were published in advance has stimulated public scrutiny of how these models work, and how they can be improved.

Our predictions will not be exactly correct; in some cases, they will not even be in the right ball park. For our predictions are based on a small number of variables and do not attempt to include numerous factors (some of them specific to given nations) that help shape mass attitudes. In order to provide a theoretically coherent explanation of the dynamics of value change, we will use a parsimonious model rather than a more complex one that might statistically explain more variance. A model that explains 75 percent of the variance with five variables is more efficient than one that explains 80 percent with ten variables. We aim at an efficient model that explains as much variance as possible with as few variables as possible; when the explanation is as complex as reality, one no longer has a theory. Our predictions will be imperfect, but we are confident that in most cases they will come much closer to the actual results than would random guesses. Our confidence is based on the fact that analysis of data from the sixty-four societies surveyed in previous waves of the Values Surveys indicates that cross-cultural differences in basic values have a surprisingly consistent relationship with socioeconomic development. Although they vary a great deal cross-nationally, the values and beliefs of mass publics vary in a roughly predictable way that reflects the revised version of modernization theory outlined in Chapter 1.

This theory postulates that (1) socioeconomic development tends to bring predictable changes in mass values. But it is not a simple linear process: industrialization brings one set of changes, while the rise of postindustrial society brings another set. Moreover, (2) cultural change is path dependent: a society's historical heritage has an enduring influence on its value system, so that societies shaped by Protestantism, Islam, or other historical forces show distinctive values today that differentiate them from societies with other cultural heritages.

Our first step is to test this model against data from the sixty-four societies surveyed in the 1999–2001 wave of the Values Surveys, predicting each society's position on two major dimensions of cross-cultural variation, the traditional/secular-rational values dimension and the survival/self-expression values dimension. Our predictive model is based on the regression analyses of Tables 2.6 and 2.7 and uses two modernization factors: (1) a country's per capita GDP and (2) the percentage of the work force employed in the industrial sector or service sector; and two factors that reflect a society's historical heritage: (3) the number of years of communist rule that it experienced, if any, and (4) the cultural zone shift factor discussed in Chapter 2. This cultural zone constant is derived from the results of the first three waves of these surveys (carried out in 1981–97) and reflects the extent to which a country with a given cultural heritage deviates from the scores predicted by the other components of the model.

We use each country's per capita GDP five years before the survey in 2000 to predict that country's scores on the two cultural dimensions. We do this in order to put the variables in the appropriate causal sequence: causes precede their effects, and our theory hypothesizes that socioeconomic development shapes a society's values. All of the other variables used to predict values – including the data from which the cultural zone constants are derived – are also based on data measured at a time before the values they predict.

As we will see, this parsimonious model predicts, with remarkable accuracy, the values actually observed in surveys of the sixty-four countries that were

carried out in 1999–2001. These are not only new surveys of previously studied countries; they also include twelve countries that had not been surveyed
previously: they are genuine out-of-sample predictions.

We then go on to predict the positions on these two dimensions that we would
expect to find in 2005 for 120 societies, many of which we have never surveyed
before. We expect that many of these countries will be included in the 2005–6
wave of the Values Surveys, but even if they are not, these predictions can be
tested by anyone who wishes to survey a given country. These predictions were
posted on the World Values Survey website in September 2004. We will test
these predictions when the relevant data become available; we publish them in
advance in order to stimulate prediction in social science. We also invite anyone
who is interested to use the formulas published here to test our model.

Our revised version of modernization theory has four components of
predictability: a society's socioeconomic development predicts where it will
fall on the cross-cultural map and the direction in which it is predicted to
move. Societies with a high per capita GDP should rank high on both the
traditional/secular-rational dimension and the survival/self-expression dimension, falling toward the upper right-hand corner of the map; societies with a low
per capita GDP should rank low on both dimensions, falling toward the lower
left-hand corner. Moreover, rich societies should gradually *shift* toward the
positive pole of both dimensions, moving toward the upper right. Low-income
societies will start near the opposite end of the diagonal and will not necessarily
show any movement. Moreover, our revised version of modernization theory
predicts that variation in the size of the industrial work force is linked with
variation in the traditional/secular-rational dimension, with a relatively large
industrial work force tending to bring a society closer to secular-rational values
than its per capita GDP alone would predict. Similarly, our theory predicts that
having a relatively large percentage of the work force in the service sector tends
to shift societies to the right on our map, bringing them closer to self-expression
values than their per capita GDP alone would predict.

But this revised theory of modernization does not depend solely on the forces
of socioeconomic development; it also takes into account the impact of a society's historical heritage, which does not predict the amount of change that will
occur, but does help predict a society's relative position on the cross-cultural
map. As we have pointed out, a society's religious tradition helps shape a society's culture, and past colonial ties also play an important role. The Spanish,
Portuguese, British, and Soviet empires have left a lasting imprint on a society's
culture. For example, the English-speaking societies tend to have more traditional value systems than one would expect of societies at their level of economic
development. Moreover, the experience of having lived under communist rule
tends to make people emphasize both secular values and survival values more
heavily than their economic level alone would predict. Socioeconomic development is a powerful predictor of a society's value system, but it needs to be
supplemented by taking the society's historical heritage into account.

When generational differences are present, they provide another indication
of whether a society is experiencing cultural change and the direction in which

it is moving. The effects of intergenerational population replacement operate slowly but steadily, and over periods of several decades they can have large cumulative effects, which can be used to predict long-term changes. But during relatively brief periods, such as the five-year span dealt with here, its effects are relatively modest and building them into our model would make it more complicated. For the sake of parsimony, we will use a simple predictive model based on two modernization factors and two historical heritage factors.

Socioeconomic development and cultural tradition share a good deal of overlapping variance. The countries of Protestant Europe and the English-speaking zone are much wealthier and have a much larger postindustrial work force than those of South Asia or sub-Saharan Africa, and it is difficult to partition the overlapping variance between culture and socioeconomic development. Thus, in the regression analyses presented in Chapter 2, socioeconomic factors (GDP per capita and the percentage of the work force employed in the industrial sector) by themselves explain 45 percent of the variance in where given societies fall on the traditional/secular-rational values dimension. This result is substantial; however, our culture zone shift factor, by itself, explains 59 percent of the variance on this dimension. The combined effects of socioeconomic factors and historical heritage factors explain fully 80 percent of the variance in a society's position on this dimension, so the heritage factors by themselves explain only an additional 35 percent of the variance, beyond what could be attributed to socioeconomic factors. But the reverse is also true: the socioeconomic variables explain only an additional 21 percent beyond what could be attributed to these societies' historical traditions. Thus, cultural heritage could be interpreted as explaining anything from 35 to 59 percent of the variation in locations on the traditional/secular-rational values dimension. If one simply split the difference, one would attribute 47 percent of the variance to cultural heritage. Similarly, the socioeconomic variables could be interpreted as explaining anything from 21 to 45 percent of the variation, and splitting the difference would attribute 33 percent of the variance to socioeconomic factors.

Similarly, the historical heritage variables alone explain 52 percent of the variance on the survival/self-expression dimension, but socioeconomic factors alone explain 61 percent of the variance on this dimension, and the combined effects of economics and culture explain 84 percent of the total variance. In this case, an economic determinist might argue that a society's cultural heritage adds only 23 percent to the variance in survival/self-expression values that is explained by socioeconomic development alone, whereas a cultural determinist might argue that socioeconomic development adds only 32 percent of the variance that is explained by cultural heritage alone. Depending on one's epistemological preferences, the explanatory power attributed to socioeconomic development could vary from 32 to 61 percent and that attributed to cultural heritage could range from 23 to 52 percent. Splitting the difference, one would attribute about 47 percent of the variance to socioeconomic development and about 38 percent to cultural heritage.

Splitting the difference is, obviously, a very crude way to decide the question, but it probably comes closer to the truth than either extreme economic or cultural determinism. Until we have a considerably longer time series of survey data, we won't be able to reach a precise answer. For now, it is clear that both cultural and socioeconomic factors explain substantial parts of the variance in where a society falls on the global map of cross-cultural variation. Our model takes both sets of factors into account.

Previous waves of the Values Surveys overrepresented societies with relatively high levels of socioeconomic development: it was much more difficult to recruit colleagues and to raise funding in poor countries than in rich ones. Consequently, most of the twelve previously unsurveyed societies for which we will advance predictions here are economically less developed – some rank among the poorest countries in the world. Moreover, previous waves of these surveys included few historically Islamic societies, and we gave high priority to covering them more adequately in the 1999–2001 wave. Consequently, six of our twelve previously unsurveyed cases are predominantly Islamic and three more are in sub-Saharan Africa (three of the new Islamic cases are located in North Africa, making a total of six new African cases). Although both regions are distinctive cultural zones, we had a relatively narrow empirical basis for projecting their values. The twelve new cases for which we will make predictions are not only new, out-of-sample cases; they also differ systematically from the database on which our predictive model is based.

Nevertheless, we will proceed to predict positions on the two basic cultural dimensions for the sixty-four countries surveyed in 1999–2001, giving special attention to the twelve countries not previously surveyed.

Developing Predictive Formulas

As Chapter 2 demonstrates, using a combination of modernization and tradition variables, one can develop models that explain very high proportions of the variance in each society's factor scores on the two key value dimensions. We will do so here, first analyzing the predictors of scores on the traditional/secular-rational values dimension, and then turning to the survival/self-expression values dimension.

Table 2.6 presents five models explaining the cross-national variation in traditional/secular-rational values, using various combinations of modernization and tradition variables. Although GDP per capita is often a good predictor of social phenomena, in this case it does not do very well by itself, explaining only 14 percent of the cross-national variance. But two modernization variables combined, GDP per capita and the proportion of the labor force in the industrial sector, explain a good deal of the cross-national variation in scores on the traditional/secular-rational values dimension, producing an adjusted R-squared of 0.45, explaining 45 percent of the cross-national variation.

Nevertheless, we must introduce a historical heritage factor to explain most of the variation in traditional versus secular-rational values. Being an ex-communist society reflects two things: the cultural impact of having experienced several decades of communism under Soviet control; and these countries' socioeconomic condition in recent years, following the collapse of communism. Adding to the equation a variable that measures the number of years a society experienced under communist rule raises the explained variance to 63 percent.

Our cultural zone deviation factor reflects the impact of a given cultural-historic heritage on the traditional/secular-rational factor, controlling for the effects of the socioeconomic variables and the ex-communist variable. Adding that factor to Model 4 makes it possible to explain fully 80 percent of the cross-national variance. The formula at the foot of Table 2.6 is derived from this analysis; one can use this formula to predict a society's position on the traditional/secular-rational values dimension. As Table 2.4 demonstrates, dozens of attitudes measured in the Values Surveys are closely correlated with a society's score on this dimension. Knowing a society's per capita GDP, the percentage of industrial workers in the labor force, and its historical heritage enables one to predict with considerable accuracy how a given public will respond to a wide range of survey questions involving religion, authority, national pride, and other topics.

Because causes precede effects, all of the independent variables used here were measured at time points before 1999–2001, when the values of the respective publics were measured. In keeping with our assumption that socioeconomic factors help shape a society's values, we find that a country's real per capita GDP in 1995 predicts its values in the 1999–2001 wave of surveys more accurately than does a measure of per capita GDP in 2000, at the time of the surveys. This outcome means that we can use the 2000 measure of per capita GDP to predict scores on the two value dimensions in 2005 – which is convenient, because we did not yet have the 2005 measures of GDP per capita when this was written.

There is an obvious ambiguity in interpreting the findings in Table 2.6. The various cultural zones have very different levels of socioeconomic development, but this procedure attributes the explanatory power shared by socioeconomic development and cultural zones to the socioeconomic variables, which may underestimate the importance of cultural zone membership. We therefore specified a fifth model, using only the cultural zone memberships, to compute an average value on the factor relative to the overall mean (a shift factor from the raw mean, rather than from the value predicted with the socioeconomic variables). Interestingly, this cultural zone factor alone explains 59 percent of the variance – more than the two socioeconomic factors in Model 2 combined. This could be interpreted to mean that cultural factors are even more important than socioeconomic ones in explaining factor scores on the traditional/secular-rational factor, but this conclusion would be risky. The socioeconomic differences between the various cultural zones probably account for a substantial portion of the variance they seem to explain, as is obvious when one controls for socioeconomic factors. It is difficult to partition the variances between socioeconomic and cultural factors conclusively, but it seems clear that both sets of factors are important, and our predictions take both sets of factors into account.

Table 2.7 analyzed the socioeconomic and cultural factors that explain factor scores on the survival/self-expression dimension. In this case, a society's GDP per capita explains so much of the variance by itself (fully 60 percent) that the addition of a second socioeconomic variable (the percent of labor in the service sector) raises the total variance explained only slightly in Model 2. But there is a significant increase in variance explained in Model 3 when the ex-communist dummy variable is added. These three factors explain 74 percent of the variance.

The addition of cultural zone factors further enhances the explanatory power of Model 4, bringing the total explained variance to a remarkable 84 percent. Again we also computed the variance explained by cultural zone membership alone and found it accounts for a substantial 52 percent; however, the socioeconomic factors are even stronger predictors of scores on the survival/self-expression dimension.

A society's cultural zone membership seems especially important in shaping traditional/secular-rational values, which are deeply rooted in long-established historical factors – above all, a society's religious heritage. But modernization variables seem to play the dominant role in shaping survival/self-expression values, which are less strongly rooted in a society's traditional cultural heritage. Hence, self-expression values rather than secular-rational values reflect the most essential cultural manifestation of modernization. This finding underlines the importance of self-expression values as the central element in a human development sequence leading from socioeconomic development to democracy, as we will demonstrate.

The formula in the footnote of Table 2.7, derived from this analysis, makes it possible to predict a society's position on the survival/self-expression values dimension from a handful of socioeconomic and cultural indicators.

Table A-1 in the Internet Appendix[1] shows how successfully the two equations we have derived from the regression analyses in Tables 2.6 and 2.7 predict a society's position on these two dimensions for all countries surveyed in 1999–2001. Table A-1 shows the factor score we predicted for each country, the score actually observed in the 1999–2001 survey, and the difference between the predicted and observed scores. The differences between the predicted scores and the observed scores range from 0.00 to 1.15, but overall the predicted values come close to the observed values. Across these sixty-four societies, the mean difference between the predicted score and the observed score on traditional/secular-rational values is only .36. The mean difference between the predicted score and the observed score on the survival/secular-rational values dimension is almost identical: .37.

Table A-2 in the Internet Appendix shows the mean error of our predictions for each society, ranking them from our most accurate predictions (South Africa

---

[1] The Internet Appendix can be found at http://www.worldvaluessurvey.org/publications/humandevelopment.html.

and West Germany) to our least accurate predictions (Puerto Rico and Sweden). Although our predictions show a wide range of accuracy, they have impressive accuracy by most standards of comparison. The mean error in prediction is .36, on a cultural map that extends from below −2.00 to above +2.00 on each dimension. Our average prediction falls within a radius of .36 of the value actually observed for that society, forming a circle that occupies about 2 percent of the map's area. These predictions are vastly better than random. And, surprisingly, our predictions are just as accurate for the twelve societies that we had never before surveyed (shown in boldface on Table A-2) as for the other societies that had been surveyed at least once before. Our model does just as good a job in predicting the values of publics that have never before been surveyed as it does in predicting the values in 1999–2001 of publics from which we have a prior reading.

How do these predictions, based on a revised version of modernization theory, compare with random predictions? Table 3.1 presents two sets of predictions for each of the twelve countries that had never before been surveyed. The first two columns on this table show the results of a genuinely random prediction: not knowing anything about the actual distributions, one predicts that the respondents will fall at the midpoint of the scale on each of the variables used to construct this map (e.g., the scale used to measure the acceptability of abortion ranges from 1 to 10, so we would predict a mean score of 5.5 for each society). Using this procedure for all ten variables in the factor analysis generates a score of 1.48 on the vertical axis (far above the actual empirical mean) and a score of −.09 on the horizontal axis (very close to the empirical mean). These random predictions are relatively far from the results actually observed: only seven of the sixty-four societies fall within one standard deviation of this predicted location; and the twelve societies in Table 3.1 deviate from their predicted scores as indicated. The mean of the two errors is 1.43. As Table 3.2 indicates, our theory-based model produces a mean prediction error of only .34 – less than one-fourth as large as the average error resulting from random predictions.

The second prediction is one that a well-informed social scientist might make: it predicts that each society will have the mean factor score on each dimension. We know that in a normal distribution about two-thirds of the sample will fall within one standard deviation of this point, so this is an excellent bet. This approach produces a mean prediction error of .99 across these twelve societies (reflecting that factor scores are standardized to have a standard deviation of 1.0). Although much less accurate than the .36 mean prediction error that our model produces for the same twelve societies, it is a considerable improvement over the random prediction in the first columns of Table 3.1. But this prediction is *not* random or a priori: one does not know the mean factor score until one has surveyed all the societies and analyzed their distributions. This approach simply selects a point that can only be known after all of the data have been collected and analyzed. Nevertheless, our model generates genuine out-of-sample, a priori predictions (including societies never before surveyed) that are far more accurate than this ex post facto "prediction."

TABLE 3.1. *Alternative Predictions for 12 Societies Not Previously Surveyed*

Country	Prediction Based on Midpoint of Each Scale		Prediction as Mean Factor Score	
	Traditional/Secular-Rational Values	Survival/Self-Expression Values	Traditional/Secular-Rational Values	Survival/Self-Expression Values
Luxembourg	.46	.30	.37	1.18
Greece	.82	-.86	.73	.62
Zimbabwe	1.37	2.81	1.46	1.33
Tanzania	1.77	1.62	1.86	.14
Vietnam	.61	1.21	.70	.27
Indonesia	.96	1.89	1.05	.41
Uganda	1.31	1.96	1.40	.48
Egypt	1.48	1.88	1.57	.40
Morocco	1.53	2.61	1.62	1.13
Iran	1.10	1.81	1.19	.33
Jordan	1.48	2.49	1.57	1.01
Algeria	1.56	2.20	1.65	.72
Mean	1.20	1.66	1.26	.67
Mean (both)	1.43		.99	

Note: Values are the difference between the predicted factor score and the observed score.

TABLE 3.2. *Theory-Based Predictions of Locations of 12 Societies Not Previously Surveyed*

Country	Accuracy of Predictions Based on Revised Version of Modernization Theory	
	Traditional/Secular-Rational Values	Survival/Self-Expression Values
Luxembourg	.40	.00
Greece	.28	.54
Zimbabwe	.04	.93
Tanzania	.50	.45
Vietnam	.03	.10
Indonesia	.02	1.14
Uganda	.19	.25
Egypt	.42	.14
Morocco	.64	.48
Iran	.15	.14
Jordan	.25	.65
Algeria	.17	.22
Mean	.26	.42
Mean (both)	.34	

Note: Values are the difference between the predicted factor score and the observed score.

Random versus Systematic Predictions

We have just examined some genuine out-of-sample predictions. Using a model based on analysis of the data from the first three waves of surveys, we predicted the positions of all sixty-four societies that were surveyed in the fourth wave, in 1999–2001. Our model includes a cultural zone deviation factor that is a constant for each cultural zone: it does not use a specific nation's position in the earlier waves to predict its position in the fourth wave. Consequently, it is a general model that not only predicts the position of countries that have already been surveyed but also predicts the positions of twelve countries that were not previously covered in the Values Surveys (for some of these countries, such as Iran, Zimbabwe, Tanzania, and Vietnam, virtually *no* previous representative national survey data were available from any source: we helped design the first national sampling frame used in some of these countries).

Despite the substantial shifts that are observed from one wave to the next, our model predicts the position of most countries in 1999–2001 rather accurately, as Figure 3.1 demonstrates. We do not attempt to show the predicted and observed locations of all sixty-four societies on this map (that information is provided by Table A-1 in the Internet Appendix). Figure 3.1 simply illustrates some representative examples. For instance, the location predicted for Finland in the fourth wave of surveys and the location actually observed appear in the upper

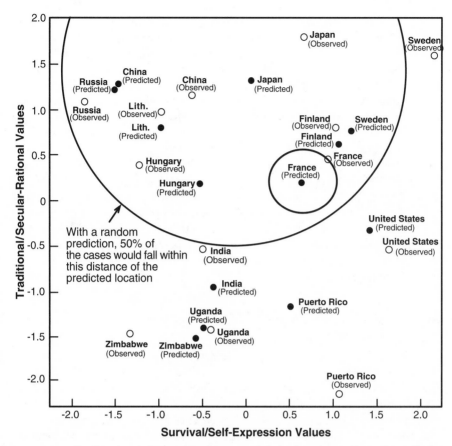

FIGURE 3.1. Predicted and observed positions on global cultural map. France's prediction is of average accuracy; the circle around France's prediction position illustrates our average prediction error. Sweden and Puerto Rico are the two *least* accurate among sixty-five predictions. Finland, Lithuania, and Uganda are among the six most accurate predictions.

right-hand quadrant, just above the circle (the predicted location is shown as a black dot, and the observed location is shown as a white dot). These two dots are very close to each other, for this is one of our most accurate predictions. Our two *most* accurate predictions (for West Germany and South Africa) are not shown, because in both cases the observed location is almost identical with the predicted location: the two dots would be indistinguishable. This figure does show our two least accurate predictions, those for Sweden and Puerto Rico. Even these two cases fall roughly in the right ball park, near the upper and lower right-hand corners of the map, respectively, but they are our worst predictions. Figure 3.1 also illustrates two more of our best predictions, showing the predicted and observed locations for Lithuania (abbreviated as Lith.) and Uganda. In each case, the predicted value is very close to the observed location.

The predicted and observed locations for France illustrate the average accuracy of our predictions: the small circle around France's predicted location on Figure 3.1 shows our model's mean range of error. The large circle in the upper half of Figure 3.1 shows the result of a random prediction, based on the procedure shown in the first half of Table 3.1 (predicting that the respondents will fall at the midpoint of each scale). Only seven of the sixty-four societies fall within one standard deviation of this predicted location. To include half of the societies would require a circle with a radius of 2.1 standard deviations. This figure provides a graphic comparison between the mean error in our model's predictions and the much greater range of error found with random predictions: the larger circle covers an area that is sixteen times as large as that of the smaller circle. The predictions generated by our model based on the data from the first three waves are not perfect, but they generally fall pretty close to the location actually observed in the fourth wave. If we had included the fourth-wave data in computing our model, we would probably be able to generate even more accurate "predictions" of these positions, but they then would not be genuine out-of-sample predictions.

Predicting the Responses of 120 Publics in 2005–2006

In the natural sciences, it is generally accepted that one can fit a model to any collection of observations, but the conclusive test of a theory is its ability to predict previously unobserved phenomena. This test is much more difficult to meet in the social sciences than in the natural sciences, because social science deals with much more complex phenomena, which are shaped by interactions between multiple levels of analysis. An interaction between two particles can be analyzed solely at the physical level; human choices involve physical, chemical, biological, psychological, economic, social, geographic, historical, and cultural factors. Nevertheless, certain regularities that have predictive value can be observed in human behavior. Predictions of future behavior will necessarily be probabilistic and only roughly accurate, but they can provide useful guidance to choices and policies.

Consequently, let us predict what the people of various societies will tell us they believe and value when the next wave of the Values Surveys is carried out in 2005–6. Our model could generate predictions for all 192 countries that are members of the United Nations, but we will limit ourselves to predicting the values of the publics of about 120 countries that, by our most optimistic assessment, might possibly be included in the 2005–6 surveys. These countries contain about 95 percent of the world's population.

We will use the data from all four waves of the Values Surveys, carried out from 1981 to 2001, in making these predictions. Consequently, we will update the cultural zone deviation factors and predictive formulas used so far in this chapter, which are based on data from the first three waves of surveys. Table A-3 in the Internet Appendix shows the revised version of the cultural zone deviation factors and the predictive formulas. Neither the factors nor the formulas differ much from the earlier versions, but we believe they should generate slightly more accurate predictions of the results from the surveys that will be carried out in 2005–6 and analyzed soon afterward.

Using the data from all available surveys, we estimated the scores on each dimension in 2005 for all societies for which previous data were available. We then used these scores as the dependent variables in regression analyses that enabled us to derive the coefficients for the new equations, to predict the scores for countries not previously surveyed. Table A-4 in the Internet Appendix shows where our model predicts that each of 122 societies will fall on the traditional/secular-rational values dimension and on the survival/self-expression dimension in 2005–6. Basic values tend to be stable, so we expect that the positions of previously surveyed countries will be reasonably close to the positions they had in 2000, apart from a tendency for rich societies to move higher on both dimensions during the five-year period from 2000 to 2005. Measurement error will also produce a certain amount of apparent movement. To maximize accuracy, the positions in 2005 of previously surveyed countries are predicted from previous data for that country, rather than from the cultural zone factor for all societies in their zone. The predicted positions of the societies that have not previously been surveyed are based on the assumption that their values will be shaped by the same factors, linked with modernization and cultural persistence that influence the values of the other societies and are reflected in our model. We will encounter some surprises: almost certainly, the publics of some societies will deviate markedly from these predictions, just as the U.S. public has more religious and traditional values than our model predicts, for reasons that are not captured in the model. This model contains only a few factors, but a society's values reflect its entire historical experience. Nevertheless, we are reasonably confident that on the whole the surveys carried out in 2005 will yield results that are reasonably close to the predictions in Table A-4 in the Internet Appendix.

Figure 3.2 shows the predicted locations of some of these societies on the cultural map. Placing all of the more than 120 societies on this map would make it unreadable (though the reader can plot the location of any additional societies that may be of interest, using the data in Table A-4 in the Internet Appendix). Figure 3.2 gives special attention to showing the predicted location of fifteen societies that have never been surveyed before, in context with a number of previously surveyed societies. Because most rich countries have already been covered in previous surveys, most of the newly surveyed countries fall on the lower half of the map, with Guatemala, Ecuador, and Paraguay falling into a cluster near other Latin American countries, and Kenya, Ethiopia, and Angola falling near the traditional pole and to the left of the midpoint of the survival/self-expression dimension. Yemen is also expected to fall in this region, but our model predicts that Kuwait, because of its high economic level, will show more-secular values than most Islamic societies. In contrast with most of the newly surveyed societies, Hong Kong is predicted to fall in the upper region – near other high-income societies such as Japan, Germany, and Slovenia. Cyprus is also a relatively high-income society, and we expect it to fall near the center, not far from Spain and Croatia. Although Cuba is a Latin American

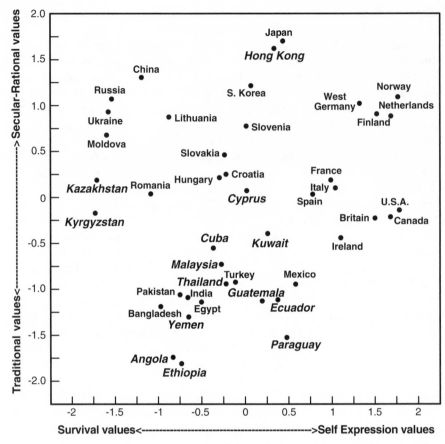

FIGURE 3.2. Predicted locations on cultural map of societies that may be surveyed in 2005–6. The predicted locations of fourteen societies that have not been surveyed previously are shown in italics.

society, it is the only one that has experienced communist rule, so our model predicts that it will be an outlier, having more secular values than most Latin American countries. Similarly, Kazakhstan and Kyrgyzstan are Islamic societies that have experienced many decades of communist rule, and our model predicts that they will be outliers from the main body of Islamic societies, showing substantially more secular-rational values than mainstream Islamic societies. Their low income levels also imply that they will tend to emphasize survival values even more than most ex-communist countries.

Predicting Responses to Specific Questions in 2005–2006

Each of the two dimensions on which our cultural map is based taps scores of important beliefs and values. Thus, if one knows a society's location on this map, one can predict its public's response to many additional questions. To illustrate this point, Table A-5 in the Internet Appendix predicts responses of 120 publics to two specific issues: the percentage of respondents in each society who will say that "religion is very important in my life"; and the percentage of respondents who will agree with the statement that "When jobs are scarce, men have more right to a job than women."

Neither of these two variables was used to construct either the traditional/secular-rational dimension or the survival/self-expression values dimensions. We present these predictions to illustrate the fact that our model makes it possible to predict the responses to many additional variables besides the ten that are used to construct these dimensions. This is possible because each dimension is strongly correlated with a wide range of additional variables, as Tables 2.2 and 2.3 demonstrated. Attitudes toward gender equality have been changing rapidly during the two decades covered by the previous Values Surveys, so in predicting attitudes toward gender equality we are not only predicting the responses of societies that have not been surveyed previously, we are also attempting to hit a moving target.

These are genuine predictions. None of these surveys had been carried out when this was written, and many of these societies have not been included in any previous wave of the Values Surveys (some of them have never been included in any previous survey).[2] As this chapter was being written, it was impossible to say how accurate these predictions would be. We can safely assume that they will only be approximately accurate, and in some cases they will be far from the mark, because our model uses only four variables among the scores of conceivably relevant factors. The fact that the United States deviates from its expected location on the traditional/secular-rational dimension (though not on the survival/self-expression dimension) reflects a significant feature of American culture that is not included in our model.

Even if our model made perfect predictions, we would still have to cope with the fact that the normal range of sampling error in measuring these items is about 5 to 6 points, so even with a perfect model, our predictions would only come within this range of the observed values. In short, a mean prediction error of 5 or 6 points is about as close to perfection as one can attain. At the other end of the scale, random predictions would produce mean errors of 30 to 33 points.

In experiments similar to those used in predicting each country's position on the two-dimensional cultural map in 2000, we predicted the responses to these two variables, using our model based on a revised version of modernization theory. The mean error in predicting the percentage saying that "religion is very important in my life" was 10.5 points; the mean error in predicting the percentage who agreed that "men have more right to a job than women" was 10.3 points. This result is imperfect but much more accurate than the results

[2] As this manuscript was being written, data were obtained from Saudi Arabia and Kyrgyzstan but not yet analyzed.

from random prediction. We also made a set of random predictions (using a random-number generator), which produced a mean error of 32 points in predicting the percentage agreeing that "men have more right to a job than women," and a mean error of 31 points in predicting the percentage saying that "religion is very important in my life." Empirically, our modernization model produces predictions that have a much smaller error margin than the results of random predictions.

This analysis applies the central assumption of all inference statistics: explanatory models are designed to reduce prediction error. Fitness statistics in regression analyses are based on comparisons between predicted and actual data: the closer the predicted values come to the actual data, the better the fit, tending to confirm the underlying theory.

Conclusion

This chapter has tested a model that enables us to predict the beliefs and values of the publics of given societies, based on a revised version of modernization theory. This model is parsimonious, utilizing two modernization factors: (1) real per capita GDP five years before the survey, and (2) the percentage of the labor force employed in given sectors; and two historical heritage factors: (3) how many years of communist rule the society experienced, and (4) a constant for each of the eight cultural zones that reflects the extent to which that zone's cultural heritage causes it to deviate from simple economic-historical determinism. The model explains more than 80 percent of the variance on each of the two major dimensions of cross-cultural variation. We used this model to predict the values of 65 societies that were surveyed in 1999–2001, including 12 societies that had not been surveyed previously. When we plotted our predictions on a two-dimensional map, we found that the predicted position of the average society falls within a small radius of its actual position – within a circle that occupies about 2 percent of the map's area. These positions reflect each public's responses to scores of important political and social questions. We then used this model to predict the positions of more than 120 societies that may be surveyed in 2005–6; and the responses of each public to two specific questions that will be asked in these surveys. These predictions were posted as part of our Internet Appendix on the website of the World Values Survey Association in September 2004. These predictions will be imperfect, as they necessarily must be; even if our model were perfect, we still would have to allow a margin for sampling error. Nevertheless, we expect these predictions will be reasonably close to the observed figures.

Our model seems to capture some of the most important factors shaping cross-national variation in mass belief systems. We have laid the groundwork for further testing and improving this kind of model. We believe that the effort to produce a predictive model of cultural change can contribute to a better understanding of how cultural change takes place and greater insight into important long-term trends.

Our predictions are probabilistic, not deterministic, and we expect them to be only roughly accurate. But the results of the analyses in this chapter make us reasonably confident that the predictions presented here will be much closer to the results actually observed in 2005–6 than random predictions. The extent to which these predictions prove accurate will provide a strong test of the validity of our revised version of modernization theory.

4

Intergenerational Value Change

As Chapter 2 demonstrated, we find massive and consistent differences between the values held by the publics of developed and developing societies. These differences suggest (but do not prove) that socioeconomic development brings systematic shifts from traditional to secular-rational values and from survival to self-expression values.

The next two chapters present additional evidence of these changes. Chapter 5 shows how the publics of postindustrial societies moved toward increasing emphasis on secular-rational values and self-expression values during the period from 1981 to 2001. This shift is direct evidence that cultural changes in the predicted directions actually are occurring, though it only covers a period of twenty years. The present chapter examines the underlying patterns of generational differences that led to these changes. For we find that in developed societies, the younger generations emphasize secular-rational values and self-expression values much more highly than do the older generations. This result is precisely what we would expect to find if intergenerational value shifts were occurring.

Under some circumstances, one might argue that these age-linked differences simply reflect life-cycle effects, not intergenerational change – claiming that people have an inherent tendency to place increasing emphasis on traditional values and survival values as they age. If such a life-cycle effect existed, the younger cohorts would place more emphasis on secular-rational values and self-expression values than the older cohorts in *any* society. But this claim is untenable in the present case, for these intergenerational differences are found in developed societies but not in low-income societies. There is no inherent tendency for people to shift toward more traditional values or to emphasize survival values more strongly as they age.[1] Likewise, there is no universal tendency for the young to

---

[1] Intergenerational population replacement tends to give that impression, however: as younger cohorts with increasingly modern values replace older cohorts with relatively traditional values, the youngest birth cohort tends to go from having *more* modern values than other cohorts, to having *less* modern values than other cohorts – not because their values have changed, but because the cohorts with less modern values have died off.

place more emphasis than the old on secular-rational values and self-expression values. The presence of intergenerational differences depends on whether a society has attained high levels of socioeconomic development. The generational differences found in developed societies seem to reflect long-term socioeconomic changes rather than life-cycle effects.

The age-related differences examined in this chapter suggest that a process of intergenerational value change has been taking place during the past six decades and more – but this is only indirect evidence of cultural change. In order to demonstrate directly that long-term cultural changes are occurring, we would need evidence from surveys that had measured these values in both rich and poor countries throughout the past sixty or seventy years. Such data are not available and will not be available for another half century. Chapter 5 examines the changes over time shown by survey evidence from the 1981–2001 Values Surveys. These surveys cover twenty years in some countries, and for most countries they cover a decade or less. This period of time is much shorter than would be needed for a conclusive test of intergenerational cultural change: over relatively short periods of time, short-term fluctuations and situation-specific period effects can easily swamp the effects of cultural change based on intergenerational population replacement. Nevertheless, the time-series data that are now available show changes in the predicted direction (toward secular-rational and self-expression values) in virtually all high-income societies but not in low-income societies. We do not find a universal shift toward secular-rational and self-expression values, such as might result from some universal process of cultural diffusion based on globalization or the internet. As our revised version of modernization theory implies, these cultural changes are linked with socioeconomic development and are *not* occurring where it is absent.

The evidence from three different types of analysis all points in the same direction, indicating that we are witnessing a process of intergenerational value change linked with socioeconomic development. If evidence from only one of these sources pointed to this conclusion, it would be less convincing. But analysis of a huge body of evidence from eighty societies, using three different approaches – comparisons of rich and poor countries, generational comparisons, and time-series evidence from the past two decades – all point to the same conclusion. Major cultural changes are occurring, reflecting a process of intergenerational value change linked with industrialization and postindustrialization.

Generational Differences and Cultural Change

The shift from agrarian to industrial society and the subsequent shift from industrial to postindustrial society are gradual processes that occur over many decades; our longitudinal evidence of trends from existing surveys covers twenty or thirty years at best, and for most low-income societies, we only have data covering periods of five or ten years. This is too short a period to provide direct measurements of intergenerational changes, which reflect changing conditions over many decades.

For the ex-communist countries (with the sole exception of Hungary, which was surveyed the first time in 1981), we only have survey data since 1989–91, because it was almost impossible to carry out independent surveys in these countries until after their authoritarian regimes had collapsed. Moreover, the years since 1990 have been an atypical period for the ex-communist societies, one shaped by the complete remodeling of their economic, social, and political systems and the breakup of the Soviet Union into fifteen successor states. In the ex-Soviet societies, real income fell to less than half its former level, the social welfare net disintegrated, law and order broke down, the communist belief system lost its credibility, and life expectancy itself fell sharply. This was a traumatic period for the ex-Soviet societies, and we would expect the short-term changes to reflect these difficult conditions. As noted in Chapter 9, this experience helps to explain why the Soviet successor states – with the exception of the Baltic countries – have been less successful in making the transition to democracy than most other former communist societies.

But during much of the twentieth century, the Soviet Union experienced high rates of economic growth. In the 1960s, commenting on the fact that socialist economies were growing at much higher rates than those of Western democracies, Khrushchev said, "We will bury you!" The threat seemed plausible to many Western observers. At that point, the Soviet Union was one of the world's two superpowers and seemed to have a dazzling future. But the years since 1990 have been a period of severe malaise and insecurity. We would expect the short-term changes among these publics to reflect these conditions. Consequently, we would expect generational comparisons to give a more accurate reflection of the long-term cultural changes that have taken place among ex-communist publics than does the time-series data from the exceptional period since 1990, which was characterized by the collapse of the communist political, economic, and social systems.

In the absence of survey data measuring these values over many decades, generational comparisons of cross-sectional surveys provide a useful indirect indication of long-term cultural change. If the basic values of a given generation tend to be established during their preadult formative years and change relatively little thereafter, then intergenerational differences in basic values may give an indication of long-term trends, especially if we have side evidence that helps us distinguish between life-cycle effects and intergenerational change.

In societies that have been shaped by high levels of existential security for sustained periods of time, we would expect to find substantial differences between the values held by older and younger generations. In such societies, the younger birth cohorts should place the most emphasis on self-expression values, while the older cohorts should continue to emphasize survival values.

We hypothesize that the spread of self-expression values does not reflect a universal process of global cultural diffusion; it is contingent on whether a society's people have experienced high levels of existential security and autonomy, or whether they have experienced economic and social collapse, as in the less successful ex-communist economies.

If these generational differences reflect socioeconomic development, we would not expect to find large generational value differences in societies that have not experienced major increases in existential security over the past several decades. In stagnant economies, we would expect the young to be just as traditional as their elders. The availability of data from fundamentally different types of societies sheds light on the interpretation of these effects, because (as we will demonstrate) we do *not* find any universal tendency for people to place more emphasis on survival values as they age: we find greater emphasis on self-expression values among the younger cohorts than among the older ones in postindustrial societies, but not in societies that have experienced little or no economic development.

For a conclusive analysis, we would need to analyze successive waves of survey data collected at numerous time points over many decades. This would enable us to disentangle life-cycle effects, period effects, and birth cohort effects. We do not have the massive longitudinal database that would be required for this. In its absence, no one approach can be absolutely conclusive, but if a combination of methods, indicators, and datasets generates findings that all point to the same conclusion, it enhances our confidence in our interpretation.

By far the longest and most detailed body of time-series data concerning value change is the one measuring materialist versus postmaterialist value priorities. These values have been measured in a large number of countries, and they have been measured in the Eurobarometer surveys almost every year from 1970 to the present. Let us start by examining the intergenerational shift from materialist to postmaterialist values. Because these values are a key component of the survival/self-expression dimension, our analysis gives an idea of what we would find with its other components if we had annual measures of them over three decades, as we do with materialist and postmaterialist values. Furthermore, this analysis is useful in another respect: it illustrates the problems of distinguishing between long-term intergenerational changes, life-cycle effects, and period effects linked with current changes in socioeconomic conditions.

The Rise of Postmaterialist Values

More than three decades ago, Inglehart (1977) hypothesized that, throughout advanced industrial societies, peoples' value priorities were shifting from "materialist" goals, which emphasize economic and physical security, toward "postmaterialist" goals, which emphasize self-expression and the quality of life. This cultural shift has been measured annually since 1970 in surveys carried out in many Western societies. A massive body of evidence demonstrates that an intergenerational shift has been taking place in the predicted direction.

This theory of intergenerational value change is based on two key hypotheses (Inglehart, 1990):

1. *A scarcity hypothesis.* Virtually everyone wants freedom and autonomy, but people's priorities reflect their socioeconomic conditions, placing the highest subjective value on the most pressing needs. Material sustenance

and physical security are the first requirements for survival. Thus, under conditions of scarcity, people give top priority to materialistic goals, whereas under conditions of prosperity, they become more likely to emphasize postmaterialistic goals.

2. *A socialization hypothesis.* The relationship between material scarcity and value priorities is not primarily one of immediate adjustment: a substantial time lag is involved because, to a large extent, one's basic values reflect the conditions that prevailed during one's preadult years. They change mainly through intergenerational population replacement. Moreover, the older generations in each society tend to transmit their values to their children; this cultural heritage is not easily dispelled, but if it is inconsistent with one's firsthand experience, it can gradually erode.

The scarcity hypothesis is similar to the principle of diminishing marginal utility in economic theory. It reflects the basic distinction between the material needs for physical survival and safety and nonmaterial needs such as those for esteem, self-expression, and aesthetic satisfaction. Because material needs are immediately crucial to survival, when they are in short supply they tend to take priority over any other needs, including postmaterialistic needs. Conversely, when material needs are securely met, they tend to be taken for granted and postmaterialistic goals receive higher priority, widening people's horizon for higher goals on the Maslowian hierarchy of motivations.

The economic history of advanced industrial societies during the past fifty years has significant implications in light of the scarcity hypothesis. For these societies are a striking exception to the prevailing historical pattern: most of their population does not live under conditions of hunger and economic insecurity. This has led to a gradual shift in which needs for belonging, esteem, and intellectual and aesthetic satisfaction have become more prominent. We would expect prolonged periods of high prosperity to encourage the spread of postmaterialist values, and enduring economic decline would have the opposite effect. Recent developments, such as relatively high unemployment, the collapse of stock markets and welfare state retrenchment, have increased economic insecurity; if this went far enough, it could undermine the prevailing sense that survival can be taken for granted and, in the long run, bring a resurgence of materialist values.

But there is no one-to-one relationship between socioeconomic development and the prevalence of postmaterialist values, for these values reflect one's subjective sense of security, not one's objective economic level per se. Moreover, one's subjective sense of security not only reflects one's own personal security but is influenced by the general sense of security that prevails in one's social context. While rich individuals and nationalities tend to feel more secure than poor ones, these feelings are also influenced by the cultural setting and social welfare institutions in which one is raised. Thus, the scarcity hypothesis must be interpreted in connection with the socialization hypothesis.

One of the most pervasive concepts in social science is the notion of a basic human personality structure that tends to crystallize by the time an individual reaches adulthood, with relatively little change thereafter. This concept permeates the literature from Plato through Freud and is confirmed by findings from contemporary survey research. Early socialization tends to carry greater weight than later socialization. A large body of evidence indicates that people's basic values are largely fixed by the time they reach adulthood and change relatively little thereafter (Rokeach, 1968, 1973; Inglehart, 1977, 1997; K. Baker, Dalton, and Hildebrandt, 1981). As Shuman and Scott (1989) argue, generations have "collective memories," imprinted in adolescence and early adulthood, that persist throughout the life cycle. If so, we would expect to find substantial differences between the values of the young and the old in societies that have experienced a rising sense of security. Moreover, although cultural traditions tend to persist through socialization, this process does not necessarily reproduce a given value system unchanged. During their formative years, people do not necessarily absorb all of the values that their societies attempt to instill in them. Individuals are most likely to adopt those values that are consistent with their firsthand experience during their formative years and drift away from values that are inconsistent with their own firsthand experience. This makes it possible for intergenerational value change to take place. If younger generations are socialized under significantly different conditions from those that shaped earlier generations, the values of the entire society will gradually change through intergenerational replacement.

Taken together, these hypotheses generate a clear set of predictions concerning value change. First, the scarcity hypothesis implies that prosperity is conducive to the spread of postmaterialist values, but the socialization hypothesis implies that neither an individual's values nor those of a society as a whole are likely to change overnight. Instead, fundamental value change takes place gradually; for the most part, it occurs as a younger generation replaces an older one in the adult population of a society.

Consequently, after an extended period of rising economic and physical security, one would expect to find substantial differences between the value priorities of older and younger groups: they would have been shaped by different experiences in their formative years. But there would be a sizable time lag between economic changes and their political effects. Ten or fifteen years after an era of prosperity began, the age cohorts that had spent their formative years in prosperity would begin to enter the electorate. Another decade or two might pass before they began to play elite roles.

Testing the Value Change Hypothesis

The value change thesis was first tested in 1970 in cross-national surveys in Britain, France, West Germany, Italy, Belgium, and the Netherlands. All six countries showed the age-group differences predicted by the socialization hypothesis. As Figure 4.1 demonstrates, in 1970 materialists outnumbered postmaterialists enormously among the oldest group; but as we move to younger groups, the proportion of materialists declines and that of postmaterialists

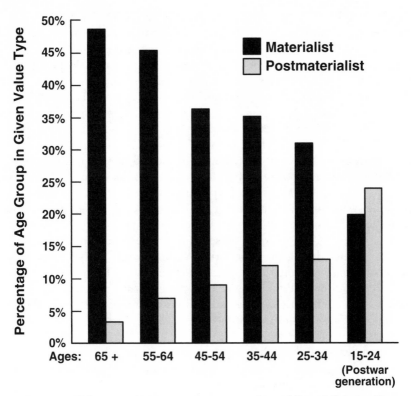

FIGURE 4.1. Value type by age group, among the publics of Britain, France, West Germany, Italy, Belgium, and the Netherlands in 1970. *Source*: European Community survey of February 1970, based on original four-item materialist/postmaterialist values battery. Reprinted from Inglehart, 1990: 76.

increases (Inglehart, 1977). Among the oldest cohort (those over sixty-five), materialists outnumbered postmaterialists by more than fourteen to one; but among the youngest cohort, postmaterialists were slightly more numerous than materialists.

Does this pattern reflect life-cycle effects, generational change, or some combination of the two? The theory predicts that we will find generational differences; but the differences that we observe between young and old could reflect some inherent tendency for people to become more materialistic as they age. If so, then, as time goes by, the values of the younger groups will eventually come to resemble those of the older groups, producing no change in the society as a whole. The only way to determine whether these age differences reflect generational change or aging effects is by following given birth cohorts over time to see if they become more materialist as they age.

Fortunately, we can do so: the four-item materialist-postmaterialist values battery has been asked in cross-national surveys in almost every year from 1970 to the present.

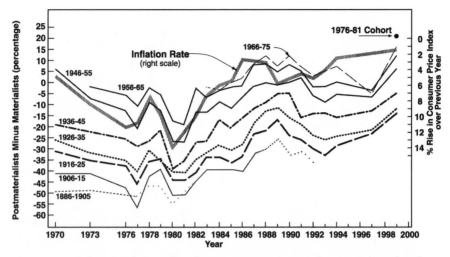

FIGURE 4.2. Cohort analysis with inflation rate superimposed (using inverted scale on right): percent postmaterialists minus percent materialists in six West European societies, 1970–99. *Source*: Based on combined weighted sample of Eurobarometer surveys carried out in West Germany, France, Britain, Italy, the Netherlands, and Belgium, in given years, using the four-item materialist/postmaterialist values index.

Figure 4.2 shows how the values of each birth cohort evolved over time, from 1970 to 1999, again using the pooled data from Britain, France, West Germany, Italy, Belgium, and the Netherlands. Each cohort's position at a given time is calculated by subtracting the percentage of materialists in that cohort from the percentage of postmaterialists. Thus, at the zero point on the vertical axis, the two groups are equally numerous (the cohort born in 1946–55 was located near this point in 1970). The proportion of postmaterialists increases as we move up; the proportion of materialists increases as we move down. If the age differences reflect a life-cycle effect, then each of the cohort lines would move downward, toward the materialist pole, as we move from left to right across this period of nearly three decades.

We find no such downward movement. Instead, the younger birth cohorts remain more postmaterialist than their elders throughout the period from 1970 to 1999: people did not become more materialist as they aged – indeed, many of these birth cohorts were slightly *less* materialist at the end of this period than they were at the start.

Moreover, if life-cycle effects were the prevailing mechanism, no overall value change would occur. But, as we will see, large value changes actually did take place from 1970 to 1999, and they moved in the predicted direction. These changes reflect the fact that each new birth cohort that enters the surveys is more postmaterialist than the previous one and remains so, producing a shift toward postmaterialist values as younger cohorts replace older ones. It is evident from Figure 4.2 that period effects are *also* present, and they produce short-term fluctuations in levels of postmaterialism that affect all age groups to roughly the same degree. Current conditions can move all birth cohorts up or down, depending on whether they are favorable or unfavorable. But in the long run, the period effects' short-term upward swings tend to cancel out their downward swings, so that they have no long-term effect. The intergenerational differences are relatively stable, so that the effect of intergenerational population replacement may move in the same direction for many decades, producing large cumulative changes.

What Causes the Period Effects?

The causes of the period effects are indicated in Figure 4.2, which shows the current rate of inflation, superimposed as a heavy shaded line above the lines for each birth cohort. Because the theory predicts that postmaterialist values will rise when inflation falls, the inflation index runs from low rates at the top of the graph to high rates toward the bottom. This makes it evident that inflation and postmaterialist values move up and down together – within a limited range of fluctuation that maintains the generational differences.

Striking period effects are evident: there was a clear tendency for each cohort to dip toward the materialist pole during the recession of the mid-1970s and again during the recessions of the early 1980s and the early 1990s. These effects are implied by our theory, which links postmaterialist values with economic security. High inflation rates tend to make people feel economically insecure, and as the graph demonstrates, there is a remarkably close fit between current economic conditions and the short-term fluctuations in materialist and postmaterialist values. High levels of inflation depress the proportion of postmaterialists. But these period effects are transient; they disappear when economic conditions return to normal. In the long run, the values of a given birth cohort are remarkably stable. Despite the fluctuations linked with current economic conditions, the intergenerational differences persist: at virtually every point in time, each younger cohort is significantly less materialist than all of the older ones. These enduring generational differences reflect differences in the formative conditions that shaped the respective birth cohorts: the older ones were influenced by the hunger and insecurity that prevailed during World War I, the Great Depression, and World War II; the younger ones have grown up in advanced welfare states, during an era of historically unprecedented prosperity and peace.

Both period effects and socialization effects exist, reflecting different aspects of reality, with the period effects reflecting the impact of short-term forces and the socialization effects reflecting the impact of long-term intergenerational changes. Each birth cohort reacts to current feelings of existential insecurity, linked with cyclical economic fluctuations. But these adaptations fluctuate around stable set points.

The generational change hypothesis, which was published long before these data were collected, predicted both the robust cohort differences and the period effects that were subsequently observed. The intergenerational value change

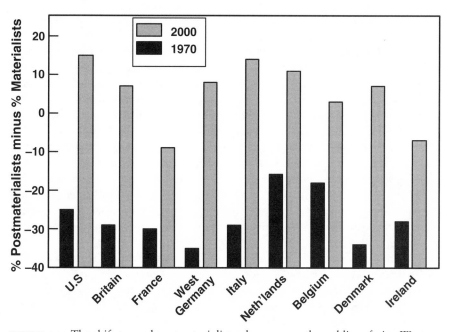

FIGURE 4.3. The shift toward postmaterialist values among the publics of nine Western societies, 1970–2000.

thesis also predicts that in the long run this should produce a shift from materialist toward postmaterialist values among the populations of these societies. More than three decades have passed since these values were first measured. Do we find the predicted value shift? As Figure 4.3 demonstrates, we do indeed.

Figure 4.3 shows the net shift observed in each of the six West European countries first surveyed in 1970, supplementing these results with data from the 1972 United States National Election Survey and from the Eurobarometer surveys that were first carried out in Denmark and Ireland in 1973, when these countries joined the European Community. The most recent data for each country come from the 1999–2001 wave of the Values Surveys. Thus, we have time-series data for these countries covering almost three decades.

We find a net shift from materialist to postmaterialist values in all nine countries. The vertical scale of this figure reflects the percentage of postmaterialists minus the percentage of materialists – which means that the zero point on this scale indicates that materialists and postmaterialists are equally numerous. In the early 1970s, materialists heavily outnumbered postmaterialists in all nine of these countries, all of which fell well below the zero point on the vertical axis. For example, in the earliest U.S. survey, materialists outnumbered postmaterialists by 24 percentage points; in West Germany, they outnumbered postmaterialists by 34 points. During the three decades following 1970, a major shift occurred: by the 1999–2001 surveys, postmaterialists had become more numerous than materialists in all nine countries. Despite substantial short-term fluctuations, the predicted shift toward postmaterialist values took place.

Figure 4.3 shows only the starting point and the end point of each country's time series. In a more detailed analysis, based on at least thirty-three surveys for each nation, Inglehart and Abramson (1999) examine the trends in each of the eight West European countries; then, using regression analysis, they demonstrate that Britain, France, West Germany, Italy, the Netherlands, Ireland, and Denmark all show large and statistically significant long-term trends from materialist to postmaterialist values from 1970 to 1994. In the eighth case (Belgium), the trend was not significant because a sharp rise of unemployment levels largely offset the effects of intergenerational population replacement. But an analysis that controls for the joint effects of inflation and unemployment demonstrates that there was a statistically significant trend toward postmaterialism in all of the West European countries for which this detailed time series is available.

The intergenerational value change thesis predicts a shift from materialist toward postmaterialist values among the populations of these societies. Empirical evidence gathered over a period of three decades fits this prediction: the large and persistent differences that we find between older and younger birth cohorts seem to reflect a process of intergenerational value change. A good deal of intergenerational population replacement has taken place since 1970, contributing to a substantial shift toward postmaterialist values. This long-term intergenerational trend would, of course, reverse itself if socioeconomic conditions changed so profoundly that new generations experienced existential insecurity throughout their formative years.

The intergenerational shift toward postmaterialist values has important implications concerning the political changes we can expect over the coming decades; as we will demonstrate, the shift toward postmaterialist values is part of a much broader cultural shift that brings increasingly strong demands for democracy (where it does not exist) and for more-responsive democracy (where it does exist).

An emerging emphasis on quality-of-life issues has been superimposed on the older, class-based cleavages of industrial society. From the mid-nineteenth century to the mid-twentieth century, politics was dominated by class conflict over the distribution of income and the ownership of industry. In recent decades, social class voting has declined and now shares the stage with newer postmaterialist issues that emphasize life-style issues and environmental protection.

The rise of postmaterialism does not mean that materialistic issues and concerns vanish. Conflicts about how to secure prosperity and sustainable economic development will always be important political issues. Moreover, the publics in postindustrial societies have developed more-sophisticated forms of consumerism, materialism, and hedonism. But these new forms of materialism have been shaped by the rise of postmaterialist values. New forms of consumption no longer function primarily to indicate people's economic class. Increasingly, they are a means of individual self-expression that people use to express their personal taste and life-style. This emphasis on self-expression is

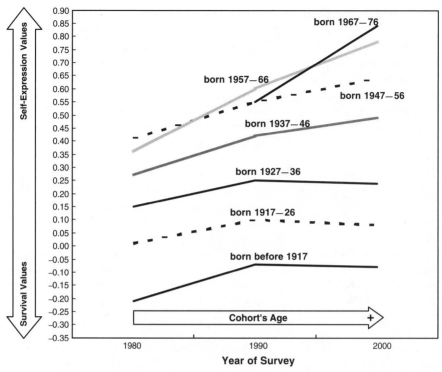

FIGURE 4.4. Emphasis on self-expression values in given birth cohorts in postindustrial societies.

an inherent feature of postmaterialism, which is the central component of self-expression values.

The evidence makes it clear that the intergenerational value differences found in postindustrial societies do *not* reflect life-cycle effects. As Figure 4.2 demonstrated, given birth cohorts did not become more materialistic as they aged. Figure 4.4 demonstrates that this pattern also holds true of the broader cultural shift encompassing postmaterialist values – the shift from survival to self-expression values.[2] From the start of this time series, younger birth cohorts placed more emphasis on self-expression values than older cohorts did, and given birth cohorts did not move away from self-expression values toward survival values as they aged from 1981 to 1999–2001 (for reasons of simplicity, these points in time are referred to as 1980 and 2000, respectively, in Figure 4.4). Throughout this period, younger birth cohorts continued to place more emphasis on self-expression values than older ones. And although each of the birth cohorts aged by twenty years during the period covered in Figure 4.4,

[2] The analyses in Figure 4.4 include all postindustrial societies that were surveyed in first, second, and fourth waves of the Values Surveys; they include Belgium, Canada, Denmark, Finland, France, Great Britain, Germany (West), Ireland, Italy, Japan, the Netherlands, Spain, Sweden, and the United States.

none of them placed less emphasis on self-expression in 1999–2001 than it did in 1981 – as would have happened if these age differences reflected life-cycle effects. Quite the contrary, we find that all birth cohorts actually came to place somewhat *more* emphasis on self-expression values as time went by. This was particularly true of the younger cohorts, who show a substantial shift toward self-expression values from 1981 to 1999–2001; the older cohorts remained relatively stable, but none of them shifted toward survival values.

We have just examined evidence of intergenerational value change in several countries from which the longest and most detailed time-series evidence is available. But all of these are rich, postindustrial democracies. What has been happening in the rest of the world? Let us examine evidence from the much larger number of societies covered in the Values Surveys.

The shift toward postmaterialist values does not reflect a global diffusion of values. Our theory attributes this shift to an intergenerational change linked with the emergence of higher levels of socioeconomic development, which implies that the shift toward postmaterialism will be most pronounced in rich postindustrial societies and may not occur in countries that have remained poor. In the 1970s survey, data from low-income societies was very scarce, and survey data from communist and other authoritarian societies was almost impossible to obtain. But the Values Surveys now provide data from a much wider range of societies.

Table A-6 in the Internet Appendix[3] shows the shifts from materialist to postmaterialist values that occurred in thirty-three additional societies not covered in Figure 4.4, from the earliest available survey to the latest available survey. In a number of cases, the earliest survey was carried out in 1981, but in many cases the earliest survey was in 1989–91 and the latest one in 1999–2001, covering a time span of only ten years (we do not include data covering less than ten years). Only fourteen of the societies in this table show positive shifts, eighteen show negative shifts (away from postmaterialist values), and the direction of these shifts reflects national income levels.

In Table A-6 asterisks appear next to the names of the "high-income" countries – those with per capita incomes more than $15,000 in 2000 (using World Bank purchasing power parity estimates). Fully ten of the fourteen high-income societies showed positive shifts during this time period. This does not include the nine additional high-income countries that were analyzed earlier; taking them into account, nineteen of the twenty-three high-income countries for which we have data moved toward increasing emphasis on postmaterialist values. But fourteen of the nineteen societies with real per capita incomes below $15,000 showed negative shifts. In other words, 83 percent of the high-income countries shifted toward postmaterialism, despite the economic difficulties of the 1990s; but 74 percent of the less prosperous countries shifted in the opposite

---

[3] The Internet Appendix can be found at http://www.worldvaluesurvey.org/publications/humandevelopment.html.

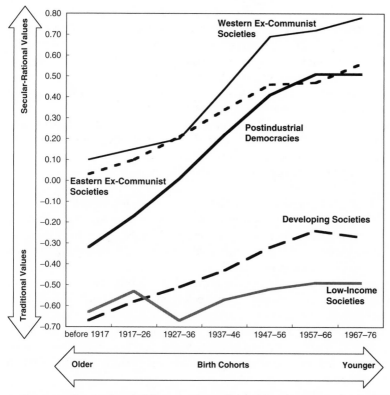

FIGURE 4.5. Generational differences in traditional/secular-rational values in five types of societies.

direction. This is typical of the pattern that emerges from analysis of cultural change in recent decades: people living in rich countries have been moving toward increasing emphasis on self-expression values and the behavior linked with them. But the world as a whole has *not* been moving in this direction – on the contrary, the publics of poor countries have retained their emphasis on survival values. Consequently, the differences between the worldviews of people living in rich and poor countries have been increasing rather than decreasing.

Intergenerational Value Differences around the World

Figure 4.5 shows the intergenerational differences in traditional/secular-rational values among seven birth cohorts, born during the seventy-year span from 1907 to 1976. Here, we are no longer examining changes over time, but simply comparing the values of different birth cohorts. Any graph that attempted to depict the age differences among scores of societies would be unreadable, so we have combined these societies into five groups, based on their economic histories during the twentieth century:[4]

Postindustrial democracies have per capita GDPs over $10,000 (based on World Bank purchasing power parity estimates in 1995). These countries experienced substantial economic growth during the twentieth century: according to data from the Penn World tables (see http://pwt.econ.upenn.edu), their real mean per capita GDP in 1992 was 6.3 times higher than it was in 1950.

Developing societies include all noncommunist countries with real per capita GDPs from $5,000 to $10,000 per year. Their long-term economic growth has been equal to that of the postindustrial democracies so that, on average, the prosperity gap between postindustrial democracies and developing societies remained constant.

Low-income societies include all noncommunist countries with a real per capita GDP below $5,000. This group experienced the least long-term growth, with real per capita GDP in 1992 being only 2.4 times higher than in 1950. These societies were poor from the start, and their relative poverty has actually increased in relation to the postindustrial world.

Western ex-communist societies, which include ex-communist societies with a Roman Catholic or Protestant heritage, belong to the World Bank's middle-income category (from $5,000 to $10,000 per capita). During the past fifty years, their economies grew significantly, so that in 1992 their income levels were 4.2 times as high as their levels in 1950. Moreover, these societies managed the transition into market economies much more successfully than the Eastern ex-communist countries.

Eastern ex-communist societies include those with an Eastern Orthodox or Islamic religious heritage, encompassing all of the Soviet successor states (except the three Baltic republics) plus Albania, Bulgaria, Romania, Serbia, and Bosnia. Starting from low-income levels in the 1950s, most of these countries attained impressive economic growth for several decades, so that in 1992 they had income levels seven times as high as in 1950. But these countries experienced growing economic difficulties after 1980, culminating in the economic collapse of the Soviet Union, which brought sharp declines in per capita income and even declining life expectancies in some cases.[5]

---

[4] See Internet Appendix (#67 under Variables) to check how the countries of the Values Surveys sample have been arranged into this fivefold classification.

[5] The best indicator of existential security during one's formative years would be a country's life expectancy levels from 1900–10 (during the childhood of our oldest respondents) to the present. Although we do not have such time-series data for most countries, we do know that life expectancies were relatively low a century ago and have risen dramatically in all societies that have experienced economic growth, improved diet and medical care, and related factors. Even in the United States (already the richest society on earth), life expectancy in 1900 was only forty-eight years; a century later, it had risen to seventy-eight years. All of the societies with high life expectancies today have experienced large increases in security since 1900. Because life expectancy is our best objective indicator of existential security, this suggests that the prevailing sense of existential security must also have risen in these countries. If this is true, we would expect to find

As Figure 4.5 indicates, the young are much less traditional than the old in postindustrial democracies and in ex-communist societies, especially the western ones.[6] But we find very little tendency for the young to be more secular than the old in the developing societies, and no such tendency at all in the low-income societies, which experienced little real economic growth since 1950. Change in socioeconomic conditions seems to play a significant role in differences across birth groups, but that is only part of the story. Note that the older birth cohorts in both the western and eastern ex-communist societies have more secular-rational values than those in any other type of society. In both types of ex-communist societies, the elders' formative years were characterized by rapid economic growth during an era when communism seemed to be surpassing capitalism. Moreover, they were subjected to powerful campaigns to eradicate religion and traditional values. Accordingly, we find steep value differences between the older and younger groups in ex-communist societies. But during the past two decades, these societies experienced economic stagnation and declining ideological fervor. The intergenerational differences flatten out and virtually disappear among the young. This was especially true in the eastern (mostly ex-Soviet and Orthodox) ex-communist societies; in the western (mostly Catholic) ex-communist countries the slope flattens, but the youngest birth cohorts in the western group are considerably more secular than their peers in the Eastern group. Conversely, the oldest groups among postindustrial societies show much more traditional values than their peers in ex-communist societies. But postindustrial societies show a steeper slope that continues longer, so that their youngest groups are as secular as their peers in the eastern ex-communist societies.[7]

strong correlations between a given society's life expectancy and the size of the intergenerational value differences in that society. We do. Intergenerational value differences are greatest in the societies with the highest life expectancies. Across sixty-one societies, the correlation between the 1995 life expectancy and the size of the intergenerational differences in traditional/secular-rational values is .56, significant at the .000 level. And the correlation between life expectancy and survival/self-expression values is .41, significant at the .001 level. Although conditions in eastern ex-communist societies have deteriorated sharply in recent years, throughout most of the twentieth century life expectancies rose markedly not only in postindustrial societies but also in most communist countries.

[6] Few low-income countries were included in the Values Surveys before the 1995–97 or 1999–2001 waves. Consequently, we limited the analyses in Figures 4.5 and 4.6 to the data on these two waves, in order to compare birth cohorts from different types of societies at the same time. See the Internet Appendix, Variables, #67 for how given countries were grouped in these five categories.

[7] Societies with traditional values also have much higher fertility rates than those with secular-rational values, which means that traditional values remain widespread despite the forces of modernization. Our traditional/secular-rational values index shows a strong negative correlation with the 1995 fertility rates of these societies (r = .75). Today, most industrial societies have fertility rates below the population replacement level. In Germany, Russia, Japan, Spain, and Italy, the average woman of child-bearing age now produces from 1.2 to 1.6 children (2.1 is the replacement rate). In contrast, low-income societies continue to have much higher fertility rates (due, in part, to the high rates of reproduction encouraged by traditional values). In Nigeria, for example, the average woman currently produces 5.5 children, and she has them earlier in

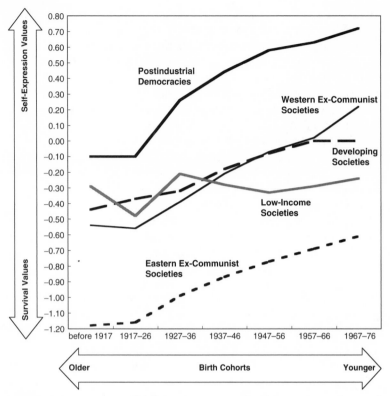

FIGURE 4.6. Generational differences in survival/self-expression values in five types of societies.

The pattern in Figure 4.5 is consistent with the expectation that we should find the largest intergenerational value differences in societies that have experienced rising life expectancies and long-term economic growth, and smaller intergenerational value differences in societies that are only beginning to do so.

Figure 4.6 shows the levels of survival/self-expression values among seven birth groups in the five types of societies. Again, we find the steepest intergenerational differences in postindustrial societies and in both eastern and western ex-communist societies, modest intergenerational differences in developing societies, and almost no difference between the values of older and younger

life, making the span between generations shorter. The fertility differences between industrial and developing societies are so large that we find two seemingly incompatible trends: most societies are industrializing, and industrialization tends to bring increasingly secular worldviews; but today more people than ever before hold traditional values. In 1970 73 percent of the world's population lived in developing countries, and 27 percent of the world's population lived in developed countries. By 1996 the developed countries contained only 20 percent of the world's population; by 2020 they will contain an estimated 16 percent of the world's population (U.S. Bureau of the Census, 1996). The peoples of most developed countries have increasingly modern values, but their societies contain a diminishing share of the world's population.

groups in the low-income societies. But Figure 4.6 contrasts with Figure 4.5 in one important respect. Eastern ex-communist societies rank much lower than other societies on the syndrome of trust, tolerance, subjective well-being, civic activism, and self-expression that constitutes this second major dimension of cross-cultural variation. This seems to reflect period effects linked with the traumatic crisis in these societies: during the past decade all eastern ex-communist societies have been in turmoil, with the peoples of the Soviet successor states experiencing the collapse of their economic, political, and social systems. Life has been insecure and unpredictable. Thus, although we find a relatively steep intergenerational slope, suggesting that the long-term trend during the past sixty years was one in which peoples' lives became increasingly secure, the peoples of eastern ex-communist societies now emphasize survival values even more strongly than the peoples of low-income societies. In other words, we find period effects superimposed on cohort effects.

The weakness of self-expression values in eastern ex-communist societies is reflected in the striking deficiency of democracy in these countries (Rose, 2001). As Chapter 8 demonstrates, self-expression values have a massive impact on the extent to which genuine democracy emerges in a society. And the relative weakness of self-expression values in the eastern ex-communist societies accurately predicts their deficiencies in democracy. The western ex-communist societies, by contrast, show stronger emphasis on self-expression values, and have attained much more effective democratic institutions than the Eastern ex-communist societies, as we will see. The postindustrial societies show by far the strongest emphasis on self-expression values, and they constitute most of the genuine democracies. Conversely, weak self-expression values lead to either nondemocracies (as in most of the low-income societies) or ineffective democracies (as in most of the eastern ex-communist societies).

Because we only have data from the 1990 and 1995 surveys for over half of these societies, we cannot perform the type of cohort analysis that would enable us to separate the effects of these long-term and short-term changes. The fact that the eastern ex-communist societies currently rank so low suggests that economic and political collapse has had a substantial impact. Evidence from the 1981 Values Survey (in which Tambov oblast, a representative region of Russia, was the only eastern communist society included) suggests that these societies had significantly higher levels of subjective well-being in 1981 than they have now. Overall levels of well-being eroded sharply with the collapse of communist systems, most of which now show levels of subjective well-being far below those of the low-income countries. Because subjective well-being is a core component of this value dimension, we suspect that the strong emphasis on survival values currently shown by the eastern ex-communist group in Figure 4.7 is linked with the collapse of the economic and social system in these societies.

There is little evidence of intergenerational change in low-income societies; the weakness of age-related differences suggests a continuing emphasis on survival values by the overwhelming majority of their people throughout the past several decades. In the eastern ex-communist societies, by contrast, we find

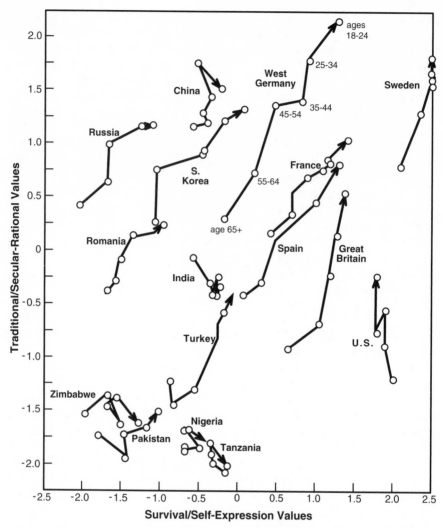

FIGURE 4.7. Generational differences on cultural map. Each arrow runs from oldest to youngest age group.

indications that successive birth groups experienced rising levels of economic security until the massive period effects linked with the collapse of communism pulled all of them sharply downward.

Figure 4.7 shows the generational differences in selected countries, plotting where the various age groups from the latest available survey fall on our two-dimensional map. West Germany[8] shows some of the largest age-related differences of any country in the world, and the values of its respective birth cohorts

---

[8] We continue to analyze data from the western region of the German Federal Republic separately from the data from the eastern region (the former German Democratic Republic), despite the

extend well across the cultural map, with the oldest cohort being located near the center of the map, and its youngest cohort at the northeast corner (we had to extend the northern and eastern boundaries used on earlier maps in order to depict the positions of the youngest West German and Swedish age groups). The six West German age groups reflect six decades of different formative experiences: the two oldest groups experienced the Great Depression (which was more severe in Germany than in any other country) and the devastation and massive loss of life of World War II. The four postwar cohorts have grown up in a Germany that has become one of the world's most prosperous societies with one of the most advanced welfare states and one of the most stable democracies.

We also find exceptionally large distances between the values of the youngest and oldest groups in Spain and South Korea. In both cases, the oldest cohorts grew up in different countries from the ones in which they now live. Their childhood was spent in unstable autocracies that had low standards of living and low life expectancies; they now live in prosperous and increasingly stable democracies.

France, Britain, Sweden, and the United States also show lesser but significant intergenerational differences. And the three ex-communist societies examined here – Russia, China,[9] and Romania – also show substantial intergenerational differences, although not as large as those in Germany, Spain, and South Korea. In almost every case where intergenerational change is taking place, it seems to be moving toward increasing emphasis on both secular and self-expression values.

But intergenerational differences are not a universal pattern. India, Nigeria, and Tanzania show no clear trends: the differences between one cohort and another are small enough to be attributed to sampling error, and they bounce from one direction to another, showing very little net movement. Pakistan and Zimbabwe show some net movement toward increasing emphasis on self-expression values, but it is modest.

Conclusion

Intergenerational value changes reflect historic changes in a society's existential conditions. Far from being universal, these changes are found only in societies in which the younger generations have experienced substantially different formative conditions from those that shaped older generations.

fact that Germany was reunified in 1990. We do so because the formative experiences of the two publics differed substantially, and these differences continue to be reflected in their values and beliefs.

9 Although China continues to be ruled by a communist party, its economy and culture have been moving away from the communist model since 1978 – to the point where well over half of its output is now produced in the market sector. In this sense, China constitutes another ex-communist country.

Cohort analysis and intergenerational comparisons indicate that we are witnessing a gradual process of intergenerational value change linked with socioeconomic development, reflecting the fact that increasingly favorable existential conditions tend to make people less dependent on religion and lead them to place increasing emphasis on self-expression. These findings reinforce the evidence from Chapter 2, which demonstrated that the publics of rich societies are much more likely to emphasize secular-rational values and self-expression values than are the publics of low-income societies. In addition, the findings converge with the time-series evidence concerning changes in postmaterialist values presented in this chapter, and the time-series evidence concerning many other variables presented in the following chapter. A huge body of evidence, using three different approaches – comparisons of rich and poor countries, generational comparisons, and time-series evidence from the past two decades – all points to the conclusion that major cultural changes are occurring, and they reflect a process of intergenerational change, linked with rising levels of existential security.

5

Value Changes over Time

In Chapter 4, we found large intergenerational differences linked with the survival/self-expression values dimension – but we did not find them everywhere. In postindustrial democracies and the western group of ex-communist societies, the young are much likelier to emphasize self-expression values than the old; smaller age differences are found in developing societies and in the eastern ex-communist group; and little or no intergenerational differences are found in low-income societies. If these intergenerational differences portend long-term shifts toward increasing emphasis on self-expression values in postindustrial societies, they have important implications. For (as the second half of this book demonstrates) increasing emphasis on self-expression values is linked with growing mass demands for democracy where it does not exist, and growing pressures to deepen democracy where it does exist.

Materialist/postmaterialist values are a key component of the survival/self-expression dimension, and, as we have just seen, the large age-related differences that were found with these values in 1970 actually *did* predict long-term changes in the prevailing values of postindustrial societies. Does this pattern hold more generally, with the age differences that are linked with survival/self-expression values predicting long-term social changes? As we will see, they do. Let us examine the changes over time found with other components of the survival/self-expression dimension, starting with its participatory component.

The Rise of Elite-Challenging Civic Action

More than twenty-five years ago, Inglehart (1977: 5, 317–21) predicted declining rates of elite-directed political mobilization and rising rates of elite-challenging mass activity among Western publics. One reason for this prediction was the intergenerational shift from materialist to postmaterialist values that we have just examined: materialists tend to be preoccupied with satisfying immediate survival needs, whereas postmaterialists feel relatively secure about survival needs and have more psychic energy to invest in other concerns. Noting that throughout advanced industrial societies, the younger birth cohorts also have higher levels of political skills than older cohorts, he concluded that the processes of value change and cognitive mobilization tend to go together: these publics are placing increasing value on self-expression, and their rising skill levels enable them to participate in politics at a higher level, shaping decisions that affect their lives rather than simply entrusting them to elites. Subsequently, analyzing data on elite-challenging political action, Inglehart (1990: 361–62) found that

postmaterialists are more likely to engage in unconventional political protest than are materialists. Moreover, one's values interact with cognitive mobilization in such a way that at high levels of cognitive mobilization, the differences between value types are magnified considerably. . . . Among those with materialist values and low levels of cognitive mobilization, only 12 per cent have taken part, or are willing to take part in a boycott or more difficult activity. Among postmaterialists with high levels of cognitive mobilization, 74 per cent have done so or are ready to do. The process of cognitive mobilization seems to be increasing the potential for elite-challenging political action among Western publics.

This prediction seemed surprising because for many years voter turnout has been declining throughout postindustrial societies, and there has been widespread speculation that declining social capital is producing politically inert publics (Putnam, 2000). We disagree with this diagnosis (for a critique, see Boggs, 2001). Instead, we find two divergent trends. On one hand, bureaucratized and elite-directed forms of participation such as voting and political party membership *have* declined; but intrinsically motivated, expressive, and elite-challenging forms of participation have *risen* dramatically. This process reflects the changing nature of social capital: social capital has not eroded but has taken a new form, leading to changing types of collective action. In industrial society, large masses of people were controlled by hierarchical political parties and machines, which marched them to the polls in disciplined fashion, leaving the elites to make the specific decisions from then on. Increasingly, people are directly expressing their preferences on specific issues such as abortion, women's and gay's rights, elite corruption, and environmental issues. Although these issues are specific, they have broad symbolic relevance, representing the life-style concerns of increasingly humanistic societies.

Barnes, Kaase, et al. (1979) predicted the spread of what was then called "unconventional political participation." They developed scales to measure both "conventional" political action, such as voting and writing one's representative in parliament; and "unconventional" political action, such as demonstrations, boycotts, and occupation of buildings. Finding that the "unconventional" forms of political action were strongly correlated with postmaterialist values and were much more prevalent among younger birth cohorts than among the old, they predicted that "unconventional" political action would become more widespread: "We interpret this increase in potential for protest to be a lasting characteristic of democratic mass publics and not just a sudden surge in political involvement bound to fade away as time goes by" (Barnes, Kaase, et al., 1979: 524).

A quarter of a century later, it is clear that they were right, contrary to widespread assumptions about the decline of civic and political activism in postindustrial societies, which are depicted as a "crisis of democracy" (Pharr and Putnam, 2000). Crisis-of-democracy theories have long predicted the weakening of representative democracies, and ultimately of the role of citizens, in Western nations. Most recently, Putnam and Goss (2002: 4) have argued that

ironically – just at the moment of liberal democracy's greatest triumph there is also unhappiness about the performance of major social institutions, including the institutions of representative government, among the established democracies of Western Europe, North America, and East Asia. At least in the United States, there is reason to suspect that some fundamental social and cultural preconditions for effective democracy may have been eroded in recent decades, the result of a gradual but widespread process of civic disengagement.

Despite these predictions, time-series data from the Political Action surveys (Barnes, Kaase, et al., 1979) together with data from the four waves of the Values Surveys, demonstrate that a substantial *increase* in elite-challenging mass activity has taken place, so much so that petitions, demonstrations, boycotts, and other forms of elite-challenging activities are no longer unconventional but have become more or less normal actions for a large share of the citizenry of postindustrial nations. We do not find a widespread pattern of civic disengagement, either in the United States or elsewhere.[1] What we find is more complex.

Our findings contradict claims that the publics of postindustrial societies are disengaging themselves from civic life in general. These claims are only partly right. We emphatically agree that Putnam (2000) was correct in claiming that people are deserting such organizations as the Elks, the Moose, and bowling leagues. Virtually all of the old-style hierarchical elite-directed organizations such as labor unions and churches are losing members. Membership in political parties is falling sharply (Dalton and Wattenberg, 2000). Big-city political machines have lost control of once-reliable blocs of loyal voters, so voter turnout is stagnant or declining (Wattenberg, 1996). Similarly, there is declining confidence in government, in state-based institutions, and in large-scale organizations among the publics of most rich democracies (see Nye, Zelikow, and King, 1997; Norris, 1999; Dalton, 2000). The publics of postindustrial societies are becoming more critical of institutionalized authority in general, and political authority in particular, and less likely to become members of bureaucratized

---

[1] Interestingly, most social capital theorists do not view elite-challenging collective action as reflecting social capital. This is inconsistent with the definition of social capital, which covers all forms of collective action networks (Coleman, 1990). Moreover, disregarding elite-challenging collective action means ignoring the importance of this form of civic activity for democracy. Both the invention of early limited versions of democracy through the liberal revolutions in the seventeenth and eighteenth centuries and the spread of modern democracies through the Third Wave were driven by elite-challenging collective action (see Markoff, 1996).

organizations. Because such organizations keep membership lists, a written record is available to show a predominantly downward trend. But this is only one side of the coin.

These same publics are becoming more likely to engage in types of action that do not leave written membership lists, because they are elite-challenging activities that emerge from loosely knit but wide-ranging civic networks. The public is not withdrawing from civic action in this broader sense. Quite the contrary, the shift toward rising levels of elite-challenging activities that was predicted more than twenty-five years ago has taken place in virtually all postindustrial societies. This trend does not indicate an erosion of social capital in general but a change in the nature of social capital, shifting from externally imposed ties based on social control mechanisms to autonomously chosen ties, which people create themselves. Church membership and trade-union membership are, to a large extent, determined by one's religious heritage or social class; being engaged in an environmentalist group or a civil rights initiative usually reflects an autonomous choice. Socializing in postindustrial societies is shifting from "communities of necessity" to "elective affinities" (U. Beck, 2002).

Elite-directed forms of mass action, such as voting and church attendance, have stagnated or declined, but elite-challenging forms of civic action have become increasingly widespread. The loosely knit networks coordinating these actions do not keep permanent membership lists. Their participation rates go unrecorded unless someone carries out surveys that actively measure them. Fortunately, the Political Action surveys, together with the Values Surveys, have done just this, and the unequivocal results flatly contradict the image of an increasingly disengaged public. It turns out that the publics of the United States and other postindustrial societies are becoming less likely to be loyal followers of oligarchically controlled organizations, but much more likely to engage in activities that express opposition to elite decisions.

A major change is taking place, characterized not by a trend toward civic inertness but by an intergenerational shift from elite-directed participation toward elite-challenging participation. As younger, better-educated, and more-postmaterialist cohorts replace older ones in the adult population, intergenerational population replacement is bringing a shift toward increasingly self-assertive and expressive publics.

Civic change is not driven by cultural change alone. It interacts with economic, social, and political developments in the given society. As we have just demonstrated, the shift toward postmaterialist values reflects both a long-term intergenerational shift and short-term period effects. Recessions brought a shift toward materialism among all cohorts, but with the return of prosperity, the respective cohorts snapped back to become as postmaterialist as ever.

We expect these underlying cultural changes to increase the potential for mass participation in elite-challenging actions. But people do not protest in a vacuum: they respond to current problems, such as war or peace, prosperity or economic collapse, the ideologies of specific political parties, and the personalities of given leaders.

Consequently, we would expect these long-term trends, based on intergenerational population replacement, and short-term period effects to continue. Intergenerational population replacement is a long-term force that works in a consistent and foreseeable direction over many decades, but its impact at any given time is increased or reduced by current economic and political events. Let us test these expectations using the data from the Values Surveys from 1981 to 1999–2001. Because this period includes the collapse of communism and the Third Wave of democratization that peaked in 1987–1995, we are dealing with an era in which we can expect some dramatic period effects. Transitions to democracy took place in dozens of countries. These transitions to democracy were driven to a considerable extent by elite-challenging mass action (Bernhard, 1993; Foweraker and Landman, 1997). "People power" helped bring democratic regimes to power in numerous countries from East Asia to Latin America and was particularly apparent in the collapse of the communist regimes – especially in the western group of ex-communist societies (L. Diamond, 1993a; Paxton, 2002). But in the aftermath of these transitions, one finds "post-honeymoon" effects (Inglehart and Catterberg, 2003). Transitions to democracy are exceptional times of mass mobilization – in the Baltic republics, for example, almost the entire population was on the streets in 1990. As the need for participation recedes after a successful transition and as the euphoria of democratization wears off, we would expect to find declining levels of mass participation, particularly in countries where democratization brought severe disillusionment.

The dynamics of democratic transitions mobilize mass support for democracy. Quite often, however, mass support for democracy is not intrinsically motivated but reflects instrumental motives, such as the belief that democracy will bring prosperity like that of the established democracies. Support for democracy is intrinsically motivated if people value democracy's civil and political liberties as ends in themselves. Self-expression values provide such an intrinsic motivation because they place high value on the civil and political liberties that are essential to free self-expression. But in many societies, overt support for democracy is strong even though self-expression values are not widespread. In these cases, people support democracy primarily for instrumental motives rather than for the liberties inherent in democracy (see Hofferbert and Klingemann, 1999). This sort of instrumental support is vulnerable if the transition to democracy brings disappointing results (see Chapter 11 for a detailed validation of this point). Disillusionment with its immediate results may lead to declining support for democracy, if support for democracy is not intrinsically rooted in self-expression values.

During the Third Wave of democratization, a widespread public belief – often reinforced by elite discourse – that democracy not only provides liberty but also improves economic well-being was a crucial factor in raising overt mass support for democracy to unprecedentedly high levels, even in societies with low levels of self-expression values. If the economy subsequently performed poorly, disillusionment with democracy occurred. Moreover, the experience of living under an authoritarian regime engendered unrealistic expectations about democracy and democratic politics: "Expectations among activists were perhaps unrealistic, incorporating a too idealistic belief in real influence from below.... [Yet] politics as it is being carried out does not, in the eyes of many, work for people" (Rueschemeyer, Rueschemeyer, and Wittrock, 1998: 101–2).

If support for democracy is primarily based on unrealistically high policy expectations rather than an intrinsically high evaluation of free choice, it may bring rising frustration among those who became active in democratic transitions. An increasing discrepancy between expectations and reality has led to disillusionment in many of the new democracies, especially where the new regimes performed poorly. On the other hand, relatively strong self-expression values provide intrinsic support for democracy, which tends to endure even if the new regime's policy outcomes are disappointing.[2] Thus, disillusionment with democracy was widespread in the eastern ex-communist societies and many Latin American societies, but not in the western group of ex-communist societies. In the former group, as we will see, disappointing policy outcomes dramatically lowered expectations about the efficacy of democratic participation and led to withdrawal from the abnormally high levels of elite-challenging participation that helped bring the transition to democracy.

Political protest is not simply a function of how much people have to complain about *objectively*. If it were, protest activities would be highest in the poorest societies and lowest in rich countries, but the exact opposite is true. In low-income societies, disappointment often leads to resignation and disengagement. But if disappointment is coupled with a widespread emphasis on self-expression values, it is likely to give rise to effective elite-challenging mass action. Ironically, what some communitarians recommend as the cure for civic disengagement, a shift *away* from self-expression values, actually would cause civic disengagement.

The Russian public, for example, manifests great concern about the level of corruption among their country's elites. But relatively weak self-expression values in Russia (and other post-Soviet societies) do not motivate people to express their dissatisfaction in sustained elite-challenging mass activities. By contrast, in Belgium – a country far less corrupt than Russia – political scandals in the late 1990s caused a huge mass mobilization in the White March

---

[2] In Chile and Spain, support for democracy did not decline despite the fact that the newly established democratic regimes showed a weaker economic performance than the previous authoritarian regimes, which had been extraordinarily successful in producing economic growth over prolonged periods. In these countries, self-expression values were widespread among the public; when this is the case, economic failures do not delegitimate democratic regimes. By contrast, authoritarian regimes always lose legitimacy if they are unable to sustain economic growth. In this case, disillusionment with authoritarian government can produce *instrumentally motivated* mass support for democracy (seeking better economic outcomes). Ironically, authoritarian regimes eventually lose legitimacy even more profoundly if they sustain economic growth for a long time, for economic development nurtures orientations that provide *intrinsic* support for democracy: self-expression values.

Movement (Walgrave and Manssens, 2000). This contrast in mass reactions to policy failure and deficient elite behavior is no accident: the Belgian public places much stronger emphasis on self-expression values than the Russian public. Mass reactions to elite failure are not simply a function of the objective magnitude of these failures but of the *criticality* of the public, which increases with rising self-expression values. This is why elite-challenging mass action is a central component of the self-expression values syndrome.

Thus, we would expect to find a long-term trend toward rising rates of elite-challenging mass activity in established democracies, especially those with high levels of self-expression values. By contrast, in new democracies that emerged during the Third Wave, we would expect a post-transition downturn of elite-challenging mass activity, partly because democratic transitions are times of exceptional mass mobilization, which are usually followed by a subsidence to normal levels. This short-term reaction, however, is unlikely to become a long-term decline in participation unless self-expression values are so weak that people react to elite failure with resignation.

In contrast with these predictions, if the crisis-of-democracy school is correct in its claims of a pervasive civic disengagement extending to all types of participation, then we should find declining rates of elite-challenging mass activity in all established democracies, particularly where self-expression values are relatively strong. For advocates of the crisis-of-democracy thesis attribute the cause of the alleged civic disengagement to the individualization trend, which is linked with rising emphasis on self-expression values (see Lawler and McConkey, 1998; Putnam, 2000; Flanagan et al., forthcoming).

To test these predictions, we fortunately have a relatively long time series of survey data available for analysis, utilizing the data from the 1974 Political Action surveys and the four waves of the Values Surveys. Let us start by examining changes in response to five measures of elite-challenging action that were developed in the Political Action survey and replicated in the Values Surveys.

Tables 5.1a–c show the percentage of the public saying that they have actually engaged in various forms of elite-challenging mass activity in each of the eight

TABLE 5.1a. *Percentage Who Have Signed a Petition, 1974–2000*

Country	Signing Petitions					Net Shift
	1974	1981	1990	1995	2000	
Britain	23	63	75		81	+58
West Germany	31	47	57	66	47	+16
Italy	17	42	48		55	+38
Netherlands	22	35	51		61	+39
United States	60	64	72	71	81	+21
Finland	20	30	41	39	51	+31
Switzerland	46		63	68		+22
Austria	39		48		56	+17
Mean	32	42	57	58	63	+30

TABLE 5.1b. *Percentage Who Have Taken Part in a Demonstration, 1974–2000*

Country	Attending Demonstrations					Net Shift
	1974	1981	1990	1995	2000	
Britain	6	10	14		13	+7
West Germany	9	15	21	26	22	+13
Italy	19	27	36		35	+16
Netherlands	7	13	25		32	+25
United States	12	13	16	16	21	+9
Finland	6	14	14	13	15	+9
Switzerland	8		16	17		+9
Austria	7		10	16		+9
Mean	9	13	19	20	21	+12

TABLE 5.1c. *Percentage Who Have Taken Part in a Consumer Boycott*

Country	Taking Part in Consumer Boycotts					Net Shift
	1974	1981	1990	1995	2000	
Britain	6	7	14		17	+11
West Germany	5	8	10	18	10	+5
Italy	2	6	11		10	+8
Netherlands	6	7	9		22	+16
United States	16	15	18	19	25	+9
Finland	1	9	14	12	15	+14
Switzerland	5			11		+6
Austria	3		5		10	+7
Mean	6	8	11	12	15	+9

Western democracies surveyed in the 1974 Political Action study and also how this behavior changed during the next quarter of a century. Table 5.1a shows the percentage that reports signing a petition.[3] Outside the United States this was still a relatively unusual activity in 1974: across the eight countries, an average of only 32 percent reported signing a petition (with the figures ranging from a low of 17 percent in Italy to a high of 60 percent in the United States). During the next twenty-five years, the percentage claiming to have signed a petition increased in every one of the eight societies and the increase was dramatic. Overall, the percentage almost doubled, from 32 percent in 1974 to 63 percent in 2000. By 2000 this had become a normal activity, something that a majority of the public in almost every country reports doing.

[3] Putnam (2000) finds an opposite trend in the United States, but the data he uses from the Roper Archive seem to be anomalous. The Values Surveys show a clear increase in signing petitions, not only in the United States but in all Western democracies for which data are available.

A similar pattern applies to the other forms of political action for which Tables 5.1b and 5.1c provide evidence. In every one of the eight countries for which we have long-term data, the percentage that reports participating in a demonstration rose from 1974 to 2000. As Table 5.1b demonstrates, the overall percentage claiming to take part in a demonstration more than doubled, rising from 9 percent in 1974 to 21 percent in 2000. The percentage reporting participation in a consumer boycott also increased in every one of these eight countries (Table 5.1c). Overall, boycotting also more than doubled, rising from 6 percent in 1974 to 15 percent in 2000. We have data on three types of elite-challenging activities across eight societies, producing a total of twenty-four tests. Among them, we find the predicted increase in all twenty-four cases. The net trend is toward rising rates of elite-challenging mass action – without exception.

The increase in elite-challenging activity is overwhelmingly a trend toward *civic* action: violent mass actions are much less widely endorsed and do not show a consistent increase. Tables A-7a and A-7b in the Internet Appendix[4] illustrate this point, showing the percentages saying, respectively, that they have taken part in an unofficial strike and those saying they have occupied buildings. These were still unconventional activities even in 2000, and the numbers engaging in them were very small.

The growth of elite-challenging activities is not universal. Our theory holds that rising rates of elite-challenging action are a component of a cultural shift from survival values toward self-expression values. This shift is not universal but is linked with high levels of socioeconomic development, so it is much more likely to be found in rich countries than in poor ones. All eight of the societies for which we have data from 1974 are high-income countries (as was typical of survey research in that era). The Values Surveys, which provide data from a much wider range of countries (though for a shorter time span), help complete the picture. Table A-8 in the Internet Appendix shows the changes in the percentages of respondents saying they have signed a petition, across all fifty of the societies for which we have data from more than one time point. This form of political action rose in thirty of these societies and declined in nineteen of them.

The pattern is far from random. As Figure 5.1 indicates, a given society's level of self-expression values explains a large proportion of its changes in elite-challenging activity: the higher the level of self-expression values, the larger the subsequent increase in elite-challenging mass action – in both old and new democracies.[5] As is nearly always the case, period effects are also present. Belgium's exceptionally steep increase, for example, reflects the White March

---

[4] The Internet Appendix can be found at http://www.worldvaluessurvey.org/publications/ humandevelopment.html.
[5] The percentage of people reporting that they have signed a petition is one of five components of our measure of self-expression values, so it might seem that testing the impact of self-expression values on changing elite-challenging activities is partly tautological. However, this is not the case because the dependent variable in this analysis reflects *changes* (not levels) in elite-challenging

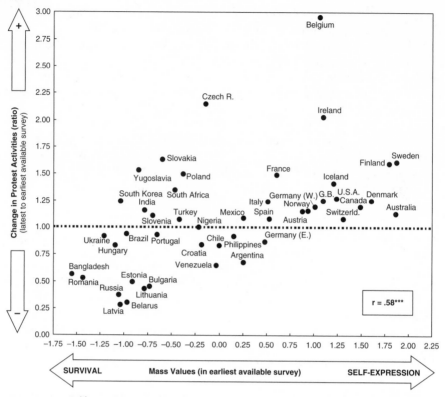

FIGURE 5.1. Self-expression values and changes in levels of elite-challenging activities, from earliest to latest available survey.

movement, a strong mass reaction to the scandals of the late 1990s. Overall, however, the pattern is clear. Post-transition decreases in elite-challenging activity were much larger in societies with weak self-expression values; they were weak or completely absent in societies with relatively strong self-expression values. In this regard, the contrast between the western and the eastern group of ex-communist societies is once more striking. Romania, Bulgaria, and Russia have weaker self-expression values than the Czech Republic, Poland, and Slovenia; and while the former experienced declining elite-challenging activities, the latter experienced *increases* in elite-challenging activities after the transition.

As Figure 5.2 illustrates, in postindustrial democracies the percentage claiming to have signed a petition rose substantially – from an overall mean of 43 percent in 1981 to an overall mean of 62 percent in 1999–2001. These are the societies with by far the strongest self-expression values. Western ex-communist societies and developing societies have weaker but still relatively strong self-expression values, which would be conducive to self-expression-driven

activities that occurred *after* the independent variable, levels of self-expression values, has been measured. Moreover, it reflects changes in all three sorts of elite-challenging activities (petitions, demonstrations, and boycotts), not in petitions alone.

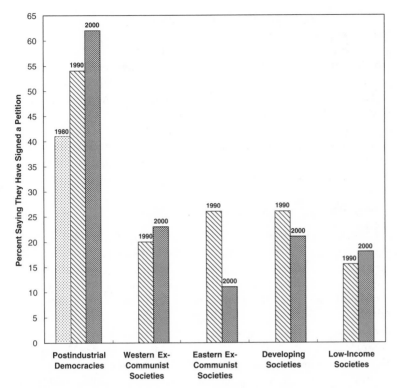

FIGURE 5.2. Changes in percentage of respondents who have signed a petition, in five types of societies.

activities, such as signing petitions. But these societies recently experienced democratic transitions, which would be expected to be followed by a post-transitional decrease in these activities. The two trends seem to cancel each other out, so that no clear overall trend is observable in western ex-communist and developing societies.

Apart from the postindustrial democracies, only the eastern group among the ex-communist societies shows a pronounced trend in signing petitions – in this case, a sharp decline from 26 percent in 1990 to 11 percent in 2000. This decline reflects the combination of a post-transition decrease of elite-challenging activities and the absence of strong self-expression values.

The trends found with signing petitions apply to elite-challenging mass activity more broadly. Comparing the changes from the two earlier surveys to the two latest ones, in the percentage that had engaged in at least one of the five elite-challenging actions, we find increases in all seventeen of the rich democracies[6] for which data are available.

---

[6] The established rich democracies in this analysis include Australia, Belgium, Britain, Canada, Denmark, Finland, France, Germany (West), Italy, Japan, the Netherlands, Norway, Portugal, Spain, Sweden, Switzerland, and the United States.

The new democracies, by contrast, show a mixed pattern. Comparing the changes that took place from the period before or during the transition to democracy to a period after the transition, we have "before" and "after" data for a total of fifteen new democracies.[7] In nine of these fifteen countries, we find declines in elite-challenging political action, but the size of the downturn varies.[8] It is largest in the eastern ex-communist group, which has the weakest self-expression values. By contrast, three societies of the western ex-communist group (Hungary, Poland, and Slovenia) show increasing elite-challenging activities and three others (Czech Republic, Slovakia, and East Germany) show only modest declines. Relatively strong self-expression values prevented these publics from having a pronounced post-transition decline in elite-challenging activities.

Other Aspects of the Shift toward Self-Expression Values

Both the shift toward postmaterialism and the rise of elite-challenging political action are components of a broader shift toward self-expression values that is reshaping orientations toward authority, politics, gender roles, and sexual norms among the publics of postindustrial societies. Postmaterialists and the young are markedly more tolerant of homosexuality than are materialists and the old, and this is part of a pervasive pattern – the rise of humanistic norms that emphasize human emancipation and self-expression. Norms supporting the two-parent heterosexual family are weakening for various reasons, ranging from the rise of the welfare state to the drastic decline of infant mortality rates. When new forms of behavior emerge that deviate from traditional norms, the groups most likely to accept these new forms of behavior are the young and the relatively secure. Postmaterialists have been shaped by high levels of existential security during their formative years and are far more favorable than materialists toward abortion, divorce, extramarital affairs, prostitution, and homosexuality.[9] Materialists, conversely, tend to adhere to traditional societal norms that favor child-rearing – but only within the traditional survival paradigm of the two-parent heterosexual family, which is reinforced by norms that stigmatized all sexual activity outside that framework.

Inglehart (1990: 195), analyzing data from the 1981 Values Surveys, found major age differences in attitudes toward gays, which led him to predict changes in these norms:

In almost every society, the young are markedly more tolerant of homosexuality than the old. In the sixteen nations as a whole, the oldest group is almost twice as likely to say that homosexuality can never be justified, as is the youngest group. . . . By itself, this

---

[7] These countries include Argentina, Chile, Mexico, Belarus, Estonia, Russia, Bulgaria, Czech Republic, Germany (East), Hungary, Latvia, Lithuania, Poland, Slovenia, and Slovakia.

[8] The Baltic societies are so small that it was possible to mobilize almost the entire adult population in 1990. Given this exceptionally high level of mass mobilization, subsequent decline was almost inevitable.

[9] The fact that postmaterialists are relatively favorable toward these topics does not mean that postmaterialists are moral nihilists. Postmaterialists are relatively *intolerant* of measures that violate civil rights, personal integrity, and human dignity.

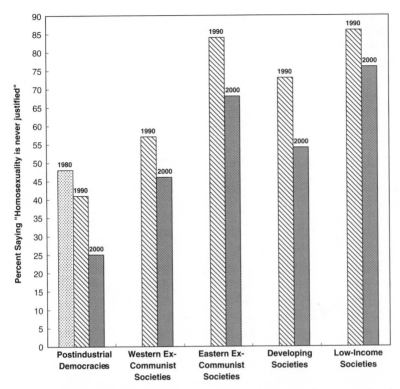

FIGURE 5.3. The decline in intolerance of homosexuality in five types of societies.

does not prove that an intergenerational shift is taking place. The age-related differences are striking but they might reflect life cycle effects rather than historical change based on cohort effects. . . . however, a life cycle interpretation seems highly implausible: it not only implies that the young will be just as intolerant of homosexuality as their elders when they get older; it also implies that in most of these countries, the majority of those who are now over 65 years of age were tolerant of homosexuality 40 or 50 years ago. This seems extremely unlikely.

Evidence from subsequent Values Surveys makes it clear that mass attitudes toward homosexuality have been changing. Table A-9 in the Internet Appendix shows the percentages saying that homosexuality is never justifiable in all fifty-one societies for which we have data from two or more time points. In the world as a whole, attitudes toward homosexuality tend to be highly intolerant: in most of these surveys, a majority of the population chooses point "1" on a 10-point scale where "1" means it is *never* justifiable and "10" means it is *always* justifiable. It is very unusual to find such highly skewed responses in survey research: they reflect the fact that, at this point in history, homosexuals are a very unpopular outgroup in most countries. But attitudes toward homosexuality have been changing rapidly in the past two decades. The percentage saying that homosexuality is "never justifiable" declined in forty-two of these fifty-one societies. The changes were most dramatic in rich countries: Figure 5.3

ranks these countries according to the relative size of the shift toward more-tolerant attitudes. Fully seventeen of the eighteen countries showing the highest shift ratios are "high-income" societies, as defined by the World Bank (the sole exception was Chile). Conversely, the three societies (Serbia, Montenegro, Croatia) showing the largest decreases in tolerance were exposed to exceptional existential threats in the wars linked with the dissolution of Yugoslavia. This reflects a pervasive tendency for existential insecurity to produce intolerance and xenophobia.

The intergenerational differences that Inglehart found in the 1981 data are clearly evident in the much broader sample examined here. As Figure 5.3 demonstrates, postindustrial democracies show much lower levels of intolerance than other types of societies. Only the western ex-communist group reached a level of tolerance in 2000 comparable to that which the postindustrial democracies already had in 1981. The rich democracies also show larger intergenerational differences than other types of societies. Among the oldest age group in the rich democracies, 70 percent reports that homosexuality is never justifiable; among the youngest group, however, less than a third as many (20 percent) takes this position. Smaller but considerable generational differences exist in developing societies (oldest cohort: 74 percent, youngest cohort: 49 percent) and in the western group of ex-communist societies (oldest cohort: 75 percent, youngest cohort: 31 percent). By contrast, the eastern group of ex-communist societies shows much smaller intergenerational differences (oldest cohort: 90 percent, youngest cohort: 80 percent), and intergenerational differences are virtually absent in low-income societies (oldest cohort: 83 percent, youngest cohort: 81 percent). Again, it is evident that a society's economic history affects changes in basic values.

Figure 5.3 shows the changes over time in each of the five types of society. The changes in the rich democracies from 1981 to 1999–2001 are truly remarkable. In 1981 almost 50 percent of the publics in the seventeen rich democracies said that homosexuality is never justifiable. Twenty years later, this figure was virtually cut in half: only 26 percent said homosexuality was never justifiable. Less dramatic but substantial changes took place in the western group of ex-communist societies and in developing countries, but the change is small in the eastern group of ex-communist societies and in low-income societies.

Figure 5.3 tends to overstate the amount of change that took place in developing and low-income countries because it is based on data from Argentina, Chile, India, Mexico, Nigeria, and South Africa – the only developing and low-income countries for which we have data on this topic from both 1989–91 and 1999–2001. We do not have time-series data on attitudes toward homosexuality from any Islamic society because our Islamic colleagues were extremely reluctant to even ask about this topic. With considerable effort, we were able to obtain readings at a single time point for ten Islamic societies and found the following percentages saying that homosexuality is never justifiable: Bangladesh, 99; Egypt, 99; Jordan, 98; Pakistan, 96; Indonesia, 95; Iran, 94; Algeria, 93; Azerbaijan, 89; Turkey, 84; and Albania, 68. Even without time-series data, it is clear that there cannot have been much movement toward growing tolerance of homosexuality in most of these countries. If the latest available survey shows that 95 percent of the public considers homosexuality to be "never" justifiable, it is obvious that no large liberalizing shift has occurred. This picture is reinforced by our data from Nigeria, where about half of the public is Islamic; where the percentage saying that homosexuality is never justifiable *rose* from 72 percent in 1990 to 78 percent in 2000. We find that dramatic shifts toward increasing tolerance of gays and lesbians have taken place in postindustrial democracies. These changes have had less impact in the ex-communist and developing countries, and almost none in the Islamic world, the region with the lowest civil rights scores (Freedom House, 2002).

Attitudes toward Gender Equality

Table A-10 in the Internet Appendix shows the percentage disagreeing with the statement "When jobs are scarce, men should have more right to a job than women." This is an excellent indicator of attitudes toward gender equality and has high loadings on the survival/self-expression values dimension, which implies that rich countries should show relatively high levels of support. This question was not asked in the first wave of the Values Surveys, so it was not used to construct the survival/self-expression values index here (which only uses items asked in all four waves of the Values Surveys). Moreover, as with tolerance toward homosexuality, younger respondents show more support for gender equality than older ones; and the generational differences in postindustrial democracies are larger than those in developing countries. This suggests that we will find a larger shift over time toward gender equality in the postindustrial democracies than in other types of societies.

Among the fifty societies for which we have data from two or more time points, 37 (or 74 percent) show rising levels of support for gender equality. Among the "high-income" countries, seventeen of twenty societies show increasing support for gender equality, and two of the countries that show decreases (South Korea and East Germany) move downward by only one percentage point. Only one of the nine countries that move downward by more than one percentage point is a high-income country (Japan). All eight of the others are developing countries.

Table A-11 in the Internet Appendix shows the percentage of the publics of sixty-two countries who disagree with the statement that "men make better political leaders than women." This question was asked only in the 1995–97 and the 1999–2001 Values Surveys, so we only have a short time series, but the results are interesting. The countries are ranked according to the percentage disagreeing that men make better political leaders than women, in the latest survey available for each country. Nine of the ten countries showing the most egalitarian attitudes are high-income countries, as defined by the World Bank; and all of the high-income countries fall in the top half of Table A-11, with 50 percent or more of their publics disagreeing that men make better political leaders than women. In the other countries, the percentage disagreeing that men make better leaders ranges from 70 to 12 percent. Among the eight countries in which fewer than 30 percent disagree with this statement, five are overwhelmingly Islamic and a sixth (Nigeria) is about half Islamic.

Table A-11 also shows the changes over time in all countries for which we have more than one time point. Among the countries in the top half of the table, all but one show shifts toward greater gender equality. Among the countries in the lower half of the table, *all* of them shift toward less gender equality. Here again, we do not find any evidence of universal cultural diffusion, producing a global shift toward the values that are socially desirable in rich democracies. Instead, we find a pattern of cultural divergence in which the high-ranking countries (which are postindustrial societies) move toward stronger emphasis on gender equality, whereas the lower-ranking countries are stagnant or move in the opposite direction.

Happiness and Interpersonal Trust

Postmaterialist values, elite-challenging political action, and tolerance of homo-sexuality are closely linked, all of them being components of the survival/self-expression dimension. The fact that both elite-challenging political action and tolerance of homosexuality are closely correlated with postmaterialism and show significant generational differences led to predictions that they would gradually increase over time through an intergenerational population replace-ment process similar to the one that has been producing a shift toward postmaterialist values. Thus, we predicted that postmaterialist values, elite-challenging political action, and tolerance of homosexuality would become more widespread in postindustrial democracies. As we have just seen, all three of these predicted changes subsequently took place.

No such predictions were made concerning two other variables that sub-sequently were also found to be components of the survival/self-expression dimension: interpersonal trust and happiness. Happiness and trust have much weaker individual-level correlations with postmaterialist values than do tolerance of homosexuality and elite-challenging political action; and they show weaker correlations with age. Although it was not predicted, happiness lev-els have been rising in most countries for which we have time-series data, as Table A-12 in the Internet Appendix demonstrates. Forty of the fifty-three coun-tries (75 percent of the total) show increases; only nine (17 percent of the total) show decreases. High-income countries are particularly likely to show increases: 88 percent of them show rising levels of happiness from the earliest to the lat-est available survey. Ex-communist countries are less likely to do so: only 61 percent of them show rising levels of happiness; among them only the western ex-communist group shows increases of more than 2 percent. This confirms our findings in Figure 6.2: increasingly favorable existential conditions nourish a sense of human autonomy, which promotes a sense of subjective well-being.

Generalized interpersonal trust is virtually uncorrelated with the respon-dent's age ($r = -.01$) and shows no upward trend – in fact, slightly more than half of the countries for which we have time-series data show declining levels of trust from the earliest available survey to the latest (see Table A-13 in the Internet Appendix). But these trends are sharply differentiated according to the type of society: 81 percent of the ex-communist societies show declining levels of trust; but only 43 percent of the high-income countries show declines. The collapse of state-run economies brought uncertainty and (especially in the ex–Soviet Union) a sharp decline in standards of living. Many ex-communist publics reacted to this uncertainty with lowered trust. These contrasting findings are consistent with a pervasive pattern in which rich democracies are much likelier to show upward trends in variables linked with the survival/self-expression dimension than are ex-communist countries (especially those in the eastern, largely ex-Soviet group) and low-income societies.

Changes on the Survival/Self-Expression Dimension as a Whole

We have examined in some detail the empirical changes observed in recent years with various components of the survival/self-expression values dimension. Now let us examine the overall pattern of changes that occurred on this dimension as a whole. Figure 4.6 shows the age-related differences found in five types of societies. More than three decades ago, the presence of such age-related differences in postindustrial democracies suggested that intergenerational population replacement would bring predictable changes in the prevailing values in these societies. The empirical evidence demonstrates that these predictions were accurate – for postindustrial democracies. Postindustrial democracies show large age-related differences, with the young emphasizing self-expression values much more heavily than the old, which implies that intergenerational population replacement should bring an overall shift toward self-expression values. As Figure 5.4 demonstrates, this is exactly what we find. From 1981 to 1990, and again from 1990 to 2000, these values became substantially more widespread among the publics of rich democracies. In 1981 this group ranked .51 of a standard deviation above the global mean[10] on survival/self-expression values. In 1990 the mean score on the survival/self-expression dimension for the publics of this same group of seventeen rich democracies had risen to a position .98 of a standard deviation above the same global mean. And by the 2000 wave, the mean score of these seventeen publics had risen to a level 1.25 standard deviations above the global mean – a net increase of .74 standard deviations in the predicted direction, on a major dimension of cross-cultural variation. The prediction based on generational change receives massive support from these findings.

But this prediction does not apply to all types of societies. The most obvious reason why it may not apply everywhere is that we do not find the same generational differences in all types of societies: these generational differences reflect

---

[10] This global mean is based on the data from all 195 surveys carried out in all four waves of the Values Surveys (so that the global mean against which we measure change is held constant in these analyses). A total of 265,037 respondents was interviewed from 1981 to 2001.

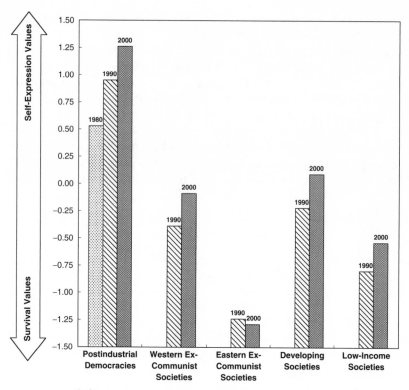

FIGURE 5.4. Shifts toward self-expression values in five types of societies.

long-term improvements in the living conditions that shaped the formative years of the respective generations, and these improvements were not experienced in all societies. As Figure 4.6 demonstrated, we find large age-related differences in the postindustrial democracies, smaller ones in the ex-communist group and in developing societies; and little or no difference between the values of different generations in the low-income societies. Consequently, the process of intergenerational population replacement would not be expected to produce much change on this dimension in the latter societies. Figure 5.4 confirms this expectation: we find a larger shift toward self-expression values in the postindustrial democracies than in other societies.

But age-related differences, even if present, do not necessarily translate into changes over time, as the eastern group of ex-communist societies demonstrates. For the amount of change observed at any given time reflects two components: generational change and period effects. Changes over time reflect both the current socioeconomic environment and the presence of generational differences. Although the generational differences are stable and persisted throughout the thirty-year period examined in Figure 4.6 in the previous chapter, during a recession all age groups become less postmaterialist; and under favorable conditions they become more so. Although intergenerational population replacement tends to push the distribution toward increasingly postmaterialist values, period effects can outweigh this effect at any given time.

The eastern ex-communist societies did show sizable age-related differences in Figure 4.6. Their dismal economic performance in recent years should not make us forget that during the early postwar decades, most of these countries had higher rates of economic growth than most Western democracies, together with relatively high levels of income equality and extensive social benefits. Even in times of stagnation, and despite notorious inefficiencies, communist societies attained relatively high levels of existential security, which are reflected in the intergenerational differences in emphasis on survival/self-expression values. But in the period from 1990 to the 2000 surveys, the economic, political, and social systems of the eastern ex-communist countries collapsed, creating massive insecurity. This is a period effect that dwarfs the impact that recent recessions had on Western countries – and it seems to have operated in a similar fashion to the period effects shown in Figure 4.2, pushing all age groups toward greater emphasis on survival values but leaving the generational differences intact.

The result is that, despite the considerable generational differences found in eastern ex-communist societies, they do not show a net shift toward increasing emphasis on self-expression values in Figure 5.4; instead, they showed a slight shift toward greater emphasis on survival values from 1989–91 to 1999–2001. The impact of intergenerational population replacement was overwhelmed by a massive period effect. Our theory implies that this effect will fade away with economic recovery: when this happens, the large intergenerational differences found in the ex-communist countries will no longer be offset by negative period effects, so that with economic recovery intergenerational population replacement will push the eastern ex-communist societies toward increasing emphasis on self-expression values. This process was already in progress before the collapse of communism, tending to delegitimize the communist regimes. Because self-expression values are strongly linked with democracy, we predict that economic recovery and generational replacement will create a long-term pressure to maintain and extend democratic institutions in the ex-communist societies, including the eastern group.

Conclusion

In recent decades, a simplistic version of globalization theory gained widespread currency, holding that the globalization of the mass media and communications networks was producing cultural convergence; we were headed toward a "global village" in which everyone was on the same wavelength. The evidence presented here demonstrates that this view is false – in fact, global trends are moving in exactly the opposite direction. The values of the publics of rich countries are changing rapidly, but those of low-income societies are changing much more slowly or not at all. As a result, a growing *gap* is opening up between the basic values of the publics of rich versus poor countries (as more-sophisticated versions of globalization imply – see, e.g., Held et al., 2003).

Socioeconomic development tends to produce intergenerational value differences and a shift toward stronger emphasis on self-expression values. The extent to which these values are present helps to explain the recent trend toward democracy, as we will demonstrate in the following chapters. But variations in self-expression values also help to explain why some countries moved closer to full-fledged democracies than others and why some countries became much more effective democracies than others. As the following chapters show, self-expression values affect both the presence and quality of democracy. This reflects our central thesis, which was summarized by the human development sequence depicted in Table I.1 in the Introduction: increasingly favorable existential conditions lead people to place greater emphasis on human freedom and choice, which generates pressures to establish and strengthen democratic liberties. This thesis of human development can be diagramed as follows:

Economic Change   →   Cultural Change   →   Political Change
(existential security)   (self-expression values)   (democratic institutions)
H U M A N   D E V E L O P M E N T

As we will demonstrate, the key cultural change is the shift from survival to self-expression values. The shift toward secular-rational values is not central to democratization. As long as the religious authorities do not attempt to control the political system, democratic institutions seem to function about equally well in religious and secular societies. The shift from traditional to secular-rational values is important in itself – so much so that a separate book has been devoted to it (see Norris and Inglehart, 2004). We do not deal with these changes here because they are not central to the rise of democracy and because they have been discussed much more fully elsewhere.

6

Individualism, Self-Expression Values, and Civic Virtues

The Psychological Roots of Human Development

In recent years, culture has entered the mainstream of psychology, with the concepts of individualism and collectivism playing prominent roles. Triandis (1995) claims that there is more cross-cultural research on individualism-collectivism than on any other psychological dimension, and Oyserman, Coon, and Kemmelmeier (2002) cite hundreds of studies dealing with it. Greenfield (2000) sees individualism-collectivism as the "deep structure" of cultural differences, from which all other differences evolved. Western social analysis has long emphasized the contrast between an individual and a collective focus. Durkheim (1988 [1893]) contrasted the intimate, fixed, and holistic ties between similar others in "segmented societies" (which he labeled "mechanical solidarity") and the looser, flexible, and specific ties between dissimilar others in "functionally differentiated" societies (which he labeled "organic solidarity"). Durkheim considered the transition from mechanical to organic solidarity a general aspect of modernization, arguing that it replaces collective patterns of self-identification with more individualistic ones. Weber (1958 [1904]) held that a key difference between Protestant and Catholic societies was the individual focus of the former versus the collective focus of the latter. Tönnies (1955 [1887]) emphasized the distinction between *Gemeinschaft* and *Gesellschaft*, or community and association. Community reflects intimate and holistic "bonding ties" that lead to very strong ingroup cohesion but also to closed, inward-looking groups. Association involves looser and more-specific "bridging ties" that connect individuals across the borders of social circles based on shared commitments to common interests. "Community" fosters collectivist identities, whereas "association" fosters individualistic identities.

The broad distinction between individualism and collectivism continues to be a central theme in psychological research on cross-cultural differences. Hofstede (1980) defined individualism as a focus on rights above duties, a concern for oneself and one's immediate family, an emphasis on personal autonomy and self-fulfillment, and basing identity on one's personal accomplishments; he developed a survey instrument that measured individualism-collectivism among IBM employees in more than forty societies. More recently, individualism has been measured cross-nationally by Triandis (1989, 2001, 2003). Schwartz (1992, 1994, 2003) measured the related concept of autonomy-embeddedness among students and teachers in scores of countries. And, as this chapter demonstrates, individualism-collectivism, as measured by Hofstede and Triandis, and autonomy-embeddedness, as measured by Schwartz, tap the same dimension of cross-cultural variation as survival/self-expression values: an emphasis on autonomous human choice.

Individualism-collectivism, autonomy-embeddedness and survival/self-expression values are all linked with the process of human development, reflecting diminishing constraints on human choice. The fact that individualism, autonomy, and self-expression values tap a common pole of cross-cultural variation is not entirely surprising. Self-expression values are defined in very similar terms to Hofstede's emphasis on personal autonomy and self-fulfillment as core elements of individualism; and Schwartz's emphasis on intellectual autonomy and affective autonomy captures core elements of self-expression values. All these variables reflect a common theme: an emphasis on autonomous human choice.

The core element of collectivism is the assumption that groups bind and mutually obligate individuals (Oyserman, 2001; Kühnen and Oyserman, 2002). In collectivist societies, social units have a common fate and common goals; the personal is simply a component of the social, making the ingroup crucial. Collectivism implies that group membership is a central aspect of identity, and sacrifice of individual goals for the common good is highly valued. Furthermore, collectivism implies that fulfillment comes from carrying out externally defined obligations, which means that people are *extrinsically* motivated, focusing on meeting others' expectations. Accordingly, emotional self-restraint is valued to ensure harmony (although such self-repression tends to lower people's subjective well-being, as we will demonstrate). In collectivist societies, social context is prominent in people's perceptions and causal reasoning, and meaning is contextualized. Finally, collectivism implies that important group memberships are seen as fixed "facts of life" to which people must accommodate – without any choice. Boundaries between ingroups and outgroups are stable, relatively impermeable, and important; and exchanges are based on mutual obligations and patriarchal ties.

Today, empirical measures of individualism, autonomy, and self-expression values are available from many societies, and they all turn out to tap a common dimension of cross-cultural variation, reflecting an emphasis on autonomous human choice. The mean national scores on these three variables show correlations that range from .62 to .70, with an average strength of .66. Factor analysis of the mean national scores reveals that individualism, autonomy, and self-expression values measure a single underlying dimension, which accounts for fully 78 percent of the cross-national variance (see Table 6.1). Triandis's measure of individualism is also strongly correlated with this dimension

TABLE 6.1. *Self-Expression Values and Individualism and Autonomy Scales Tap a Common Dimension*

The Individualism/Autonomy/Self-Expression Dimension: Emphasis on Intrinsic Human Choice (Principal Component Analysis)	78% Variance Explained
Inglehart: Survival vs. self-expression values	.91
Hofstede: Individualism vs. collectivism rankings	.87
Schwartz: Autonomy vs. embeddedness (mean of student/teacher samples)	.87

(r = .88), but it makes little sense to add it to this factor analysis because his scores are based on Hofstede's data, supplemented with estimated scores for a number of additional countries.[1]

High levels of individualism go with high levels of autonomy and high levels of self-expression values. Hofstede's, Schwartz's, Triandis's, and Inglehart's measures all tap cross-cultural variation in the same basic aspect of human psychology – the drive toward broader human choice. They also measure something that extends far beyond whether given cultures have an individualistic or collective outlook. Societies that rank high on self-expression tend to emphasize individual autonomy and the quality of life, rather than economic and physical security. Their publics have relatively low levels of confidence in technology and scientific discoveries as the solution to human problems and are relatively likely to act to protect the environment. These societies also rank relatively high on gender equality and tolerance of gays, lesbians, foreigners, and other outgroups; show relatively high levels of subjective well-being and interpersonal trust; and emphasize imagination and tolerance, as important things to teach a child.

But individualism, autonomy, and self-expression are not static characteristics of societies. They change with the course of socioeconomic development. As we have seen, socioeconomic development brings rising levels of existential security (especially in its postindustrial phase), which leads to an increasing emphasis on individualism, autonomy, and self-expression. Birch and Cobb (1981) view this process as reflecting an evolutionary trend toward the "liberation of life." We describe it as a process of human development in which the most typically "human" ability – the ability to make autonomous choices – becomes an ever more central feature of modern societies, giving them an increasingly humanistic orientation. As we will see, this syndrome of individualism, autonomy, and self-expression is conducive to the emergence and survival of democratic institutions.

This common dimension underlying individualism, autonomy, and self-expression is remarkably robust. It emerges when one uses different measurement approaches, different types of samples, and different time periods. Hofstede found it in the late 1960s and early 1970s, analyzing the values of a

[1] Hofstede's power distance rankings are also strongly related to this dimension: r = −.72.

cross-national sample of IBM employees. Schwartz measured it in surveys of students and teachers carried out from 1988 to 2002; and Inglehart first found it in an analysis of representative national samples of the publics of forty-three societies surveyed in 1989–91; the same dimension emerged in representative national samples of sixty societies, interviewed in 1995–97; and in surveys of the publics of more than seventy societies carried out in 1999–2001. This dimension seems to be an enduring feature of cross-cultural variation, so much that one could almost conclude that it is difficult to *avoid* finding it if one measures the basic values of a broad sample of cultures.

Individualism, Autonomy, and Self-Expression as Evolving Phenomena

Most cultural-psychological theories have treated the individualism-collectivism polarity as a static attribute of given cultures, overlooking the possibility that individualist and collectivist orientations reflect a society's socioeconomic conditions at a given time. Our theory holds that the extent to which self-expression values (or individualism) prevail over survival values (or collectivism) reflects a society's level of socioeconomic development: as external constraints on human choice recede, people (and societies) place increasing emphasis on self-expression values or individualism. This pattern is not culture-specific. It is universal.

The most fundamental external constraint on human choice is the extent to which physical survival is secure or insecure. Throughout most of history, survival has been precarious for most people. Most children did not survive to adulthood, and malnutrition and associated diseases were the leading cause of death. Although these conditions are remote from the experience of Western publics today, existential insecurity is still the dominant reality in most of the world. Under such conditions, survival values take top priority. Survival is such a fundamental goal that if it seems uncertain, one's entire life strategy is shaped by this fact. Low levels of socioeconomic development not only impose material constraints on people's choices; they also are linked with low levels of education and information. This intellectual poverty imposes cognitive constraints on people's choices. Finally, in the absence of the welfare state, strong group obligations are the only form of social insurance, imposing social constraints on people's choices.

In recent history a growing number of societies have attained unprecedented levels of economic development. Diminishing material, cognitive, and social constraints on human choice are conducive to a shift from emphasis on survival values to emphasis on self-expression values – and from a collective focus to an individual one, with extrinsic motivations giving way to intrinsic motivations.

The finding that cross-national cultural variation reflects variations in individual psychology is fundamental. It indicates that sociocultural change follows processes that are deep-rooted in human psychology, a finding that many cultural theorists ignore. The subjective sense of human autonomy becomes stronger as objective existential constraints on human choice recede. This has further consequences, as we will demonstrate. Mass emphasis on human choice tends to favor the political system that provides the widest room for choice: democracy. Thus, democracy is not simply a matter of institutional rationality. It is an evolving institutional manifestation of a broader human development process that is ultimately anchored in human nature.

The Psychological Force toward Human Self-Expression: Subjective Well-Being

As objective constraints on human choice relax, the desire for self-expression takes higher priority in a society. Aspirations for choice and self-expression are universal human aspirations: attaining them brings feelings of self-fulfillment, as Abraham Maslow pointed out long ago (Maslow, 1988 [1954]). Maslow's claim that self-expression is linked with stronger feelings of self-fulfillment has been demonstrated empirically by psychological research showing that self-steering people who are driven by intrinsic motivations tend to be happier than people driven by extrinsic motivations, regardless of their society's emphasis on collectivism or individualism (Schmuck, Kasser, and Ryan, 2000). Similarly, Chirkov et al. (2003) demonstrate that individual autonomy is related to feelings of well-being among people in both individualist and collectivist cultures.

Humans have an inherent need to express themselves. If this need is suppressed by existential insecurity or restrictive social norms, people feel less fulfillment and report lower levels of overall life satisfaction. Empirical data from the Values Surveys indicate that having opportunities for self-expression is linked with relatively high levels of life satisfaction. In each of 191 national representative surveys, conducted in 73 diverse societies ranging from the United States to Uganda, China, Iran, Brazil, Sweden, and Poland, one finds a highly significant correlation between individuals' life satisfaction and their perception of how much choice they have in shaping their lives.[2] The mean individual-level correlation within nations is $r = .37$. This correlation has a small standard error ($SE = .07$), implying that the linkage between life satisfaction and the sense of choice does not significantly differ for the nation within which it is measured. Moreover, as Figure 6.1 demonstrates, the linkage between life satisfaction and the sense of choice exists across cultural zones. It is not a unique feature of Western Protestant societies. We find some variation in the strength

---

[2] Life satisfaction in the Values Surveys is measured on a 10-point rating scale from 1, "completely dissatisfied," to 10, "completely satisfied." Choice perception is also measured on a 10-point rating scale based on the following question: "Some people feel they have completely free choice and control over their lives, while other people feel that what they do has no real effect on what happens to them. Please use this scale where '1' means 'none at all' and '10' means 'a great deal' to indicate how much freedom of choice and control you feel you have over the way your life turns out." In 191 surveys in which these variables can be created, one finds a highly significant positive correlation. The average within-survey correlation is $r = .37$. Pooled across all surveys, the individual-level correlation is $r = .40$ ($N = 248,000$). At the aggregate level of nations, the correlation is $r = .78$.

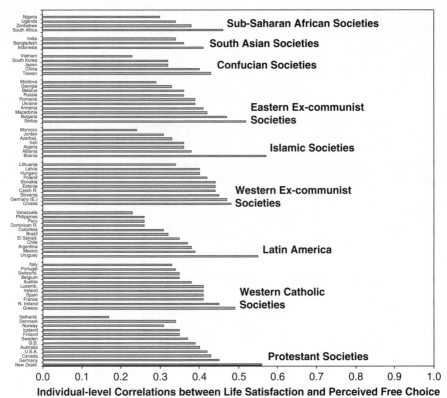

FIGURE 6.1. Correlations between life satisfaction and the sense that one has free choice (at the individual level).

of this linkage in each cultural zone, but it is significant in all cultural zones. In some non-Western societies, moreover, the linkage between life satisfaction and the sense of choice is stronger than in some Western societies. Thus, the linkage between life satisfaction and freedom of choice is stronger in China, Indonesia, and Zimbabwe than in the Netherlands, Denmark, Iceland, or Finland.

The linkage between life satisfaction and a sense of human choice is universal because the desire for autonomous choice is anchored in human psychology, with freer choice bringing higher satisfaction even in collectivist cultures. The aspiration for choice is not peculiar to individualistic Western cultures but exists everywhere. What *does* differ is the amount of external constraint that given societies impose on their people's freedom of choice. And these differences are reflected in different levels of life satisfaction. Societies can instill cultural norms that strongly discourage people from exercising autonomous choices, but they tend to diminish the prevailing level of life satisfaction.

The linkage between the sense of free choice and life satisfaction is particularly strong at the societal level, as Figure 6.2 demonstrates. Across nations

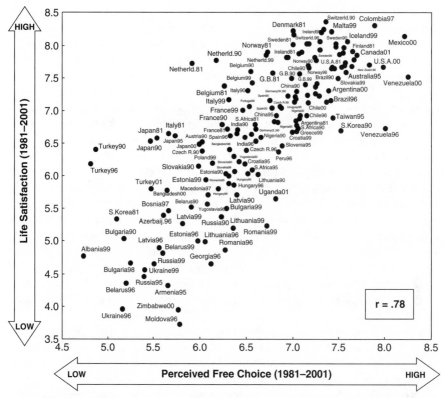

FIGURE 6.2. Life satisfaction by country and year and the feeling that one has free choice (at the societal level).

and time, the prevailing mass sense of human choice explains 61 percent of a society's level of life satisfaction. Human happiness flourishes in climates of free choice. Given individuals may not be conscious of the linkage between autonomous choice and happiness, but those who feel they have relatively high levels of control and choice over their lives systematically report higher levels of life satisfaction. The finding that autonomous choice tends to make people happier constitutes a driving force in the process of human development. This force favors norms and institutions that enhance human freedom.

The Civic Nature of Self-Expression Values

Existential threats drive people to seek safety in closely knit groups. This fosters intimate and holistic bonding ties, which narrows people's solidarity to the circle of extended kin (Geertz, 1963). The closed nature of ingroups favors intimate interpersonal trust at the expense of generalized interpersonal trust. This has a pervasive impact on the nature of social ties, or social capital: under conditions of insecurity, social capital is bonding rather than bridging.

Consequently, the debate about whether social capital is declining in postindustrial societies is overlooking an important point. Social capital is not declining in these societies but is shifting from one form to another. No society can exist without social ties. What differs is the character of these ties. Bonding social capital and bridging social capital tend to compete with each other and cannot be maximized simultaneously. There is an inescapable trade-off between the intensity and the extensiveness of people's social ties, with intense ingroup ties limiting one's capacity to engage in looser ties with many others (Fukuyama, 2000).[3] Thus we disagree with Putnam's (2000) view that declining engagement in formal associations in the United States indicates an erosion of social capital. His findings reflect the decline of the specific *type* of bonding social capital. But, at the same time, bridging social capital has been increasing, as self-organized and elite-challenging collective actions have become markedly more widespread. The nature of social capital is changing in postindustrial societies. Growing individualization makes people increasingly socially independent: the social ties in which they engage reflect their autonomous choices rather than conformity to externally imposed groups. Shaping social ties in postindustrial societies becomes increasingly a matter of autonomous choice (U. Beck, 2002; Florida, 2002). Ties are more and more intrinsically shaped rather than externally imposed.

Closed groups develop conformity among insiders and discrimination against outsiders (Monroe, Hankin, and van Vechten, 2000). Conformity among insiders has deindividualizing effects, making people readier to support limitations on individual liberties for the sake of group discipline (Pettigrew, 1998). Similarly, discrimination against outsiders has dehumanizing effects, depriving outsiders of human rights – sometimes to the extent of making genocide seem acceptable for the welfare of the ingroup. Survival values are a rational human reaction to existential threats: when resources are so scarce that it is a question of one group or the other surviving, discrimination against outsiders, strong mutual obligations, and insider favoritism[4] are inevitable. Xenophobia becomes widespread when threats to survival dominate people's lives. Survival values are functional under these conditions, but they force people to adopt a morality that focuses on the well-being of one's ingroup rather than that of humanity as a whole. Survival values emphasize bonding social capital, which is often used in discriminatory ways. The tendency to discriminate against outsiders leaves survival values with a largely anticivic imprint.

---

[3] This reflects a trade-off between intensity and extensiveness in human cooperation, linked with an equilibrium between cooperation and competition. If competition becomes fiercely intensive (e.g., in a civil war), cooperation within the competing camps becomes correspondingly intensive (people cooperate so intensely that they even sacrifice life for each other). If competition becomes less severe, people can lower the intensity of their cooperation with insiders and extend the circles of their cooperation with outsiders. However, cooperation as a sum of its intensity and extension tends to remain constant even though the nature of cooperation changes dramatically.

[4] Tribalism, nepotism, and familism are obvious forms of insider favoritism.

Survival values have been examined from a variety of perspectives. Rokeach (1960) explored the "closed mind," which – according to Popper (1966 [1945]) – leads to a "closed society" governed by the "spirit of the horde." Putnam (1993) emphasizes the uncivic character of "bonding ties," Banfield (1958) studied the values of "amoral familism," and Monroe et al. (2000) examined the twin phenomena of ingroup favoritism and outgroup discrimination. All of these are manifestations of a broader syndrome of survival values, which tends to be present in their most extreme form when a group's survival is threatened. Hence, what Hofstede (1980) describes as "collective identities" and what Kühnen and Oyserman (2002) describe as "interdependent" self-conceptions are not simply static psychological attributes of given cultures. These psychological traits reflect the dominance of survival values, under conditions of existential insecurity. These values emphasize collective discipline over individual liberty, group conformity over human diversity, and state authority over civic autonomy.

Conversely, self-expression values tend to become more widespread when existential threats recede. Self-expression values emerge as people grow up experiencing existential security and individual autonomy, reducing the need for group protection. This weakens pressures for group conformity. People adopt increasingly independent conceptions of themselves. Creating ties to other people is no longer a matter of external constraints but a matter of intrinsic choice, which helps people move beyond the narrow boundaries of extended kinship. Bridging ties replace bonding ties, and generalized trust replaces intimate trust. People become less likely to accept restrictions of individual liberties for the sake of group conformity and become more likely to view other types of human beings as intrinsically valuable individuals. Accordingly, self-expression values make people more supportive of individual liberties and human rights. Self-expression values have an antidiscriminatory and humanistic tendency. This gives these values a largely procivic character.

Social scientists have examined various aspects of this phenomenon, using different labels, such as the open mind, bridging ties, independent self-conceptions, individualism, and altruism. From the perspective of human development, these are all facets of a broader phenomenon that we describe as self-expression values. Self-expression values become increasingly widespread when existential constraints on human choice recede, giving more room for the universal human aspirations for self-realization and individual autonomy to emerge. From the human development perspective, this wide variety of psychological and cultural traits does not represent idiosyncratic aspects of given cultures but tends to be linked with socioeconomic conditions.

In keeping with this reasoning, "regulatory focus theory" in experimental psychology argues that the social situation shapes people's orientations (Förster, Higgins, and Idson, 1998). If the social situation is charged with insecurity and threats, people's orientations are channeled into a "prevention focus" in which they apply survival strategies in trying to avoid harmful losses and failures. But if the social situation is secure and offers opportunities for achievement, people's orientations are directed into a "promotion focus" that emphasizes striving for initiative, creativity, and self-expression. From this perspective, socioeconomic development is crucial because it changes the social situation of entire populations, so that the "promotion focus" becomes the modal type of orientation in a society. Thus, rising self-expression values can be interpreted as reflecting the growing social dominance of a promotion focus. Cultural change follows fundamental psychological mechanisms.

In the literature on the virtues that make good democratic citizens (see Sullivan and Transue, 1999; Galston, 2001), theorists and researchers have identified two polarities, which have been discussed separately: xenophobia versus altruism in people's orientations toward outsiders (e.g., noncitizens); and authoritarianism versus liberalism in people's orientation toward insiders (e.g., fellow citizens). These two distinctions converge in the broader polarization between survival versus self-expression values. The discriminatory impulse of survival values combines a xenophobic tendency toward outsiders with an authoritarian tendency among insiders. Conversely, the humanistic impulse of self-expression values combines a cosmopolitan tendency that favors universal human rights with a libertarian tendency that favors individual liberties.

In the discussion of civic virtues, individualism and humanism have often been seen as contradictory. But this view is based on the false assumption that individualism should be equated with asocial egoism. From this perspective, it is argued that individualism has anticivic consequences (Lawler and McConkey, 1998; Flanagan et al., forthcoming). This view can be traced back to classical Greek times when the Epicureans praised self-interest, while the Stoics praised charity (see Coleman, 1990: 302). But the contradiction between individualism and humanism is mistaken. In fact, individualism tends to go together with a *humanistic* orientation, not an *egocentric* one. It is no accident that the philosophy of humanism, which took shape during the Renaissance in the fifteenth century, emerged from the prosperous urban centers of Flanders and Lombardy when preindustrial capitalism gave these societies a more individualistic outlook than any other society of the time (Jones, 1985).

Conclusion

We have argued that cross-cultural variation in fundamental psychological characteristics – including collectivism versus individualism, embeddedness versus autonomy, and prevention focus versus promotion focus – are closely linked with the survival versus self-expression values dimension. Individualism, autonomy, promotion focus, and self-expression reflect a common underlying theme, emphasizing autonomous human choice. This has two implications. First, the polarity between survival values and self-expression values is anchored in human psychology: it is a dimension that applies to all cultures, although they vary greatly in which pole they emphasize. Second, the widely prevailing view among cultural psychologists that traits such as individualism rather than collectivism are fixed traits of given cultures should be modified: they do indeed reflect a given cultural heritage to some extent, but the emphasis can change over time. To a large extent, the emergence of humanistic orientations reflects human development. No society is immune to human development. Quite the contrary, as the preceding chapters have shown, self-expression values are linked with socioeconomic development. They are not a static feature of cultures, but an evolving phenomenon linked with a universal logic: subjective emphasis on human freedom increases as external constraints on intrinsic choice recede.

The rise of emancipative orientations, such as individualism, autonomy, promotion orientation, and self-expression values, reflects the process of human development. This has desirable civic consequences, because rising emphasis on autonomous human choice is inherently conducive to antidiscriminatory conceptions of human well-being. Finally, emancipative orientations are inherently people-centered, which is a major reason why rising emphasis on self-expression values is strongly linked with democracy. This means that the emergence and flourishing of democracy itself is part of the broader process of human development – as the remainder of this book will demonstrate.

PART II

THE CONSEQUENCES OF VALUE CHANGE

7

The Causal Link between Democratic Values and Democratic Institutions

Theoretical Discussion

Rising self-expression values transform modernization into a process of human development, giving rise to a new type of humanistic society that promotes human emancipation on many fronts. This transformation has a number of important societal consequences. One of them is that it encourages the emergence and flourishing of democratic institutions. This chapter outlines this process, discussing the causal linkage between mass self-expression values and democratic institutions. Building on previous work by Welzel (2002), Chapter 8 tests the propositions and conclusions developed here, using quantitative empirical analyses.

From the perspective of human development, the crucial element of democratization is that it empowers people. Democracy provides civil and political rights, entitling people to freedom of choice in their private and public actions (see Dahl, 1973, 2003; Rose, 1995; Sen, 1999: 152–54). Human development is not linked with all forms of democracy to the same degree; it is most specifically linked with the liberal aspect of democracy that institutionalizes human choice.

The Third Wave gave birth to a large number of new democracies that were initially greeted with enthusiasm (Pye, 1990; Fukuyama, 1992). Subsequently, however, a growing number of observers have noted that many of the new democracies show severe deficiencies in their actual practice of civil and political liberties (Ottaway, 2003). Widespread concern has been expressed about "low intensity democracies," "electoral democracies," "defective democracy," or "illiberal democracies" (D. Collier and Adcock, 1999; Bollen and Paxton, 2000; Merkel et al., 2003; O'Donnell, Vargas Cullel, and Iazzetta, 2004). Many writers emphasize the need to distinguish between merely formal democracy or electoral democracy and genuinely effective liberal democracy (see, e.g., Gills and Rocamora, 1992; O'Donnell, 1996; Bunce, 2000; Heller, 2000; Rose, 2001). Using this distinction, a crucial point becomes evident. Formal democracy can be imposed on almost any society, but whether it provides genuine autonomous choice to its citizens largely depends on mass values. And among the values linked with effective democracy, self-expression values prove to be the most crucial of all, as this and the following chapter will demonstrate.

TABLE 7.1. *Correlations between Socioeconomic Development Indicators and Self-Expression Values*

Correlates	Correlation with Percentage Index of Self-Expression Values, Mid-1990s[a]
Per capita GDP in 1995 PPP (World Bank, 2000)[b]	.86*** (73)
Human Development Index, 1995 (UNDP, 1998)	.75*** (69)
Index of Social Progress, 1995 (Estes, 1998)	.65*** (72)
Postindustrialization, 1990 (work force in services minus industry)	.74*** (71)
Index of Socioeconomic Resources, early 1990s (Vanhanen, 1997)	.88*** (73)

[a] Earliest available survey from Values Surveys II–IV (1989–2001). Average measure is in 1995. Significance level: *p < .10; **p < .01; ***p < .001.
[b] PPP = purchasing power parity.

The Centrality of Self-Expression Values

The preceding chapters have shown that mass emphasis on self-expression values is a major dimension of cross-cultural variation. A society's emphasis on self-expression values is closely linked with its socioeconomic and political characteristics. Tables 7.1 and 7.2 demonstrate this point, showing the correlations between a percentage index indicating how widespread self-expression values are in a given society[1] and various measures of socioeconomic development (Table 7.1) and democracy (Table 7.2).[2] This measure of self-expression values is strongly correlated with the factor scores used in Part I of this book (r = .96), but it is used here for two reasons: the percentage of a public scoring high on these values has an intuitively clearer meaning than that of factor scores; and because we are not making comparisons over time in this section of the book, we are no longer constrained by the need to use only those variables that were included in all four waves of the Values Survey but can use the most effective measurement that is available.

[1] This percentage index is a weighted average of the percentages of its five components (weighted for their factor loadings): (1) postmaterialistic aspirations for civil and political liberty; (2) tolerance of others' liberty, as indicated by tolerance of homosexuality; (3) elite-challenging civic activity, as indicated by signing petitions; (4) generalized interpersonal trust; and (5) emphasis on subjective well-being measured by life satisfaction. For exactly how the percentage index is constructed, see the Internet Appendix, #49 under Variables. The percentage scale gives an intuitive idea of how widespread self-expression values are in societies. This is important if one considers self-expression as a social force that provides a source of collective actions. For more details, see the Internet Appendix, at http://www.worldveluessurvey.org/publications/humandevelopment.html.
[2] For measurement details on the remaining variables used in Tables 7.1 and 7.2, see under Variables in the Internet Appendix, #04 (postindustrialization), #05 (GDP per capita), #06 (Human Development Index), #07 (Index of Social Progress), #08 (socioeconomic resources), #16 (constitutional democracy), #17 (electoral democracy), #18 (liberal democracy), #20 (elite integrity), #21 (effective democracy).

TABLE 7.2. *Correlations between Measures of Democracy and Self-Expression Values*

Correlates	Correlation with Percentage Index of Self-Expression Values, Mid 1990s[a]:
Presence of democracy	
Constitutional Democracy, 1998–2001 (Polity IV data)	.62*** (66)
Electoral Democracy, 2001 (Vanhanen, 2003)	.75*** (71)
Liberal Democracy, 2000–2002 (Freedom House, 2003)	.75*** (73)
Quality of democracy	
Civil Society Index, 2000 (Anheier et al., 2004)	.85*** (31)
Gender Empowerment, 2000 (UNDP, 2002)	.85*** (55)
Elite Integrity, 2000–2002 (Anti-Corruption scores, World Bank, 2003)	.89*** (73)
Effective democracy (Presence of Democracy × Quality of Democracy):	
Liberal Democracy × Elite Integrity	.90*** (73)

[a] Earliest available survey from Values Surveys II–IV (1989–2001). Median measure is in 1995.
Significance level: *p < .10; **p < .01; ***p < .001.

The proportion of people in a society who emphasize self-expression values correlates strongly with measures of both socioeconomic development and democratic institutions, suggesting that there is a common dimension underlying these three phenomena. In fact, they are three pieces of a puzzle in which the integrating theme is human development: socioeconomic development, self-expression values, and democratic institutions work together to broaden autonomous human choice.

How do these three components accomplish this? The process starts with socioeconomic development, which reduces constraints on autonomous human choice by increasing people's economic, cognitive, and social resources. Economic resources include wealth and income (i.e., financial capital) that make people materially more independent. Cognitive resources derive from access to information and formal education (i.e., human capital), which make people intellectually more independent. Social resources (i.e., social capital) increase when social complexity allows people to connect and disconnect more freely with others, which makes them socially more independent. Socioeconomic development increases all three types of resources by raising incomes and educational levels and diversifying human interaction. Together, economic, cognitive, and social resources constitute "socioeconomic" resources. Increasing socioeconomic resources broaden the range of actions that people can perform, giving them the *objective capabilities* to act according to their own choices.

Because socioeconomic development tends to make people materially, intellectually, and socially more independent, it nurtures a sense of existential security and autonomy. A growing sense of existential autonomy leads people to give priority to humanistic self-expression values that emphasize human emancipation, giving liberty priority over discipline, diversity over conformity, and autonomy over authority. As growing socioeconomic resources broaden the range of activities that people can choose, self-expression values broaden the range of activities to which they aspire. In short, objective capabilities of choice promote subjective aspirations for choice.

Rising self-expression values lead people to demand the institutions that allow them to act according to their own choices. Accordingly, self-expression values motivate people to seek the civil and political rights that define liberal democracy. For these rights legally entitle people to pursue their own choices in their private and public activities. In short, subjective aspirations for choice lead to demands for entitlements to choice.

Human development advances with the growth of three components: (1) objective capabilities, based on socioeconomic resources, that enable people to act according to their own choices; (2) subjective motivations, based on self-expression values, that emphasize acting according to one's autonomous choices; (3) and legal entitlements, based on civil and political liberties, that allow people to act on the basis of their autonomous choices. These three components have a common focus on autonomous human choice. Table I.1 in the Introduction summarized this concept of human development.

The preceding chapters have explored the first major linkage in the human development process, that between socioeconomic development and self-expression values. The following chapters examine the second major linkage of this humanistic process, that between self-expression values and democratic institutions. As Table 7.2 illustrates, self-expression values are strongly linked with all of the widely accepted measures of democracy. But the strength of the linkages varies according to how directly a given indicator of democracy taps the core element of freedom: the degree to which people have genuine choice in their daily lives.

The Polity IV indicator measures "constitutional democracy" based on Eckstein and Gurr's (1975) concept of "authority patterns." This indicator is based on institutional provisions for the competitiveness of political recruitment, constraints on executive power, and openness of political competition (Gurr and Jaggers, 1995; Marshall and Jaggers, 2000).[3] This index focuses on procedures regulating the formal operation of state institutions that direct societies. This top-down perspective certainly taps an important element of democracy, but it focuses on an aspect that is relatively distant from the extent to which ordinary people have effective freedom in their daily lives. Hence, constitutional democracy shows the weakest linkage with mass self-expression values of the various indicators: r = .62.

Vanhanen's (1997, 2003) index of "electoral democracy" is a combined index of the inclusiveness and competitiveness of national parliamentary

---

[3] For more details on variable definitions, coding procedures, and data sources, see the project's website: http://www.bsos.umd.edu/cidcm/inscr/polity.

elections, with the index yielding higher scores as voter turnout becomes higher and the power concentration of parliamentary parties becomes lower.[4] This index comes closer to measuring people's effective choices because it is not restricted to constitutional provisions but focuses on a real aspect of people's choice, actual parliamentary elections. Hence, electoral democracy shows a stronger linkage with mass self-expression values than constitutional democracy: $r = .75$.

The measures published by Freedom House also are more relevant to people's effective choices than the Polity IV index of constitutional democracy, because Freedom House measures democracy bottom-up rather than top-down: it indicates the extent to which people are entitled to civil and political rights.[5] Like "electoral democracy," this measure of "liberal democracy" is more closely linked with mass self-expression values ($r = .75$) than is constitutional democracy.

Figure 7.1 shows the linkage between self-expression values and liberal democracy, as measured by the Freedom House scores – the most widely used indicator of democratic freedom. The relationship is remarkably strong, especially when one considers the fact that the two variables are measured at different levels and by completely different means: self-expression values tap the values of individuals, as measured by independent surveys in each of scores of societies, whereas the Freedom House scores are expert ratings of the extent to which the institutions of given societies provide political rights and civil liberties. Despite these fundamental differences in their nature, the relationship between these variables is strong and highly significant. In one important respect, the relationship even seems to be deterministic: without exception, any society in which more than half the population emphasizes self-expression values scores at least 90 percent of the maximum score on liberal democracy.

The measures of electoral democracy developed by Vanhanen and the measures of liberal democracy developed by Freedom House are unquestionably useful, but they both have significant limitations. The Vanhanen index narrowly ignores anything outside elections; and the Freedom House scores are limited because they measure only the extent to which civil and political liberties are institutionalized, which does not necessarily reflect the extent to which these liberties are actually respected by political elites. Recent literature has emphasized the distinction between formal democracy and genuine liberal democracy

---

[4] Because this index is solely based on electoral data, we classify it as an index of "electoral democracy," rather than of democracy itself. This does not mean that we consider elections unimportant, but one should be aware of the "electoral fallacy" (Linz and Stepan, 1996: 4), which all too easily equates democratic elections with democracy itself. Elections are one of the central aspects of democracy, but they do not reflect whether the civil rights that are essential to liberal democracy are present. For more details on measurement, see the Internet Appendix, #17 under Variables.

[5] The concept of liberal democracy (see Berlin, 1969; Rose, 1995) includes both "negative" freedom from the state (civil liberties) as well as "positive" freedom over the state (political liberties). Hence, our measure of liberal democracy always uses the *combined* Freedom House scores for civil and political liberties. For measurement details, see http://www.freedomhouse.org.

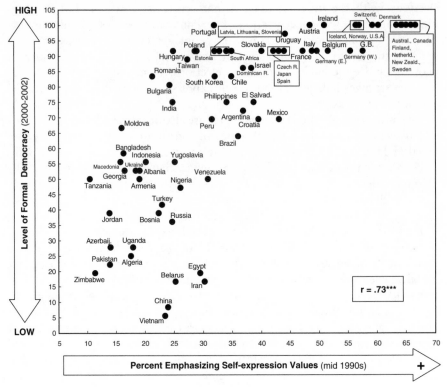

FIGURE 7.1. Self-expression values and formal democracy.

(Ottaway, 2003; O'Donnell et al., 2004). In order to tap the latter, we need a measure of "effective democracy," which reflects not only the extent to which formal civil and political liberties are institutionalized but also measures the extent to which these liberties are actually *practiced* – indicating how much free choice people really have in their lives. To construct such an index of effective democracy, we multiply the Freedom House measures of civil and political rights by the World Bank's anticorruption scores (Kaufman, Kraay, and Mastruzzi, 2003), which we see as an indicator of "elite integrity," or the extent to which power holders actually follow legal norms (see Chapter 8 for a more detailed discussion of this index). When we examine the linkage between this measure of genuine democracy and mass self-expression values, we find an amazingly strong correlation of r = .90 across seventy-three nations. This reflects a powerful cross-level linkage, connecting mass values that emphasize free choice and the extent to which societal institutions actually provide free choice.

Figure 7.2 depicts the relationship between this index of effective democracy and mass self-expression values. The extent to which self-expression values are present in a society, explains fully 80 percent of the cross-national variance in the extent to which liberal democracy is actually practiced. These findings

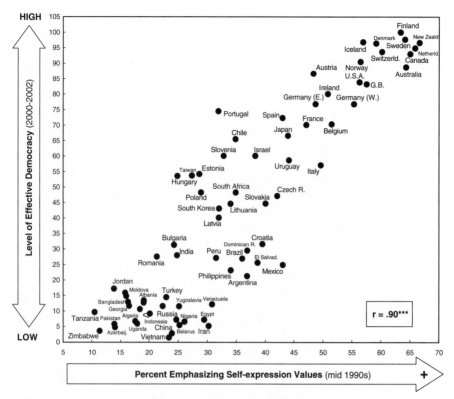

FIGURE 7.2. Self-expression values and effective democracy.

suggest that the importance of the linkage between individual-level values and democratic institutions has been underestimated. Mass preferences play a crucial role in the emergence of genuine democracy (Welzel, Inglehart, and Deutsch, 2004).

As Figure 7.1 suggests, "formal" democracy tends to emerge when more than 30 percent of the public emphasizes self-expression values. And, as Figure 7.2 suggests, genuinely effective democracy tends to emerge when at least 45 percent of the public emphasizes self-expression values. These are only probabilities, of course: as long as the ruling elite controls the army, it can repress mass pressures for democracy. But the statistical relationships are surprisingly strong: a society's level of self-expression values accounts for fully 80 percent of the variance in its level of effective democracy.

The linkage between mass self-expression values and formal democracy is strong and consistent, having only a few outliers, but these outliers are significant. China and Vietnam show considerably lower levels of democracy than their publics' values would predict. Both countries have authoritarian regimes that had greatly increased the latitude for individual choice in the economic realm and are currently experimenting with local-level democracy, but their one-party regimes are extremely reluctant to allow competition at the national level. These regimes are under growing societal pressure to liberalize, and we predict that they will become liberal democracies within the next fifteen to twenty years. The success of their economic reforms is giving rise to societal pressures that tend to erode their one-party regimes. Authoritarian rulers of some Asian societies have argued that the distinctive "Asian values" of these societies make them unsuitable for democracy (Lee and Zakaria, 1994; Thompson, 2000). In fact, the position of most Asian countries on Figures 7.1 and 7.2 is about where their level of socioeconomic development would predict. Japan ranks with the established Western democracies, both on the self-expression values dimension and on its level of democracy. And South Korea's position on both dimensions is similar to those of other relatively new democracies such as Chile and Uruguay. The publics of Confucian societies are more supportive of democracy than is generally believed.

On the other hand, less than 30 percent of the public emphasizes self-expression values in our sample of Islamic societies, which rank second lowest among the major cultural groups (slightly above the Orthodox ex-communist societies). The goal of democracy may be attractive to Islamic societies (and it actually *is*, as Chapter 11 demonstrates), but their levels of tolerance and trust and the priority they give to self-expression fall short of what is found in all established democracies. But we do not find an unbridgeable chasm between Islamic societies and the rest of the world. The belief systems of these Islamic countries fall roughly where one would expect them to be located, on the basis of their level of socioeconomic development. The most developed of them, Turkey, is now in the transition zone along with other countries such as the Philippines, South Africa, Poland, and Slovenia that have recently undergone transitions to democracy. Iran is a significant exception insofar as it has a lower level of democracy than the values of its public suggest. Among all Islamic countries, Iran shows the strongest liberalizing pressures from within its society. This tension leads us to expect that growing mass support will eventually help the liberalizing forces to overcome authoritarian theocratic rule, bringing the country on a path to liberal democracy.

Which comes first – a democratic political culture or democratic institutions? The extent to which people emphasize self-expression values is closely linked with the flourishing of democratic institutions. But what causes what? We suggest that democratic institutions have a relatively minor effect on self-expression values, which are primarily shaped by socioeconomic development. But rising self-expression values should have a major impact on democratic institutions because these values are inherently relevant to the civil and political liberties that constitute democracy.

To demonstrate that these causal linkages hold true requires a complex empirical analysis that will be presented in the following chapter. But previous research indicates that socioeconomic development leads to democracy, rather than the other way around (although this research does not demonstrate the intervening role of cultural change). Thus, the causal direction of the relationship between socioeconomic development and democracy has been analyzed by

Burkhart and Lewis-Beck (1994), using empirical data from 131 countries. On the basis of Granger causality tests, they conclude that socioeconomic development causes democracy, but that democracy does not cause socioeconomic development. Helliwell (1993) reaches similar conclusions. Moreover, Przeworski and Limongi's claim (1997) that socioeconomic development merely helps existing democracies to survive but does not help establish new democracies has been refuted by Boix and Stokes (2003), who demonstrate that socioeconomic development helps both existing democracies to survive *and* new democracies to emerge. The analyses in Chapter 8 confirm that this is true and demonstrate that culture is the intervening variable, explaining *why* socioeconomic development leads to democracy: it does so mainly because it gives rise to mass self-expression values.

This causality is probabilistic, not deterministic. The social world is complex and rarely works through monocausality. For example, the relationship between smoking and lung cancer is an established stochastic relationship. Although there are many individual exceptions, on average, smoking markedly increases the risk of cancer. Likewise, we argue that – other conditions being equal – rising self-expression values strongly increase the probability that a society will become democratic (if it not yet is) or will remain democratic (if it already is). Individual exceptions exist, but they do not refute the fact that rising self-expression values are a major force in promoting democracy.

Culture and Institutions: What Determines What?

The question of causal primacy is central to one of the most controversial debates in the research on democratization: Does a culture that sustains democracy primarily result from well-designed democratic institutions? Or does a prodemocratic political culture spring from other causes and give rise to effective democratic institutions? These questions are still unresolved. As Dahl (1998: 35) noted, "The exact nature of the relationship among socioeconomic modernization, democratization, and the creation of a democratic culture, is almost as puzzling today as it was a quarter century ago." Ever since Almond and Verba's (1963) pathbreaking civic culture study, students of political culture have argued that mass values play an important role in strengthening democracy. Influential writers have claimed that trust, tolerance, and feelings of efficacy represent "civic virtues" that enable democratic institutions to function effectively (Lasswell, 1958b; Sniderman, 1975; Putnam, 1993; Gibson, 1997; Inglehart, 1997; Pettigrew, 1998; Dalton, 2000; Newton, 2001; Norris, 2002). Likewise, Eckstein (1966) and Eckstein et al. (1996) argue that a democratic system will become stable only if people have internalized democratic norms and practice them in their daily relationships (see also Nevitte, 1996; and for an overview of the literature, see Sullivan and Transue, 1999).[6]

---

[6] The basic assumptions of the political culture approach go back to Montesquieu (1989 [1748]) and to Aristotle, both of whom argued that a society's institutions reflect the specific "virtues"

The basic claim of the political culture school is that political institutions and mass values must be congruent in order to produce stable and effective regimes. Thus, an authoritarian regime is unlikely to function effectively if it is under strong pressure from social forces that seek to institutionalize human autonomy, choice, and self-expression. Citizens who strongly value human self-expression tend to withdraw support from a regime that restricts their freedom of expression, forcing such regimes to bear the costs of "aspiration suppression" (Kuran, 1991), which grow as the public comes to place increasing emphasis on self-expression values. Growing suppression costs tend to make authoritarian rule less and less effective, leading to intraelite tensions and the growth of dissident groups and antiregime movements (see Welzel, 1999: 105–13; Paxton, 2002: 256–57). Similarly, liberal democracy is unlikely to be consolidated or to operate effectively if it exists in a culture dominated by survival values, which subordinate human freedom to social conformity and state authority. Under such conditions, charismatic leaders find it easy to foment threat perceptions among the public, to nourish social group pressures, and to foster compliance with authoritarian rule – even to the point that people support the abolition of their own liberties.

The evidence shown in Figures 7.1 and 7.2 seems to confirm these propositions: the extent to which formal democracy is present – and, even more so, the extent to which democracy is effective – largely depends on how strongly the public emphasizes self-expression values. To be precise, across a sample of seventy-three societies from the second to fourth Values Surveys, cross-national variation in self-expression values explains 52 percent of the variation in formal democracy and 80 percent of the variation in effective democracy. Given the temporal order of the variables involved, with self-expression values measured from two to twelve years *before* the two versions of democracy, one would need very strong additional evidence to interpret this linkage as reflecting the causal impact of democracy on values.

Confronted with the evidence in Figures 7.1 and 7.2, what arguments might a scholar who is convinced that democratic institutions cause prodemocratic values invoke in order to defend this claim? One line of reasoning would be to argue that these two figures do not control for the fact that self-expression values are themselves shaped by the prior existence of democracy, so that the effect that these values seem to have on subsequent democracy simply reflects democracy's

that prevail among its citizens. Tocqueville (1994 [1837]), in his study of early American democracy, reached a similar conclusion: the functioning of institutions in the United States reflected the "civic spirit" of its people. Herodotus and Thucydides established this idea much earlier in their discussions of the cultural differences between the Greek and Persian peoples and between the peoples of Athens and Sparta, arguing that the contrasting virtues that these societies emphasized accounted for the distinctive characteristics of their polities. Thus, the insight that political systems reflect the prevailing values of their publics has been recognized since political analysis began; its relevance continued to be recognized by modern political scientists such as Almond and Verba (1963), who introduced it into empirical research. This insight's persistence over time reflects the fact that it is an enduring part of reality.

autocorrelation over time. Accordingly, if one controls for prior democracy, the impact of self-expression values on subsequent democracy would disappear (as the following chapter demonstrates, this does not happen).

We test these and other alternative interpretations using quantitative techniques in Chapter 8. In this chapter, we develop the substantive arguments concerning why it is more plausible that the dominant causal direction in the relation between human values and democratic institutions runs from values to institutions rather than the reverse.

One way to explain the strong linkage between mass self-expression values and democratic institutions would be to assume that prodemocratic values are *caused* by the presence of democracy, emerging through "habituation" or "institutional learning" from living under democratic institutions (Rustow, 1970; Muller and Seligson, 1994; Jackman and Miller, 1998). In other words, democracy makes people tolerant, trusting, and happy and instills postmaterialist aspirations for civil and political liberty. This interpretation is appealing and suggests that we have a quick fix for most of the world's problems: adopt a democratic constitution and live happily ever after.

Unfortunately, the experience of most of the Soviet successor states does not support this interpretation. Since their dramatic move toward democracy in 1991, the people of most of these societies have *not* become more trusting, more tolerant, happier, or more postmaterialist (Inglehart and Baker, 2000). As Figures 7.1 and 7.2 demonstrate, Russia and the eastern group of ex-communist countries (Albania, Armenia, Azerbaijan, Belarus, Bosnia-Herzegovina, Bulgaria, Georgia, Macedonia, Moldova, Romania, Serbia-Montenegro, and Ukraine) rank even lower on self-expression values than *any* of the Islamic countries for which we have data, and far lower than the more advanced Islamic societies such as Turkey or Iran. This is not uniformly true of ex-communist countries: some of the western group of ex-communist societies (especially East Germany, the Czech Republic, Slovakia, Croatia, and Slovenia) show relatively strong emphasis on self-expression values – indeed, slightly higher than the public of such earlier-established democracies as Portugal. These are prosperous societies in which the postcommunist transition went relatively smoothly. But virtually all of the Soviet successor states show lower levels of emphasis on self-expression values than most Islamic societies, despite the fact that their publics are living under democratic institutions that are absent in all of the Islamic countries except Turkey. Whether democracy takes root seems to depend on the strength of self-expression values far more than on simple habituation through living under democratic institutions. Although the extent to which a prodemocratic culture is present varies greatly from one society to another, no cultural zone seems immune to pressures for democracy. Despite the presence of "Asian values," or an Islamic cultural heritage, the emergence of postindustrial society is conducive to rising emphasis on self-expression, which in turn seems to bring rising mass demands for democracy.

Even the best-designed institutions need a compatible mass culture. Institutions cannot function well unless the public internalizes a set of norms consistent with these institutions. This is particularly true of democratic institutions, which depend on mass acceptance and support. Indeed, the democratic institutions of one of the world's most effective and stable democracies, Great Britain, exist *only* as a set of informal norms, without a written constitution. If one had to choose between a superbly written democratic constitution that did not have mass acceptance and a set of democratic norms that had never been enacted as laws but were deeply internalized by the people, the latter would clearly be preferable. Actual practices differ dramatically from institutional norms when a society's prevailing values contradict them, rendering them irrelevant. This is one of the most fundamental insights of the political culture approach: one cannot assume that making democracy work is simply a matter of having the right constitutional arrangements.

Illustrative Contrasts

The tendency for democracy to go with high levels of socioeconomic development has become one of the most extensively validated statistical linkages in the social sciences (see Lipset, 1959a; L. Diamond, 1992; Boix and Stokes, 2003). Nevertheless, various critics have argued that the modernization thesis does not hold up, pointing to deviant cases to support their claim: for example, it is frequently pointed out that India is a democracy although it is a low-income society; and conversely, Singapore and various oil-exporting societies are rich but not democratic. A closer examination of these cases shows that they do not contradict modernization theory.

Modernization theorists have viewed socioeconomic development as a broad syndrome of changes in people's living conditions, involving the reduction of poverty, rising educational levels, and the diversification of social relations, all of which tend to make people more autonomous in their daily activities. The oil-exporting countries became rich through rent-seeking economies where wealth is highly concentrated in the hands of the ruling elite; this process did not involve modernization and did not make people more autonomous in shaping their lives. The dominance of oil revenues in these societies has not led to the rise of individual autonomy for the masses; it has made people more dependent on state-controlled oil monopolies. Hence, the liberating effects that modernization produces are largely absent in the oil-exporting countries, contributing only weakly to emancipative values and democratic institutions, which is exactly what modernization theory suggests.

Singapore is a seemingly deviant case in the other direction. For forty years, it has had the world's highest rate of economic growth and has emerged from poverty to become a high-income society. Unlike the oil-exporting states, Singapore *has* modernized. In the short run, its remarkable economic success helped legitimate its restrictions on political competition. But in the long run it is producing a social infrastructure that should give rise to growing demands for democracy. Singapore is currently classified as "partly free" by Freedom

House. We predict that Singapore will fully adopt democracy within the ten years following this book's publication.

Conversely, India is indeed remarkably democratic for its level of development, and a rich literature has been devoted to explaining why it is such a striking exception to the overall pattern: among the sixty-four societies that the World Bank defines as "low income," only two, including India, are defined as "free" by Freedom House; conversely, among the fifty-one "high-income" societies, almost all are "free." India illustrates the fact that, although formal democracy is much more probable at high levels of development than at low ones, this relationship is probabilistic, not deterministic. In addition, although India is a striking exception insofar as it is a poor country with a working democratic constitution, it has been questioned whether India is a genuinely liberal democracy whose leaders allow people to practice effectively the civil and political rights to which the constitution theoretically entitles them (see Heller, 2000). In fact, India's score on effective democracy is about where one would expect it to be on the basis of its level of economic development or its public's emphasis on self-expression values (see Figure 7.2).

The fact that democracy failed to survive in Weimar Germany, although it was a highly industrialized country, is also sometimes raised to refute the modernization thesis, but this argument misses the point. As a result of the hyperinflation of the early 1920s and the Great Depression of the 1930s, Germany suffered an economic disaster more severe than virtually any other country in the world (Vermeil, 1956: 120; James, 1986: 311–28). Unemployment was severe in the United States at the time, but only half as widespread as in Germany, where it was compounded by a prior hyperinflation that wiped out the life savings of almost the entire middle class. Economic disaster, not economic prosperity, led to the collapse of democracy in Weimar Germany (James, 1986: 45–48; Lieberman, 1998: 184–94).

Under severe existential pressures, prodemocratic values that emphasize human self-expression cannot take root. Existential insecurity is conducive to emphasis on survival values, driving people to seek the protection offered by strong leaders, rigid authority, and group discipline. This enhances the appeal of charismatic extremists who play on feelings of anxiety and threats from foreign or domestic enemies. Weimar Germany had inherited an authoritarian culture from the militaristic Prussian-dominated society that existed before World War I. Long-term economic prosperity might have nourished a sense of existential security and human autonomy, from which values supportive of democracy might have developed, but unfortunately events moved in exactly the opposite direction. Recurrent economic crises reinforced Germany's traditionally authoritarian culture, preventing the emergence of emancipative values (Conradt, 1980; Dalton, 1988: 3–6). Accordingly, Weimar was a "democracy without democrats" (Bracher, 1971 [1955]).

Cultural patterns can change, as is illustrated by the contrasting outcomes of Germany's two attempts to install democracy, after World War I and after

World War II. Democracy did not fail in Weimar Germany simply because of badly designed institutions. The 5 percent hurdle for parliamentary representation and the weaker presidency adopted after World War II were good ideas, but constitutional factors such as these were not what determined the failure of democracy in the Weimar Republic and the successful emergence of stable democracy under the Bonn Republic. If Weimar had enjoyed an economic miracle like Bonn's, Hitler would almost certainly not have come to power: even the limited prosperity of the late 1920s had virtually eliminated the Nazi Party as a serious contender, but the Great Depression brought it back with a vengeance. Conversely, if Bonn had endured the Great Depression, it is unlikely that the gradual but steady intergenerational shift toward a democratic political culture would have occurred, as has been documented in the literature (Boynton and Loewenberg, 1973; K. Baker et al., 1981). The empirical evidence suggests that a prolonged period of economic prosperity was needed in order to generate the sense of existential security and autonomy from which self-expression values arise. Unfortunately, events moved in exactly the opposite direction during the Weimar era, giving extremist leaders an opportunity to foment the xenophobia and antidemocratic feelings that helped Hitler to seize power in 1933.

By the same token, Germany's postwar democracy succeeded not simply because it had a well-designed constitution. Bonn started with better conditions because the Nazi system had culminated in unequivocal disaster that discredited fascism; and the dismal performance of Soviet-type socialism in East Germany helped to discredit the other main authoritarian alternative. But this alone did not produce the emancipative values that provide intrinsic support for democracy. Quite the contrary, Bonn initially had an antidemocratic culture similar to that of Weimar (see Almond and Verba, 1963; Conradt, 1980; Dalton, 1988: 8). The key factor needed to transform this authoritarian culture into a democratic culture was a prolonged period of economic prosperity that generated a sense of existential security and human autonomy. The contrast was striking: in Weimar, recurrent economic disasters hindered efforts to develop a democratic culture; in Bonn, sustained economic growth led to a democratic transformation.

In comparing Weimar and Bonn, the differences in existential living conditions are more fundamental than the differences in constitutional details. The Weimar constitution was considered a model of institutional design at the time. Democracy would certainly have survived in a post-1945 Germany equipped with the Weimar constitution – and the Weimar Republic would probably have crumbled even with the Bonn constitution.

These contrasting cases illustrate a sequence in which existential constraints nurture a culture of social control and civic conformism, dominated by survival values. Such a situation does not preclude the emergence of liberal democracy, as the Indian example shows, but it makes it much less likely. People absorbed in sheer physical survival tend to place less emphasis on human emancipation, so that they more readily accept – and sometimes even demand – restrictions on the civil and political liberties that define democracy. Conversely, socioeconomic development reduces existential constraints on human autonomy by increasing people's economic, cognitive, and social resources. This tends to be reflected in a culture of self-expression that views democracy as the form of government best suited to maximize autonomous choice.

Putnam (1993) has presented interesting evidence of how cultural factors influence democratic institutions. Northern and southern Italy live under the same political institutions, but these institutions work far more effectively in northern Italy than they do in southern Italy – reflecting the more deeply rooted civic culture of the more urban, commercial North. Early sociologists, such as Émile Durkheim (1988 [1893]), Ferdinand Tönnies (1955 [1887]), and Georg Simmel (1984 [1908]), pointed out that market-based urban societies diversify human transactions, extend interpersonal exchange beyond intimate bonds, and enhance the importance of contractual relations against clientelistic relations (see also Granovetter, 1973; Coleman, 1990). Contractual relations are largely horizontal. They cut through vertical clientelistic bonds and bridge social groups; they diminish an individual's exposure to the conformity pressure of close-knit groups; they lower an individual's dependence on external authority and, by doing so, reduce social constraints on human autonomy and choice. These tendencies, in turn, tend to promote individual self-esteem, generalized interpersonal trust, and other civic virtues that are conducive to democracy (Dahl, 1973: 33–47). These features of a horizontal middle-class society are linked with more widely dispersed resources and tend to produce the bridging sort of social capital linked with self-expression values.

Southern Italy, by contrast, was not a market-based middle-class society. Even today, much of southern Italy shows many features of a society dominated by hierarchical patron-client relations, with mafialike clan structures. These structures are linked with scarce resources, which impose rigid constraints on human autonomy, pressing people into closely knit networks held together by strict group discipline and governed by rigid authority patterns. As Banfield (1958) has argued, the functioning of such vertical societies undermines civic virtues, nourishing "amoral familism." Existential constraints on human autonomy are reflected in an emphasis on conformist survival values. Existential insecurity fuels threat perceptions, leading people to have closed minds, with low tolerance and little trust of outsiders (Rokeach, 1960); under such conditions, people seek order, discipline, and strong authority (see Lerner, 1958; Inkeles and Smith, 1974).

The Italian regional governments set up in the 1970s functioned much more effectively in northern Italy than in southern Italy. This contrast clearly does not reflect institutional differences because exactly the same institutions were adopted throughout Italy at the same time. The contrasting performance of these institutions reflects regional cultural differences that can be traced to different existential constraints on human autonomy, which are based on fundamentally different socioeconomic conditions.

This interpretation was foreshadowed to some extent by earlier versions of modernization theory. When Lerner (1958), Lipset (1959a), Dahl (1973: 79), and Huntington (1991: 69) try to explain *why* economic development is conducive to democracy, each of them refers to the intervening role of mass values: socioeconomic development is conducive to democracy because it tends to shape mass values in ways that make them less compatible with autocracy and more functional for democracy. None of these writers pursued this argument farther because when they were writing, survey data from a wide range of societies was not available to enable them to test this thesis, but the logic of this argument is so strong that it has been articulated repeatedly.

Clearly, becoming rich does not, in itself, create democracy. If it did, Kuwait would be a long-established democracy. There must be some intermediate mechanism, such as cultural change. The logic of this argument is that as people emerge from the struggle for sheer subsistence, they become economically, cognitively, and socially more independent. This increases people's sense of autonomy, leading them to place increasing emphasis on freedom of choice and eventually to demand the civil and political liberties that constitute democracy – even if people have no experience with democracy so far. Socioeconomic development widens the repertory of people's possible actions, giving higher priority to self-expression values. Rising self-expression values put institutions under increasing pressure to provide freedom of choice, eroding the legitimacy of authoritarian rule.

The linkage between socioeconomic development, rising self-expression values, and the implementation of civil and political liberties can be seen among individuals. Survey research has repeatedly shown that people with higher incomes and education are most likely to emphasize political self-expression and are most inclined to practice their liberties through political participation (Inglehart, 1977; Verba, Nie, and Kim, 1978; Barnes, Kaase, et al. 1979; Brint, 1984; Scarbrough, 1995; Nevitte, 1996; Dalton, 2001; Welzel, 2002; Norris, 2002). As Verba et al. (1978: 73) noted: "In all nations, people tend to convert socioeconomic resources into participation." This linkage between socioeconomic resources, self-expression values, and the practice of democratic liberties is not only present at the individual level. It exists at the societal level as well, as Tables 7.1 and 7.2 demonstrate: in societies where people have more socioeconomic resources, self-expression values are more widespread than in societies where people have fewer resources. And in societies in which self-expression values are more widespread, civil and political liberties are more strongly institutionalized and these liberties are more genuinely respected by the elites. Rising emphasis on self-expression values implies a shift of legitimacy from authoritarian regimes to democratic regimes because only democracies provide the freedom that self-expression values demand. Thus, the shift from survival values to self-expression values favors democracy.

Elite-Focused and Institution-Focused Parochialism

The linkage between socioeconomic development, rising self-expression values, and democratic institutions is fundamental. Without recognizing this linkage, the emergence and strengthening of democracy cannot be understood. But many researchers dealing with the Third Wave of democratization have not only overlooked this linkage but insisted that the emergence of democracies is not linked with broader social forces, such as socioeconomic development or rising self-expression values. This tendency is illustrated by Karl and Schmitter (1991: 270), who claim that "Searching for the causes of democracy, from probabilistic associations with economic, social, cultural, psychological or international factors has not so far yielded any general law of democratization, nor is it likely to do so in the near future, despite the recent proliferation of cases." This claim is demonstrably false, as the next chapter will show. Its advocates and many others (see O'Donnell and Schmitter, 1986; DiPalma, 1990; Marks, 1992; Przeworski, 1992; Casper and Taylor, 1996) claim to have overcome the social determinism that they see in modernization theory, but they have replaced it with something equally problematic: elite-centered or institution-centered determinism (for a critique, see Foweraker and Landman, 1997; Gasiorowski and Power, 1998).

Elite-centered determinism implies that the emergence and survival of political institutions is determined by the behavior of elites, particularly their institutional choices: "If political leaders...are understood to be the founders of democracy, then they also function, after that initial breakthrough, as its sustainers or its underminers" (Bunce, 2000: 709). This claim assumes that power holders are independent from the values and beliefs of the population they rule (see also Higley and Burton, 1989; Higley and Gunther, 1992). In this view, elite behavior is autonomous from mass influences. Ironically, this assumes that mass preferences really don't matter in democracy – when the whole point of democracy is that they *do*. Similarly, institution-focused determinism maintains that the failure and success of democracies depends on the enactment of suitable institutional arrangements rather than on broader social forces (see Mainwaring, O'Donnell, and Valenzuela, 1992; Linz and Valenzuela, 1994; Lijphart and Waisman, 1996). These elitist and institutionalist accounts view effective democracy as a matter of enacting the right institutional arrangements by enlightened elites. The public is reduced to a passive spectator.

Advocates of these approaches assume that well-functioning democratic institutions are a precondition rather than a consequence of a mass culture that supports democracy (Muller and Seligson, 1994; Jackman and Miller, 1998; Seligson, 2002). Rustow (1970), for instance, claims that a civic culture that supports democracy cannot emerge in a nondemocratic system; when a democratic mass culture emerges, it results from "habituation" to previously established democratic institutions. Habituation can only occur if suitable institutional arrangements are enacted, so that elections, government formation, and legislation function without friction. People will then learn to appreciate these institutions and internalize their norms: effective democracy is primarily a matter of institutional arrangements.

Similarly, in a critique of Putnam (1993) and Inglehart (1997), Jackman and Miller (1998: 53–57) claim that a prodemocratic civic culture is "endogenous" to well-functioning democratic institutions: a mass culture that supports democracy is produced by well-functioning democratic institutions. Economic development might help to produce prodemocratic values, but only if democratic institutions are already in place. According to this argument, mass values that support democracy can only emerge in societies that have democratic institutions: it rules out the possibility that democratic mass values can emerge within authoritarian societies.

This assumption is demonstrably false. It is contradicted by the fact that in modern history demands for political self-expression, representation, and suffrage arose before modern democracy was established in response to rising socioeconomic resources that made people economically, cognitively, and socially more independent (Markoff, 1996). Mass support for democracy did not result from preexisting democracy – it *led* to democracy. The very origin of democracy was public resistance to autocracy (Finer, 1999). Representation and suffrage evolved through the liberal revolutions of the seventeenth and eighteenth centuries. These revolutions were led by autonomous social groups: the commercial middle classes of free farmers and merchants. These groups were driven by emancipative values and held that their existential independence was a matter of "natural" rights – rights that had to be defended against attempts of central authorities to impose taxes on people without their consent: "no taxation without representation," as it was termed at the Boston Tea Party in 1773 (see Downing, 1992; Tilly, 1997).

Moreover, as the following chapter demonstrates, a generational shift toward growing mass emphasis on self-expression values arose within authoritarian societies, from Poland to Taiwan, and led to mass demands for democracy *before* democratic institutions were adopted. Both the historical invention of modern democracy and its recent spread have emancipative roots, linked with the liberal revolutions of the eighteenth century and the liberation movements of the Third Wave (Markoff, 1996). The very essence of democracy is that it reflects people power and not simply the constitutional choices of enlightened elites (Foweraker and Landman, 1997). Most democratization processes in history succeeded because they were supported by mass-based liberation movements and freedom campaigns. Democratization attracts ordinary people because it empowers them with civil and political liberties. This goal is most important to people who are motivated by emancipative values that emphasize human self-expression. Self-expression values in turn emerge naturally when diminishing existential constraints nourish a sense of human autonomy. This process can and does take place even in authoritarian systems. And it makes people intrinsically supportive of the idea of democracy, even if they have no experience with its practice.

In some cases, democratic institutions were installed as the result of wars and not of modernization. In Weimar Germany, postwar Germany, postwar Italy, and postwar Japan, democratic institutions were imposed on the population by foreign armies. But none of these "merely accepted" postwar democracies became an effective democracy unless the public began to support it intrinsically because of rising emancipative values that emphasize human self-expression.

Externally imposed democratization is not typical of the Third Wave (nor was it typical of the invention of democracy). Aside from Grenada, all cases of Third Wave democratization were propelled by emancipative forces *within* societies. As we will demonstrate, mass self-expression values motivated these emancipative forces. This allows for two hypotheses. First, rising self-expression values facilitate the adoption of democracy, if the transition is led by internal forces rather than being externally imposed. Second, regardless of which way democracy emerged, rising self-expression values are necessary to transform the new democratic institutions into a genuinely effective democracy. Formal democracy can be imposed even when self-expression values are not widespread (although this is unlikely); but unless mass values emphasizing human self-expression are widespread, genuinely effective democracy is almost impossible to emerge, as we will demonstrate.

The major waves of democratization reflect powerful mechanisms of transnational diffusion (Huntington, 1991). This was particularly apparent when democracy spread to country after country in the Third Wave of democratization in Latin America, East Asia, and Eastern Europe during the 1980s and 1990s (Starr, 1991; L. Diamond, 1993a). The recent spread of democracy was clearly facilitated by the fact that a successful working model already existed, and people did not have to invent democracy anew. But diffusion did not spread uniformly across the world. Some societies were far more receptive than others, which was largely determined by internal factors, such as the presence of social forces emphasizing human self-expression. Nearly all of the high-income societies (except rich oil-exporting countries) already were democratic by 1989, so almost all of the democracies that emerged since then were middle-income societies, as defined by the World Bank. Almost none of the new democracies emerged in low-income societies (even if one counts Nepal and Mongolia as democracies). Similarly, within what was once Yugoslavia, Slovenia adopted democratic institutions earlier and more thoroughly than Croatia, while Croatia did so earlier and to a greater extent than Serbia – reflecting their different levels of economic development and their different receptivity to democracy. As we will demonstrate, the strength of self-expression values plays a major role in shaping a society's receptiveness to democracy.

Modernization and Regime Change

The thesis that socioeconomic development is conducive to democracy was an established claim of modernization theory: "the more well-to-do a nation, the better the chance that it sustains democracy" (Lipset, 1959a: 32). So far, however, only a few quantitative studies have dealt with the impact of socioeconomic development on *transitions* to democracy (see Hannan and Carroll, 1981; Burkhart and Lewis-Beck, 1994; Muller and Seligson, 1994;

Inglehart, 1997: chap. 6; Przeworski and Limongi, 1997; Welzel and Inglehart, 2001; Welzel, 2002). Most quantitative studies analyze *levels* of democracy at a given time or the number of years under democratic rule.[7] These analytical designs leave it uncertain whether socioeconomic development only sustains existing democracies or whether it also promotes the emergence of new democracies.

Recognizing this difference, Przeworski and Limongi (1997) focused on the emergence of democracies. Using a global sample, they classified political regimes as either democratic or autocratic and then identified all cases of regime changes from autocracy to democracy between 1950 and 1990. Their major conclusion is that socioeconomic development may be conducive to the survival of existing democracies but not to the establishment of new democracies (pp. 176–77). The authors claim that this finding invalidates modernization theory, confirming the elite-focused approach of O'Donnell and Schmitter (1986) according to which democratization is "an outcome of actions, not just conditions" (p. 176).

To reach this conclusion, Przeworski and Limongi compare regime changes from autocracy to democracy across seven categories of per capita income. They find that autocracies in the richest category of countries are not more likely to switch to democracy than are autocracies in poorer countries (p. 160) – which they interpret as disproving the claim that socioeconomic development is conducive to transitions to democracy.

This conclusion is false. It ignores the huge differences in regime stability between rich and poor countries. Poor countries tend to be much more unstable than rich ones, so they have far more regime changes in *both* directions. Poor countries show relatively large numbers of shifts toward democracy simply because they are unstable, but these changes are more than offset by even larger numbers of shifts *away* from democracy.

It is crucial to measure the extent to which regime changes in one direction are offset by changes in the *opposite* direction, in order to reach any meaningful conclusion about the impact of economic development on the process of democratization. The relevant question is whether economic development produces more changes toward democracy than toward autocracy. Modernization theory implies that economic development does exactly this.

Using Przeworski and Limongi's own data (p. 162, table 2), we calculated the balance between shifts toward democracy and shifts toward autocracy – dividing the number of changes toward democracy by the number of changes toward autocracy. The higher this ratio is, the more heavily shifts toward democracy outweigh shifts toward autocracy. We calculated this ratio for each of Przeworski and Limongi's seven income groups. The results of this exercise produce an entirely different picture from the one they present.

---

[7] More-recent studies include Arat (1991), Hadenius (1992), Helliwell (1993), Lipset et al. (1993), Burkhart and Lewis-Beck (1994), Barro (1997), Vanhanen (1997), Gasiorowski and Power (1998), and Boix and Stokes (2003).

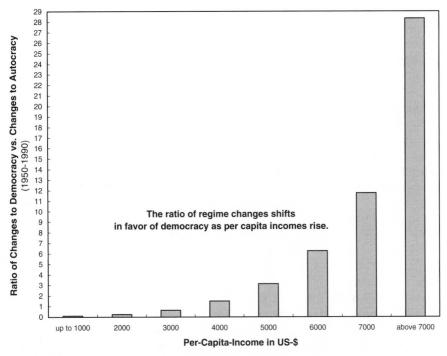

FIGURE 7.3. The balance of regime changes along rising income groups.

Figure 7.3 demonstrates that the balance of regime changes shifts strongly and monotonically in favor of democracy as income rises. In countries with per capita incomes less than $1,000, changes toward democracy emerge only one-tenth as often as changes toward autocracy. But in countries with per capita incomes greater than $7,000, changes toward democracy occur twenty-eight times as often as changes toward autocracy. Each $1,000 unit increase in per capita income roughly *doubles* the proportion of changes toward democracy, in relation to changes in the opposite direction. Thus, with rising income levels, regime selection increasingly favors democracy.

Taking the balance of regime changes into account reverses Przeworski and Limongi's conclusions: socioeconomic development does contribute to the emergence of democracy and it does so dramatically. Socioeconomic development is an evolutionary force that acts on the regime selection process, introducing a strong bias in favor of democracy. Working from a different perspective, Boix and Stokes (2003) provide another convincing refutation of Przeworski and Limongi's findings. Democratization reflects societal conditions and not simply the choices of elites. As Geddes (1999: 117) puts it, "Przeworski and Limongi interpret their findings as a challenge to modernization theory, although it seems to me a revisionist confirmation – in fact, the strongest empirical confirmation ever."

The Limits of Socioeconomic Modernization

As we have pointed out, socioeconomic development is only part of the story. Getting rich does not automatically make a country democratic; if it did, the oil-exporting countries would be model democracies (see M. Ross, 2001). Instead, we argue that the impact of socioeconomic development on democracy works primarily through its tendency to give rise to cultural changes that place increasing emphasis on human emancipation and self-expression.

The choices of elites and international events, such as the end of the Cold War, are also unquestionably important: though a number of East European countries had already developed the mass-level preconditions for democratization, these mass preferences were thwarted as long as the threat of intervention by the Red Army was present (Huntington, 1984). But as soon as that threat was withdrawn, internal societal factors that had seemed irrelevant, such as mass values, suddenly became crucial elements in deciding whether democracy would emerge.

As we have seen (see Tables 7.1 and 7.2 and Figures 7.1 and 7.2), socioeconomic development, self-expression values, and democratic institutions are closely linked with each other. The evidence is based on strong zero-order correlations, but a causal interpretation requires more-conclusive tests considering the temporal order of causes and effects and controlling for alternative explanatory variables. Inglehart (1997), for instance, demonstrated a strong correlation between self-expression values in 1989–91 and the number of years that a country experienced under democratic rule since 1920. He interpreted this relationship as reflecting the causal impact of self-expression values on democratic institutions, arguing that cross-national differences in self-expression values are relatively enduring over time, so the differences found in 1990 probably give a good indication of cultural differences that already existed during the period from 1920 to 1990. But this crucial assumption could not be demonstrated because survey data from earlier than 1981 did not exist. The following chapter deals with this problem.

Although Inglehart's theory focuses on cultural change, his argument here emphasizes the *persistence* of culture, which is not at all contradictory. With evolving phenomena such as culture, persistence and change are two sides of the same coin. The value systems of societies tend to change gradually, as we have seen, but the *relative* positions of given societies remain constant over long periods of time. Culture is an inertial phenomenon characterized by accumulated change that proceeds steadily but slowly. Consequently, a given society's starting point tends to be reflected in its subsequent location. Evolving phenomena such as culture typically show such a *combination* of change and persistence. As we saw in Chapter 1, starting from different levels most of the societies included in the Values Survey have moved slowly toward increasing emphasis on self-expression values, except where economic stagnation or collapse has sustained the persistence of survival values. Insofar as socioeconomic development takes place, steady cultural change is the prevailing pattern. Nevertheless, the various countries' relative levels of self-expression values are remarkably stable: we find a correlation of r = .89 between levels of self-expression values in 1981 and 1989–91 among the twenty-one countries surveyed at both time points. Similarly, the correlation between societies' self-expression values in 1989–91 and 1995–97 is r = .94 among the thirty countries surveyed at both time points. The inertia inherent in cultural change tends to perpetuate cross-national variation in values even while change occurs.

Conclusion

This chapter discussed deviant cases used in attempts to refute the thesis that socioeconomic development fuels cultural changes that favor the emergence, survival, and strengthening of democracy. Although deviant cases are important, and demonstrate that economic development is not the only factor involved, they in no way refute the fact that there is an extremely strong probabilistic relationship between development and democracy. Similarly, a discussion of Germany's two attempts to install democracy after World Wars I and II illustrates the importance of the contrast between the economic disasters that led to the failure of democracy in the Weimar Republic and the economic miracle that contributed to the success of democracy in the Bonn Republic.

The early limited versions of modern democracy derived from civic resistance to absolute state power in the liberal revolutions of the seventeenth and eighteenth centuries. Thus, prodemocratic cultural forces initially emerged under authoritarian societies – which flatly contradicts the claim that democratic institutions must already be in place in order to produce a culture that supports them. Also, in the Third Wave transitions broadly based mass support for democracy had emerged within authoritarian societies, and mass action played an important role in the transitions to democracy.

There is no logical reason why – and no mechanism for *how* – the sheer presence of democratic institutions could instill self-expression values in people. These values reflect an emphasis on human autonomy that is nurtured by favorable socioeconomic conditions. These values do not necessarily become widespread under democratic institutions (as the Weimar case illustrates), and they have frequently emerged within authoritarian societies, in both early and recent history. The strong empirical linkage that we find between mass self-expression values and democratic institutions seems to reflect the fact that self-expression values are conducive to democratic institutions – precisely the type of institutions that provide the civil and political liberties that self-expression values emphasize.

Przeworski and Limongi's analysis, though widely believed to invalidate modernization theory, does not hold up under closer scrutiny. Their own data demonstrate that the balance between changes toward autocracy and changes toward democracy shifts dramatically in favor of democracy with rising levels of development. High levels of modernization confer an increasingly strong selective advantage on democracy. Modernization by itself does not install democracy, for modernization is only an impersonal process with no collective actors involved. Some intervening motivational factor is necessary to produce the social forces and collective actions that work in favor of democratization. Self-expression values constitute this factor: they motivate collective actions directed toward democratization (as Chapter 9 demonstrates).

In short, we argue that: (1) socioeconomic development brings increasingly favorable existential conditions; (2) this gives rise to mass self-expression values, which place a high priority on human freedom and choice; (3) these values mobilize social forces that seek the adoption of democracy, if it is not yet in place, and favor the survival and deepening of democracy, if it is already in place. The next chapter tests these hypotheses empirically.

8

The Causal Link between Democratic Values
and Democratic Institutions
Empirical Analyses

Institutional versus Cultural Explanations

The preceding chapter discussed the causal linkage between mass values and democratic institutions from the perspective of a theory of human development. This chapter tests these theoretical expectations empirically, using measures of democratic institutions and mass values from scores of societies. The strong link between mass values and democratic institutions has been explained both institutionally and culturally – and the two interpretations have radically different implications.

The institutional explanation argues that living under democratic institutions causes prodemocratic values to emerge among the public. The cultural explanation reverses the causal arrow, arguing that prodemocratic mass values are conducive to the emergence and survival of democratic institutions. Conceivably, there could be reciprocal effects in the relationship between democratic institutions and democratic mass values, in which case the key question is whether the causal arrow is stronger in one direction than the other. The institutional explanation holds that a society's prior democratic experience has the stronger causal effect on its mass culture. The cultural explanation claims that a society's mass values have the stronger causal effect on its subsequent democratic performance.

The previous chapter outlined some theoretical reasons why the cultural explanation of the relationship between mass values and democracy is more plausible than the institutional explanation. In this chapter we examine a broad base of evidence, using quantitative analyses to test whether the empirical evidence supports the cultural or the institutional explanation. Our analysis focuses on "liberal" democracy because our theory implies that human development is inherently linked with the liberating aspects of democracy. We proceed in four steps.

First, we examine the extent to which the civil and political rights that constitute liberal democracy are formally institutionalized. The Third Wave of democratization spread liberal democracy into a number of new countries.

Focusing on the changes that occurred during this period makes it possible to carry out a longitudinal test of the relation between self-expression values and liberal democracy. We can test whether self-expression values measured *during* the Third Wave had a stronger effect on liberal democracy *after* the Third Wave, or whether these values were mainly the result of how much liberal democracy was present *before* the Third Wave.

Second, we address one of the fundamental – but never tested – assumptions of political culture theory: the congruence thesis. According to this thesis, political institutions are unlikely to endure unless they are consistent with the underlying mass culture. Consequently, shifts toward democracy will reflect how much incongruence was present between mass demands for democracy and the absence of democratic institutions: the more strongly mass demands for democracy exceed the extent to which democratic institutions were present, the more likely it is that a shift toward democracy will occur. We also test the converse thesis, that democratic regimes will not persist if they are linked with a predominantly authoritarian mass culture. We measure both types of incongruence and test whether it helps to explain the shifts toward democracy that occurred during the Third Wave.

Third, the institutionalization of civil and political liberties is a necessary component of liberal democracy, but it is not sufficient to make democracy genuinely effective. Liberal democracy is effective only if elites exercise state power in ways that respect and reflect people's rights. Effective democracy must be based on the rule of law (Rose, 2001). Hence, we use measures of law-abiding elite behavior to locate societies on a continuum that reflects varying degrees of *effective* democracy. This continuum indicates the extent to which civil and political liberties are formally institutionalized *and* effectively respected by political elites. We then use this measure to test whether prior self-expression values or a society's democratic tradition plays the main role in shaping the extent to which a country has effective democracy.

Fourth, since the distinction between formal democracy and effective democracy only makes sense if there *are* significant discrepancies between these two versions of liberal democracy, we examine this discrepancy directly. We find that self-expression values operate as a social force that helps reduce the gap between formal and effective democracy.

These analyses test the dependence of liberal democracy on self-expression values from four different perspectives. And all four tests point to the same conclusion, indicating that self-expression values have a major causal impact on liberal democracy.

Defining Democracy

How one measures democracy partly depends on one's theoretical focus (D. Collier and Adcock, 1999). Our approach – the concept of human development – focuses on freedom of choice. From this point of view, the liberal aspect of democracy is most important because civil and political liberties entitle people to exert free choices in their private and public actions (Berlin, 1969; Rose, 1995, 2001; Sen, 1999). Civil and political liberties empower citizens to make autonomous choices in shaping their lives. Throughout history, the quest for civil and political liberties has provided a major motivation for people to struggle for democracy, seeking political self-determination (Macpherson, 1977; Markoff, 1996; Foweraker and Landman, 1997; Shapiro, 2003). Mass involvement in liberation movements and freedom campaigns is an essential element of democratization (Bernhard, 1993; Casper and Taylor, 1996; R. Collier, 1999; McAdam, Tarrow, and Tilly, 2001).

Civil and political liberties define the latitude for choice that people have to shape their lives according to their own values. Voting rights are a significant part of the story but only one part, so it would be inappropriate to focus narrowly on them. Electoral democracy can easily be abused to hide severe deficiencies in the actual practice of civil and political liberties. Under the formal structure of an electoral democracy, authoritarian mechanisms can determine what actually happens, as is true in many of the Soviet successor states (Rose, 2001). People power does not lie solely in voting rights and universal suffrage but requires a broader set of civil and political liberties. According to Isaiah Berlin (1969), these liberties include rights to private decision-making freedom ("negative" freedom *from* state authority) and rights to political decision-making freedom ("positive" freedom *over* state authority).

Przeworski and Limongi (1997) use a dichotomous classification that simply divides political regimes into democracies and nondemocracies. Apart from serious conceptual and methodological flaws (on this point, see the powerful critique by Elkins, 2000), this approach might be appropriate if one were merely interested in electoral democracy. For a country either does have or does not have freely elected representatives and governments (D. Collier and Adcock, 1999). But such binary simplicity does not apply to liberal democracy (Bollen and Paxton, 2000). Instead of being *entirely* present or absent, elements of liberal democracy are present or absent in varying *degrees*. There are huge differences in the extent to which the countries that would be dichotomously classified as nondemocracies actually implement or repress liberties. In a dichotomous classification, for instance, Singapore would be classified as a nondemocracy, equating it with North Korea, although virtually all observers would agree that North Korea represses civil and political liberties far more severely than Singapore. Liberal democracy is a matter of degree, spanning the continuum from the complete absence of civil and political liberties to their full presence. In liberal democracy, elections are only one important component among many.

We combine the Freedom House scores for civil and political liberties (Freedom House, 2002)[1] to measure the extent to which liberal democracy is

---

[1] Freedom House measures the presence of individual freedom on scales from 1 to 7 for "civil liberties" and "political rights." On both of the two freedom scales, 1 indicates the highest and 7 the lowest level of liberty. We reversed these scales so that higher figures indicate a larger set of liberties. Then we added both scales in order to create an overall index of liberal democracy,

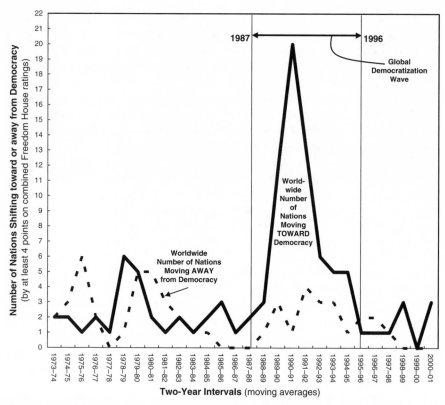

FIGURE 8.1. Shifts to and from democracy in the world as a whole, 1973–2001.

officially present – at least on paper. Although alternative measures exist, such as the Polity scores developed by Marshall and Jaggers (2000), we use the Freedom House scores because our theoretical perspective focuses on human choice. From this perspective, decision-making freedom and the rights protecting it are the most essential elements of democracy. Thus, the degree to which liberal democracy is formally present is measured on a scale of 0 to 12 as follows:

$$\text{Civil and Political Liberties}_t = (\text{Civil Liberties}_t + \text{Political Liberties}_t) - 2$$

(0 to 12 scale)   (1 to 7 scale)   (1 to 7 scale)

Tracking the Third Wave of Democratization

Using this measure of the formal existence of liberal democracy, Figure 8.1 shows when significant shifts toward and away from democracy occurred from

ranging from 0 to 12 (actually from 2 to 14, so we subtracted 2 to have 0 as the minimum). Then we standardized the maximum (12) to the value of 100 to provide a percentage scale of the level of liberal democracy. For the validity of the Freedom House measures and their strong correlations with alternative measures of democracy, see Bollen and Paxton (2000).

1972 to 2002. Separate trend lines show the number of countries moving toward more democracy (by gaining civil and political liberties) and the number of countries moving toward less democracy (by losing civil and political liberties) in a given year. Huntington (1991) dates the beginning of the Third Wave back to the mid-1970s when transitions to democracy occurred in Portugal, Spain, and Greece. But writing earlier – in 1984 – he did not detect a democratic trend; at that time, he answered the question "Will more countries become democratic?" with a no. Nevertheless, in his 1991 book he argues retrospectively that the transitions in Portugal, Spain, and Greece were the start of the Third Wave. In fact, these were precursors of a democratization wave that was still to come, as the evidence in Figure 8.1 indicates.

The empirical evidence in Figure 8.1 does not support Huntington's timing of the Third Wave. As it shows, up to 1987 changes toward more democracy in some countries were offset by changes toward *less* democracy in other countries, with an average of two to three regime changes per year in either direction. Thus, there was no global shift toward liberal democracy before 1987: the transitions to democracy in southern Europe in the 1970s were counterbalanced by changes in the opposite direction elsewhere. Other recent analyses point to the same conclusion (Kurzman, 1998).

Figure 8.1 shows no major worldwide shift toward more democracy until the late 1980s. But starting around 1987, a virtual "explosion of democratization" (Doorenspleet, 2000) took place within a period of eight years, establishing a major historical watershed between the levels of democracy before 1987 and after 1996.

Our analyses recognize this historically important period, analyzing the impact of values on democracy when favorable international conditions made transitions to democracy possible. Analyzing the numerous changes that occurred during this period makes it possible to carry out a broad-based test of the extent to which a prodemocratic culture leads to the emergence of democratic institutions, or whether democratic institutions produce a prodemocratic culture. We hypothesize that cultural factors shape levels of democracy more strongly than democratic institutions shape culture. This implies that given levels of self-expression values influence subsequent levels of democracy more strongly than previous levels of democracy influence given levels of self-expression values. Our analysis will focus on the global shift between the levels of democracy that were present before 1987 and the levels that were present after 1996. We will analyze the changes that occurred during this period, in scores of countries around the world. In order to dampen the effect of random fluctuations before 1987 and after 1996, we use the democracy levels during the six-year periods before and after these two dates, as our "before" and "after" baselines. In other words, we examine the changes that took place between the average democracy level that was present from 1981 to 1986 and the average democracy level that was present from 1997 to 2002. Using time-sequential regression analyses, we measure (1) how strongly given levels of self-expression values influenced subsequent levels of democracy during 1997–2002; we then compare this with (2) how strongly prior levels of democracy during 1981–86 influenced subsequent levels of self-expression values – controlling for socio-economic development and autocorrelation over time, in both cases.

Statistical Analysis of Causality

Identifying the causal direction in a statistical relationship is complicated. But it is possible, provided one has data that allow one to model three fundamental conditions of causality: temporal order, spuriousness, and autocorrelation (see Cox and Wermuth, 2001).

Temporal order implies that the effect of an independent variable X on a dependent variable Y can only be considered causal if X is measured prior to Y, because causes must precede effects. For example, a strong correlation between self-expression values and democracy cannot be interpreted as a causal effect of self-expression values on democracy if self-expression values are measured at the same time or later than democracy. If self-expression values cause democracy, they must be in place before democracy.

The second condition, spuriousness, requires us to test whether the impact of an independent variable X on a dependent variable Y holds up when one controls for relevant third variables. This is necessary in order to rule out the possibility that the effect of X on Y is merely an artifact of a third variable Z, which is causing both X and Y. In this case the effect of X on Y would be spurious. If this is true, the impact of X on Y will disappear when one controls for Z. For example, the effect of self-expression values on democracy could not be considered causal if it disappears when one controls for levels of socioeconomic development. In this case, socioeconomic development would act as the common cause of both self-expression values and democracy, but self-expression values themselves would not cause democracy – they would show an impact on democracy only insofar as they were linked with socioeconomic development.

Autocorrelation, the third condition, requires us to test whether the impact of X on Y holds up when one controls for prior measures of Y. If it does not, X adds nothing in explaining changes in Y over time. Thus, an effect of self-expression values on democracy could only be considered causal if it holds up when one controls for earlier measures of democracy. This is known as "Granger-causality" (Granger, 1969): if the levels of a variable are almost entirely explained by prior levels of this variable, exogenous factors can have no strong causal impact (little variance is left for them to explain).

In the following, we model each of the three conditions of causality, first separately and then simultaneously, in regressions in which we reverse independent and dependent variables, varying their temporal order accordingly.

We have measures of self-expression values in the relevant time period for sixty-one countries with diverse cultural backgrounds, including a large number of countries that became democratic in the Third Wave, such as South Korea, Taiwan, Chile, Poland, Hungary, Russia, and South Africa. These values were measured around 1990 and 1995, at times within the historical transition period shown in Figure 8.1.[2] Thus, our measures of self-expression values were taken *after* our pre-transition measure of democracy (in 1981–86) and *before* our post-transition measures of democracy (in 1997–2002). In order to locate the measure of self-expression values as early as possible in the transition period, we used the measure made around 1990 whenever it was available – which applies to forty-one societies.[3] For the remaining twenty societies, we used the measure from 1995. Using the latter measure is feasible because of the strong temporal autocorrelation between aggregate measures of self-expression values in the early and mid-1990s: there is an r = .94 correlation for the thirty countries for which both measures are available. Accordingly, self-expression values measured around 1995 are a good indicator of the level of self-expression values slightly earlier around 1990.[4] The bulk of measurements were made near the earlier date so that on average self-expression values are measured in 1992 (we will refer to this as the "early 1990s measure"). In every case, self-expression values are measured prior to the post-transition level of democracy during 1997–2002, that is, before the new democracies of the Third Wave stabilized on their post-transition level of democracy.

Because causes must precede their effects, we use the temporal ordering of "pre-transition" (1981–86), "mid-transition" (early 1990s), and "post-transition" (1997–2002) in time-sequential regressions in which we test pre-transition democracy as a predictor of mid-transition self-expression values; and mid-transition self-expression values as a predictor of post-transition democracy. If the institutional interpretation of the relationship between self-expression values and democracy is correct, then pre-transition democracy should have a stronger impact on mid-transition self-expression values than these values have on post-transition democracy. If the cultural interpretation is correct, and self-expression values are conducive to democracy, the opposite should hold true.

But this model is still too simple. In order to test the causal direction in the relationship between two variables, one not only must bring the independent and dependent variables into the correct temporal order, so that the independent variable is measured earlier than the dependent variable. One must also test whether the impact of the prior variable on the subsequent variable holds up when one controls for other possibly relevant variables. In this case, we know that both self-expression values and liberal democracy are strongly correlated with socioeconomic development – which means it is quite conceivable that

---

[2] For reasons of temporal order, the following analyses are restricted to the countries for which the second and third waves of the Values Surveys gathered data at the early or mid 1990s.

[3] In order to identify for which country the data are taken from which round of the Values Surveys, see Internet Appendix, note 4. For this and subsequent references to the Internet Appendix, see http://www.worldvaluessurvey.org/publications/humandevelopment.html.

[4] This statement holds true, even though self-expression values declined in ex-communist societies (especially the Soviet successor states). For even in these cases, societies did not leave their ballpark position in relation to other societies.

socioeconomic development causes both. To test whether this is true, we must test whether the relation between self-expression values and democracy remains significant when we control for the influence of socioeconomic development. Hence, we will use socioeconomic development as an additional independent variable in the regression of self-expression values on prior democracy and the regression of democracy on prior self-expression values.

One more step is needed to enable us to draw conclusions about the causal direction of the relationship between liberal democracy and self-expression values. We must take into account the fact that variables tend to be autocorrelated over time. A variable may be strongly path-dependent, so that earlier levels of this variable explain most of the variation in later levels, leaving little variance to be explained by other factors. We expect this to be the case with self-expression values because we know that levels of these values are strongly correlated over time (reflecting the fact that they accumulate in a gradually evolving process). Accordingly, we do not expect that prior levels of democracy will explain much of the variance in self-expression values once we have controlled for prior levels of self-expression values. On the other hand, as we have seen, levels of democracy did change drastically during the Third Wave, which means that pre-transition and post-transition measures of democracy are less strongly correlated over time, leaving a good deal of variance to be explained by exogenous factors, such as self-expression values. Empirical analyses will show if these expectations are supported by the evidence.

Step 1: Explaining the Presence of Formal Democracy

Are self-expression values conducive to democracy, or does democracy give rise to a culture that emphasizes self-expression values? Figures 8.2a–c summarize the results of six regression models that test these two alternatives. In each of these graphs, the regression models in the upper half use self-expression values measured in the early 1990s as a predictor of post-transition democracy measured over 1997–2002. The graphs in the lower half examine the opposite causal possibility, using pre-transition democracy measured over 1981–86 as a predictor of self-expression values in the early 1990s.

In the two models of Figure 8.2, we use Vanhanen's index of "power resources" as an additional predictor (Vanhanen, 1997). This is an index of socioeconomic resources indicating the level and distribution of material, cognitive, and social resources. It includes measures of property and income distribution, which tap economic resources; aggregate measures of education, which tap the distribution of cognitive resources; and indicators of social complexity, which measure the social resources available to individuals who are exposed to the diverse human interactions of complex societies.[5] This index provides a

---

[5] For details on the indicators Vanhanen uses to create his indices, see the Internet Appendix, #08 under Variables.

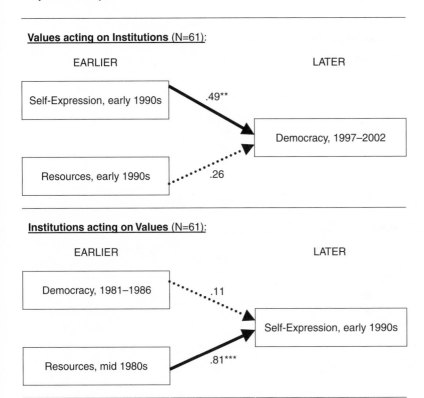

FIGURE 8.2a. What causes what? Temporal order test, controlling for third variable.

broad-based measure of a society's socioeconomic resources, or modernization, and it is measured prior to the respective dependent variable.[6]

In the two models of Figure 8.2b, a measure of the respective dependent variable at an earlier time is introduced as an additional predictor to control for this variable's autocorrelation over time. Finally, in the two models in Figure 8.2c, both socioeconomic resources and the prior measure of the dependent variable are used as predictors.

The results of this exercise are straightforward. First, controlling for socioeconomic resources, mid-transition self-expression values have a highly

---

[6] In Part I we wanted to analyze the impact of socioeconomic development on values separately for the three types of resources provided by socioeconomic development. Here in Part II we are interested in socioeconomic development as a control factor for which we only need one overall indicator. This explains why we introduce Vanhanen's compact index of socioeconomic resources at this point. We consider this index preferable to the Human Development Index because its multiplicative combination of resources avoids averaging them out in an additive combination. The Human Development Index (UN Development Program, 1995, 2000), by contrast, combines its component measures additively. Moreover, the Human Development Index does not include a measure of social complexity that could serve as a proxy for the proliferation of social resources.

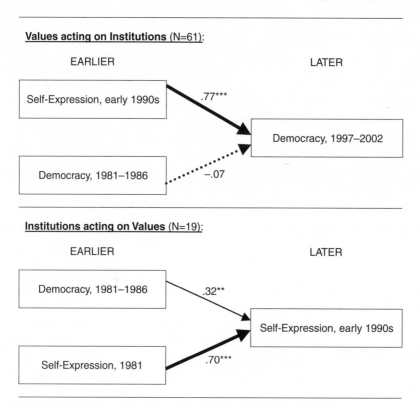

FIGURE 8.2b. Temporal order test, controlling for autocorrelation.

significant impact on post-transition democracy (Figure 8.2a, upper model). This impact is even stronger than the impact of socioeconomic resources on post-transition democracy. Hence, the impact of self-expression values on democracy is not an artifact of socioeconomic development. Although self-expression values are themselves shaped by socioeconomic resources, they have a significant independent impact on democracy.

Second, when we control for socioeconomic resources, pre-transition democracy has *no* significant impact on mid-transition self-expression values (Figure 8.2a, lower half), whereas socioeconomic resources do have a pronounced impact on these values. Thus, although a society's earlier level of democracy shows a strong zero-order correlation with its subsequent level of self-expression values (r = .78), this linkage is an artifact of socioeconomic development: the correlation only exists because democracy is linked with socioeconomic development, and this correlation vanishes when one holds development constant.

Figure 8.3 gives a graphic view of this finding. Controlling for socioeconomic resources, the figure illustrates the fact that we find much stronger

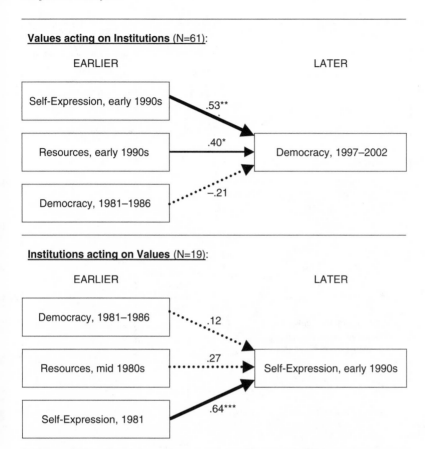

FIGURE 8.2c. Temporal order test, controlling for third variable *and* autocorrelation.

correlations between self-expression values and *subsequent* measures of democracy than between self-expression values and *prior* measures of democracy: in other words, the relationship is much stronger when we view self-expression values as *causing* democracy than when we view democracy as causing self-expression values. We find a steep leap in the strength of the correlations when the switch occurs from democracy being measured temporally *before* self-expression values to democracy being measured contemporaneously and after self-expression values. Controlling for socioeconomic development, the temporally prior measures of democracy are virtually uncorrelated with the early-1990s measure of self-expression values; but the contemporaneous and subsequent measures of democracy, show highly significant and strongly positive correlations with self-expression values. This indicates that the variation in self-expression values that exists independent of socioeconomic resources is not affected by prior levels of democracy. Conversely, this independent variation in

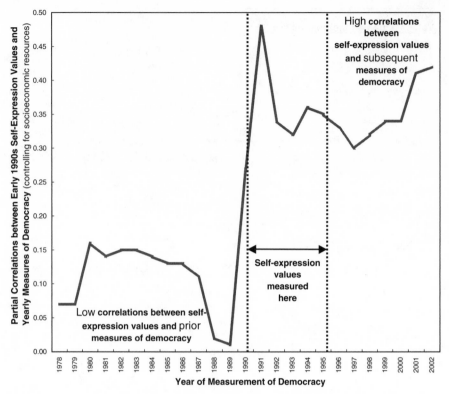

FIGURE 8.3. Correlation between self-expression values and prior and subsequent levels of democracy.

self-expression values *does* affect subsequent levels of democracy, even when we control for socioeconomic resources.[7] Moreover, because the strength of the correlations in Figure 8.3 increases, it is clear that liberal democracy and self-expression values have moved into closer correspondence to each other. However, only the democracy measures change in this analysis, whereas self-expression values remain constant. Hence, the dynamic in Figure 8.3 demonstrates that levels of democracy adjust to a society's given emphasis on self-expression values – which indicates a causal impact of individual-level values on societal-level institutions.

Figure 8.2b examines the relationship between self-expression values and democracy, controlling for the temporal autocorrelation of the dependent variable, democracy. As it indicates, mid-transition self-expression values show a strong and highly significant impact on post-transition democracy, even if

---

[7] We ran a partial correlation procedure in which we correlated the early 1990s measure of self-expression values with various annual measures of democracy, controlling for Vanhanen's late-1980s measure of socioeconomic resources.

we control for pre-transition democracy (Figure 8.2b, upper half).[8] And pre-transition levels of democracy have no significant impact on post-transition democracy, controlling for midtransition self-expression values. These results reflect the fact that democracy underwent major changes in many countries during the transition period – and that the *amount* of change depended to a considerable degree on the strength of self-expression values that were present in the society at the start of the transition. Conversely, when we control for the temporal autocorrelation in self-expression values, pre-transition democracy has a relatively weak impact on mid-transition self-expression values (Figure 8.2b, lower half),[9] reflecting the fact that self-expression values are strongly path-dependent, leaving little variance to be explained by prior democracy.

Introducing both controls simultaneously confirms the previous results, as Figure 8.2c demonstrates. Self-expression values measured near the start of the transition period have a significant and powerful impact on post-transition democracy, while socioeconomic resources have a weaker but still significant impact on democracy (Figure 8.2c, upper half). By contrast, when we control for self-expression values and socioeconomic resources, pre-transition levels of democracy have no significant impact on self-expression values (Figure 8.2c, lower half). Self-expression values depend above all on their own prior levels and are also significantly influenced by socioeconomic development, but they are not influenced by pre-transition levels of democracy. A culture that emphasizes self-expression values does not seem to reflect the prior existence of liberal democracy, but it is conducive to liberal democracy.

If we take into account the historical sequence of the Third Wave, the relationship between liberal democracy and self-expression values cannot be interpreted as due to the impact of democratic institutions on mass values. The evidence from scores of countries flatly contradicts the institutional explanation of this relationship. Controlling for temporal order, spuriousness, and autocorrelation, self-expression values have a significant and strong causal impact on subsequent democracy, but the reverse is not true. The evidence strongly supports the cultural explanation, rather than the institutional explanation, of the relationship between mass values and democratic institutions.

---

[8] Hadenius and Teorell (2004) undertake a similar analysis, but they use the 1990 Freedom House measure of democracy to control for the temporal autocorrelation of democracy. This procedure does not take into account the pattern of historic regime changes shown here, so it does not adequately separate pre-transition and post-transition measures of democracy. Instead, the 1990 measures refer to a point in time at which democracy was a moving target in many countries. To take the Third Wave into account, one must control for the autocorrelation of post-transition levels of democracy with pre-transition levels of democracy.

[9] In the lower half of Figures 8.2b and 8.2c, in which we control for the temporal autocorrelation of self-expression values, the sample is reduced to those countries that participated in the first Values Surveys conducted in 1981. In these cases, postmaterialistic liberty aspirations could not be calculated on the basis of three items (see Internet Appendix, #43 under Variables) but only on the basis of two items (because of changes in the questionnaire). This means that the percentage index of self-expression values has been calculated on a slightly different basis for the 1981 data.

The .89 correlation between aggregate measures of self-expression in 1981 and 1990 is based on twenty-one countries that were measured at both times.[10] Most of these countries are long-established Western democracies. Is the strong temporal autocorrelation that we find between self-expression values in 1981 and 1990 unique to stable democracies? Apparently not, for we also have data from four societies that were surveyed in 1981 but were not yet democracies – South Korea, Hungary, South Africa, and Mexico. These countries show no less stability in their self-expression values than is found in stable democracies. Among established democracies, self-expression values changed on average by 10 percent of their accumulated level from 1981 to 1990. In Hungary they changed by 12 percent, in Mexico by 5 percent, in South Africa by 4 percent, and in South Korea by 0.5 percent. Because these changes account for a minor proportion of the levels in self-expression values that had accumulated over time, these changes affect a society's relative position very little, so that societies with relatively strong self-expression values in 1981 still had relatively strong self-expression values ten years later. Relative temporal stability in self-expression values characterizes all types of societies, even the Soviet successor states, in which we measured considerable declines in self-expression values over recent years. Despite this decline, these societies stayed in pretty much the same position that they had earlier, relative to other societies.

These findings invalidate the assumption that the self-expression values found in transition countries are produced by these transitions. The reverse is true: they helped *cause* these transitions. It is no coincidence that transitions have stopped or have been reversed in precisely those countries with the weakest self-expression values (e.g., the Soviet successor states except the Baltic countries).

Step 2: Explaining Shifts toward and away from Democracy

Let us test the thesis that self-expression values are conducive to democracy from another perspective. Here, we build on a fundamental premise of the political culture approach that has never been tested directly: the congruence thesis. Eckstein (1966), Eckstein and Gurr (1975), Almond and Verba (1963) and many other social scientists claim that the stability of political regimes depends on the degree of congruence between political institutions and mass values: political institutions must be consistent with the citizens' value orientations or they will not be seen as legitimate, and their stability will be low. The greater the incongruence between mass values and political institutions, the more unstable the regime will be. If this premise is correct, it suggests that regime changes operate as a function of the incongruence between institutions

---

[10] As noted in the previous note, the aggregate measures of self-expression values are based on slightly different component measures for 1981 and 1990. Despite this inconsistency, the correlation is strong over both points in time.

TABLE 8.1. *Congruence and Incongruence in the Supply of Freedom and the Demand for Freedom*

	Cultural DEMAND for Freedom	
	WEAK DEMAND: Survival values Prevail	STRONG DEMAND: Self-Expression values Prevail
Institutional SUPPLY of Freedom HIGH SUPPLY: Wide range of civil rights	Incongruence (supply higher than demand): unstable democracy	Congruence (both supply and demand high): stable democracy
LOW SUPPLY: Narrow range of civil rights	Congruence (both supply and demand low): stable nondemocracy	Incongruence (demand higher than supply): unstable nondemocracy

and culture: the larger the incongruence, the larger subsequent regime change will be.[11] If regime changes occur, they should tend to be greatest in countries that start out with the largest gaps between culture and institutions. From this perspective, regime changes tend to correct the discrepancies between culture and institutions.

One can view the linkage between democratic institutions and self-expression values as reflecting the congruence between the supply and the demand for freedom. Democratic institutions represent an institutional supply of freedom because democracy institutionalizes civil and political liberties; and self-expression values create a cultural demand for freedom because these values emphasize freedom of choice. This makes it possible to identify two forms of incongruence, depending on the relationship between the supply and demand for freedom.

Table 8.1 illustrates this in a fourfold typology. Incongruence between the institutional supply of freedom and the cultural demand for freedom can occur in both democracies and authoritarian states. An authoritarian state has low incongruence if people emphasize survival values, placing little emphasis on human self-expression. Here, a low cultural demand for freedom coincides with a low institutional supply of freedom. In democracies, by contrast, there is low incongruence if people emphasize self-expression values, creating a strong cultural demand for freedom, which is congruent with the broad institutional supply of freedom.

The incongruence between culture and institutions can also be large. If the citizens of a society with high levels of democracy place low emphasis on human freedom, there is an institutional oversupply of freedom. If shifts toward more or less democracy follow an incongruence-reducing logic, one would expect a

[11] This reasoning applies to societal-led regime changes but not to externally imposed regime changes.

shift *away* from democracy in this case, diminishing the institutional oversupply of freedom. Conversely, in an authoritarian state where the public places strong emphasis on self-expression values, a move toward democracy would reduce incongruence, increasing the level of freedom so that it comes into closer correspondence with the underlying cultural demand.

The following formula enables us to calculate the incongruence between the supply of freedom and the demand for freedom, reflecting the discrepancy between levels of liberal democracy and self-expression values:

$$\text{Incongruence}_t = \text{Supply of Freedom}_t - \text{Demand for Freedom}_t$$
$$\text{(liberal democracy)} \quad \text{(self-expression values)}$$

The incongruence between the institutional supply of freedom and the cultural demand for freedom is calculated by subtracting the demand from the supply. Because we want to measure the incongruence that was present before the transition period, we use the pre-transition measures of democracy from 1981–86 to indicate the supply of freedom. To calculate the cultural demand for freedom, we use self-expression values measured around 1990 as an approximation of how strong these values were *before* the transition. This measure will be roughly accurate because the strength of self-expression values at a given time gives a strong indication of corresponding values at a slightly earlier time, as the regression models in Figure 8.2 demonstrated.

We cannot simply subtract our raw measure of self-expression values from the pre-transition democracy measures because the two variables are measured on different scales: we must transform them into comparable scales in order to calculate the difference between democracy and self-expression values. For this purpose we normalized both variables, standardizing both scales to their empirical maximum, which was equated as 1.0. We then subtracted self-expression values from democracy, yielding an incongruence scale from -1 to $+1$, on which -1 represents a situation in which there is a maximum of liberal democracy and a virtual absence of self-expression values, while $+1$ indicates the reverse. Accordingly, the higher one moves on the incongruence scale from -1 to $+1$, the stronger the tendency for self-expression values to match or surpass the level of democracy (i.e., the cultural demand for freedom grows in relation to the institutional supply of freedom). Thus, a score of -1 marks the maximum possible demand-deficit for freedom; while a score of $+1$ marks the maximum demand-surplus for freedom. Our sample includes a number of stable Western democracies in which the levels of democracy have remained constant since measurement began. Apparently, these societies are at an equilibrium, with supply and demand for democracy in balance. Thus, it is no coincidence that the zero point on the incongruence scale – where the supply of democracy exactly equals the demand for democracy – is the mean incongruence value of these stable Western democracies.[12]

---

[12] For details on construction of the incongruence scale, see the Internet Appendix, #50 under Variables.

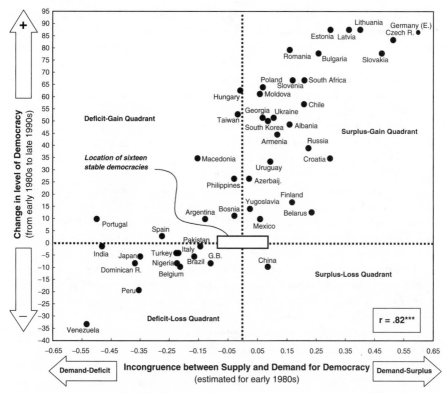

FIGURE 8.4. Impact on democracy of incongruence between supply of freedom and demand for freedom.

The incongruence scale that results from these transformations is a continuum that reflects the extent to which the demand for freedom exceeds, or falls short of, its supply. According to our hypothesis, a society's score on the incongruence scale should predict both the direction and the extent to which a society experienced subsequent changes toward more or less democracy: countries with positive scores on the incongruence scale should move toward more democracy, whereas countries with negative incongruence scores would be most likely to move toward less democracy. Moreover, moves toward democracy should be greatest among the countries with the highest positive scores on the incongruence scale (similarly, moves toward less democracy should be greatest among the countries with the highest negative scores on the incongruence scale). In short, regime changes should operate as a function of the incongruence between freedom-supply and freedom-demand, so that the changes that took place during the Third Wave of democratization will reflect the degree of incongruence between the supply and demand for freedom that existed immediately before these changes occurred.

These predictions are right on target, as Figure 8.4 demonstrates: the more the cultural demand for freedom exceeded its institutional supply around 1986, the greater were the subsequent moves toward more democracy, from 1987 to 2002.[13] The reverse relationship holds also true: the more the cultural demand for freedom fell short of its institutional supply, the larger the moves toward less democracy. Large moves toward more democracy occurred only among societies having a demand-surplus for freedom. And almost no losses in levels of democracy occurred among societies where the demand exceeded the supply (China being the sole exception). Overall, the incongruence between a society's demand for freedom and its supply of freedom explains fully 73 percent of the variance in changes toward higher or lower levels of democracy during the Third Wave. This is a dynamic model explaining the *process* of democratization, not just the absence or presence of democracy.

Figure 8.4 also shows that the losses among countries with a demand-deficit were smaller than the gains among countries with a demand-surplus, reflecting the fact that the overall trend during the Third Wave was toward more democracy. This overall trend can also be explained by the incongruency approach: there were far more societies in which the demand for freedom exceeded its supply than there were societies in which the demand for freedom fell short of its supply. But there *were* some countries in the latter category (such as Venezuela and Peru), and they were precisely the cases in which one finds declining levels of democracy during this period.

Figure 8.4 provides a basis for predicting what would be expected to happen in specific cases. China was one of the few countries that ran counter to our predictions. As Figure 8.4 indicates, there was a tension between the demand for freedom and its supply in China, implying that there was potential societal pressure for democratization. These forces manifested themselves in the Democracy Movement of 1989, when demonstrators took over Tiananmen Square in Beijing, demanding greater freedom of expression. For a few months the government wavered, but in June 1989 the top leaders ordered the army to repress the movement. Tanks were used in the subsequent massacre of protestors. The repression of the Democracy Movement demonstrates the fact that mass demands for freedom do not always succeed. Determined authoritarian elites can repress mass pressures, as long as they control the military. But sheer repression is costly and ultimately dangerous. In 1989 the Democracy Movement was mainly concentrated among the younger and more educated segments of the urban population, in a society that was still predominantly rural. China already is a society in which mass demands for freedom exceed the institutional supply. If socioeconomic development continues at the current pace (as it shows every sign of doing), mass emphasis on self-expression will become even more widespread, and will probably also begin to permeate the military and the younger party elites, making it increasingly difficult to resist democratization. We predict that China's socioeconomic liberalization process

---

[13] The change score in democracy measures the difference between the pre-transition level of formal democracy (in 1981–86) and the post-transition level (1997–2002), subtracting the former from the latter. See the Internet Appendix, #19 under Variables.

and its experimentation with local-level democracy will spill over to the national level so that China will make a transition to a liberal democracy within the next two decades.[14]

It is virtually impossible to interpret the relationship depicted in Figure 8.4 as reflecting the impact of democratic institutions on self-expression values. In Chapters 1 and 2, we demonstrated that changes in self-expression values occur steadily but slowly. Hence, the self-expression values measured around 1990 must have accumulated over a long period of time, and these levels existed shortly before the sudden regime changes occurred. It is logically impossible that regime changes could have created the levels of self-expression values that existed earlier. The causal arrow can only run from accumulated self-expression values toward the sudden regime changes. Consequently, the moves toward democracy reflect a catch-up to accumulated mass demands: the supply of freedom moved toward greater congruence with the societies' underlying demands for freedom.

This pattern confirms the point that was demonstrated by Figures 8.2a–c, showing that – when we control for third variables and temporal autocorrelation – the relation between self-expression values and liberal democracy operates primarily in one direction: from values to democracy. Previous levels of democracy show no impact on self-expression values when we control for the temporal autocorrelation of self-expression values; but, conversely, self-expression values do have a substantial impact on democracy levels, even when we control for the temporal autocorrelation of democracy.

Step 3: Explaining Levels of Effective Democracy

Our central claim is that self-expression values transform modernization into a process of human development, giving rise to humanistic societies that emphasize human emancipation. Part of this process is the emergence of civil and political liberties where they do not yet exist and the deepening and increasing effectiveness of these liberties where they are already in place.

Civil and political liberties are a necessary component of liberal democracy, but unless they are actually practiced by ruling elites, they merely establish formal democracy. To make civil and political liberties an effectively practiced reality requires that governing elites accept the rule of law, and the extent to which this is true varies greatly from one society to another. Social scientists

---

[14] To be sure, there are clear violations of human rights, and the Chinese Communist Party does not yet accept open opposition. China is not an electoral democracy. But it is also clear that the economic, administrative, and local political reforms have increased people's autonomy and choice in shaping their lives. Political liberties at the local level and civil liberties in the socioeconomic and cultural sphere have been significantly widened in China. This is not reflected in China's Freedom House ratings, which remain at the bottom of the scale. This is another indication that Freedom House tends to give a country low freedom scores in general, as long as it does not have competitive elections at the national level.

too readily equate formal democracy with genuine effective democracy. In actual practice they rarely coincide, and the gap varies from a relatively modest difference to a discrepancy that makes democracy a hollow pretense. From the start, civil and political rights were designed to limit state power and despotic government (Finer, 1999). But to make this effective, civil and political rights also require honest, law-abiding elites. Corruption, broadly understood, reflects nepotism, favoritism, and other illegal mechanisms used by elites to circumvent the rule of law and abuse their power for their own benefit, depriving ordinary people of their legal rights (Sandholtz and Taagepera, 2005). Similarly, formal democracy alone is not enough to guarantee that violations of human rights will be avoided; elite integrity is required for human rights to become a reality (Davenport and Armstrong, 2004).[15] Elite corruption often reaches a point that renders democratic norms totally ineffective (Stiglitz, 2002). Hence, our next step is to examine the relation between self-expression values and *effective* versions of liberal democracy.

The term "effective" democracy, as used here, does not refer to whether democracy is successful in its policy outcomes. It refers to being effective concerning the defining elements of liberal democracy – civil and political rights. Effective democracy in this sense means the extent to which formally institutionalized civil and political rights are effective in actual practice – that is, respected in the elites' use of state power (Rose, 2001).

So far we have used the Freedom House ratings to measure civil and political rights. These ratings measure the institutional absence or presence of civil and political rights but *not* the effective practice of these rights by the state. Unless governing officials and decision makers respect these rights when they exercise power, they exist only on paper. In order to measure effective democracy, one needs to take into account the extent to which formal civil and political liberties are made effective by the rule of law.[16]

Effective democracy reflects the extent to which officeholders use their power in ways that do not deprive ordinary people of their formal rights as citizens. Thus, the most serious violation of effective democracy is elite corruption (Linz

---

[15] Davenport and Armstrong (2004) demonstrate that gradual increases in formal democracy have no consistent diminishing effect on human rights violations, confirming that mere formal democracy does little to guarantee that either the political rights *or* the human rights of the citizens are genuinely respected by the power holders: elite integrity must also be present.

[16] Rose (2001) also advances this argument. In measuring effective democracy, however, he simply averages measures of the formal presence of civil rights and rule of law. Such an additive combination is theoretically inappropriate because it allows high levels of rule of law to compensate for low levels of civil and political rights. Thus, a country would come out with a medium level of effective democracy, even if it has no civil and political rights at all, if its elites behave according to the existing laws. Until recently, Singapore would have been an example. For this reason, we use a weighing procedure in which measures of rule of law are used to grade given measures of civil and political rights. This does not allow high scores in rule of law to compensate for low scores in civil and political rights. In the best case, a high rule-of-law score simply reproduces a given civil- and political-rights score.

and Stepan, 1996; Heller, 2000; Brzezinski, 2001; Brown, 2001; Fairbanks, 2001; Rose, 2001; Shevtsova, 2001). By definition, corruption means that officeholders do not provide people the services to which the law entitles them. Instead, elites provide services only to privileged people who can afford to buy them by paying bribes or doing favors. This violates the rule of law and equal rights. Corruption tends to establish conspiratorial networks held together by mutual obligations, fueling nepotism, favoritism, and clientelism. Corruption distributes privileges in highly discriminatory and selective ways, disenfranchising the masses. Corruption undermines people power. It is the opposite of rule of law. It can undermine civil and political rights to the point of making them meaningless.

In order to measure effective democracy, one needs to measure not only the extent to which civil and political rights are institutionalized but also the degree to which officeholders actually *respect* these rights. The first of these two components is measured by the Freedom House scores. Although these measures are intended to measure genuine civil and political rights, they neglect the extent to which these rights are actually practiced by law-abiding elites. Freedom House tends to rate a society that holds free elections as "free," giving it scores at or near the top of the scales. Thus, the new democracies in Eastern Europe are given scores as high as those of the established democracies of Western Europe, although any in-depth analyses (see Rose, 2001) indicate that these new democracies are far more corrupt in actual practice than their Freedom House scores would indicate. Because the Freedom House scores tend to equate formal democracy with effective democracy, it is necessary to supplement them, in order to measure the extent to which democratic institutions are actually effective, providing the citizens with genuine freedom of choice.

The "control of corruption" scores developed by the World Bank (Kaufman et al., 2003) provide the most comprehensive and methodologically most sound measure of law-abiding and honest elite behavior, or "elite integrity." These measures are calculated from expert polls and population surveys that reflect perceptions of the extent to which officeholders abuse public power for private benefits. A sophisticated "unobserved components" method is used to make corruption perceptions from twenty-five different sources comparable across countries and to summarize them into a single-factor scale, in which high scores indicate the absence of corruption, or elite integrity. We transformed the World Bank control-of-corruption scores into a scale from 0 to 1.0.[17] We use this measure of elite integrity to grade the formal democracy scores (having transformed the combined Freedom House scores into a percentage scale in which the maximum is equated to 100). Because we use the most recent Freedom House and World Bank scores from 2000–2, we obtain a measure of effective democracy in 2000–2.[18] This procedure yields an index of effective democracy

---

[17] For measurement details on elite integrity, see the Internet Appendix, #20 under Variables.
[18] See also the Internet Appendix, #21 under Variables.

that measures effectiveness-weighted formal democracy:[19]

Formal Democracy * Elite Integrity
(percentages)   (fractions from 0 to 1)

Although elite integrity multiplies the effectiveness of given civil and political liberties, it cannot compensate for the absence of civil and political liberties. As a grading factor, elite integrity cannot do more than reproduce a given level of formal democracy. Even if we have a maximum elite integrity level of 1.0 (no elite corruption), this factor cannot raise a low level of formal democracy but simply maintains it. However, a low degree of elite integrity can devalue a high level of formal democracy, reflecting the fact that there are large variations in the extent to which effective democracy is actually present among societies categorized as formal democracies.

A high level of formal democracy is a necessary condition for reaching a high score on effective democracy, but it is not sufficient. Imagine a country with a constitution that guarantees a full set of civil and political rights; if this country is governed by corrupt elites who do not respect these rights, it renders them irrelevant. In such a case, even the highest score for formal democracy can be downgraded, falling near zero if the elite integrity scores are near zero. Thus, a society can obtain a low score in effective democracy for one of two reasons: either it has no formal democracy, so even perfect elite integrity would not produce effective democracy; or it has formal democracy, but low elite integrity renders it ineffective. In *both* cases people are deprived of their rights. This measure provides a meaningful representation of reality – and of the extent to which people actually have effective choice.

In short, effective democracy measures not only the extent to which a society has liberties on paper but the extent to which these liberties are actually practiced by the state and its officials. This variable spans a continuum ranging from little or no real democracy to fully effective democracy.

As Figure 8.5 illustrates, it is more difficult for a country to obtain a high score on effective democracy than on formal democracy. Formal democracy translates into effective democracy in a curvilinear way: a relatively large variation on the lower half of the formal democracy scale produces a relatively small variation in effective democracy, whereas a small variation in the top quartile on the formal democracy scale translates into large variations in effective democracy. These results reflect the fact that formal democracy is a necessary condition to create

[19] Hadenius and Teorell (2004) criticize this measurement, arguing that it reflects conceptual confusion because it combines two different things. This is similar to arguing that table salt is a conceptual confusion because it is a combination of sodium and chlorine, a caustic metal and a greenish gas, which are two very different things. In fact, completely different things can and frequently do interact to produce significant outcomes. Hadenius's critique would be more relevant if we had simply averaged formal democracy and elite integrity, which we did not do because they *are* two different things. But formal democracy and elite integrity can and do interact to produce effective democracy. Their multiplicative combination – in which neither can substitute for the other – measures precisely this interaction.

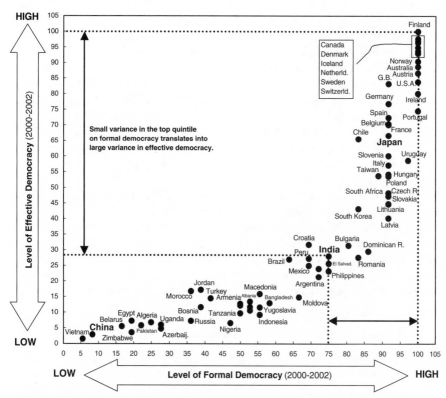

FIGURE 8.5. Formal democracy versus effective democracy.

effective democracy: only nations scoring high in civil and political rights (i.e., above the 75th percentile) can reach high scores on effective democracy. But civil and political rights are not a sufficient condition for effective democracy: not all countries scoring high in civil and political rights also score high on effective democracy because it depends on their level of elite integrity. Elite integrity is a crucial factor in differentiating between formal and effective democracy.

This reflects an important aspect of reality. For example, Freedom House assigns Latvia and Slovakia the same scores on formal democracy as Britain or Germany (about 90 percent of the maximum score in each case), but Britain and Germany score considerably higher on effective democracy than Latvia and Slovakia (about 75 percent of the maximum score compared to about 35 percent). If we took the formal democracy measure at face value, we would conclude that Latvia and Slovakia are just as democratic as Britain and Germany. But in reality, they have relatively corrupt elites who devalue the constitutional rights their people theoretically possess (see Rose, 2001; Sandholtz and Taagepera, 2005). Conversely, while there is large variation in levels of formal democracy among lower-income countries, ranging from below the 10th percentile in the case of China to the 75th percentile in the case of India, widespread elite corruption diminishes these differences considerably: China scores at the 5th percentile on effective democracy and India just below the 30th percentile. Taking into account the effectiveness of a society's civil and political rights, the situation in India is somewhat closer to that of China than to that of Japan, although India ranks much higher on formal democracy than China. Effective democracy is a more demanding and more meaningful measure than formal democracy: it reflects how much freedom people actually have rather than how much freedom they have on paper. Because effective democracy is what people are actually seeking when they emphasize self-expression values, we expect these values to be even more closely linked with effective democracy than with formal democracy.[20]

Figure 7.2 confirmed this point. We have already seen evidence in Figure 7.1 showing that self-expression values are significantly linked with formal democracy. But as Figure 7.2 illustrates, these values are even more closely linked with effective democracy. The strength of self-expression values explains 80 percent of the cross-national variance in subsequent measures of effective democracy, with no striking outliers (not even India). However, additional analyses are necessary before we can conclude that this relationship is causal.

Self-Expression Values and Effective Democracy

As before, we apply Granger causality to test whether self-expression values have an impact on subsequent measures of effective democracy, controlling for temporally prior measures of democracy. Because measures of effective democracy are not available earlier than 1998 (when the World Bank's "control of corruption" measures begin), we use the length of time that a society has been governed by democratic institutions – or "democratic tradition" – as a surrogate. The length of the democratic tradition is a key factor, according to a number of prominent theorists who argue that the emergence of intrinsically democratic values depends on how long democratic institutions have endured (see Rustow, 1970; Linz and Stepan, 1996). According to these writers, the longer democratic institutions persist, the more they become an indispensable part of a society's collective identity among both elites and masses. If this argument is correct, the prodemocratic nature of self-expression values is simply a consequence of how long a society has lived under democratic institutions, which means that these values will have no impact on effective democracy when we control for their linkage with the democratic tradition. We test this hypothesis here. Moreover, following Bunce (2000: 715–17) and Kopstein and Reilly (2000), who argue that spatial diffusion acts as an autonomous determinant on democracy, we examine diffusion within cultural

[20] China scores at the 5th percentile of effective democracy while a simple dichotomous classification would code it as categorically nondemocratic. This more refined coding is more informative as it shows exactly *how* undemocratic China is, rather than simply saying that China is nondemocratic.

zones as an additional control predictor, controlling for exogenous effects due to regional diffusion.

The analyses in preceding chapters have shown that economic, cultural, and political variables vary greatly across cultural zones. Indeed, a mere eight cultural zones capture about 85 percent of the cross-national variance in a society's socioeconomic resources, its self-expression values, and its degree of effective democracy across more than seventy nations. This finding suggests that socioeconomic development, mass values, and institutions cannot be considered as merely endogenous properties of nations but also reflect exogenous diffusion processes, penetrating and homogenizing the nations of given cultural zones (see Starr, 1991; L. Diamond, 1993a; Whitehead, 1996; Kopstein and Reilly, 2000). In order to control for diffusion effects, we include the cultural zone averages on the dependent variables as an additional control factor (for a similar procedure, see Gasiorowski and Power, 1998).

For instance, in predicting self-expression values in the early 1990s, we use the average level of self-expression values in each cultural zone as an additional predictor, assigning each country the mean self-expression values score of all other countries in its cultural zone, excluding the country's own value.[21] This ensures that we assign each country an average score that is independent of its own score. Similarly, in predicting subsequent levels of effective democracy, we include each region's average level of effective democracy as an additional predictor. Thus, we model each dependent variable as a function of its diffusion within cultural zones.

Let us emphasize that these averages have been calculated in a way that makes them exogenous to each country, with each country's own score being excluded from calculating the cultural zone average assigned to that country. This means that we assign a slightly different cultural zone average to each country in that culture zone. Empirically this makes little difference, but conceptually it is important because the notion of exogenous effects is crucial to the concept of diffusion (Starr, 1991).

Table 8.2 shows regression results from our first series of models. They predict self-expression values as measured in the early 1990s, using the following independent variables: the length of the society's democratic tradition prior to 1990 (i.e., the number of years of democracy it experienced before that date);[22] the society's level of socioeconomic development prior to 1990 (using the Vanhanen measure of the level and distribution of socioeconomic resources); and the cultural zone levels of self-expression values. The first four models are bivariate regression models, and the following ones are multivariate

---

[21] For details of measuring the cultural zone average of self-expression values, see the Internet Appendix, #51 under Variables.

[22] To construct the measure of years of democracy, we used the "Autocracy-Democracy" scale provided by the Polity IV project (Marshall and Jaggers, 2000). We calculated for each country the number of years in which it scored at least +7. For more details, see the Internet Appendix, #23 under Variables.

TABLE 8.2. *The Impact of Democracy on Self-Expression Values, Controlling for Socioeconomic Development and Cultural Diffusion*

Predictors	Dependent Variable: Percent High on Self-Expression Values in Early 1990s[a]					
	Model 1	Model 2	Model 3	Model 5	Model 6	Model 7
Number of years under democratic government up to 1990	.79*** (9.83)			.15[n.s.] (1.53)	.42*** (5.14)	.08[n.s.] (.91)
Index of socioeconomic resources in late 1980s		.90*** (15.97)		.78*** (7.99)		.58*** (6.15)
Cultural zone level of dependent variable			.82*** (10.93)		.55*** (6.76)	.35*** (4.86)
Adjusted R²	.62	.81	.67	.81	.77	.85

Note: Entries are standardized regression coefficients (T-values in parentheses). Significance levels: * p < .100; ** p < .010; *** p < .001; n.s., not significant. Test statistics for collinearity, heteroskedasticity, and influential cases are all below critical thresholds.
[a] Earliest available survey from Values Surveys II–III (1989–91 to 1995–97). Average measure is in 1992. N = 61.

combinations, controlling the effect of the democratic tradition for one of the other predictors.

The models shown in Table 8.3 reverse the causal direction from the models in Table 8.2, testing the impact of self-expression values in the early 1990s on subsequent levels of effective democracy in 2000–2, controlling for socioeconomic development, prior democratic tradition, and the cultural zone level of effective democracy.[23] In order to test our hypothesis, we compare the results from Tables 8.2 and 8.3.

Model 1 in Table 8.2 suggests that a nation's democratic tradition has a highly significant impact on its subsequent emphasis on self-expression values. Specifically, the number of years under democracy explains 62 percent of the subsequent cross-national variation in self-expression values – provided we don't control for any other variable. This effect is substantial. However, it explains considerably less variance in self-expression values than is explained by the level of socioeconomic resources (81 percent). More important, it is also considerably less than the degree to which self-expression values explain subsequent levels of effective democracy (80 percent), as Model 1 of Table 8.3 demonstrates. Most decisively, the impact of the democratic tradition on self-expression values drops to an insignificant level when we control for

[23] For details on measuring this variable, see the Internet Appendix, #22 under Variables.

TABLE 8.3. *The Impact of Self-Expression Values on Democracy, Controlling for Socioeconomic Development, Democratic Tradition, and Cultural Diffusion*

Predictors	Dependent Variable: Level of Effective Democracy in 2000–2002							
	Model 1	Model 2	Model 3	Model 4	Model 5	Model 6	Model 7	Model 8
Percent high on self-expression values in early 1990s	.89*** (15.33)				.59*** (4.97)	.80*** (8.38)	.63*** (7.02)	.57*** (4.56)
Index of socioeconomic resources in early 1990s		.87*** (13.34)			.35*** (2.94)			.33* (2.67)
Years under democratic government up to 1995			.75*** (8.82)			.12[n.s.] (1.29)		.04[n.s.] (.41)
Cultural zone level of dependent variable				.84*** (11.67)			.33*** (3.64)	
Adjusted R^2	.80	.74	.56	.69	.82	.80	.83	.80

Notes: Entries are standardized regression coefficients (T-values in parentheses). N = 61. Significance levels: * p < .100; ** p < .010; *** p < .001; n.s., not significant. Test statistics for collinearity, heteroskedasticity, and influential cases are below critical thresholds.

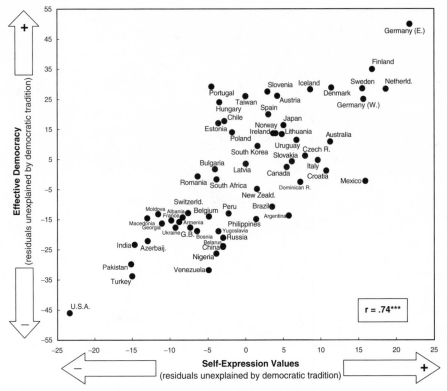

FIGURE 8.6a. Impact of self-expression values on effective democracy, controlling for time spent under democracy.

socioeconomic resources. When we do so, the length of a society's democratic tradition explains no variance in self-expression values beyond what socioeconomic resources explain alone, as one sees when one compares Models 2 and 5 in Table 8.2.

Conversely, the impact of self-expression values on a nation's subsequent level of effective democracy remains highly significant against all controls, even when we control for the number of years it has spent under democracy. In fact, the country's democratic tradition adds nothing to the impact of self-expression values on effective democracy, as a comparison of Models 1 and 6 in Table 8.3 demonstrates. This is, once again, a positive test of Granger-causality: self-expression values have a highly positive impact on democracy, even when we control for democracy's correlation with previous measures of itself.[24]

These findings argue against institutional explanations of democratic mass values. It is not true that such fundamental prodemocratic orientations as

---

[24] Granger (1969) argues that the effect of a predictor on a dependent variable is causal, if this effect holds against temporally prior measures of the dependent variable. Our findings meet this requirement, showing that self-expression values have a significant impact on democracy, even controlling for preceding measures of democracy.

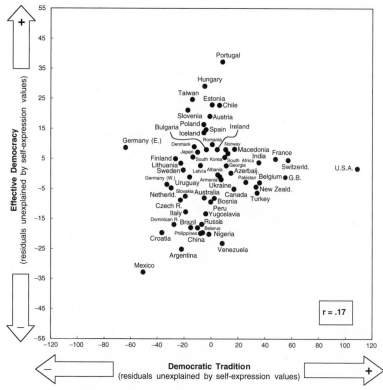

FIGURE 8.6b. Impact of time spent under democracy on effective democracy, controlling for level of self-expression values.

self-expression values can only emerge from long experience under democratic institutions. These values can arise even in the most authoritarian societies, and they have a much stronger impact on a society's subsequent democratic performance than does its previous experience with democracy. The strength of self-expression values in a society does not depend on prior democracy but is strongly influenced by the society's level of socioeconomic resources. Figures 8.6 and 8.7 illustrate these facts graphically.

Figure 8.6a depicts the impact of self-expression values on effective democracy, controlling for the length of the society's democratic tradition. We find that societies having higher levels of self-expression values than their democratic tradition would suggest also have higher levels of effective democracy than their democratic tradition would suggest (see the locations of East Germany, Denmark, Finland, Sweden, the Netherlands, and West Germany). By the same token, societies with weaker self-expression values than their previous experience with democracy would suggest also have lower levels of effective democracy than their experience with democracy would suggest (see the locations of the United States, Belgium, India, Venezuela, or Nigeria). Overall, the independent variation in self-expression values explains 53 percent of the

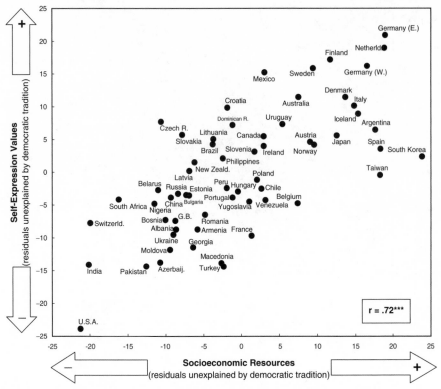

FIGURE 8.7a. The impact of socioeconomic resources on self-expression values, controlling for length of time spent under democracy.

independent variation in effective democracy. Self-expression values have an impact on effective democracy, even when we control for how long people have lived under democratic institutions.

Figure 8.6b depicts the impact of the democratic tradition on effective democracy, controlling for each society's level of self-expression values. As is immediately apparent, this figure resembles a random scatterplot. A good deal of variation in democratic traditions is independent of a society's level of self-expression values, but it explains only an insignificant 4 percent of the independent variation in effective democracy: societies having a longer democratic tradition than their self-expression values would suggest do not have more effective democracy than their self-expression values would suggest. Thus, decoupled from the strength of self-expression values, the length of a society's democratic tradition has no significant impact on the degree of effective democracy. The democratic tradition is linked with effective democracy insofar – and almost only insofar – as it is linked with strong self-expression values. Consequently, this impact vanishes almost completely when we control for levels of self-expression values.

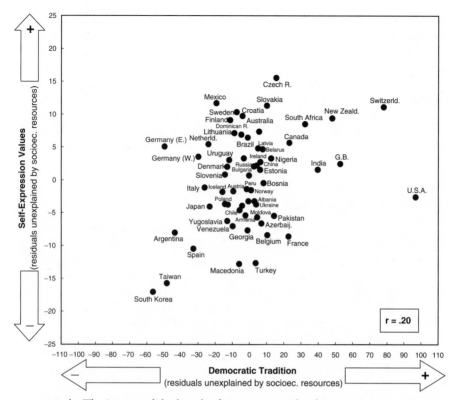

FIGURE 8.7b. The impact of the length of time spent under democratic institutions, on self-expression values, controlling for socioeconomic resources.

Figure 8.7a treats self-expression values as the dependent variable, illustrating how it is influenced by the level of socioeconomic resources, controlling for the length of the democratic tradition. As this figure demonstrates, societies having more socioeconomic resources than their democratic tradition would suggest also have stronger self-expression values than their democratic tradition would suggest (see the locations of East Germany, the Netherlands, South Korea, and Argentina). Similarly, societies with lower levels of resources than their democratic tradition would suggest also have weaker self-expression values than their democratic tradition would suggest (see the locations of the United States, India, Turkey, South Africa, and Switzerland). Overall, the variation in socioeconomic resources that is independent of the length of a society's democratic tradition explains 54 percent of the independent variation in self-expression values. Thus, a society's socioeconomic resources have a substantial impact on its strength of self-expression values, and this effect is largely independent of how long the society has lived under democratic institutions.

Figure 8.7b shows the impact of the democratic tradition on self-expression values, controlling for socioeconomic resources. There is variation in the democratic tradition that is independent from a society's resources, but it explains only an insignificant 4 percent in the independent variation of self-expression values. The number of years of democracy that a society has experienced has no significant impact on self-expression values when we control for its level of socioeconomic resources.

These findings solve Dahl's puzzle of what determines what, cited in Chapter 7. They indicate that the syndrome of human development emerges through a sequence in which growing socioeconomic resources tend to fuel emancipative social forces, reflected in rising self-expression values, which in turn are conducive to democracy.

The Role of Other Structural Factors

Socioeconomic development is the most widely accepted determinant of democracy in the democratization literature. Our results confirm that socioeconomic development has a significant impact on democracy, but one that is weaker than the impact of self-expression values: to a large extent, it is linked with democracy because it brings changes in values that are conducive to democracy. Moreover, we controlled the impact of self-expression values on a society's subsequent democratic performance for this society's prior democratic tradition and the regional diffusion of democracy. Neither of these factors made the impact of self-expression values insignificant.

Does this result hold up when we control for additional structural factors that have also been discussed as determinants of democracy in the literature? Leaving aside other mass attitudes (which we examine in Chapter 11), widely discussed structural determinants of democracy include international influences, religious tradition, and societal cleavages (for an overview, see Bollen and Jackman, 1985; Gasiorowski and Power, 1998; Berg-Schlosser and Mitchell, 2000; Doorenspleet, 2004).

Among the international factors, world system theory holds that socioeconomic development will be conducive to democracy *only* if a country has a favorable position in the world economy, being able to trade on a par with the capitalistic centers (Wallerstein, 1974). From a different perspective, free-trade theory concludes that countries that are able to accumulate wealth through free trade will naturally develop liberal tendencies because they are constantly exposed to diverse new ideas from outside (Bollen and Jackman, 1985; McNeill, 1990; Landes, 1998). Whether a society has a favorable position in the world market is indicated by the per capita value of its exports: the higher this value, the better a country's position. Accordingly, one would expect a high per capita value of exports to have a positive impact on liberal democracy.[25]

Social cleavage factors have been discussed extensively in the democratization literature. Sharp class divisions, social polarization, and extremely uneven

---

[25] For measuring the per capita value of exports in 1990, see the Internet Appendix, #09 under Variables.

distributions of wealth are considered hostile to democracy (Muller, 1997). So-cial inequality causes the powerful upper classes to fear that democracy will enable the lower classes to carry out redistributive measures that will dispossess them. This gives the upper classes a powerful incentive to block genuine democracy. Conversely, a more equal distribution of wealth leads to the dominance of politically moderate middle classes, which have less to fear and more to gain from democracy. Consequently, relatively equal distributions of wealth should have a positive impact on democracy (Boix, 2001).[26]

When there are extreme imbalances in the distribution of wealth, states tend to establish strong coercive capacities, because the privileged classes need coercive power to protect their status against redistributional claims of the lower classes (Dahl, 1973). Accordingly, the presence of strong coercive state capacities should have a negative impact on democracy, in particular when state expenditure for coercive means comes at the expense of expenditure for public welfare.[27]

Ethnic fractionalization is also considered hostile to democracy (Muller and Seligson, 1994). Ethnic diversity can be used to create hostilities between ethnic groups, undermining the democratic idea of a community of equals; consequently it has been claimed that ethnic fractionalization has a negative impact on democracy.[28]

A final structural factor is a society's religious tradition. Many writers have attributed an individualistic worldview to Protestantism (Bollen and Jackman, 1985). This implies that liberal democracy with its emphasis on individual rights should find the most fertile ground in Protestant societies. If this is true and a society's Protestant imprint is reflected in its percentage of Protestants, it should have a positive impact on democracy. By contrast, a specifically antidemocratic tendency has been attributed to Islamic societies (Huntington, 1996). If this is true as well and a society's Islamic imprint is reflected in its percentage of Muslims, it should have a negative impact on democracy. If these measures are combined into a percentage difference index that becomes increasingly positive the more Protestants outweigh Muslims, a positive impact on democracy would be expected.[29]

Table 8.4 demonstrates what happens when we introduce each of these structural factors, in addition to self-expression values. Following the principle of Granger causality, we control for how long a society's democratic tradition has lasted in order to identify the impacts of these variables on subsequent democracy insofar as they operate independently from a society's prior democracy.

[26] To measure the inequality of income distribution, we used the Gini index at around 1990. For more details, see the Internet Appendix, #10 under Variables.

[27] To measure how far state expenditure for coercive means goes at the expense of expenditure for public welfare, we calculated the difference in state budgets invested into the military and into health and education. For more details, see the Internet Appendix, #13.

[28] We used indices of ethnic and linguistic fractionalization provided by Alesina and Devleeschauwer (2002) and Roeder (2001). For details, see the Internet Appendix, #11 under Variables.

[29] For measurement details, see the Internet Appendix, #14 under Variables.

TABLE 8.4. *The Impact of Self-Expression Values on Democracy, Controlling for Various Sociostructural Factors*

Predictors	Dependent Variable: Level of Effective Democracy in 2000–2002					
	Model 1	Model 2	Model 3	Model 4	Model 5	Model 6
Years under democratic government up to 1995	.14 (1.51)	.24* (2.58)	.17 (1.62)	.10 (1.10)	.17* (1.88)	.15 (1.65)
Percent high on self-expression values in early 1990s	.65*** (5.95)	.67*** (7.11)	.71*** (6.72)	.64*** (5.93)	.56*** (5.31)	.61*** (4.77)
Per capita value (U.S.$) of exports in 1990	.18* (2.18)					
Ethnolinguistic fractionalization index in 1985		−.20** (−3.45)				
Income inequality (Gini coefficient) in 1995			−.16* (−2.36)			
Years of schooling aged 20–24 in 1992				.25** (2.88)		
Government expenditure for welfare minus army in 1990					.30*** (4.25)	
Percent Protestants minus Muslims in 1990						.21* (2.20)
Adjusted R² (N)	.83 (59)	.83 (61)	.79 (51)	.84 (54)	.85 (51)	.81 (61)

Notes: Entries are standardized regression coefficients (T-values in parentheses). Significance levels: * p < .100; ** p < .010; *** p < .001; n.s., not significant. All test statistics for collinearity, heteroskedasticity, and influential cases are within acceptable limits.

The results shown in Table 8.4 indicate that a number of the structural factors proposed in the literature do have significant additional impacts on effective democracy, but none of them reduces the impact of self-expression values on effective democracy to an insignificant level. Indeed, none of these factors has an impact as strong as that of self-expression values. Hence, we can conclude that the impact of self-expression values on democracy is not an artifact of the other structural factors discussed in the democratization literature.

Step 4: Explaining Discrepancies between Formal and Effective Democracy

Distinguishing between formal and effective democracy only makes sense if there *are* significant discrepancies between these two versions of liberal

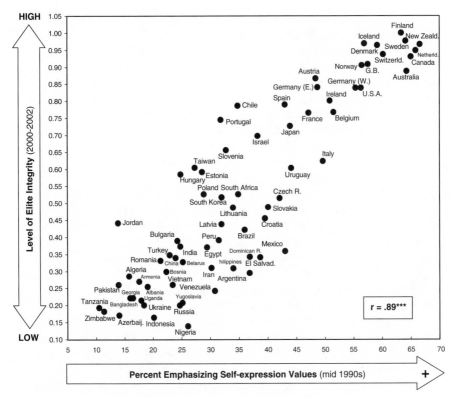

FIGURE 8.8. The impact of self-expression values on elite integrity.

democracy. As Figure 8.5 demonstrates, dramatic discrepancies do indeed exist between formal and effective democracy.

Elite integrity makes the entire difference between formal democracy and effective democracy: the discrepancy between formal and effective democracy reflects deficiencies in elite integrity. Relatively high levels of elite integrity bring a society's level of effective democracy up to its level of formal democracy, but low levels of elite integrity degrade a society's level of effective democracy far below its level of formal democracy. Hence, in order to understand how self-expression values affect discrepancies between effective and formal democracy, one must examine the impact of self-expression values on elite integrity.

As Figure 8.8 demonstrates, self-expression values have a strikingly strong effect on subsequent measures of elite integrity, explaining 79 percent of the cross-national variation in elite integrity. This implies that rising self-expression values operate as a social force that closes the gap between effective and formal democracy, by reinforcing elite integrity – the factor that diminishes the difference between formal democracy and effective democracy.

The impact of self-expression values on formal democracy is somewhat different, as Figure 7.1 demonstrated. On one hand, the effect is strong and highly significant, explaining roughly 50 percent of the variation in formal democracy. In addition, the effect seems to work in a specific direction: strong self-expression values are a sufficient condition to produce formal democracy, because any society that ranks above the 33rd percentile on the self-expression values scale (i.e., at or above the level of Venezuela) scores at or above the 60th percentile on formal democracy – without exception. On the other hand, the impact of self-expression values on formal democracy is weakened by the fact that strong self-expression values are not a necessary condition for formal democracy: free elections can be held almost anywhere, and the 80th percentile in formal democracy can be reached even by societies below the 25th percentile in self-expression values.

Bulgaria, Romania, and India are cases where we find high levels of formal democracy, even though self-expression values are weak. But in all these cases, weak self-expression values are linked with severe deficiencies in elite integrity, making their high levels of formal democracy translate into low levels of effective democracy. In other words, high levels of formal democracy tend to be rendered ineffective if they exist in a society where the public places weak emphasis on self-expression. By contrast, when self-expression values are strong, elite integrity also tends to be high, making given levels of formal democracy effective. Thus, high levels of formal democracy are virtually always effective if the public places strong emphasis on self-expression values. Self-expression values are a social force that closes the gap between formal democracy and effective democracy by fueling elite integrity.

From another perspective, weak self-expression values imply strong survival values, which drive people to seek protection in closely knit groups and to create strong bonding ties, cultivating favoritism for insurance against the risks of life. Favoritism provides a fertile ground for corruption. Corruption comes to be the standard behavior that people expect from elites in a survival culture. By contrast, the emancipative nature of self-expression values encourages nondiscriminatory and universal conceptions of human well-being. The rise of an emancipative culture brings increasing mass disapproval of favoritism and corruption. Thus, when formal democracy is combined with widespread self-expression values, strong social forces create pressures for high elite integrity, making formal democracy effective. Rising self-expression values bring social pressures that tend to close the gap between formal and effective democracy.

Conclusion

This chapter examined the impact of self-expression values on democracy from several different perspectives. We found that self-expression values are significantly linked with various measures of democracy, including constitutional democracy, electoral democracy, and liberal democracy. From the human development perspective, liberal democracy is particularly significant, and our analyses focus on it, differentiating between formal and effective versions of liberal democracy. We then demonstrated that: (1) self-expression values have a strong causal impact on the emergence of formal democracy, but (2) these values have an even stronger impact on the emergence of effective democracy, and (3) self-expression values are conducive to elite integrity, the factor that closes the gap between formal and effective democracy. Causal effects in the reverse direction, that is, from democratic institutions to self-expression values, were found to be negligible. These findings strongly support a cultural explanation of democracy and disconfirm an institutional explanation of political culture. They indicate that rising self-expression values play a central role in the trend toward democracy.

9

Social Forces, Collective Action, and International Events

We have just seen strong evidence that mass self-expression values promote the emergence and effectiveness of democracy. But cultural changes by themselves are not the entire story. For example, one could argue quite plausibly that the Third Wave of democratization would never have occurred, if Mikhail Gorbachev had not abolished the Brezhnev doctrine, and unless the United States had supported democratization in such countries as the Philippines and South Korea. For democratization is not brought about by impersonal mass tendencies, such as self-expression values, but by collective actions in which specific actors, including elites and counterelites, play the key roles.

It would be absurd to argue that cultural changes automatically produce institutional changes such as democratization, but they do seem to be an important contributing factor. The question is, How do rising self-expression values interact with elite-level events, such as Gorbachev's decision not to intervene militarily in Eastern Europe to prop up tottering communist regimes, in bringing about and strengthening democracies? To answer this question, we must deal with three types of causal factors (see Tilly, 1984).

First, changing international circumstances, exemplified by such events as the Washington consensus or the end of the Brezhnev doctrine, play key roles in launching international waves of democratization (Pridham, 1991; L. Diamond, 1993a; W. I. Robinson, 1996; Markoff, 1996; Whitehead, 1996). The impact of these international events is obvious to anyone who has dealt with questions of democratization, but they are only part of the story. For suitable societal conditions are required for democracy to take root in any given country. The United States provided assistance to prodemocracy movements in the Philippines and South Korea and also to such movements in Iran and Pakistan. But a given amount of assistance was far more successful in some countries than in others, for reasons that reflect internal conditions. Similarly, the Soviet Union's abolition of military support for communist regimes in Central Eastern Europe in the late 1980s opened an opportunity that made democratization possible. But this opportunity gave rise to very different outcomes in different societies. The end of the Brezhnev doctrine applied equally to Poland and Romania, but different internal conditions led to different outcomes: Poland moved quickly to a fully consolidated and reasonably effective democracy, whereas Romania still has to struggle toward such an achievement.

A society's internal conditions can develop to a point where the country is ripe for democratization, but authoritarian elites can block this process, particularly if they are supported by external powers. Once this external support fades, authoritarian elites will be exposed to the democratizing forces within their societies – *if* such forces have emerged. International events can either block or mobilize democratizing forces within a society. However, they can only mobilize democratizing forces that already exist; they cannot create them. If these forces are not in place or are not yet strong enough (as seems to be the case in China, Vietnam, Saudi Arabia, and other authoritarian societies that manage to survive in an increasingly anti-authoritarian international environment), favorable international conditions will have no effect.

Regardless of what happens on the international scene, democratization takes place through collective action, such as mass demonstrations, liberation campaigns, and bargaining processes at the elite level, where power holders and regime opponents negotiate the details of a transition process (among others, see O'Donnell and Schmitter, 1986; Karl and Schmitter, 1991; Higley and Gunther, 1992; Bernhard, 1993; Casper and Taylor, 1996; Foweraker and Landman, 1997). But descriptions of collective action sequences have limited explanatory power, even if they are reconstructed into more general typologies. For collective actions are an integral part of transition processes themselves. They describe *how* transitions proceed, but they do not explain *why* they occur.

Democratization always takes place through collective actions, whether the process is shaped by mass mobilization or by elite bargaining. People who make important decisions are defined as elites, so by definition elite actions are always the proximate factor in bringing about democracy – but this does not mean that elites operate in a vacuum. Quite the contrary, their actions are usually conditioned by more deeply rooted social forces such as those tapped by mass self-expression values: these forces shape collective actions, channeling them into corridors that make some outcomes – such as effective democracy – more likely than others. We view social forces as mass tendencies that motivate collective actions, directing them toward particular outcomes, such as the various institutional configurations in which effective democracy can be realized. Collective actions conduct transitions. But social forces channel collective actions in a specific direction.

This notion of social forces is consistent with that expressed in theories of social movements and mass mobilization. Tilly's resource-mobilization theory (1978) holds that resources are needed to mobilize social forces. And modernization provides people with the economic, cognitive, and social resources needed to constitute social forces. But resources alone do not determine the direction in which social forces will move and the aims they will pursue. Mass attitudinal tendencies also play a crucial role, making people prefer some goals over others. McAdam (1986), for instance, demonstrated that mobilization in the Mississippi Freedom Summer in 1964 not only involved resource mobilization but depended on motivational mobilization of what he called "attitudinal affinities." Movement activists help frame the goals that mobilize people (Benford and Snow, 1988). But which political goals are most likely to attract people depends on McAdam's attitudinal affinities, which make people more receptive to some goals than others. Thus, people who emphasize self-expression values will be more receptive to the symbols of civil rights than to those of the strong leader, whereas people with survival values are likely to respond in the opposite fashion.

Self-expression values are mass attitudinal tendencies that emphasize civil and political liberties and genuinely effective democracy. These values do not themselves install democratic institutions or make them effective. But they channel collective actions into directions that make democratic outcomes increasingly likely. The strong impact of self-expression values on effective democracy exists because these values help generate the collective actions that create and sustain democracy. This conclusion is inescapable because democracy is always created and sustained by collective actions. If self-expression values did not help generate the collective actions that eventually establish and deepen democracy, these values could have no significant effect on the emergence and effectiveness of democracy.

Any democratic transition reflects the interaction of three types of causal factors: international events *stimulate* given social forces within societies; social forces *channel* collective actions toward certain political outcomes; and collective actions *execute* the processes producing these outcomes. Thus, there is an interaction of *stimulating* factors (international events), *channeling* factors (social forces), and *executing* factors (collective actions). In this interaction, social forces constitute the most fundamental factor. They provide the root cause of such processes as democratization, whereas collective actions provide the proximate cause. To reach a deeper understanding of democratization, we must not only look at its proximate causes; we must also examine its root cause: social forces. These forces are reflected in mass attitudinal tendencies, such as self-expression values.

Rhythms of Change

As Chapter 8 demonstrated, levels of democracy and self-expression values show sharply contrasting degrees of stability. Self-expression values tend to accumulate slowly, showing only minor changes within short time intervals. Consequently, self-expression values at one point in time provide a pretty accurate prediction of self-expression values at a slightly later point in time. By contrast, levels of democracy changed drastically in many societies during the Third Wave: the autocorrelation of democracy over time is considerably weaker, which means that we must turn to other factors (such as self-expression values) to explain shifts toward democracy. These differences in temporal stability imply different logics of change, which must be taken into account in interpreting causal relationships.

The pattern of sudden regime changes that manifested itself during the Third Wave contrasts with the inertia of socioeconomic and cultural change, both of which tend to move continuously but slowly. Political regimes can change from autocracy to democracy overnight, but societies need decades to move from poverty to prosperity, or from a culture emphasizing survival values to a culture emphasizing self-expression values.

Gradually changing variables, such as socioeconomic development, show a great deal of inertia. The gains or losses in any year are minor in comparison with the stocks that have been accumulated up to that point. Annual increases in a society's GDP always constitute a small percentage of that society's GDP. Gradually changing variables like these show substantial changes only over the long run. We will refer to such variables as "cumulating variables." By contrast, explosively changing variables, such as democratization and other institutional changes, show long periods of constancy but can suddenly make dramatic moves that completely alter the situation, bringing historical breakthroughs. We refer to these variables as "break variables." The difference in the dynamics of change between cumulating variables and break variables affects the interpretation of their causal relationship in two ways.

First, the causal relationship between a cumulating variable and a break variable is not continuous: it becomes manifest only at the moment when the break variable suddenly makes a major leap. Apart from these leaps, one rarely sees any change in a break variable. To analyze such changes, one must concentrate the analysis on the particular time during which the break variable suddenly made massive changes. This makes standard time-series techniques inadequate because they treat each time interval equally, mixing leaps in the break variable that appear at one point with prolonged periods of constancy during which nothing happens. The episodic character of changes in a break variable must be dealt with by focusing on specific periods of change, instead of averaging them out across the many years in which a break variable stays at constant levels. Our analyses in Chapter 8 reflect this strategy. Instead of analyzing democracy on a year-to-year basis, we concentrated on the major wave of changes that sharply separates the period before 1987 from the one following 1996.

Second, the sudden leaps that a break variable shows in a specific period of time do not reflect corresponding leaps in a cumulating variable, for cumulating variables do not leap. Whether a country's economy has recently grown by 1 or 3 percent will not determine whether the country makes a sudden leap into democracy. But whether a country's average per capita income has accumulated to $500 or to $10,000 before the leap can play a decisive role in whether the country shifts to democracy. As recent analyses have shown (Boix and Stokes, 2003), almost no low-income country shifted to democracy in the Third Wave – but a large number of middle-income countries did: Chile was much likelier to leap to democracy than Benin. Cumulating variables, such as socioeconomic development and cultural change, are inertial, not necessarily showing any change during the brief period in which a break variable changes drastically.

Due to their gradual but continuous pattern of change, cumulating variables show large variation in the levels that have accumulated up to any given point in time. Differences in current growth rates are relatively small compared to the differences in levels of per capita income, where the wealthiest nation in our sample is two hundred times richer than the poorest nation.

Some examples of cumulating variables versus break variables were discussed in Chapter 1, where we saw that intergenerational cultural changes that took place over many decades suddenly culminated in an institutional breakthrough, such as the legalization of divorce in Spain, Italy, and Ireland, or the legalization of same-sex marriages in the Netherlands, Germany, and Canada. In such cases, any attempt to explain the institutional breakthrough in terms of recent attitudinal changes would be pointless. Recent attitudinal changes concerning homosexuality were actually greater in Nigeria than in the Netherlands; but in Nigeria only 8 percent of the public had tolerant attitudes toward homosexuality, whereas in the Netherlands 78 percent of the public did – so the Netherlands was where the institutional breakthrough occurred. An analysis of recent attitudinal changes would not only show weak effects, it would often point in the wrong direction.

Short-term changes in cumulating variables, such as self-expression values, are modest and would not have a significant impact on drastic changes in break variables. When decisive regime changes occur, recent minor fluctuations in people's self-expression values are irrelevant. What matters is whether self-expression values have reached a *level* at which they are relatively widespread, because it is the extent to which a public emphasizes self-expression values that determines the strength of a public's demand for freedom. This was also reflected in our analyses: we explained change in levels of democracy by the level of self-expression values, not by *changes* in the level of self-expression values.

In short, the analysis of changes toward higher or lower levels of democracy must recognize three major points. First, regime changes are unique events, establishing major historical breakthroughs. They do not emerge gradually over many years but emerge within sharply focused periods, sometimes occurring only once in a country's history. Accordingly, any large-scale analysis of regime changes must focus on periods when major waves of regime changes occur. Second, if one wants to explain the impact of a cumulating variable such as self-expression values on regime changes, recent fluctuations in the cumulating variable are irrelevant; what matters are the levels of cumulating variables. Short-term changes in cumulating variables are generally insignificant, compared to the levels that have been accumulated at a given point in time. Third, one should recognize that the impact of a cumulating variable on regime changes is usually conditional, interacting with external conditions that activate their effect. For these reasons, the standard type of time-series analysis is inappropriate for analyzing regime changes, which is why we have used a different approach in the causal analyses in this and the preceding chapter.

External Stimulating Factors

Cumulating variables alone do not explain sudden leaps in a break variable; they interact with relevant external events. With democratization in Eastern Europe, the relevant external event was the nullification of the Brezhnev doctrine. As long as communist regimes were backed up by the Red Army,[1] no regime change was possible – no matter how much emphasis people placed on self-expression. But once Gorbachev announced that the Red Army would no longer intervene to support communist regimes in 1988, internal forces, such as mass emphasis on self-expression values, had an immediate impact, causing major and enduring moves toward democracy where these values were widespread (e.g., Poland, Czech Republic, Slovenia) but smaller and less successful changes where these values were not widespread (e.g., Belarus, Russia, Serbia). The regime changes were sudden. The social and cultural changes that conditioned them reflected long periods of gradual growth.

Relatively widespread self-expression values in such countries as Chile, South Korea, and Hungary could not initiate regime changes toward more democracy as long as these countries' authoritarian regimes obtained financial, military, and political support from one of the two superpowers. But once this support was withdrawn, self-expression values were no longer irrelevant and could affect these societies' political regimes, which gave way to democracy soon after external conditions had changed. Right-wing authoritarian regimes in Southeast Asia, Latin America, and Africa that had previously been supported by the United States lost this support after the Washington consensus in the mid-1980s (see Pridham, 1991; Gills and Rocamora, 1992; Pridham and Vanhanen, 1995; W. I. Robinson, 1996; Whitehead, 1996; Randall and Theobald, 1998). From then on, the United States began to support civil rights movements all over the world, and the World Bank began to tie credits to conditions of "good governance." At this point, authoritarian regimes lost Western support (with the exception of some oil-exporting countries, such as Saudi Arabia). Accordingly, most of the regime shifts toward democracy in East Asia (the Philippines, South Korea, Taiwan, Thailand, Indonesia), Latin America (Chile, Panama, Guyana, Paraguay, Suriname), and Africa (Benin, Ghana, Mali, South Africa, Zambia) started after the late 1980s and not earlier (Diamond, 1993b).

The members of the Warsaw Pact lost their external guarantee even more abruptly in 1988, when Gorbachev declared that the Red Army would no longer intervene to support communist regimes in Central and Eastern Europe (Diamond, 1993b; W. I. Robinson, 1996). The subsequent collapse of communism and the breakup of the Soviet Union were sudden, but there was a wide

---

[1] Similarly, during the Cold War the United States supported a number of authoritarian anticommunist regimes.

range of outcomes. In some cases, the result was renewed authoritarian rule, as in Belarus and Central Asia; in others, it led to "authoritarian democracies," as in Russia and Serbia; and in others, it led to genuine democracies, as in Slovenia, the Czech Republic, and the Baltic states. As we demonstrated, these outcomes largely reflected the level of self-expression values that was present in a given society at the start of the transition.

This interaction between external conditions and internal conditions was grasped by Huntington years before the collapse of communism (1984: 211) when he concluded that "in terms of cultural tradition, economic development and social structure, Czechoslovakia would certainly be a democracy today (and probably Hungary and Poland) if it were not for the overriding veto of the Soviet presence." This diagnosis was right on target. It implied that without the threat of Soviet intervention, the internal social forces in these countries would affect their existing institutions, which is exactly what happened. External support for autocracies ended abruptly after 1988, removing a blocking factor that had hindered transitions to democracy in societies where the internal conditions already were ripe. Once this blocking factor vanished, differences in value orientations that had seemed irrelevant for decades suddenly played a decisive role in transitions to democracy.

Our reasoning is compatible with value-expectancy theory in mobilization research (Klandermans, 1984). Value-expectancy theory argues that mobilizing movement activities reflects the interaction between people's expectation that these activities have a reasonable chance to succeed and the extent to which people value the movement's goals. People will not participate in social movements if they expect that their activities have no chance to succeed, even if they fully support the movement's goals. But they also will not participate if they do not value those goals, regardless of their expectations of success.

The interaction between international events, such as the nullification of the Brezhnev doctrine, and given levels of self-expression values reflects this same logic. For people to take part in a prodemocracy movement, they must expect that their actions have a reasonable chance of attaining a democratic regime. If this expectation is absent, they will not participate, even if they support the goal of democratization. This helps explain why given self-expression values remained ineffective as long as the Brezhnev doctrine was in force: mass expectations that their protests would succeed against Soviet tanks were close to zero. But mass aspirations for democracy, rooted in self-expression values, became effective immediately after the threat of Soviet military intervention was withdrawn. The dramatic change in external conditions activated self-expression values that were already present, but it could not create them. Because these values had emerged in varying degrees in different societies, the same external changes produced very different degrees of democratic mobilization.

The product of values multiplied by expectations is close to zero when the expectations are close to zero, rendering the value term irrelevant. This was the situation before 1988. But as expectations change, the product of expectations and values becomes dependent on the value term, so that after 1988, differences in self-expression values explain differences in mass mobilization in democracy movements and democratic outcomes.

Regime changes can be understood as the interaction between internal conditions and relevant external events, with external factors often being able to block or stimulate the impact of internal conditions. Accordingly, our analyses focus on changes from before to after the Third Wave, when relevant external events made internal factors relevant. Our analyses recognized the importance of external international factors in two ways: by analyzing regime changes when international changes allow them to happen; and by taking spatial diffusion into account, in examining the extent to which a given country's regime change reflects changes in its vicinity.

Undemocratic regimes do not necessarily need external support to survive. Undemocratic regimes continue to survive without external support in such countries as China and Belarus, where prodemocratic social forces are still relatively weak. The same is true of regimes that are formally democratic but severely deficient in democratic standards, such as their civil rights performance. But as we have demonstrated, in countries where undemocratic regimes and ineffective democracies persist without external support, the mass culture places relatively weak emphasis on self-expression values. By the same token, as we have seen, undemocratic regimes and ineffective democracies are unlikely to persist without external support today, once self-expression values have become widespread in the society.

Mass Culture and Elite Behavior

How do self-expression values condition the collective actions that bring about democratization? From O'Donnell and Schmitter's (1986) seminal work onward, many researchers have argued that elite-managed collective actions are always the immediate cause of regime transitions to democracy (Karl and Schmitter, 1991; Higley and Gunther, 1992; Marks, 1992; Przeworski, 1992; Linz and Stepan, 1996). Accordingly, transitions to democracy can be seen as the result of "defender-challenger games" (Casper and Taylor, 1996) between the elites in office and the counterelites who challenge them. Even if large-scale mass mobilizations involve broader segments of the population, a relatively small number of political elites and activists play the key roles. The same argument is made for regime stability: democratic regimes are stable if the elites agree that democracy is "the only game in town" (Linz and Stepan, 1996: 4).

The insight that regime stability and regime change result from collective actions in which political elites and counterelites play the key roles focuses narrowly on the proximate causes of democratization, ignoring the broader social forces that channel their actions into specific directions. It even verges on tautology to argue that a transition from an autocracy to a democracy succeeded because the prodemocratic challengers played their cards better than the antidemocratic defenders. It is true that elite behavior is always the proximate factor in bringing about regime change, but this gives no insight concerning the broader social forces that caused the elites to act as they did (Huntington, 1991: 36). The fact that the fate of political regimes "is an outcome of actions, not just conditions" (Przeworski and Limongi, 1997: 176) does not mean that these actions are not shaped by broader social forces, such as mass self-expression values.

It is true by definition that creating, implementing, and crafting democratic institutions is something done by elites. But this means that there is only one possible way in which self-expression values can have the strong impact on democracy that the previous analyses have shown they have: mass preferences must influence elite behavior. Because elite behavior is the proximate cause of democratization, the impact of self-expression values on democracy indicates that mass culture influences elite behavior. The question is, How?

There are two possible ways in which the emancipative social forces tapped by self-expression values can promote elite behavior that is conducive to democracy. The first possibility derives from the properties of a society in which self-expression values are widespread. By definition, such a society contains a large proportion of people who value human emancipation and who are inclined to actively protest against unacceptable elite action. In a society with widespread self-expression values, people are likely to join mass social movements and support public campaigns that put pressure on elites to respond to their demands and respect their rights. Furthermore, because self-expression values tend to emerge with high levels of socioeconomic development, a public emphasizing these values tends to have the resources needed to help make its demands effective. Hence, one way in which mass-level self-expression values impact on elite behavior is that these values produce mass pressure on elites. Such pressure can take the form of mass movements, public campaigns, and protest activities – all of which can put effective pressure on state-anchored elites (see L. Diamond, 1993b; Markoff, 1996; Paxton, 2002: 256).

Authoritarian elites usually have enough power to repress mass demands, as long as they control the military and are willing to use coercion. But the resources that people invest, and the determination with which they invest them in freedom campaigns and liberation movements, can offset a regime's coercive power (Dahl, 1973; Markoff, 1996; Tilly, 1997). Massive and intense freedom campaigns demonstrate civilian power against a coercive state, implying that the regime will be confronted with high suppression costs if its elites opt to use military means. Being confronted with higher suppression costs affects the risk calculation on the part of the elites, increasing the likelihood that they will hesitate to opt for suppression (Marks, 1992: 50–55; Karklins and Petersen, 1993; Gibson, 2001). If mass demonstrations for democracy in 1989 China had spread across all major cities and had involved all groups of the population, it would have been less likely that the Communist Party leaders would have been able to suppress the movement. Conversely, if mass demonstrations for democracy in 1989 Czechoslovakia and the GDR had been concentrated solely in Prague and East Berlin and were only supported by a thin student population, the Communist Party leaders would have faced lower risks when trying to send troops against demonstrators.

One cannot simply conclude that elites only need the will to stay in power and to defend their position by all means, in order to guarantee an authoritarian regime's survival. Authoritarian elites usually want to stay in power; the question is whether they can. The strength of mass opposition is a crucial factor in this respect, and the evidence suggests that widespread self-expression values nurture democratic mass opposition against authoritarian regimes, whereas weak self-expression values limit it. This helps to explain why the democracy movement failed in China in 1989 but succeeded in Czechoslovakia in 1989.

Another reason why rising self-expression values work against authoritarian regimes is that generational value changes occur not only among the masses but also among the elites. If the younger elite cohorts come to emphasize self-expression values, the emancipative nature of these values erodes their belief in the legitimacy of using force against peaceful civil rights movements. Elites almost always want to stay in power but not necessarily at any price. Emancipative norms tend to lower the price that elites are willing to pay for staying in power, eliminating military force against a civilian opposition as a legitimate option. Consider once more the regime challenges in China and Czechoslovakia in 1989: the Chinese elites sent troops against peaceful demonstrators, whereas the Czech elites did not. As we have pointed out, the demonstrations for democracy were more widespread and intense in Czechoslovakia than in China so that any attempt to repress the demonstrations by force meant a much larger risk in Czechoslovakia than in China. But it is also likely that elites in Czechoslovakia opted against the use of force because stronger emancipative norms (which were certainly present in the society as a whole) made them less ready to use repression than Chinese elites. Moreover, they may have sensed that lower-level elites might not follow orders to shoot demonstrators if they considered the action illegitimate (which was exactly what happened in the GDR in 1989; see Friedheim, 1993). But why would elites in Czechoslovakia have held stronger emancipative values than Chinese elites?

Elites and masses differ in many ways. Previous studies have shown that elites' orientations differ systematically from those of the general public (Dalton, 1985; Iversen, 1994). But the national context affects both elites and masses, with growing prosperity transforming both elite and mass values. This is reflected in the fact that the value differences between elites and masses within nations are much smaller than the value differences across nations, as we will demonstrate. Self-expression values tend to be emphasized by the elites of a given society even more strongly than by the general public. Because these values are associated with the high levels of economic security and education that characterize elites, this outcome is not surprising – but it has important implications. It suggests that as self-expression values emerge among mass publics, they also tend to emerge among the elites of that society. This means that if a

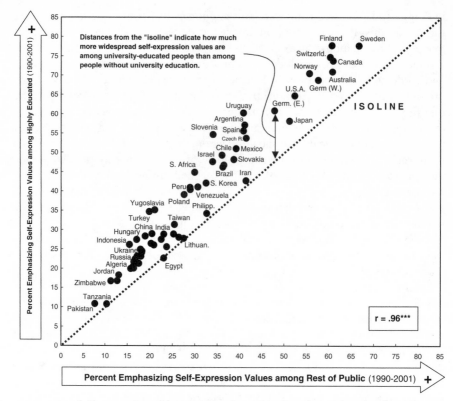

FIGURE 9.1. Self-expression values among the university-educated and among the rest of the public.

society's mass culture becomes more hostile to favoritism, corruption, and authoritarianism, elite culture is likely to do so as well.

We do not possess samples of the elites from the more than eighty societies included in the Values Survey, but in virtually every society the political elites are primarily recruited from people with higher education. Hence, we treat the value orientations of the university-educated as a rough indicator of the value orientations of elites, expecting the university-educated to place more emphasis on self-expression values than the general publics of their society.

The evidence in Figure 9.1 strongly supports this expectation. The horizontal axis of this figure shows for each country the percentage of ordinary citizens who emphasize self-expression values. The vertical axis shows the percentage emphasizing self-expression values among those with at least some university education.[2] The "isoline" marks the locations on which each public would

---

[2] The Values Surveys ask respondents to indicate their level of formal education (V227) on a scale from 1 to 9 in which 8 means "some university education" and 9 means "a university degree." We summed these two categories to identify the university-educated.

fall if self-expression values were equally widespread among the university-educated and ordinary citizens. Deviations from the "isoline" indicate the margin by which self-expression values are more widespread among the educated than among ordinary citizens. Downward deviations from the "isoline" indicate how much *less* widespread self-expression values are among the university-educated than among the general public of their country; upward deviations indicate how much *more* widespread these values are among the educated strata.

As Figure 9.1 shows, virtually all national publics fall above the "isoline," which means that the university-educated place stronger emphasis on self-expression values than the average citizen. One might interpret this finding as indicating that university education tends to promote an emancipative orientation, reflected in stronger emphasis on human self-expression. Or this could simply reflect the fact that the university-educated have grown up with higher levels of existential security than the mass public as a whole.

In any case, the margins by which the educated deviate from the population (reflected in the length of the distances from the "isoline") are relatively small and more or less constant, averaging about 7 percentage points. The range of cross-national differences is about ten times as large as this. No distance from the "isoline" even remotely approaches the huge cross-national differences that range from Tanzania at the lower left of the overall distribution to Sweden at the upper right end. Differences in emphasis on self-expression values *between* nations are much greater than the differences between the educated and non-educated *within* nations. In fact, fully 92 percent of the cross-national variation in self-expression values among the university-educated can be explained by the corresponding mass-level values in the same countries. Although there is an almost universal tendency for the educated to place more emphasis on self-expression values than the general public, this effect is constrained by a strong tendency for elite values to correspond to the broader public's values within a given society. Elites tend to reflect the values prevailing in their society.

Overall, the values of the broader public have a much stronger impact on the self-expression values of the educated than has their higher level of education. In other words, the educated do not simply impose their values on the publics: these values reflect the society's level of socioeconomic development. Each society's elite is recruited from its own society and rarely runs very far ahead of (or behind) the prevailing values of that society.

These findings suggest that mass culture and elite culture tend to coincide in their most fundamental values, which has important implications. To some extent, the population may not even need to push the elites to adopt mass-responsive and law-abiding behavior; the same factors that tend to develop self-expression values among the masses tend to instill these values in succeeding elite cohorts.

One can explain elite choices by rational risk calculations to some extent, but one should not forget that elite perception of choices is culture-bound. Cultural norms and internalized values clearly limit the scope of choices that are taken into rational calculation. In other words, cultural norms and internalized values shape an individual's cost-benefit ratio with respect to particular choices (Lal, 1998). Options violating one's internalized norms cause additional costs that make the choice of these options less likely. These costs are psychological and are manifest in the emotional pain that one experiences when acting against one's internalized values. Depending on the strength of an internalized value, the psychological costs that such a violation would cause can outweigh the material benefits linked with this violation. For example, in some societies the value of premarital chastity can be so strongly internalized that a girl would rather sacrifice her life than lose her virginity. Similarly, the value of tolerance can be so deeply internalized that one would refuse to discriminate against one's most hated enemies, even if one could directly benefit from doing so. Thus, the British government does not consider using troops to suppress the opposition, even if it were feasible. This is not the result of a deliberate calculation. The prime minister and his cabinet do not decide against using troops because they have considered this option and calculated that it would not work; they do not even take that option into consideration. This option – a very common one in much of the world – is completely outside their universe of culturally legitimate options. This is why it seems absurd to discuss whether the British prime minister would even think about using troops to repress the opposition. It is beyond consideration. By 1989 this seems to have also become true in Czechoslovakia – but not in China.

Path Analysis

In the preceding section, we argued that mass values affect democracy through their impact on elite behavior. Self-expression values, in other words, have an impact on effective democracy because they promote the elite integrity that makes formal democracy effective. This can now be tested in two ways. If we are right, self-expression values should have an even stronger impact on effective democracy than on formal democracy because effective democracy includes elite integrity. On the other hand, if we decompose effective democracy into its two components – formal democracy and elite integrity – self-expression values should only have an indirect impact on formal democracy, operating mainly through their impact on elite integrity, which in turn should be the proximate cause of formal democracy.

The path analysis in Figure 9.2 confirms these assumptions. As is evident, the impact of self-expression values on formal democracy becomes insignificant when we control for elite integrity. In keeping with expectations of elite theorists, elite integrity turns out to have the only significant impact on formal democracy; however, elite integrity itself is *not* an independent factor, as elite theorists tend to assume. Instead, elite integrity is strongly influenced by mass self-expression values. In multivariate analysis, socioeconomic development has an additional impact, because a given level of self-expression values will produce stronger pressures for elite integrity if people have more resources. But

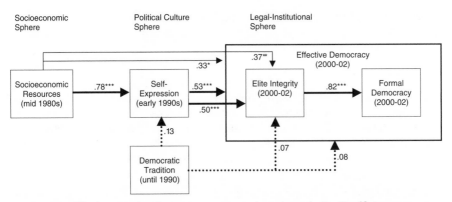

FIGURE 9.2. The human development sequence: A path analysis. Coefficients are standardized path coefficients. Bold arrows indicate strongest effect on respective dependent variable. Interrupted arrows show insignificant effects. There is no overall fit for this fully identified model. Dropping the effects of "Years of Democracy," the Adjusted Goodness of Fit Index is .88, showing that the impact of the democratic tradition is negligible. Number of cases: N = 68

the duration of a society's democratic tradition has no significant impact: not on self-expression values, not on elite integrity, and not on formal democracy. The habituation theory of how a democratic culture emerges finds no empirical support whatever. Instead, the path model depicted in Figure 9.2 shows a sequence that starts with socioeconomic development, moves to self-expression values and then to elite integrity, and ends in effective democracy – confirming the diagram we depicted at the end of Chapter 7 and confirming the human development sequence shown in Table I.1.

It would be illogical in the extreme to interpret the strong linkage we find between mass self-expression values and elite integrity as meaning that elite integrity creates a mass culture of tolerance, liberty aspirations, emphasis on subjective well-being, trust, and an elite-challenging outlook – not only because elite integrity was measured almost ten years after self-expression values, but because such broad and deeply rooted values as these reflect long-term processes of intergenerational change. Elites can appeal to such values but not create them. Even if they *could*, it is difficult to imagine why elites would want to create a public that is self-assertive, demanding, and defiant toward elite authority – all of which are defining characteristics of self-expression values. The rational self-interest of elites lies in having a compliant public that defers to institutionalized authority, rather than being critical of it. Hence, there is no reason to suppose that the strong linkage between self-expression values and elite integrity exists because elite integrity produces mass values that emphasize tolerance, liberty, and elite-challenging behavior. Self-expression values constitute a powerful force pressing for elite integrity – either by instilling these values in the elites themselves or by exposing elites to such pressures from the broader public. We suspect that both factors are at work. The only logical interpretation of the evidence is that self-expression values work to maximize elite integrity.

Cultural Change and Collective Action

Advocates of the actor-centered approach argue that one cannot explain the implementation and consolidation of democracy by factors that are exogenous to the collective actions through which these processes proceed (O'Donnell and Schmitter, 1986: 16; Karl and Schmitter, 1991: 270). They assert that collective action-driven processes can only be explained by reconstructing these actions. Accordingly, Przeworski and Limongi (1997: 176) claim that all processes affecting the stability of political regimes are "about actions, not just conditions." This is true but shortsighted: it ignores the fact that actions have preconditions. To be sure, to *describe* a process one must reconstruct the sequence of actions that generate it, but one cannot *explain* a process by actions that are endogenous to the process itself. Any such explanation inevitably becomes circular. And indeed, the central insight of much of the actor-centered research on democratization has been summed up in the claim that "the implementation and stabilization of democracies depends on the superiority of actors with pro-democratic interests over actors with anti-democratic interests" (Rössel, 2000: 629). This insight is true but trivial. In retrospect, it is always clear that the winners were stronger then the losers, but this gives no insight into the broader social forces that help explain *why* the winners were stronger. Collective actions need to be considered in context with the broader social forces that help shape them. The strong linkage between mass self-expression values and the emergence and strengthening of democracies helps explain *why* prodemocratic actors have become increasingly likely to be the winners.

This study was not designed to investigate the specific processes of collective action through which self-expression values act on democratic institutions in each society. Instead, we have examined the *outcomes* of collective actions – specifically, changes in levels of formal democracy and varying degrees of effective democracy. If self-expression values affect these outcomes, it can only happen because these values engender collective actions that eventually produce these outcomes. Because collective actions are always the immediate cause of changing political institutions, this premise does not have to be tested: we can safely assume that it is true.

Precisely *how* self-expression values engender the collective actions that produce and sustain effective democracy in any given case can best be examined by case studies such as those undertaken by Rueschemeyer et al. (1992), Casper and Taylor (1996), or Foweraker and Landman (1997). Case studies of collective actions in given societies are needed if we are to understand the entire process. They constitute an important task, but a huge one that could not possibly fit into this book, which focuses on the broader population-system linkage within which collective actions operate. Nevertheless, we outline some general ways in which self-expression values help shape the emergence of collective actors that press for democracy. Because the emancipative thrust of self-expression values generates demands for the civil and political rights that define liberal democracy, self-expression values tend to channel collective actions in favor of democratization in the following ways.

First, the strength of self-expression values among the population determines the size of the pool from which prodemocratic political activists emerge, with increasingly widespread self-expression values increasing the pool of potential activists. In nondemocratic regimes, these political activists form a counterelite, creating dissident networks that build the core of a civil society whose sheer existence undermines authoritarian controls (Bernhard, 1993; Markoff, 1996; Paxton, 2002). Civil-societal networks constituted by circles of democratic dissidents played a crucial role in many of the Third Wave democratization processes, and these processes tend to have been more successful where the dissident circles were relatively wide in scope and large in numbers (L. Diamond, 1993b; Joppke, 1994; Foweraker and Landman, 1997).

Relatively widespread self-expression values among the population also increase the chances that dissidents can mobilize large segments of the public for mass campaigns demanding civil and political rights and democratic elections. Such mass mobilizations were a crucial factor in many recent regime transitions, especially in Argentina, the Philippines, South Korea, the Baltic countries, Czechoslovakia, East Germany, Hungary, Russia, and Indonesia, where large parts of the population went to the streets, demonstrating for freedom of expression and demanding democratic elections. In 1989 China, by contrast, demonstrations for democracy were mainly concentrated in one place (Tiananmen Square) and mainly supported by the relatively small student population. At that time, the democracy movement had a relatively small potential mass base in the country as a whole, reflecting the fact that self-expression values were not yet widespread in China, as our 1990 survey demonstrates.

Widespread mass campaigns for democracy are particularly important if the incumbent political elite is united in its will to stay in power, as was the case in China, Czechoslovakia, and East Germany. More-widespread and more-intense campaigns imply that the regime faces high suppression costs if the elites opt to use military means. This affects the elites' risk calculations. It also implies a higher risk that local officials and troop commanders will disobey orders to shoot (Marks, 1992). Being ordered to shoot peaceful protestors can place great psychological strain on the shooters; and an order to shoot is even less likely to be obeyed if it means killing many thousands of protesters at many places throughout the entire country. Thus, widespread mass campaigns may induce authoritarian power holders to give way to free elections, either because they correctly anticipate that they can no longer mobilize sufficient force to suppress the opposition, as happened in the Philippines, South Korea, and Czechoslovakia; or because they attempt to do so but fail, as happened in East Germany, where the communist dictator Erich Honecker ordered the military to shoot the demonstrators, but the order was disobeyed by local elites (Friedheim, 1993). In short, the spread of self-expression values among the population influences the size of the mass base of the democratic opposition and the costs and risks of suppression, increasing the probability of a successful transition to democracy.

Sometimes the ruling elite is divided into one camp of conservative defenders of the status quo and another camp of liberal reformers who show some willingness to make concessions to the democratic opposition (Przeworski, 1992; Marks, 1992). Here too, the strength of self-expression values and the consequent strength of the mass basis of the democratic opposition makes a difference, because a broadly based democratic opposition gives the reformers a viable alliance option, strengthening their bargaining position and making it more likely that the conservative camp will make concessions – as happened in Spain, Poland, Chile, and South Africa (Casper and Taylor, 1996).

Widespread self-expression values among the population also make it more likely that a liberal reform camp will establish itself among the ruling elites. For if self-expression values are relatively widespread among the society, it is more likely that the younger generation of the ruling elite will themselves be influenced by these values, eroding their belief in the legitimacy of coercive methods and making it more likely that they will split off as liberal reformers. This is what happened in Hungary, Mexico, and Taiwan, where it became obvious that the elite successor generation had much more liberal ideas than the founders of the socialist regime, the PRI, and the Kuomintang regime, respectively (L. Diamond, 1993b). Once the reform elites came to hold increasing numbers of top positions, its leaders began to initiate democratic reforms. In this case there was no need for a strong democratic opposition on the streets because changing values infiltrated the elites themselves. This is most likely to happen in authoritarian regimes that have tried to meet the challenge of the knowledge society by expanding university education and by recruiting the next generation of elites on the basis of professional qualification instead of ideological loyalty, as happened in Hungary and Taiwan (for Hungary, see Konrad and Szelenyi, 1991; for Taiwan, see Domes, 1990).

In conclusion, not only the formation of a strong democratic opposition but also the emergence of liberal reformers among the ruling elite seems to become increasingly likely when self-expression values become increasingly widespread among the population.

In regimes that already are democratic (at least formally), self-expression values also play an important role. When self-expression values are relatively widespread, people are more inclined to protest against unpopular elite actions and to practice the liberties to which they are formally entitled. People with strong self-expression values also tend to have the means to make their protests effective, because these values are most likely to emerge in societies with abundant socioeconomic resources. Moreover, as self-expression values spread among the broader public, they tend to infiltrate the mass media, making succeeding cohorts of journalists more critical and more likely to scrutinize elite corruption and state failure more closely. Self-expression values produce a social force that pressures democratic elites to be more responsive and accountable, strengthening democracy and making it more effective. Table 9.1 summarizes our propositions on how self-expression values condition collective actor constellations that are relevant to democracy and democratization.

Figure 9.3 demonstrates that self-expression values do indeed help shape a society's capacity for collective action. The vertical axis in this figure is an index that measures the strength of civil society, based on data from the Global Civil Society project (Anheier, Glasius, and Kaldor, 2001).[3] It is clear that publics placing relatively strong emphasis on self-expression values tend to have stronger civil societies. This evidence supports our claim that rising self-expression values are positively linked with a public's capacity to carry out collective action.

If one considers the implications of this finding for authoritarian regimes, it suggests that rising self-expression values contribute to the proliferation of dissident circles, civil rights movements, and public demonstrations of people power against authoritarian government. When authoritarian regimes face a regime challenge, successful democratic transitions are more likely to occur if relatively widespread self-expression values fuel civil rights movements and freedom campaigns. The approach used by Casper and Taylor (1996) in their transition case studies confirms these expectations. Casper and Taylor analyzed twenty-four initially authoritarian regimes in which the question of regime change was on the agenda at some time between the early 1980s and mid-1990s, and the outcome produced one of three results: (1) continued authoritarianism, in which the incumbent authoritarian regime survived or a new authoritarian regime was installed; (2) deficient democratization, in which electoral democracy was adopted but restrictions on people's liberties continued; and (3) complete democratization, in which electoral democracy emerged, bolstered by a full set of civil and political rights as measured by Freedom House (Casper and Taylor, 1996: 41). Excluding all long-established democracies, we used Casper and Taylor's criteria to classify the societies included in the Values Surveys sample into one of these three categories.[4]

---

[3] The index summarizes data on membership in voluntary associations, the organizational density of nongovernmental organizations, tolerant attitudes to immigrants, and child education, as well as participation in protest activities, creating an overall index of the strength of civil society (for index construction and data sources, see the website: http://www.lse.ac.uk/depts/global/yearbook). This measure is partly overlapping with our measure of self-expression values because both include participation in signing petitions. To avoid depicting a partly tautological relationship in Figure 9.3, we recalculated self-expression values under exclusion of petition signing. See also the Internet Appendix, #24 under Variables. For references to the Internet Appendix, see http://www.worldvaluessurvey.org/publications/humandevelopment.html.

[4] As "continued authoritarianism," we classified all societies scoring below the 50th percentile in formal democracy over 2000–2. Societies at or above the 50th percentile but below the 75th percentile are classified as "deficient democratization." Societies scoring above the 75th percentile are classified as "completed democratization." Note that long-established democracies are excluded from this classification of transition outcomes. For the countries belonging to these categories, see the Internet Appendix, #68 under Variables.

TABLE 9.1. *How Self-Expression Values Channel Collective Action and Agency toward Democracy*

Rising self-expression values					
in nondemocracies increase			in democracies increase		
the pool of civil rights activists and radius of dissident circles.	mass support for civil rights movements.	the probability of the formation of liberal reform elites.	the pool of social movement activists.	mass support for new social movements.	the proportion of mass-responsive elites.
All this makes democracy more likely to be adopted.			All this makes existing democracies more effective.		
Rising self-expression values help to bring about and strengthen democracy.					

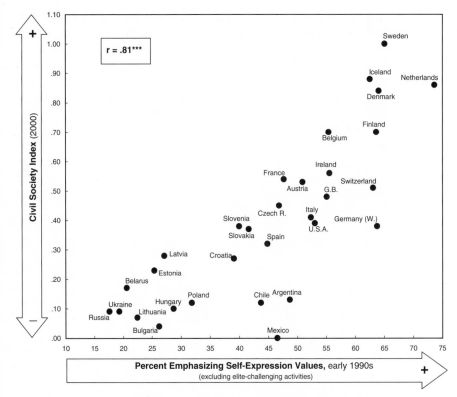

FIGURE 9.3. Self-expression values and the strength of civil society.

These three types of societies differ significantly in the extent to which self-expression values are emphasized: (1) the eighteen societies in the "continued authoritarianism" category fall on average at the 21st percentile on self-expression values; (2) the sixteen societies that experienced "deficient democratization" fall at the 27th percentile on self-expression values; and (3) the nineteen societies that achieved "complete democratization" fall on average at the 34th percentile. Deficient democratization appears to be an intermediate zone between the two extremes, which show almost no overlap: most of the societies under continued authoritarianism score between the 14th and 25th percentile in self-expression values, whereas most societies with complete democratization score between the 29th and 38th percentile on self-expression values. These findings indicate that differences in mass emphasis on self-expression values tend to channel collective actions toward different degrees of democracy, as the theory of human development suggests.

Conclusion

Our focus on the direction and strength of the linkage between self-expression values and democratic institutions does not rule out alternative approaches, such as those emphasizing elite bargaining and class coalitions. Quite the contrary, our model complements these approaches, which explore the mediating factors that tie societal characteristics to mass tendencies. The residuals of our models provide a rough indicator of the impact of these mediating factors. If so, one would conclude that these factors account for about 25 to 30 percent of the variation in democratization and effective democracy. This is a significant part of the story, but it is less than is explained by mass values.

Democracy, and especially effective democracy, is too deep-rooted a social phenomenon to be simply the product of enlightened elite choices and clever institutional arrangements. Democracy is not merely a matter of elite consensus or institutional rationality. It is firmly anchored in a broad syndrome of human development that links modernization with rising mass emphasis on self-expression, and self-expression values with democracy.

10

Individual-Level Values and System-Level Democracy
The Problem of Cross-Level Analysis

Misinterpretations of the Ecological Fallacy

As we have seen, socioeconomic development brings rising emphasis on self-expression values, which is conducive to liberal democracy. We have analyzed these linkages at the societal level, using the proportion of people emphasizing self-expression values in each nation, to measure the impact of mass attitudes on democracy. Because democracy exists only at the societal level, this is the appropriate level (indeed, the *only* possible level) at which to analyze the process, although these values were originally measured at the individual level. But the analysis of cross-level linkages, such as the one between individual-level values and societal-level democracy, is somewhat unusual (since it requires comparable survey data from scores of societies, which are rarely available) and it remains widely misunderstood. Thus, for example, Seligson (2002) claims that the strong aggregate-level correlations that Inglehart has found between political culture and stable democracy are "spurious" because Seligson does not find strong correlations between Inglehart's individual-level indicators of political culture and individual-level support for democracy, claiming that the cross-level linkage between mass values and democracy represents an "ecological fallacy."

Everyone has heard of the ecological fallacy, a problem that can arise when individual-level data are aggregated to the societal level. But the problem is often misunderstood, even by prominent social scientists. Because aggregating individual-level data to the societal level is done in this book's most central analyses, let us take a closer look at how it works.

More than fifty years ago, in his classic article on the ecological fallacy, W. S. Robinson (1950) pointed out that the relationships between two variables that exist at the aggregate level are not necessarily similar to those that exist at the individual level: the individual-level correlation may be much weaker or may even reverse its sign, working in the opposite direction from the relationship found at the aggregate level. To illustrate this fact, before the civil rights era, the U.S. legislative districts that had the highest percentage of African Americans tended to elect strongly segregationist candidates. If one naively assumed that the same relationship between race and political preferences existed at both the individual level and the aggregate level, one would conclude that African Americans supported racial segregation. Needless to say, this interpretation was false: they opposed it, but their legislative districts were dominated by racist whites who were virulently segregationist (partly because they felt threatened by the large numbers of African Americans in their districts).

The relationship between any two variables is not necessarily the same at the individual level as at the aggregate level. This was true half a century ago, it is true today, and it will be true tomorrow – but it has been and still is misinterpreted (Inglehart and Welzel, 2003). Quite frequently, people refer to the ecological fallacy as if it meant that aggregating individual-level data to the societal level is somehow tainted, elevating Robinson's finding into the injunction, "Thou shalt not aggregate individual-level data and treat them as a societal-level phenomenon." This is mistaken. If it were taken seriously, it would invalidate most of the work on democratic theory, which focuses on the linkage between mass tendencies in individual-level preferences and democratic institutions at the system level. The individual-level preferences are aggregated into a societal-level phenomenon sometimes referred to as "the will of the people" or "majority rule." Mass preferences have an impact on democratic institutions, which exist only at the societal level. Unless these cross-level linkages work, democracy cannot function. The literature on political culture is based on the assumption that aggregated individual-level values and beliefs have an impact on societal-level phenomena such as a society's level of democracy. This book tests this assumption empirically, on a more extensive basis than has been done previously. The injunction to be drawn from Robinson's findings might better be stated as, "Sometimes aggregating individual-level data to the societal level is exactly what you need to do – but Thou shalt not blindly assume that relationships work the same way at both levels."

Ironically, Robinson's lesson is sometimes interpreted to mean the exact opposite: it is alleged that relationships *must* work in the same way at both aggregate and individual levels – and if they do not, the aggregate-level finding is somehow "spurious." This is a complete misunderstanding. The central point of the ecological fallacy thesis is that strong aggregate-level relationships are *not* necessarily reproduced at the individual level. When Robinson was writing, districts with large percentages of African Americans (then located mainly in the South) generally elected segregationist candidates; but this relationship was not reproduced at the individual level – African Americans themselves did not vote for segregationist candidates. This did not mean that the aggregate-level relationship was somehow "spurious"; no one questions the fact that districts with large numbers of African Americans really *did* elect the worst sort of segregationists, in a pattern of repression that endured for decades. Although they worked in opposite directions, both the individual-level and the aggregate-level phenomena were genuine and had important consequences.

Similarly, in contemporary France the vote for the xenophobic Front Nationale (FN) tends to be highest in districts with high percentages of Islamic immigrants. This does not mean that the immigrants are supporting the FN. They are not. And conversely, the fact that the immigrants are not voting for the FN does not mean that the linkage between ethnicity and politics is somehow "spurious:" the presence of a relatively high percentage of immigrants in a district does tend to inflate the vote for the FN, even though the correlation between vote and immigrant status reverses its polarity from one level of analysis to another.

Deciding whether a relationship is genuine or spurious on the basis of whether the relationship exists at *another* level of analysis is exactly what Robinson warned us *not* to do: it is an unwarranted cross-level inference. Whether a relationship is spurious can only be determined by evidence at the *same* level of analysis. Thus, Przeworski and Teune's (1970: 73) well-known claim that an "ecological correlation" is spurious if it is not reflected at the individual level within each aggregate unit is simply untrue. Seligson (2002) cites this dictum as authority when he argues that the societal-level linkages we have found between mass values and democracy are spurious, because (he claims) at the individual level these values are not linked with overt support for democracy.

The first failure in this argument is the belief that the linkage between aggregated individual-level values and democratic institutions at the societal level must be the same at the individual level, and if it is not, the aggregate-level linkage is invalidated. Furthermore, Seligson tests his claim that the correlation between mass values and democracy does not exist at the individual level by examining the correlation between individual-level values and overt support for democracy. In doing so, he equates individual-level support for democracy with democracy itself – which exists only at the societal level. This is an unwarranted cross-level inference. As Chapter 11 demonstrates, overt support for democracy often reflects nothing more than shallow lip service to a socially desirable term: in equating this with democracy itself, Seligson himself is making precisely the type of cross-level inference that the ecological fallacy literature warns against. In fact, self-expression values are linked with individual-level support for democracy, as will be demonstrated in Chapter 11, but this is beside the point here. The point is that, at the societal level, self-expression values have a major impact on effective democracy while overt mass support for democracy has no impact, when we control for self-expression values (see Chapter 11). Concluding that linkages between mass values and democracy are spurious because these linkages are not reflected in the same way at the individual level implies a profound misunderstanding of cross-level analysis.

Mass Tendencies and System Characteristics

Let us ask, What is the meaning of aggregated data, such as the percentage of a public emphasizing self-expression values? Is this percentage a genuine societal characteristic? This percentage is calculated from the responses of individuals. But for any given individual, the percentage is almost completely determined by the responses of the other individuals. Thus, aggregate data represent mass tendencies that are almost entirely exogenous to each of the individuals from which they are calculated. The proportion of people emphasizing self-expression values is not an individual-level characteristic; it is a collective property, as is the case with a genuine system characteristic such as democracy. Collective properties can and do impact on democratic institutions at the societal level – the *only* level at which they can be analyzed.

In contrast to aggregate measures of self-expression values, democracy is a system characteristic that cannot be disaggregated to the individual level. In this sense, *mass tendencies* and *system characteristics* are different types of societal-level phenomena, but both *are* societal-level phenomena. The fact that mass attitudinal tendencies and democracy are societal-level phenomena of a different nature does not invalidate their relationship; it makes it particularly interesting. This type of relationship lies at the heart of democratic theory, which is inherently concerned with linkages between mass preferences and the system of government. Not only is it perfectly valid to analyze the linkages between aggregated individual-level variables and system-level characteristics; if one is interested in the central questions of democratic theory, this is the *only* way in which they can be analyzed empirically.

Explaining Cross-Level Differences

One can find quite different linkages between any two variables at the individual and the societal levels. When such differences are present, they do not invalidate the relationship that exists at either of the two levels. But the ways in which linkages differ between the societal level and the individual level help illuminate the nature of the social mechanisms that produce them. There are three ways in which linkages that exist at the societal level can differ from linkages between the same variables at the individual level. They indicate minority effects, context effects, and a combination of effect thresholds and central tendencies.

Societal-Level and Individual-Level Linkages with Opposite Signs
A linkage existing at the societal level can have an opposite sign at the individual level, as W. S. Robinson (1950) pointed out long ago. As we have noted, although at the district level there was a strong *positive* correlation between the proportion of African Americans and support for segregationist policies, at the individual level there was a *negative* relationship between being African American and supporting segregationist policies.

This kind of a deviation of societal-level correlations from individual-level correlations indicates minority effects: the negative individual-level correlation between immigrants and support for segregationist policies at the individual level does not translate into a similar societal-level correlation, as long as immigrants remain a minority.

Societal-Level Linkages That Do Not Exist at the Individual Level
There can be a linkage between two variables at the societal level, but the same variables may show no significant linkage at the individual level. An

example is the relationship between unemployment and support for the Nazis in late Weimar Germany. At the constituency level there was a strong correlation between the proportion of jobless people and the vote for the Nazis (Falter, 1991). But at the individual level, there was little or no correlation between unemployment and Nazi support.

In this case, rising unemployment increased support for the Nazis among the people of given districts, regardless of whether the respondents were jobless or not. People did not necessarily support the Nazis because they themselves were unemployed, but because many others in their district were unemployed, creating a climate of threat conducive to xenophobia and extremism. Accordingly, the positive correlation between unemployment and Nazi support was not reflected in differences between individuals within the same district. But it was apparent between districts: those districts with higher unemployment rates also had a higher vote for the Nazis, and as unemployment levels rose over time, the Nazi vote rose as well.

This sort of a deviation between individual-level and societal-level correlations reflects a *context effect*: a given characteristic, such as unemployment, affects people's behavior as a property of the context, not of the person itself.

Strong Societal-Level Linkages That Are Weak at the Individual Level

Another possibility is that a strong correlation at the societal level is significant and has the same sign but is considerably weaker at the individual level. Correlations between variables usually *are* much weaker at the individual level than at the societal level. The reason for this is the joint operation of central tendencies and effect thresholds. Because this elementary phenomenon is often poorly understood, we discuss it in more detail.

Effect Thresholds and Central Tendencies

Variation in an independent variable X almost never translates perfectly into a corresponding variation in the dependent variable Y. Practically all social relationships are probabilistic, showing a range of uncertainty within which small variations in X are not necessarily reflected in correspondingly small variations in Y. Only variations in X that are large enough to exceed a certain threshold are reflected in corresponding variations in Y, indicating the existence of an *effect threshold*: variation in X must exceed this threshold in order to have an impact on Y (Inglehart and Welzel, 2003). This phenomenon is comparable to the tolerance in the reaction to the movement of the steering wheel of a large truck. Only if a turn of the steering wheel exceeds this tolerance will the wheels on the street react in the intended way. This tolerance can be small, but to a certain extent it almost always exists, reflecting the threshold that a cause has to exceed in order to produce an effect. Only entirely deterministic effects do not have such thresholds. So far, no such deterministic effect has been demonstrated in the social sciences (Sekhon, 2004).

The existence of effect thresholds is particularly important in combination with central tendencies among populations. For central tendencies bound individual-level variations within a limited range, so that the variation in X may rarely exceed the threshold beyond which its impact on Y becomes apparent. This necessarily leads to small individual-level correlations between X and Y *within* populations.

Social units such as nations that create common collective identities among their constituents have strong central tendencies. This means that the social characteristics of the individuals within given nations tend to be bounded within a limited range. Some outliers with extreme deviations from the majority will be present, but the great majority of individuals cluster within a limited range of the median citizen. But these central tendencies often differ dramatically from unit to unit, which means that one will find much larger variances between individuals from different units than between individuals from the same units. For example, life satisfaction among both Swedes and Russians is relatively concentrated, with both Russians and Swedes being close to their national mean, while these means differ drastically between the two nations: the median Swede is much more satisfied (scoring 8.1 on a 10-point scale) than the median Russian (who scores 3.9). At the same time the two populations are so strongly concentrated around their mean levels of satisfaction that they scarcely overlap. This exemplifies how pronounced central tendencies can be.

Figure 10.1 gives an illustration of this type of pattern. It shows a positive relationship between two variables (in this example, socioeconomic resources and self-expression values), where both variables show centralized distributions within nations and large differences between these nations' central tendencies. In such a case, most individuals within any given nation fall within the range in which variations in socioeconomic resources are small and do not necessarily create similar small variations in self-expression values.

The effect threshold in the relation between socioeconomic resources and self-expression values is depicted by the horizontal distance between the left and right boundary of the confidence interval in Figure 10.1. At any point of the left boundary of the confidence interval from which one starts to travel to the right (i.e., toward greater resources), it remains uncertain that the next dot one meets scores higher in self-expression values, as long as one's travel remains within the effect threshold. But as soon as the effect threshold is surpassed, it is almost certain that the next dot scores higher in self-expression values. As Figure 10.1 illustrates, effect thresholds can be large, even in a strongly linear relationship. This result necessarily produces relatively small individual-level correlations *within* nations. But *between* nations there is much more variation in people's socioeconomic resources, and the effect threshold beyond which corresponding variations in self-expression values occur is surpassed by a much larger proportion of individuals. Consequently, the pooled individual-level correlation will be much larger than the individual-level correlations within nations. As Figure 10.1 illustrates, when two variables have relatively centralized distributions among individuals within the same nations, but large differences between nations, one will find much stronger linkages at the societal level than within any given country.

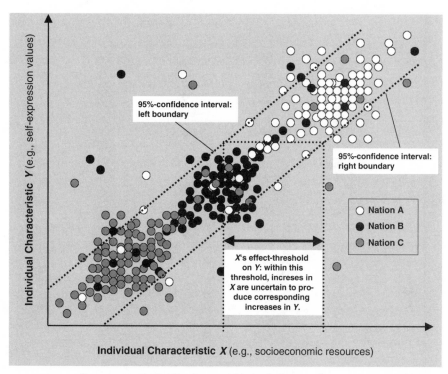

FIGURE 10.1. Concentrated distributions *within* and dispersed concentrations *between* nations (illustrative model).

Moreover, individual-level measures, especially survey data, contain a large component of random measurement error (see Converse, 1970; Inglehart, 1977; Page and Shapiro, 1993; Erikson, MacKuen, and Stimson, 2002). Aggregating data to the societal level tends to eliminate this measurement error because random deviations around a national mean tend to cancel each other out. This diminishes the random term in the correlation, so that the correlation systematically becomes larger when one moves from the individual level to the societal level.

In short, correlations tend to be smaller at the individual level within nations than at the pooled individual level, if (as is usually the case) there is a wider range of variation in the pooled sample than within given nations. Moreover, correlations are smaller at the pooled individual level than at the societal level, if (as is usually the case) individual-level data contain random measurement error that gets canceled out through aggregation. Figure 10.2 demonstrates these two points, showing real-world data for the various attitudes generating self-expression values. The linkage between these attitudes is weakest by far at the individual level within nations, where every component of the self-expression values syndrome shows its weakest factor loadings. This linkage is considerably stronger at the pooled individual level where the components' factor loadings

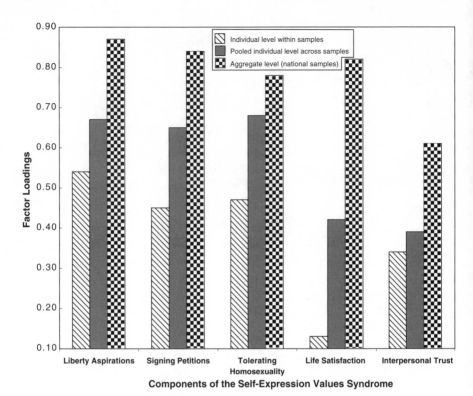

FIGURE 10.2. Factor loadings of the components of self-expression values, at three levels of analysis.

are larger. And it is strongest at the societal level, where every component of the self-expression values syndrome shows its strongest factor loadings.

The fact that a societal-level linkage is not reflected at the individual level does not invalidate the societal-level linkage. For example, the individual-level linkage between tolerance of homosexuality and life satisfaction is completely insignificant in most national samples of the Values Surveys. But at the societal level, we find a highly significant relationship between levels of tolerance and life satisfaction ($r = .50$, $N = 194$ nations per wave). Accordingly, societies whose people are more tolerant of homosexuality have higher levels of life satisfaction. This does not mean that people are more satisfied with their lives because they themselves are relatively tolerant of homosexuals. Instead, societies in which tolerance is widespread have a friendlier social climate that affects all members of that society, increasing the overall level of life satisfaction. Thus, tolerance does not impact on life satisfaction as a personal characteristic but as a characteristic of one's society: people are not more satisfied with their lives because they *themselves* are tolerant, but because they live in a society in which the *general social climate* is more tolerant. Such contextual effects do not manifest themselves in differences between individuals within the same society; they become manifest only when one compares different societies. Hence, the impact of attitudes that are shaped by the social context should be analyzed at the societal level – the level at which they are relevant to democratic institutions.

The Equivalence of Mass Values across Cultures

As we have shown, important social processes function very differently at different levels of analysis. Nevertheless, it is important to be sure that our measures of individual-level values tap similar things in different countries. The Values Surveys use standardized questions to measure values in countries with widely varying cultural backgrounds. They face the problems inherent in all comparative research, such as the fact that given words can have different meanings in different cultural contexts. The Values Surveys address this problem by avoiding situation-specific questions with meanings that vary greatly from one setting to another; and questions that are so remote from people's daily lives that respondents are unable to express a clear preference. Instead, these surveys focus on universal questions – such as life satisfaction, tolerance, religiosity, or gender equality – that are relevant to people's daily lives almost everywhere and to which almost everyone is likely to have an attitude that is relevant to their own life experiences.

Whether the questions asked by the Values Surveys have equivalent meanings across different types of societies can be tested empirically. We have indeed sometimes found that given questions asked in these surveys have fundamentally different meanings in different settings: when one analyzes their relationships with the other variables, one finds that they have different connotations and different demographic correlates.

As a particularly crucial example, let us examine the cross-cultural comparability of a central cultural measure used in this book: postmaterialist aspirations for personal liberty ("free speech") and political liberty ("more say"). These liberty aspirations are the central component of self-expression values, showing the strongest factor loadings of any component of this syndrome. Liberty aspirations tap the essence of self-expression values, focusing on human choice.

Liberty aspirations reflect a specific component of postmaterialist orientations. Postmaterialism as a whole includes not only liberty aspirations but also ecological and idealistic orientations that emphasize environmental protection and a humane society. Liberty aspirations are part of this complex, but they are more specifically relevant to democracy, since they emphasize personal and political freedom. Accordingly, this analysis will focus on liberty aspirations using three of the six postmaterialist items: "protecting freedom of speech," "giving people more say in important government decisions," and "seeing that people have more say about how things are done at their jobs and in their communities."

The priority that respondents assign to each of these items (i.e., top priority, second priority, or no priority) generates scores on a 6-point index,

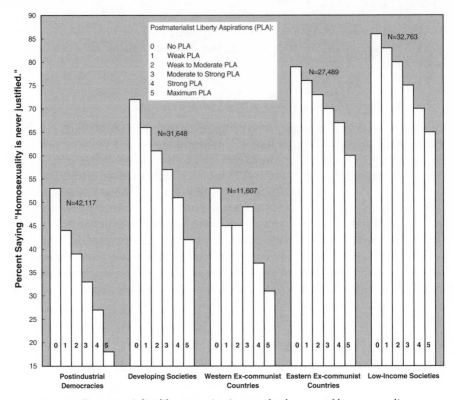

FIGURE 10.3. Postmaterialist liberty aspirations and tolerance of homosexuality.

with o indicating the lowest and 5 the highest level of liberty aspirations.[1] The average scores of national samples produce a continuous scale, measuring the overall strength of liberty aspirations among a population. These mean scores represent a nation's central tendency on liberty aspirations, because in each nation most of the population is closely distributed around the national mean; we never find bimodal or polarized distributions.

One indication of whether liberty aspirations have equivalent meanings in different types of societies is whether they show similar linkages with other attitudes. As we will see, although the absolute levels of postmaterialist liberty aspirations vary dramatically from society to society, its attitudinal correlates are strikingly similar across different types of societies.

Figures 10.3–10.6 illustrate the individual-level linkages between postmaterialist liberty aspirations and several other attitudes in different types of societies, comparing the patterns found in postindustrial democracies, western and eastern ex-communist countries, developing societies, and low-income

---

[1] For measurement details, see the Internet Appendix, #43 under Variables. For this and subsequent references to the Internet Appendix, see http://www.worldvaluessurvey.org/publications/humandevelopment.html.

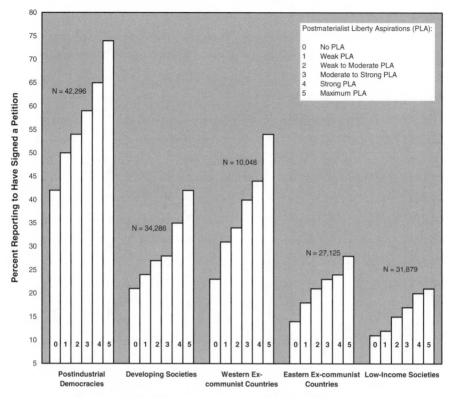

FIGURE 10.4. Postmaterialist liberty aspirations and elite-challenging activity.

countries.[2] Within each type of society, the respondents are grouped into six categories based on the strength of their liberty aspirations. The six bars in each type of society represent rising levels of liberty aspirations as one moves from left to right: the leftmost column shows respondents with minimal liberty aspirations, followed by respondents with weak, weak-to-moderate, moderate-to-strong, strong, and maximum liberty aspirations in the rightmost column.

Comparing the heights of these columns, one sees how strongly a particular attitude is present (1) among respondents with different liberty aspirations in the same type of society, and (2) among respondents with the same liberty aspirations in different types of societies. Whether postmaterialist liberty aspirations are linked with other attitudes in the same way in different types of societies is indicated by the similarity of the column profiles. The more similar these patterns are, the more similar is the linkage between liberty aspirations and other important attitudes, and the more equivalent is the meaning of liberty aspirations across different types of societies.

---

[2] See the Internet Appendix, #67 under Variables, for the classification of countries into these categories.

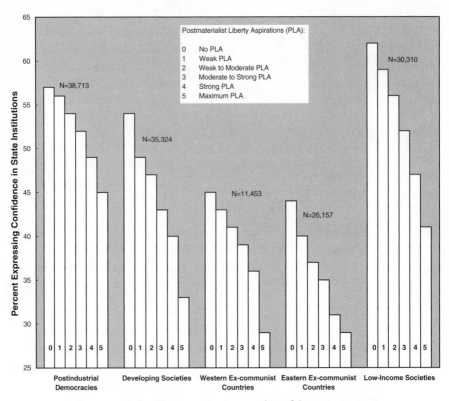

FIGURE 10.5. Postmaterialist liberty aspirations and confidence in institutions.

Figure 10.3 depicts the individual-level relationship between liberty aspirations and tolerance of homosexuals in postindustrial democracies, western and eastern ex-communist countries, and developing and low-income societies. As is evident, the column profile is similarly structured in each type of society: the column heights decrease systematically from left to right, reflecting the fact that fewer and fewer people reject homosexuality as never justifiable with rising levels of postmaterialist liberty aspirations in *every* type of society.[3]

The column profiles do not differ between different types of societies, which indicates that the inner logic of the relationship between liberty aspirations and tolerance is not a function of the type of society in which it is observed. Instead, it is universal: people with weaker liberty aspirations score below their society's mean level of tolerance; people with stronger liberty aspirations score above their society's mean level of tolerance. In contrast to the column profiles, the column levels *do* differ consistently between the five types of societies. Tolerance levels are consistently highest in postindustrial democracies, within each category of liberty aspirations. Accordingly, a given strength of liberty aspirations

---

[3] See the Internet Appendix, #44 under Variables, for how tolerance of homosexuality is measured.

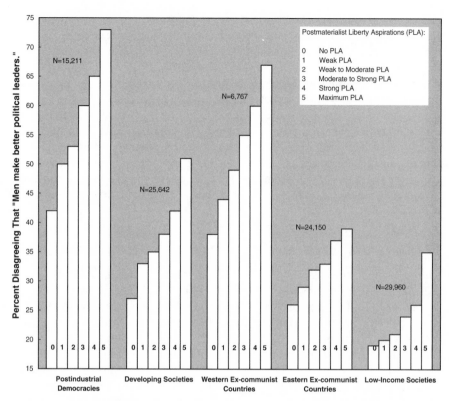

FIGURE 10.6. Postmaterialist liberty aspirations and support for gender equality.

does not fix people's tolerance at an absolute level that is constant throughout all types of societies. Instead, liberty aspirations shift people's tolerance above or below a given society's baseline, which varies. Overall, postindustrial democracies show the highest level of liberty aspirations and the highest level of tolerance, whereas low-income societies show the lowest levels in liberty aspirations and the lowest levels of tolerance, as human development theory suggests. But regardless of a society's mean level of liberty aspirations and tolerance, stronger liberty aspirations make individuals more tolerant in any type of society.

The same pattern applies to the relationship between postmaterialist liberty aspirations and elite-challenging activities, which is shown in Figure 10.4.[4] The column heights increase systematically from left to right, reflecting the fact that elite-challenging activities increase with rising levels of liberty aspirations in each type of society. Similarly, people's confidence in state institutions (i.e., police, legal system, and parliament) decreases systematically with their liberty

---

[4] Elite-challenging activity is measured by signing petitions. See the Internet Appendix, #45 under Variables.

aspirations (Figure 10.5).[5] Furthermore, as Figure 10.6 demonstrates, liberty aspirations are systematically linked with emphasis on gender equality:[6] in each type of society, people's emphasis on gender equality increases with their liberty aspirations.

The striking similarity between the column profiles shown in Figures 10.3, 10.4, 10.5, and 10.6 indicates that postmaterialist liberty aspirations are related to many important attitudes and values in similar ways, regardless of the type of society in which the survey was carried out. We could extend the list in considerable detail (for additional illustrations, see Inglehart and Abramson, 1999), but the underlying principle is evident. The meaning of liberty aspirations and self-expression values seems to be basically similar across different types of societies, justifying the cross-national comparisons we have undertaken in this book.

Conclusion

The widespread belief that societal-level linkages are "spurious" unless they also exist in the same form at the individual level reflects a basic misinterpretation of the ecological fallacy problem. Whether a linkage is spurious or not can only be decided at the level where the linkage exists, and not by unwarranted cross-level inferences.

If it were true that the strong societal-level linkage between self-expression values and democracy was not reflected at the individual level, it would not invalidate the societal-level linkage. In fact, searching for this linkage at the individual level is pointless since democracy is a societal-level phenomenon that does not *exist* at the individual level. If democracy is influenced by people's value orientations, only mass tendencies in these value orientations can exert such an influence – which they do, as we have seen.

The linkages between the various components of self-expression values are considerably weaker at the individual level within nations than at the societal level, as is true of most configurations of attitudes. This does not invalidate the linkages at the societal level. It reflects systematic differences between individual-level linkages and societal-level linkages, and the fact that some linkages are more contextual than individualistic in character. In analyzing democracy, these contextual linkages (not individualistic ones) are relevant.

Finally, a central component of self-expression values – postmaterialist liberty aspirations – is linked with various other attitudes in the same way in all types of societies for which data exist, indicating that self-expression values have similar connotations in all societies. When comparing the strength and distribution of self-expression values in different societies, we are comparing comparable things.

---

[5] For measuring confidence in state institutions, see the Internet Appendix, #52 under Variables.

[6] Emphasis on gender equality is measured by rejecting male superiority in political leadership. See the Internet Appendix, #66 under Variables.

11

Components of a Prodemocratic Civic Culture

Rival Theories of Political Culture

From the start, scholars of political culture have claimed that the functioning and survival of democratic institutions at the system level is closely linked with individual-level value orientations (Lerner, 1958; Almond and Verba, 1963; Eckstein, 1966). Thus, the notion of a population-system linkage that ties political institutions to mass tendencies in individual-level values is essential to the entire literature on political culture. From this perspective, the fate of a political system is largely determined by its people's political attitudes and value orientations. Aristotle in the fourth century B.C. and Montesquieu (1989 [1748]) in the eighteenth century argued that different forms of government reflect the kinds of virtues that prevail among a people. Awareness of this insight reemerged in explanations of the Nazi takeover in Weimar Germany, with many observers concluding that this disaster could be traced to the fact that Weimar was a "democracy without democrats" (Bracher, 1971 [1955]).

Starting from the premise that mass orientations were crucial to democracy, Almond and Verba (1963) launched the first comparative empirical survey of the mass attitudes linked with the stability and functioning of democracies. They concluded that a healthy mixture of "subject orientations" and "participant orientations" was conducive to a "civic culture" that helps democracies to flourish. Subsequent comparative empirical studies emphasized the importance of individual-level attitudes and values, in sustaining democratic institutions at the system level (among others, see Barnes, Kaase, et al., 1979; K. Baker et al., 1981; Putnam, 1993; Klingemann and Fuchs, 1995; Inglehart, 1997; Pharr and Putnam, 2000; Dalton, 2001; Norris, 2002). The emergence of new democracies in Latin America, Southeast Asia, and Central Eastern Europe stimulated another avalanche of political culture studies (among many others, see Gibson, Duch, and Tedin, 1992; Hofferbert and Klingemann, 1999; Gibson, 2001; Mishler and Rose, 2001; Bratton and Mattes, 2001; Newton and Norris, 2000; Diamond, 2003). Nearly all of these studies hold that mass tendencies in individual-level attitudes and value orientations are important for the functioning of democracy at the system level. This assumption is the basic justification underlying research on political culture.

Despite the centrality of this claim, few studies have actually tested it (e.g., Putnam, 1993; Muller and Seligson, 1994; Inglehart, 1997: chap. 6; Newton, 2001; Paxton, 2002). Most political culture studies simply assume that certain individual-level attitudes are important for democracy at the system level, and this assumption is used to justify analyses of the individual-level determinants of these attitudes. But the assumption that mass tendencies in these attitudes have system-level effects remains based on faith, in most analyses of political culture. It is rarely tested, although if it were not true there would be little point in doing research on political culture.

Instead of taking it for granted that mass tendencies in certain attitudes and value orientations have system-level effects on democracy, this chapter tests this claim empirically. Because very few studies have actually tested this claim, it is not surprising that the thesis that mass attitudes promote the functioning and persistence of democracies has been questioned. There has been a continuing debate about the causal direction underlying the relationship between mass attitudes and democratic institutions. Rustow (1970), for example, argued that mass support for democracy can result from disappointing experiences with authoritarian rule, but that "intrinsically" democratic values that reflect a deeply rooted commitment to democratic norms can only emerge through habituation – that is, learning democratic norms through practice under existing democratic institutions. According to Rustow, democratic mass values are not a precondition for functioning democracies but a *consequence* of them. Similarly, in a sharp critique of Putnam (1993) and Inglehart (1997), Jackman and Miller (1998) claimed that a democratic mass culture results from living under democratic institutions, instead of being conducive to them (see also Muller and Seligson, 1994).

In Chapter 8 we examined these contradictory arguments, hypothesizing that self-expression values reflect an intrinsic commitment to democratic norms, such as liberty and tolerance. Accordingly, we tested empirically whether self-expression values are shaped by previous experience under democratic institutions or whether these values help shape subsequent democratic institutions. The results are unequivocal: controlling for socioeconomic development, prior democratic institutions have only a minor impact on self-expression values; but self-expression values have a strong and significant impact on subsequent democratic institutions, even holding socioeconomic development constant. Likewise, controlling for temporal autocorrelation, self-expression values show a significant impact on democratic institutions, but the reverse is not true. These findings suggest that the main causal arrow operates from mass values to democratic institutions, and not the other way around.

Because the evidence indicates that mass values affect democracy, it is important to know precisely *which* mass values affect democracy most strongly. Human development theory implies that self-expression values should be most crucial for democracy, but other social scientists emphasize other values and attitudes. This chapter analyzes empirical evidence from scores of societies to determine which mass orientations have the strongest impact on democracy.

Three Competing Approaches

The research on political culture falls into three main approaches, with adherents of each approach emphasizing different types of mass values as most important in strengthening democracy. We label these approaches the legitimacy approach (or system-support approach), the communitarian approach (or social capital approach), and the human development approach (or emancipative approach).

In a highly influential work, David Easton (1965) argued that all political systems need legitimacy, which they obtain if their public supports the system's specific institutions and the system as a whole. Accordingly, adherents of the legitimacy approach argue that mass support for a given system of governance, and mass confidence in its specific institutions, provide political systems with the legitimacy that they need to operate effectively (see Gibson, 1997; Klingemann, 1999; Mishler and Rose, 2001; Seligson, 2002). Advocates of this approach consider mass support for democracy to be crucial in delegitimizing autocracy and legitimizing democracy (see Chanley, Rudolph, and Rahn, 2000; Newton and Norris, 2000; Anderson and Tverdova, 2001; Newton, 2001).

Two other approaches – the communitarian and the human development approach – follow the tradition of the civic culture school in arguing that making democracy work requires more than just having confidence in institutions and preferring democracy to alternative systems of government; it requires a broader set of civic values.

The communitarian approach emphasizes values that link the citizens to daily public life and strengthen their social ties and their loyalty to the community (Bell, 1993; Etzioni, 1996). According to Putnam (1993, 2000), such communal orientations create social capital and are reflected in people's activities in voluntary associations and in their trust in their fellow citizens. Thus, communitarians and social capital theorists emphasize membership in voluntary associations and interpersonal trust as the communal ground on which democracies flourish (see Norris, 2002: chap. 8). Another school in the communitarian debate emphasizes the citizens' conformity to laws and their loyalty to rules of good conduct, or what they call "civic honesty" or "trustworthiness," as the moral resource that sustains and strengthens democracy (Crozier, Huntington, and Watanuki, 1975; Levi and Stoker, 2000; Rothstein, 2000). In contrast to dictatorships, democracies have only limited repressive ability in order to enforce laws. Thus, more than any other system of government, democracy depends on citizens' voluntary compliance, or what we will call "norm obedience."

The human development approach shares with the communitarian approach the belief that civic values, rather than just specific orientations toward the political system and its institutions, are important for democracy. Human development theory is a theory of the societal conditions that restrict or widen people's choices. Democracy is a key one of these conditions. It institutionalizes civil and political liberties, providing people legal guarantees to make free choices in their private and public activities. And since human choice is at the heart of democracy, the civic values that make it work effectively are those that emphasize human choice, which we term self-expression values. Thus, not all communal values and forms of social capital are equally important to democracy, but above all those that are motivated by people's aspiration for human freedom and choice. Self-expression values tap this dimension. These values are most intrinsically directed toward the emancipative essence of democracy.

Interpersonal trust, norm obedience, and activity in associations certainly reflect communal values and social capital, but they do not necessarily reflect emancipative values and the forms of social capital motivated by them. Communal values can be authoritarian and xenophobic, producing "bonding" rather than "bridging" forms of social capital; bonding forms of social capital exist in the form of inward-looking networks that expose people to group pressure, rather than emancipating them. From the perspective of human development theory, these forms of communal values and social capital would not operate in favor of democracy; only emancipative values and the bridging forms of social capital they motivate do so. Emancipative values give priority to individual liberty over collective discipline, human diversity over group conformity, and civic autonomy over state authority. Bridging forms of social capital are motivated by emancipative values. They diminish people's dependence on inward-looking groups while integrating them into webs of looser but more diverse human interactions.

Not all forms of communal values and social capital are conducive to democracy's focus on human choice. Democracy requires values that emphasize human self-expression, which is intrinsically directed against discrimination and specifically focused on the liberating elements of democracy. The human development approach does not endorse Almond and Verba's claim (1963) that a strong component of "subject orientations" is an integral part of a democratic civic culture. Quite the contrary, we argue that weak or ineffective democracy does not reflect a lack of collective discipline, group conformity, and norm obedience. It is more likely that insufficient civic disobedience and self-expression make the job of authoritarian rulers all too easy. Not a more compliant but a more emancipative outlook is what most societies need to become more democratic.

Self-expression values include a postmaterialist emphasis on personal and political liberty, civilian protest activities, tolerance of the liberty of others, and an emphasis on subjective well-being reflected in life satisfaction. Interpersonal trust also belongs to this syndrome of self-expression values (see Figure 10.2).[1]

---

[1] This statement applies solely to *generalized* interpersonal trust, not to *intimate* interpersonal trust. The former is less intensive but has a broader social radius, which is important in sustaining the diversity of human interactions that keep complex modern societies working. Intimate interpersonal

However, we hypothesize that its linkage to democracy is indirect, operating through its linkage with other components of the self-expression values syndrome – above all, liberty aspirations. Among the various components of the self-expression values syndrome, postmaterialistic aspirations for personal and political liberty are most directly focused on human choice and the rights that guarantee it. Consequently, we hypothesize that these liberty aspirations are most closely associated with democracy.

In short, three distinct approaches emphasize three different aspects of mass culture as being most conducive to democracy. First, the legitimacy approach (or system support approach) emphasizes institutional confidence and support for democracy. Support for democracy is considered particularly crucial in delegitimizing autocracy and legitimizing democracy, regardless of the motivations and values underlying support for democracy. Second, the communitarian approach (or social capital approach) emphasizes norm conformity, associational activity, and interpersonal trust as producing the community bonds and civic loyalties that enable democracy to flourish. Third, the human development approach emphasizes self-expression values, particularly liberty aspirations, as the mass orientation most intrinsically relevant to democracy and its emphasis on human choice.

Analytic Strategy

What mass orientations are most crucial to democracy? Tables 11.1 and 11.2 present correlation and regression analyses that measure the impact on democracy of each of the orientations we have just discussed. Let us emphasize that our measures of both formal and effective democracy were made in 2000–2, whereas all of the political culture predictors were measured five to ten years earlier: this temporal ordering allows us to interpret the effects we find as reflecting the influence of political culture on democratic institutions.[2] Moreover, the regressions in Table 11.2 control for the temporal autocorrelation of democracy, introducing the duration of a society's experience with democracy up to the mid-1990s as an additional predictor, to control for the possibility that democracy in 2000–2 simply reflects prior levels of democracy – and for the possibility that the linkage between mass values and democracy is simply an artifact of these values' dependence on prior democracy. The duration of a society's experience with democracy generally has a positive influence on its subsequent democratic performance (Wessels, 1997). Controlling this effect,

---

trust, by contrast, is limited to closely knit groups that can exist in isolation from each other with no bridging ties. Intimate interpersonal trust does not produce the kind of social capital that is needed for the diverse interactions of complex societies.

[2] As in the analyses of Chapter 8, all attitudinal data are taken from the earliest available survey of the Values Surveys II (1989–91) and III (1995–97). We do this in order to keep attitudinal data temporally prior to our dependent variables, formal and effective democracy, measured in 2000–2.

we examine whether given mass values have genuinely independent impact on subsequent measures of democracy.

Holding the democratic tradition constant also helps us control for the influence of Western culture, which could be a factor because Western societies have the longest democratic tradition. Accordingly, we examine the effects of given mass values on democracy insofar as they are independent from a Western democratic heritage.

The tables in this chapter are organized so that one sees the effects of the specific types of mass values on a society's democratic performance, differentiating between formal and effective versions of liberal democracy. It is clear from these tables that the explained variance in merely formal democracy is considerably lower than the explained variance in effective democracy, which indicates that formal democracy is a less socially rooted phenomenon than effective democracy – a finding that has already been explored in detail in Chapter 8. Aside from this, the same pattern applies to both formal democracy and effective democracy: the mass values that provide the strongest explanation of effective democracy also provide the strongest explanation of formal democracy. Because effective democracy is the more crucial dependent variable, our interpretation focuses on explaining it.

The Legitimacy Approach

Confidence in institutions has been declining for several decades, in almost all advanced Western democracies (Pharr, Putnam, and Dalton 2000; Newton and Norris, 2000; Newton, 2001). Because it is often assumed that high confidence in institutions is crucial to democracy, this sharp decline of confidence has drawn much attention, reviving the thesis of a legitimacy crisis that Crozier et al. (1975) articulated in the 1970s. But *is* a high level of confidence in institutions actually crucial to the flourishing of democracy? Do lower levels of confidence in institutions produce less effective democracies? In order to answer these questions, we measured each public's average level of confidence in core institutions of the state ("confidence in state institutions") and in all types of institutions for which confidence had been asked ("overall confidence in institutions").[3]

Confidence ratings are positively correlated across all types of institutions, and factor analyses reveal no polarity between confidence in different types of institutions: summarizing institutional confidence over various institutions is meaningful. Using them, the first two rows in Table 11.1 illustrate that there is virtually no significant relationship between people's confidence in institutions and a society's subsequent democratic performance across various types of societies.

---

[3] For details on measurement, see the Internet Appendix, #52–53 under Variables. For this and subsequent references to the Internet Appendix, see http://www.worldvaluessurvey.org/publications/humandevelopment.html.

TABLE 11.1. *Correlates of Democracy Emphasized by Three Approaches (earliest available survey)*

Correlates	Correlations with Formal Democracy 2000–2002	Correlations with Effective Democracy 2000–2002
Legitimacy approach		
Confidence in state institutions (early 1990s)	.13 (61)	.33** (61)
Overall confidence in institutions (early 1990s)	−.12 (61)	−.04 (61)
Approval of democracy (mid-1990s)	.38** (60)	.42** (60)
Democracy-autocracy preference (mid-1990s)	.57*** (60)	.68*** (60)
Communitarian approach		
Voluntary activity in social associations (early 1990s)	−.06 (60)	−.06 (60)
Overall voluntary activity in associations (early 1990s)	−.13 (60)	−.11 (60)
Norm obedience (early 1990s)	.13 (61)	.25* (61)
Interpersonal trust (early 1990s)	.37** (61)	.63*** (61)
Human development approach		
Postmaterialist liberty aspirations (early 1990s)	.70*** (61)	.80*** (61)
Tolerance of sexual liberty (early 1990s)	.50*** (60)	.67*** (60)
Signing petitions (early 1990s)	.64*** (61)	.76*** (61)
Life satisfaction (early 1990s)	.59*** (61)	.73*** (61)
Self-expression values syndrome (early 1990s)	.72*** (61)	.89*** (61)

Note: Early 1990s: data from earliest available survey of Values Surveys II–III (1989–91 or 1995–97). Mid-1990s: data from earliest available survey of Values Surveys III–IV (1995–97 or 1999–2001). Significance levels: *p < .10; **p < .01; ***p < .001.

Confidence in institutions, however, may not operate in the same way across different types of societies but is conducive to democracy only within the limits of a democratic heritage. In this case the impact of confidence in institutions would only become evident if one controls for prior experience under democracy. We do so in the regression analyses in Table 11.2, which control for a society's prior democratic tradition. But even holding prior democracy constant, public confidence in institutions has no significant impact on a society's subsequent democratic performance. This holds true whether one analyzes the impact of confidence in state institutions or confidence in all types of institutions. Indeed, if public confidence in institutions has any impact, it tends to be negative rather than positive, as the negative signs of the various correlation and regression coefficients indicate.

TABLE 11.2. *Explaining Democracy by Political Culture Predictors from Three Rival Schools (separate regressions, each controlled for democratic tradition up to 1995)*

Predictors	Formal Democracy 2000–2002		Effective Democracy 2000–2002	
	Beta	Partial R²(%)	Beta	Partial R²(%)
Legitimacy approach				
Confidence in state institutions (early 1990s)	−.09	02	.06	00
Overall confidence in institutions (early 1990s)	−.18*	05	−.13	00
Approval of democracy (mid-1990s)	.20*	05	.16*	05
Democracy-autocracy preference (mid-1990s)	.38**	15	.38***	20
Communitarian approach				
Voluntary activity in social associations (early 1990s)	−.09	00	−.11	00
Overall voluntary activity in associations (early 1990s)	−.10	00	−.08	00
Norm obedience (early 1990s)	−.03	00	.04	00
Interpersonal trust (early 1990s)	.09*	00	.31**	15
Human development approach				
Postmaterialist liberty aspirations (early 1990s)	.61***	29	.54***	37
Tolerance of homosexuality (early 1990s)	.28**	07	.37***	20
Signing petitions (early 1990s)	.50***	17	.46***	23
Life satisfaction (early 1990s)	.40**	13	.42***	23
Self-expression values syndrome (early 1990s)	.77***	32	.80***	55

Note: Early 1990s: data from earliest available survey of Values Surveys II–III (1989–91 or 1995–97). Mid-1990s: data from earliest available survey of the Values Surveys III–IV (1995–97 or 1999–2001). For number of cases in each regression, see Table 11.1. Significance levels: *p < .10; **p < .01; ***p < .001.

Surprising as it may seem in the light of the literature on this subject (see Pharr et al., 2000), public confidence in institutions does not seem to affect a society's democratic performance in any systematic way. High or low levels of confidence in institutions can be found in any type of political system, regardless of its democratic performance. Some long-standing authoritarian states, such as China, show high levels of confidence in institutions, whereas some long-established democracies, such as the United States, show low levels of confidence in institutions. Public confidence in institutions does not systematically differ between societies that have a long or a short experience with democracy. And it has no significant impact on a society's subsequent democratic performance, regardless of whether we control for prior democracy. This finding casts serious doubt on the importance that has been ascribed to confidence in institutions and its recent decline in most developed societies. It confirms the interpretation (advanced in Chapter 4) that the decline of confidence in institutions does not pose a threat to democracy. On the contrary, it reflects the emergence of less deferential, more elite-challenging publics in modern societies, which we interpret as conducive to democracy.

Our findings suggest that high levels of public confidence in institutions are not a valid indicator of a prodemocratic civic culture. By the same token, low levels of public confidence in institutions do not necessarily pose a threat to democracy. This does not mean that confidence in institutions is entirely irrelevant; it may be relevant in more specific ways that have not been tested here. But even if this were the case, it remains true that confidence in institutions has no consistent impact on democracy that operates in the same way across all units of observation. This finding invalidates confidence in institutions as a *general* indicator of a prodemocratic civic culture.

Although mass confidence in institutions is unrelated to democracy at the system level, this might not be true of people's support for democracy in general. Intuitively, one would assume that mass support for a democratic system creates pressures to attain or sustain democracy. No doubt, this is why many regional survey programs, including the New Democracies Barometer, the Latinobarometer, and the Afrobarometer, have included questions on people's satisfaction with, and approval of, democracy. We will examine these measures. But we agree with Klingemann (1999) and Rose (1995), who argue that one should not only examine people's support for democracy but also their rejection or support for nondemocratic alternatives. Thus, we measure people's preference for democracy versus autocracy by subtracting their approval of autocracy from their approval of democracy, producing a measure that reflects people's net preference for democracy. Measuring regime preferences in this way is important because some people do not have a clear understanding of democracy, expressing strong support for both democratic and nondemocratic forms of government. In such cases, the individual's support for democracy is offset by their support for authoritarian regimes, indicating that they have mixed views. By contrast, other people express strong support for democracy *and* strong rejection of authoritarian forms of government, showing a strong net preference for democracy. These people are classified as "solid democrats."[4]

One would expect agreement with the statement that "democracies are the best form of government" should show a significant positive correlation with subsequent measures of both formal and effective democracy, and it does, as Table 11.1 shows. But if we control for prior democracy, this impact becomes

---

[4] For details on how we measured approval of democracy, see the Internet Appendix, #55 under Variables; for the democracy-autocracy preferences, see #56; for solid support of democracy, see #57.

insignificant, as Table 11.2 shows. By contrast, people's preferences for democracy over authoritarian alternatives show a different pattern. The bivariate correlations in Table 11.1 show a significant positive linkage between a public's system preference for democracy over autocracy and subsequent measures of formal and effective democracy. If we control for prior experience under democracy, the effect remains highly significant, explaining 25 percent of the variation in effective democracy that is unexplained by prior democracy.

Low levels of confidence in public institutions can and do go together with strong preferences for democracy over autocracy. Even if people live in a democracy and strongly prefer democracy to authoritarian rule, they may be critical of how specific institutions are currently run by their elites – which results in low confidence in these institutions. This is the case in many Western democracies today: overwhelming majorities of the public support democracy over alternative forms of government, but at the same time express low confidence in institutions and low satisfaction with how democracy is functioning (Klingemann, 1999; Newton, 2001). Living under high degrees of existential security leads people to place priority on self-expression and democracy, but, at the same time, they become increasingly critical of authority.

Declining confidence in institutions does not necessarily reflect an erosion of democratic values. And clearly, these orientations are not valid indicators of a prodemocratic civic culture. Preferences for democracy versus autocracy, by contrast, *do* seem to be a valid indicator of a prodemocratic civic culture, and one that operates in the same fashion across all units of observation.

The Communitarian Approach

Both the social capital and the communitarian school emphasize the importance of voluntary associations, arguing that they sustain the communal life and the civil society on which strong democracy rests (Putnam, 1993, 2000; Norris, 2002: chap. 8). This view can be traced to Tocqueville (1994 [1837]), who viewed voluntary associations as the "schools of democracy." We created two indices measuring a society's level of voluntary activity in associations, one measuring the percentage of people being active in specifically social associations and another measuring the percentage of people being active in any kind of voluntary association.[5]

As Tables 11.1 and 11.2 indicate, a society's level of activity in associations shows no significant effect on its level of democracy whatever, regardless of whether we control for prior democracy. Voluntary activity in associations does not explain a significant amount of variation in either formal or effective democracy. This finding holds for activity in social associations and overall activity in associations. Like public confidence in institutions, voluntary activity in associations does not affect democracy in any consistent way – and probably for the same reasons. Neither public confidence in institutions nor activity in

---

[5] For measurement details, see the Internet Appendix, #61 and #62 under Variables.

TABLE 11.3. *The Impact of Self-Expression Values on Democracy, Controlling for Other Political Culture Indicators*

Predictors	Dependent Variable: Effective Democracy, 2000–2002				
Years under democracy before 1990	.12 (1.16)	.11 (1.20)	.13 (1.38)	.11 (1.12)	.08 (.85)
Percent emphasizing self-expression values in early 1990s	.80*** (8.04)	.72*** (7.36)	.78*** (7.99)	.80*** (8.36)	.72*** (6.89)
Overall confidence in institutions in early 1990s	.01 (.23)				.05 (.85)
Democracy-autocracy preference in mid-1990s		.15* (2.11)			.16* (2.03)
Activity in associations in early 1990s			−.07 (−1.06)		−.05 (.79)
Norm obedience in early 1990s				.05 (.75)	.04 (.69)
Adjusted R²	.80	.83	.79	.80	.82
N	61	60	59	61	58

Notes: Entries are standardized beta-coefficients with T-values in parentheses. Significance levels: *p < .10; **p < .01; ***p < .001.

associations is necessarily linked with democracy's focus on human choice. Simply knowing a society's level of activity in associations does not tell us whether its people support authoritarian principles or democratic principles. Germany was noted for its high rates of activity in voluntary associations under the kaisers, but until postwar times Germany's flourishing associational life did not help foster democracy.

This finding would surprise anyone who assumes that active membership in associations plays a key role in making democracy possible, but the empirical evidence is unequivocal: it gives no support to this assumption, even if a society's democratic heritage is held constant in order to test whether associational activity helps only within the limits of existing democracy. This result does not necessarily mean that the level of people's associational activity is entirely irrelevant to democracy, but its relevance may depend on the type of *values* motivating these activities.

The finding that voluntary activity in associations is not inherently favorable to democracy leads us to examine the values that are claimed to be conducive to democracy. Within the communitarian camp, it has been argued that a public whose citizens show a high level of trustworthiness and follow social norms and obey the laws is particularly important for democracies. These values have been described as "trustworthiness," "civic morality," or "civic honesty" (Coleman, 1990; Scholz and Lubell, 1998; Tyler, 1998; Uslaner, 1999; Levi and Stoker, 2000; Rothstein, 2000; Rose-Ackerman, 2001). Following these writers, we created an index of "norm obedience" based on people's disapproval of dishonest behavior, such as cheating on taxes or avoiding transport fares.[6]

Tables 11.1 and 11.2 demonstrate that norm obedience has no significant relationship with formal or effective democracy, regardless of whether we control for prior democracy. The problem of norm obedience is the same as with confidence in institutions and voluntary activity in associations: it is not specific to democracy's emancipative focus on human choice. Such obedience can reflect loyalty to democratic norms, but it can also reflect Adolf Eichmann's loyalty to Nazi procedures. Norm obedience is not necessarily a sign of civic health. If strong disapproval of norm violations is widespread, this could simply reflect awareness of the fact that high rates of norm violations have become a major problem in one's society – as is suggested by the fact that the Russians score higher on norm obedience than the Finns. In any case, norm obedience shows no impact on a society's democratic performance and does not seem to be a valid indicator of a prodemocratic civic culture.

Interpersonal trust, by contrast, *does* show a significant positive linkage with both formal and effective democracy (Table 11.1). When we control for prior experience with democracy (Table 11.2), the impact of interpersonal trust on formal democracy becomes less significant, but its impact on effective democracy remains highly significant, explaining 15 percent of the cross-national variance.[7] Interpersonal trust does have a significant impact on effective democracy and seems to be a valid indicator of a prodemocratic civic culture.

So far we have a mixed picture. Two indicators emphasized by the legitimacy approach, public confidence in institutions and approval of democracy, have no consistent impact on democracy; while one indicator, preferences for democracy over autocracy, does have a consistent and significant impact on democracy. Similarly, two indicators emphasized by the communitarian camp, voluntary activity in associations and norm obedience, turn out to have no consistent impact on democracy, whereas another indicator, interpersonal trust, has a significant impact on democracy.

The Human Development Approach

When we examine the indicators emphasized by our emancipative version of human development theory, the evidence is unequivocal. As Tables 11.1 and 11.2 illustrate, every component of the self-expression values syndrome has a highly significant impact on a society's subsequent democratic quality, regardless of whether we control for prior democracy. We have already seen that

---

[6] For measuring norm obedience or disapproval of dishonest behavior, see the Internet Appendix, #63 under Variables.

[7] Following Norris (2002: chap. 8) in combining civic trust with civic activism in associations in order to create an overall index of social capital does not improve the explanation of a society's democratic performance. All of the impact of the overall social capital index comes from civic trust and none from activism.

this is true of interpersonal trust, which belongs to this syndrome, though it is its weakest component. But the other components of self-expression values show even stronger effects on democracy, and they explain considerably more of the variation in effective democracy, controlling for the length of time a society has lived under democratic institutions. This outcome is especially true of the orientation that focuses most directly on human freedom: postmaterialistic aspirations for personal and political liberty. Liberty aspirations show the strongest partial effect on a society's democratic quality, explaining 37 percent of the variance in effective democracy that is unexplained by the length of a society's democratic tradition.

Elite-challenging activities also have a significant independent impact on democracy, reflecting that these activities put pressure on elites to be more responsive and helped to topple authoritarian regimes and establish many of the Third Wave democracies, such as those in the Philippines, South Korea, South Africa, or the Czech Republic (Bernhard, 1993; L. Diamond, 1993a; Foweraker and Landman, 1997; Paxton 2002: 255–57). But although elite-challenging activities often exert pressure for democracy, they also can be directed toward undemocratic goals, if they are not linked with self-expression values. This explains why elite-challenging activities have a slightly smaller impact on democracy than liberty aspirations – the central element of the syndrome of self-expression values. In addition, even though elite-challenging activities can put institutions under pressure for democracy, these activities are in turn facilitated when democratic institutions are in place, simply because democratic institutions provide the civil and political rights that make elite-challenging activities legal, lowering the risks of participating in them. Elite-challenging activities are therefore influenced by prior experience under democracy, so the democratic tradition captures part of the impact of elite-challenging activities on subsequent measures of effective democracy. But even if we control for how long a society has experienced democracy, elite-challenging activities still have a significant independent impact on subsequent democracy. Elite-challenging activities are not just a product of democracy; they are also a motor of democratization, especially when they are motivated by self-expression values (Welzel et al., 2005). Again, this confirms democracy's rootedness in people power.

As we have seen, interpersonal trust has a significant impact on democracy, but this effect is considerably weaker than that of liberty aspirations. The same applies to two other components of self-expression values: tolerance of homosexuality and life satisfaction, a measure of people's emphasis on subjective well-being. The reason why tolerance of homosexuality and life satisfaction show a more modest impact on democracy is similar to the case of interpersonal trust: neither trust nor satisfaction nor tolerance is as sharply focused on civil and political freedom as are liberty aspirations. Nonetheless, trust, life satisfaction, and tolerance do have some impact on democracy, as parts of the broader syndrome of self-expression values. This leads us to examine the impact of this syndrome as a whole.

The broad syndrome of self-expression values links liberty aspirations with protest activism, tolerance of homosexuality, subjective well-being, and interpersonal trust. As the factor loadings in Figure 10.2 indicate, postmaterialist liberty aspirations have the highest loadings on self-expression values, followed by elite-challenging activities, life satisfaction, tolerance of homosexuality, and interpersonal trust, which has the weakest loading. This creates an asymmetrical linkage with democracy, which is shaped most strongly by liberty aspirations and least strongly by interpersonal trust. But even though this linkage is asymmetrical, the self-expression values syndrome as a *whole* shows a stronger impact on democracy than any of its components, including liberty aspirations. As Table 11.2 demonstrates, the strength of self-expression values explains 55 percent of the variation in effective democracy, controlling for how long a society has lived under democratic institutions. The whole is greater than the average of its parts.

The crucial finding is the fact that the self-expression values syndrome explains far more of the variance in effective democracy than any of the other variables emphasized in the political culture literature. The multivariate regressions shown in Table 11.3 strikingly confirm this point. If we control for the self-expression values syndrome, *none* of the attitudes that are not part of this syndrome has a significant impact on democracy; but the impact of self-expression values remains highly significant and is almost completely undiminished when we control for the other political culture indicators, regardless of which one we use. Comparing these findings with those in Table 8.4 indicates that the impact of self-expression values on democracy is not an artifact of its linkages with any other societal factor, whether structural or cultural. Although all prominent theories in the political culture literature emphasize other factors, self-expression values seem to play the central role. Many other factors are indeed correlated with democracy, but this is true mainly insofar as they are linked with self-expression values. Decoupled from self-expression values, other political culture factors seem irrelevant to democracy.

These findings support the interpretation that the rise of a culture that emphasizes human self-expression constitutes the single most important force in strengthening democracy. Considered in this light, effective democracy can be understood as the institutional manifestation of social forces emphasizing human choice and self-expression – as our theory of human development holds. Self-expression values seem to be the most crucial component of a democratic civic culture.

The Centrality of Liberty Aspirations

All components of the self-expression values syndrome show significant linkages with democracy. This syndrome involves postmaterialist aspirations for human liberty, interpersonal trust, elite-challenging activities, tolerance of outgroups, and an emphasis on subjective well-being. These attributes go together because they reflect a culture in which survival is sufficiently secure that out-groups do not seem threatening, people feel safe enough to trust others, and self-reliance, creativity, and initiative take high priority. Increasingly, freedom of expression and freedom of choice are highly valued, both for oneself and for others.

Strong emphasis on human choice lies at the core of the self-expression values syndrome. This fact becomes clearer when we focus on postmaterialist liberty aspirations, which emphasize personal and political freedom. These aspirations are the most directly relevant to human choice. Liberty aspirations are a postmaterialist phenomenon that tends to be most widespread in postindustrial societies. But liberty aspirations are not unique to postindustrial societies. They exist to varying degrees in all societies, and the extent to which they are present tends to shape a society's affinity to democracy.

The relationship that other mass attitudes have with liberty aspirations reflects how closely these attitudes are related to the emancipative essence of democracy – self-expression values, or their opposite, social conformism. Attitudes that are positively correlated with liberty aspirations have a positive impact on democracy; those that are uncorrelated do not. This is why some of the attitudes emphasized by the communitarian and the legitimacy approaches were found to have no impact on democracy, while others did.

For example, public confidence in institutions has no impact on democracy (see Table 11.2), reflecting the fact that confidence in institutions is unrelated to liberty aspirations. Confidence in institutions can be as strong in authoritarian societies as it is in democratic societies. Thus, mass liberty aspirations are essentially uncorrelated with public confidence in state institutions ($r = .05$, $N = 61$), and they have a *negative* (though insignificant) correlation with overall confidence in institutions ($r = -.18$, $N = 61$). By contrast, our multi-item indicator of mass preferences for democracy over autocracy has a significant impact on democracy, reflecting that these preferences correlate strongly and significantly with liberty aspirations at $r = .53$.

Similarly, none of the types of voluntary activities in associations showed a significant impact on democracy, reflecting that voluntary activity in associations is not significantly linked with liberty aspirations. But mass levels of subjective well-being, elite-challenging activities, and tolerance all show significant effects on democracy, reflecting that all these components are strongly correlated with liberty aspirations, generating the self-expression values syndrome.

Figure 11.1 summarizes these findings, showing that the linkage between a given political culture indicator and effective democracy is a linear function of the given indicator's linkage with liberty aspirations. Indicators that are positively linked with liberty aspirations also show a positive correlation with democracy, and those that are negatively linked with liberty aspirations are negatively linked with democracy – and the stronger an indicator's linkage with liberty aspirations, the stronger its linkage with democracy. This finding

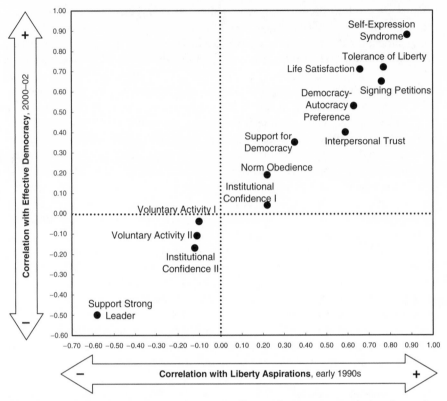

FIGURE 11.1. Mass attitudes are linked with effective democracy mainly insofar as they are linked with liberty aspirations.

confirms our emancipative version of human development theory, indicating that democracy is an institutional reflection of mass emphasis on human choice and freedom.

Institutional Confidence and Interpersonal Trust

It is significant that confidence in institutions and interpersonal trust have different relationships with liberty aspirations. This finding is consistent with Putnam's (1993) distinction between "horizontal" trust and "vertical" trust.

Confidence in institutions is vertically oriented because it reflects trust in institutionalized hierarchies through which authorities exert power over the public. As Putnam argues, strong forms of vertical trust are typical of societies with strong hierarchical ties. These ties strengthen the intensity of trust but at the same time restrict its social radius: one's trust focuses narrowly on the authority of leaders but does not include equals outside one's primary group (see also Banfield, 1958; Fukuyama, 1995, 2000).

By contrast, generalized interpersonal trust is horizontally oriented because it reflects trust between equal citizens. Horizontal trust characterizes egalitarian middle-class societies in which people are linked with each other by webs of diverse economic and civic interactions. Horizontal trust is not necessarily intensive, but its social radius is relatively large. Horizontal trust reflects the "strength of weak ties" in that it is "bridging" rather than "bonding" (see Granovetter, 1973). Because horizontal trust reflects and creates autonomously motivated civic interactions, it is linked to emancipation rather than conformism. Accordingly, horizontal trust is more conducive to civic cooperation that puts elites under democratizing pressure than is vertical trust. Strong vertical trust can help make people obedient to dictatorial power.

Rokeach (1960) and Rosenberg and Owens (2001) argue that high levels of trust in other people indicate an "open-minded" social climate, which is typical of societies that emphasize liberty. This explains the positive societal-level linkage between interpersonal trust and liberty aspirations. By definition, societies in which liberty aspirations are strongly emphasized are driven by an emancipative spirit, which in turn implies a critical orientation toward hierarchies and authorities (Nevitte, 1996). This explains the weak but negative linkage between liberty aspirations and confidence in institutions. Because liberty aspirations reflect autonomy from or even defiance toward institutionalized authority, they diminish public confidence in institutions – particularly insofar as this confidence reflects an authoritarian outlook.

According to some social capital theorists, interpersonal trust between citizens and public confidence in the working of institutions should go together (see Newton, 2001). In fact, they do not, because they are linked in opposite ways to liberty aspirations.

Conformist and Challenging Forms of Civic Activism

Postmaterialist liberty aspirations help us to distinguish between different kinds of trust as well as between different kinds of civic engagement. Elite-challenging forms of activism – such as participating in demonstrations, boycotts, and petitions – are positively linked with mass liberty aspirations: the percentage of people that have signed a petition, attended a demonstration, or joined a boycott correlates with postmaterialist liberty aspirations at a highly significant level ($r = .62$). Elite-challenging activities reflect a critical citizenry whose members are able and willing to put incumbent authorities under pressure to respond to their demands.

Hence, we find that mass liberty aspirations are positively linked with elite-challenging activity; but voluntary activity in formal associations shows a slightly negative relationship with liberty aspirations (see Figure 11.1). In keeping with this fact, elite-challenging activism does have a significant impact on democracy, but activity in associations does not, as Tables 11.1 and 11.2 demonstrated.

Many traditional associations, in particular churches, labor unions, and political parties, are bureaucratically organized and dominated by small circles of leaders. They reflect Michels's (1962 [1912]) Iron Law of Oligarchy. Consequently, as liberty aspirations have become more widespread in postindustrial societies, membership in these traditional bureaucratic associations has been declining (see Putnam, 2000; Norris, 2002: chap. 9). Florida (2002) describes this as the "end of the organizational age" in which large-scale organizational machines produced regimented troops of uniform followers. This does not mean that people with strong liberty aspirations are political nihilists who only seek to maximize their private goals. On the contrary, in liberty-oriented societies people tend to engage in expressive forms of civic activity that allow more individual autonomy and self-determination. These activities, which allow people to engage and disengage as they choose, have become considerably more widespread during recent decades (see Norris, 2002: chap. 10). As Chapter 4 demonstrated, the proportion of people taking part in petitions, demonstrations, and civic boycotts rose markedly from 1974 to 2001 in all eight Western societies from which data are available (see also Dalton, 2001; Welzel, Inglehart, and Deutsch, 2004).[8] The overall level of civic activity in modern democracies has not declined; it remained constant or increased (Norris, 2002: chap. 8). But it has shifted away from conformist forms of participation, toward elite-challenging forms of expressive activity. These activities have become such an integral part of people's usual repertory that they are no longer considered unconventional and no longer attract much coverage in the mass media.

Until now, social capital theorists have mainly measured activity in formal associations in order to assess levels of civic cooperation, ignoring the relevance of elite-challenging activities, although these activities also reflect the operation of societal networks, coordinated collective action, and civic cooperation – the core of the definition of social capital from Bourdieu (1986) to Coleman (1990) to Putnam (1993). We would even argue that elite-challenging activities are a better indicator of the civic type of social capital that works to the benefit of democracy than are conventional civic activities. For elite-challenging activities reflect a liberty-oriented and critical public that is able to organize resistance and mobilize people power. History has shown that this is the most effective antidote to authoritarian methods and despotic leaders.

The impact that various indicators of political culture have on a society's subsequent democratic performance reflects how closely these indicators are linked with liberty aspirations, as Figure 11.1 demonstrated. This finding emphasizes

---

[8] The data from the Roper Institute that Putnam (2000) presents as evidence that people are becoming less likely to sign petitions in the United States contradict the results from the World Values Surveys, which show a clear increase in rates of participation in petitions in the United States, and in virtually all other Western democracies. Since a similar pattern of growth is found in all Western democracies for which data are available, this seems to be the prevailing trend.

the emancipative nature of democracy: democracy works best in a culture that emphasizes human choice.

Intrinsic and Instrumental Support for Democracy

Most of the research on the linkages between mass attitudes and democracy has focused on measuring overt support for democratic institutions. This is understandable: the most obvious and direct way to measure support for democracy would be to ask people if they favor democracy, and whether they prefer it to other forms of government. But, as we have seen, certain other attitudes, which constitute the syndrome of self-expression values, are even *better* indicators of the extent to which a given society's political culture is conducive to democracy than is overt support for democracy itself.

A decade has passed since the Third Wave of democratization brought an avalanche of new democracies into being, raising the question, How solid is support for democracy in these countries? In the intervening years, public support for democracy has faded in some countries, many of which are democratic in name only. Studies of Russian political culture (Gibson and Duch, 1994; Miller et al., 1994; Gibson, 1996, 1997, 2001; Fleron and Ahl, 1998; Rose, 2000) have pointed out that a solid majority of the Russian people supports democratic institutions. With varying nuances, these studies concluded that the outlook for democracy was good.

Although this literature is perfectly correct in finding that most Russians have favorable attitudes toward democracy, when these findings are examined in broader cross-cultural perspective, one finds that support for democracy is relatively weak in Russia – indeed, it is weaker than in almost any other country among the more than seventy societies covered by the Values Surveys. Moreover, by some important indicators, prodemocratic orientations among the Russian people became weaker, not stronger, during the 1990s. To some observers, it is unclear how long even the pretense of electoral democracy will survive in the Soviet successor states, apart from the Baltic republics (Brzezinski, 2001).

The prospects for democracy in Islamic countries also have been questioned, with some writers arguing that the basic values of Islamic publics may be incompatible with liberal democracy (Huntington, 1996). Contrary to this claim, we find surprisingly widespread support for democracy among the twelve Islamic publics included in the 1999–2001 wave of the World Values Surveys. But how reliable are the standard indicators of support for democracy?

Several major empirical research programs monitor public support for democratic institutions, including the New Democracies Barometer, the New Russia Barometer, the Latinobarometer, the Afrobarometer, and the Values Surveys. Some degree of consensus has developed concerning which items are most effective, so that certain questions, measuring overt support for democracy, are regularly utilized in these surveys. These questions seem well designed, and they demonstrate internal consistency: people who say they favor democracy on one indicator tend to favor democracy on other indicators. But our faith in these measures rests entirely on their face validity: no one has demonstrated that a high level of mass support for these items actually is conducive to democratic institutions.

Today, overt support for democracy is widespread among publics throughout the world. In country after country, clear majorities of the population endorse democracy. In the last two waves of the Values Surveys, an overwhelming majority of the population in virtually every society described "having a democratic political system" as either "good" or "very good." In the median country, fully 92 percent of those interviewed gave a positive account of democracy. The Russian public ranked lowest, with 62 percent expressing a favorable opinion of democracy. The next lowest figure was found in Pakistan, where 68 percent favored democracy. Although Pakistan ranks relatively low, most of the Islamic countries surveyed rank relatively high: in Albania, Egypt, Bangladesh, Azerbaijan, Indonesia, Morocco, and Turkey, from 92 to 99 percent of the public endorses democratic institutions – a higher proportion than in the United States. Islamic publics may be anti-Western in many respects but, contrary to widespread belief, the democratic ideal has powerful appeal in the Islamic world.

At this point in history, democracy has an overwhelmingly positive image throughout the planet. This has not always been true. In the 1930s and 1940s, fascist regimes won overwhelming mass approval in many countries; and for many decades, communist regimes had widespread support. But in the past decade, democracy has become virtually the only political model with global appeal. Although Francis Fukuyama may have exaggerated in calling this "The End of History," we do seem to be living in a genuinely new era in which the main alternatives to democracy have been discredited.

Research on political culture was motivated by the assumption that prodemocratic attitudes are conducive to democratic institutions. If this is true, democracy should be most prevalent in countries where prodemocratic attitudes are widespread. But this is an empirical question, not something that can simply be assumed. And the evidence indicates that, although mass responses to these questions do tend to be correlated with democracy at the societal level, many of them are weak predictors.

Overwhelming majorities agree that "Having a democratic political system is a good way of governing this country," but this item turns out to be a relatively modest predictor of societal-level democracy, showing correlations of only .38 and .42 with the formal and effective versions of actual democracy in Table 11.1. The Albanians and the Armenians are likelier to agree with this item than are the Swedes and the Swiss. The well-designed multi-item index, which measures system preferences for democracy versus autocracy, has stronger explanatory power than any of its components, as Table 11.1 also demonstrates. This index shows a .57 correlation with formal democracy and a .68 correlation with effective democracy. Countries that rank high on support for democracy and rejection of authoritarian rule tend to be effective democracies. Thus, the standard items used to monitor mass support for democracy cannot be taken at face value, but a well-designed multi-item index does provide a good predictor of how democratic a given society actually is.

But several component attitudes of self-expression values (none of which refers explicitly to democracy) are even stronger predictors of effective democracy than this index of explicit support, as the bottom half of Table 11.1 demonstrates. The extent to which a society has an underlying culture of elite-challenging action and the extent to which its people give high priority to subjective well-being, freedom of speech, and self-expression are even more powerful predictors of effective democracy than whether people say they prefer democracy to autocracy. Liberty aspirations are the strongest single predictor of how democratic a society is. People emphasizing human liberty value democratic freedom intrinsically and do not support democracy only insofar as it is linked with prosperity. Thus, liberty aspirations show a .80 correlation with a society's level of effective democracy – a far stronger linkage than any of the items that measure explicit support for democracy; indeed, it is a much more powerful predictor of system-level democracy than the four-item index measuring people's preference for democracy over autocracy.

Perhaps the most surprising finding is the fact that mass preferences for democracy over autocracy have no independent impact on democracy, when we control for self-expression values (see Table 11.3). The items used to measure system preferences explicitly ask about support for democracy and for authoritarian alternatives. In terms of face content, they might seem to provide ideal measures of a democratic political culture, but empirically they prove to be much weaker predictors of democracy than are self-expression values. This finding is important and by no means obvious. To illustrate it, Figures 11.2a and 11.2b show the impact of system preferences for democracy versus autocracy and self-expression values on effective democracy, with mutual controls.

Based on evidence from all four waves of the Values Surveys, Figure 11.2a shows the impact of self-expression values on effective democracy, controlling for the percentage of people expressing strong preferences for democracy over autocracy (the "solid democrats") in each society. As this figure indicates, societies with more widespread self-expression values than their percentage of solid democrats would suggest also have higher levels of effective democracy than their percentage of solid democrats would suggest (see the locations of Finland, New Zealand, Sweden, Switzerland, and Australia). Conversely, societies with less widespread self-expression values than the percentage of solid democrats would suggest have lower levels of effective democracy than their percentage of solid democrats would suggest (see the locations of Nigeria, Yugoslavia, Azerbaijan, Turkey, and Venezuela). Overall, variation in the strength of self-expression values that is independent of the percentage of solid democrats explains 76 percent of the variation in effective democracy that is independent of the percentage of solid democrats. Self-expression values have a very strong impact on effective democracy, even if we control for the percentage of solid democrats.

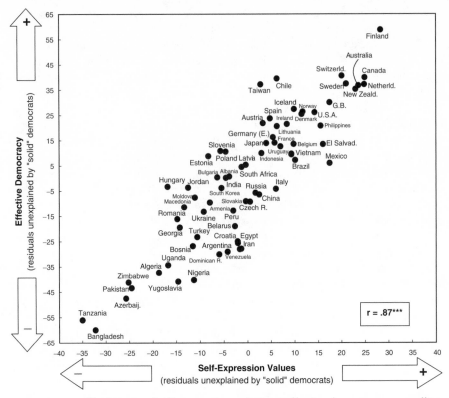

FIGURE 11.2a. The impact of self-expression values on effective democracy, controlling for each country's percentage of "solid democrats."

Figure 11.2b shows the impact of mass preferences for democracy versus autocracy (the percentage of "solid democrats") on effective democracy, controlling for the strength of self-expression values. There is a weak relationship that only exists because of one single leverage case: Vietnam.[9] Without Vietnam, there would be no relationship at all. Anyway, the percentage of solid democrats in such societies as Hungary, Nigeria, or Croatia is much higher than the strength of self-expression values in these societies would suggest, whereas countries like Mexico, Russia, or Taiwan have a lower percentage of solid democrats than the strength of self-expression values in these countries would suggest. Much of the variance in the percentage of solid democrats is independent of the strength of self-expression values. But this independent variation in the proportion of solid democrats accounts for only 12 percent in the variation of effective democracy. Thus, decoupled from self-expression values,

[9] The very low percentage of "solid democrats" in the case of Vietnam reflects a very high percentage of respondents expressing support for the army rule. In a country in which the army is a symbol of national liberation, these figures require a different interpretation. However, we display data as they are, not eliminating cases that do not fit into the pattern.

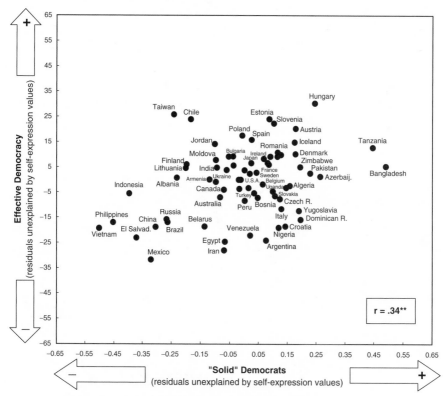

FIGURE 11.2b. The impact of percentage of "solid democrats" in a country, on its level of effective democracy, controlling for its level of self-expression values.

preferences for democracy over autocracy do not have a strong impact on effective democracy. These preferences are linked with effective democracy mostly insofar as they are linked with self-expression values.

The relationship between self-expression values and seemingly solid support for democracy is revealing, as Figure 11.3 demonstrates. Self-expression values explain about 25 percent of the variance in the percentage of solid democrats. But this effect reflects a curvilinear relationship, indicating that widespread self-expression values are a sufficient but not necessary condition to create majorities of solid democrats. If more than 43 percent of the public emphasizes self-expression values (which is Mexico's level), a majority of its citizens will be "solid democrats." There are no exceptions: above this level of self-expression values, one invariably finds a majority of solid democrats. But the reverse does *not* hold: societies whose citizens place relatively low emphasis on human self-expression can show either high or low levels of overt support for democracy, ranging from almost 0 percent in Vietnam to 95 per cent in Bangladesh. Lip service to democracy can be based on a variety of motives, including the belief that being democratic means being rich and powerful. Accordingly, public

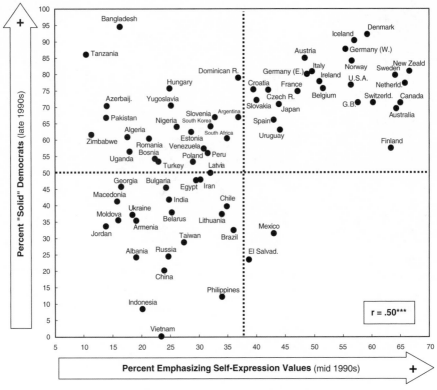

FIGURE 11.3. The impact of self-expression values on overt support for democracy.

support for democracy does not necessarily reflect a culture that emphasizes human choice.

At the individual level, support for democracy tends to be linked with self-expression values because almost everyone who places strong emphasis on self-expression also supports democracy. But many who do not emphasize self-expression values support democracy for other reasons, such as the belief that democracy means being secure and prosperous. These other motives are instrumental; they do not reflect a high valuation of democracy per se; they reflect support for democracy insofar as it is thought to be linked with prosperity and order. This type of support can quickly vanish if a society's experience under democracy is disappointing. Our findings suggest that overt mass support for democracy leads to effective democracy only insofar as it is linked with self-expression values.

The fact that various other attitudes can motivate people to express overt support for democracy has been demonstrated by Bratton and Mattes (2001). Using survey data from the Afrobarometers, Bratton and Mattes found that individual-level support for democracy is strongly linked with performance evaluations, especially those concerning economics and law and order: people

TABLE 11.4. *Explaining Individual-Level Support for Democracy by Instrumental and Intrinsic Motives*

Dependent Variable: Democracy-Autocracy Preference	Emphasis on Self-Expression Values	Performance Expected of Democracy	Adjusted R^2	N
Postindustrial democracies				
Intrinsic	.26	–	.07	13,119
Instrumental	–	.39	.15	27,950
Combined	.20	.38	.21	12,307
Developing societies				
Intrinsic	.13	–	.02	18,831
Instrumental	–	.33	.11	21,082
Combined	.12	.34	.14	17,571
Western ex-communist societies				
Intrinsic	.22	–	.05	4,835
Instrumental	–	.41	.17	11,333
Combined	.15	.38	.19	4,586
Eastern ex-communist societies				
Intrinsic	.17	–	.03	16,816
Instrumental	–	.48	.23	21,654
Combined	.11	.45	.23	15,580
Low-income societies				
Intrinsic	.02	–	.00	18,576
Instrumental	–	.27	.07	19,845
Combined	.02	.26	.07	17,088

Note: Entries are standardized beta-coefficients. All coefficients significant at the .001 level.
Source: Data taken from Values Surveys III–IV (1995–2001).

who believe that democracies are more successful than other regimes in managing economic development and reducing social tensions tend to prefer democracies to other types of political systems. We replicated this analysis with data from the Values Surveys, with similar results (see Table 11.4): what people believe about the policy performance of democracies[10] (which taps instrumental support) is a stronger predictor of their system preference for democracy than is their emphasis on self-expression values (which tap intrinsic support). This pattern is universal since it holds true for all five types of societies: in all types of societies, from postindustrial societies to ex-communist societies to low-income societies, instrumental support motives explain more of people's system preferences for democracy than do intrinsic support motives. To be sure, people with strong self-expression values strongly support democracy, but people who place little emphasis on self-expression values also express support for democracy, if

[10] We measure performance evaluations of democracy referring to such statements as "democracies run the economy badly," or "democracies are bad at maintaining order." The polarity of these items has been reversed. For details, see the Internet Appendix, #65 under Variables.

they believe that democracies are good at running the economy and maintaining order.

Support for democracy does not necessarily reflect intrinsic support, even when one's measure is a well-designed multi-item index of net preferences for democracy over autocracy. Overt support for democracy reflects intrinsic support only insofar as it is linked with self-expression values, and this linkage captures only a minor part of the variance in support for democracy. In many countries, support for democracy is heavily inflated by instrumental motives. Precisely because the questions used to measure self-expression values make no explicit reference to democracy, they are not inflated by the tendency to give lip service to democracy, which has become a socially desirable term. Overt support for democracy itself is not the most important ingredient in a prodemocratic civic culture. More important still are the motives underlying this support, indicating whether support is merely instrumental or reflects the intrinsic commitment to democracy that is tapped by self-expression values.

The contemporary world is no longer divided between those who favor and those who oppose democracy; the vast majority favors democracy, and the main distinction now is whether people support democracy for instrumental or intrinsic reasons. In postindustrial democracies, intrinsic supporters constitute the great majority of those who support democracy. In eastern ex-communist countries and low-income societies, on the other hand, although high proportions of the public express overt support for democracy, intrinsic supporters constitute only a small share of this group.[11] These societies are precisely where we find the lowest actual levels of democracy. Indeed, among fifty-seven countries for which these variables are available, cross-national variation in *instrumental* support for democracy correlates negatively, at $-.51$, with subsequent measures of effective democracy. But variation in intrinsic support for democracy correlates at $+.84$ with effective democracy. Rising self-expression values provide intrinsic support for democracy – the kind of support that is most crucial for democracy to emerge and survive.

Summary

Our findings point to three conclusions:

1. We find strong evidence that a broad set of civic values focusing on freedom and self-expression are more important to democracy than is overt support for democratic institutions. This is true because democracy is not merely an institutional phenomenon; it also involves citizens.

---

[11] To make these calculations, we dichotomized the "solid supporters" of democracy (see the Internet Appendix, #57). Those placing relatively strong emphasis on self-expression values (i.e., those scoring above zero on the factor scale) were classified as "intrinsic supporters"; those with weaker emphasis on self-expression values fell into the other group (see the Internet Appendix, #58).

As Tocqueville, Almond and Verba, Eckstein, Putnam, and others have argued, making democracy work requires civic values among the public.

2. Among the civic values, trust in other people is important for democracy, but mainly through its linkage with other components of self-expression values such as liberty aspirations, which have a more direct relationship to democracy. Postmaterialist liberty aspirations reflect an intrinsic preference for democratic procedures and rules and an intrinsic, not an instrumental, preference for democracy.

3. Mass participation in the classic bureaucratically organized associations and public confidence in hierarchically organized institutions often reflect an emphasis on social conformism rather than on autonomy. Because human autonomy is at the heart of democracy's focus on choice, attitudes that emphasize social conformism are not positively linked with democracy at the system level.

Democracy is not just a set of rules that depend solely on institutional engineering. It is an inherently normative concept that emphasizes free choice, autonomy, and emancipation (see Macpherson, 1977; Donnelly, 1993). To put these norms into practice requires more than lip service to the now-fashionable term democracy. It requires a commitment to human choice and autonomy, which is tapped by self-expression values. These values give priority to individual liberty over collective discipline, human diversity over group conformity, and civic autonomy over state authority. Unless support for democracy is coupled with these emancipative values, it is virtually irrelevant to effective democracy at the system level. Effective democracy is not simply a matter of institutional arrangements; it reflects deep-rooted normative commitments. These commitments take on new prominence with the shift from survival values to self-expression values, reshaping the emphasis of social forces from social conformism to civic emancipation, in keeping with the logic of human development. Our indicator of self-expression values was developed only in recent years and undoubtedly can be improved. But it seems to be the most powerful indicator of a democratic civic culture that is currently available.

12

Gender Equality, Emancipative Values, and Democracy

Gender Equality as an Aspect of Human Development

The rise of gender equality is another aspect of the process of human development that is comparable in importance to the global trend toward democracy and closely linked with it. Since the dawn of history, women have had an inferior social position in virtually every society. The role of women was largely limited to the functions of reproduction and caretaking; public decision making and political power were predominantly male domains (Daly, 1978; Ember and Ember, 1996: 124; Nolan and Lenski, 1999: 102; Fulcher and Scott, 2003: 164–68). Even today, men still dominate most areas of economic and public life.

But in the postindustrial phase, a trend toward gender equality becomes a central aspect of modernization (Inglehart and Norris, 2003: 29–48). This transformation of established gender roles is part of a broader humanistic shift linked with rising self-expression values, bringing increasing tolerance of human diversity and antidiscrimination movements on many fronts (see Fulcher and Scott, 2003: 179–91).

Gender equality has become crucial to the quality of democracy. Democracy is based on the idea that all human beings are valuable, regardless of biological characteristics such as race and sex (Birch and Cobb, 1981; Rose, 1995; Sen, 1999; Dahl, 2003). The idea of democracy aims at empowering people as if societies were made through a social contract between equals, all of whom have the same potential for making autonomous and responsible choices (Sen, 1999: chap. 6). Thus, any discrimination based on race or sex conflicts with the democratic idea of human equality (McDonagh, 2002; Welzel, 2003).

Human development reflects the degree to which societal conditions allow people to develop their potential for choice (Anand and Sen, 2000; Welzel, 2002; Welzel, Inglehart, and Klingemann, 2003). Consequently, gender equality is a sensitive measure of how far human development has advanced in a society. Even today, women are confronted with societal disadvantages that make it more difficult for them than for men to develop their talents in careers

272

outside the household (Inglehart and Norris, 2003). Objectively, women have the same talents as men and could develop them beyond their traditionally limited roles. Subjectively, they have been socialized to accept these role limitations throughout history.

But history has recently taken a fundamentally new direction. In postindustrial societies, women no longer accept their traditional role limitations, and female empowerment has moved to a high place on the political agenda (Inglehart, Norris, and Welzel, 2002). Gender equality has become a central element in the definition of human development, for it is an essential aspect of human equality, like civil and political liberties and human rights. Never before in the history of civilization have women enjoyed more equality and more freedom in choosing their education, their careers, their partners, and their life-styles than in contemporary postindustrial societies. This change is recent. Although it can be traced back to the introduction of female suffrage in some countries after World War I, female empowerment only recently became a pervasive trend. It is reflected in a massive tendency toward increasing female representation in national parliaments and in a shift toward emancipative value orientations in which the traditional belief that "men make better political leaders than women" is fading dramatically – at least in postindustrial societies. This increasing emphasis on gender equality is part of a humanistic change that propels antidiscriminatory forces, fueling human development and the quality of democracy.

We argue that gender equality – along with tolerance of outgroups, such as people of other races, foreigners, and homosexuals – is becoming an essential element of democracy. Is this an ethnocentric claim, imposing Western cultural standards on the rest of the world? At first glance, it may seem so, because Western societies currently emphasize these values more strongly than most other societies. But they are not inherently Western values. A few generations ago, they were just as foreign to Western publics as they now seem to some non-Western publics; indeed, until relatively recently, some non-Western societies were more tolerant toward some of these outgroups than were Western publics. Emphasis on gender equality and tolerance toward gays and other outgroups has emerged in postindustrial societies around the globe through a process of intergenerational value change – and the older birth cohorts in these societies are still relatively close to their peers in less-developed societies (Inglehart and Norris, 2003). The idea that democracy requires broadly inclusive standards such as gender equality is becoming increasingly prominent: it is linked with a pervasive humanistic shift in which rising self-expression values transform modernization into a process of human development.

Democracy emerged historically long before gender equality became an issue. But when modern democracy emerged in Great Britain and the United States, it was a limited version that accepted slavery, property requirements for voting, and the exclusion of women from political rights. Those societies would not be considered democracies by today's standards. For democracy is not a static concept. It evolves over time. Cultural changes are transforming the very

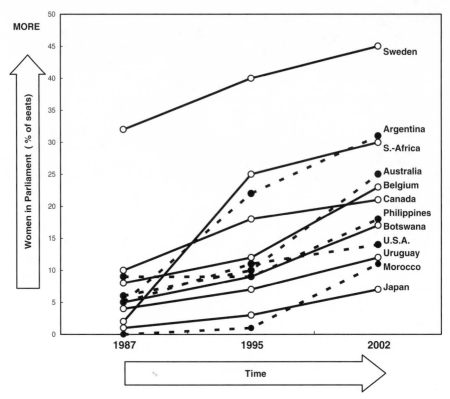

FIGURE 12.1. The growth of women's representation in parliament in selected countries.

definition of democracy, and gender equality is becoming a central component of what constitutes democracy.

Figures 12.1 and 12.2 demonstrate these points. Using data from the Inter-parliamentary Union (IPU), Figure 12.1 shows that female representation in national parliaments has been increasing during the past fifteen years in many countries with diverse cultural backgrounds. Although this trend occurs at different levels and advances at different rates in different countries, the overall pattern is clear: female representation is increasing rapidly, from Belgium to Botswana.

Figure 12.2 plots public rejection of the statement that "men make better political leaders than women," by sex, age, and a society's level of economic development. Women in both poorer and richer societies reject this statement more than men. But the gender difference in poor societies is relatively small and considerably smaller than the differences between poor and rich societies: men in rich countries reject the statement in much higher proportions than do women in low-income societies. Thus, it is clear that beliefs about gender roles do not simply follow the rational self-interest of the given gender. These beliefs are changing, but they are deeply rooted in a society's culture: in

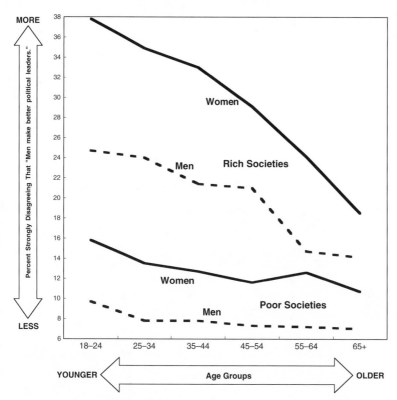

FIGURE 12.2. Generational differences in support for gender equality in rich versus poor countries.

patriarchic cultures, both men and women have relatively patriarchic orientations. Conversely, in more-modern cultures, even men have relatively egalitarian orientations toward gender roles.

Increasing emphasis is being placed on gender equality, especially in rich societies, and it is occurring largely through intergenerational replacement. Consequently, we find large age-differences, with members of the younger generations being much less likely to believe in male superiority than are members of the older generation. These differences, too, are much larger than the gender differences: younger men in rich societies have more egalitarian gender orientations than older women in rich societies. This explains why the gender issue has become salient only recently: the changes that are driving it have been at work for some time, but it emerged as a powerful political force only after sufficient generational replacement had occurred to transform the adult electorate. In addition, the gender gap has become much larger among the younger generations, with younger women moving toward more egalitarian gender attitudes more quickly than younger men. Nevertheless, in the world as a whole, even among younger women we do not yet find an absolute majority that strongly rejects

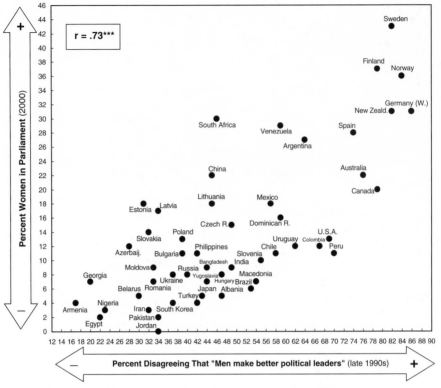

FIGURE 12.3. Mass attitudes toward gender equality, and women's representation in parliament.

the idea of male superiority, although in some societies, such as Sweden and the Netherlands, such majorities exist among both men and women.[1]

The long-standing belief that "men make better political leaders than women" is changing, as younger generations replace older ones. This belief is not just a matter of lip service. It has important political consequences.

As Figure 12.3 demonstrates, in countries where the public rejects the idea that men make better political leaders, much higher proportions of women actually get elected to parliament. The extent to which this belief is present is an even stronger predictor of the number of women in parliament than is the society's level of democracy (Inglehart et al., 2002), which suggests that cultural

---

[1] If one combines percentages who "fairly" or "strongly" disagree with the statement that "men make better political leaders than women," one obtains considerably larger percentages of disagreement. We have based Figure 12.3 on the percentages of people who "strongly disagree" with the idea of male superiority because we think this is a better indicator of deeply anchored convictions. See the Internet Appendix, #66 under Variables. For this and subsequent references to the Internet Appendix, see http://www.worldvaluessurvey.org/publications/humandevelopment.html.

norms have even more impact than democratic institutions on the percentage of women in parliament. Moreover, although richer countries have higher proportions of women in parliament than poorer ones, this seems mainly to reflect the fact that socioeconomic development leads to cultural changes. Regression analysis indicates that a society's economic level explains only 30 percent of the variance in the percentage of women in parliament. Mass support for gender equality plays the main explanatory role: both the trend toward democracy and the shift toward gender equality in parliament reflect underlying cultural changes that are transforming society (Inglehart et al., 2002).

Traditional Causes of Gender Inequality

How were men able to dominate economic and political life in virtually all societies throughout recorded history? To begin with, human sexual dimorphism gave rise to the trivial but fundamental fact that men on average have more physical strength than women and produce more testosterone, which is linked with aggression, whereas only women can bear and nurse children. In the resulting sexual division of labor, men performed the martial survival functions, particularly hunting and fighting, while women performed child-rearing and care-taking functions. With high infant mortality rates, it was necessary to produce a large number of children in order to reproduce the population; and with life expectancies of thirty-five to forty years, by the time a woman had borne and raised four to six children, she was nearing the end of her life. This role division tied women to the household, while men dominated all activities outside the household, including politics. For politics begins with the organization of coercive power for defense and the enforcement of law and order. As long as the organization of defense and security remained the dominant state activity, women were excluded (Service, 1962; Flannery, 1972; Daly, 1978; Carneiro, 1988; Fedigan, 1991; Peterson and Wrangham, 1997). Moreover, in both agrarian and industrial societies, production activities involved heavy physical work, which led men to dominate these activities. Women were largely excluded from economic life outside the household until major economic activities increasingly began to involve intellectual rather than physical activities (Daly, 1978; Nolan and Lenski, 1999).

Recent technological advances and the functional differentiation of state activities have transformed all of these factors. In the knowledge society, muscular strength is virtually irrelevant to production: it depends on creativity, skill in handling people, and intellectual ability – in all of which women are at least as talented as men. Moreover, in postindustrial societies infant mortality has dropped to very low levels; life expectancy has more than doubled; and birth control technology makes it possible to choose how many children a woman has, and when. Women no longer spend most of their adult lives bearing and raising children. Finally, even the military function has become divorced from muscular strength. Military success no longer depends on having masses of strong, aggressive men: increasingly, it is fought at a distance, and success depends on skillful planning and high technology – or, better still, effective diplomacy. Moreover, with the expansion of its welfare functions, organizing the means of coercion ceased to be the focus of the modern state. As this happened, the male monopoly of politics began to erode.

These technological and organizational transformations have fundamentally changed the character of power, in keeping with the general trend of human development: power is decreasingly physical and coercive, and increasingly communicative and intellectual. The consequences of these changes, in terms of gender equality in economic and political life, have been surfacing only recently, reflecting the fact that deep-rooted cultural characteristics such as gender roles tend to change gradually, largely through intergenerational population replacement.

Throughout industrial society, and even more strongly in postindustrial societies, large intergenerational differences exist in attitudes toward gender equality (Inglehart and Norris, 2003). They reflect a "Rising Tide" of change toward greater societal acceptance of gender equality in particular and human equality in general. Increasing gender equality is a major aspect of the human development trend.

Additional factors help explain the dramatic changes in gender roles that are emerging, especially in postindustrial societies, including those related to modernization, institutions, and culture. In this chapter, we outline these explanations and test them empirically, using the gender empowerment index developed in the *Human Development Report* by the United Nations Development Program (2000) as our dependent variable.[2]

New Factors Promoting Gender Equality: The Welfare State

The traditional coercive state gave males a monopoly in politics (Carneiro, 1988). And the transition from the coercive state to the welfare state has played an important role in opening economic and public roles to women. The welfare state takes on caretaking responsibilities, reducing the risks of aging, sickness, unemployment, and homelessness. These developments have freed modern families from the need to have many children in order to reproduce the population, raised life expectancy, and provided education for women as well as men, enhancing women's options for activities outside the household. The institutionalization of caretaking responsibilities also worked to the advantage of women, with public schools, health care, and pension systems unburdening them from many of their traditional responsibilities within the household (Poggi, 1978). Modern women do not need to tie themselves to a family or a male breadwinner in order to earn a living. Accordingly, the welfare state loosens women's ties

---

[2] The "gender empowerment measure" developed by the United Nations Development Program reflects female representation in parliaments, in management positions, and in administrative functions, as well as gender equality in salaries. For details, see the Internet Appendix, #26 under Variables.

TABLE 12.1. *Correlates of Gender Empowerment*

Correlates	Pearson Correlation with Gender Empowerment Index 2000 (N)
Percent emphasizing self-expression values, early 1990s	.86*** (50)
Public welfare investment minus military investment, 1990	.77*** (48)
Welfare state regimes (Esping-Andersen, 1990)	.60** (17)
Internet hosts per 1,000 inhabitants, 1998	.67*** (49)
Years under democratic government up to 1995	.65*** (50)
Consociationalism, first dimension (Lijphart, 1999)	.11 (23)
Percent Protestants minus Muslims 1995	.74*** (50)

Note: Significance levels: *p < .100; **p < .010; ***p < .001.

to the household, allowing them to play a more prominent role in the broader circles of economic, political, and societal life (Sainsbury, 1996; Liebert, 1999; Hirschmann, 2001; Tronto, 2001).

The expansion of the welfare state also reflects the emergence of a new social contract. Before the rise of mass democracies and welfare states, traditional states mainly operated as tribute-taking machines. They used their coercive power to extract any economic surplus from the people, to satisfy the interests of the power holders (Jones, 1985; J. Diamond, 1997: 265). By contrast, democratic welfare states that are held responsible to the public reinvest extracted resources for the welfare of the broader public – the very definition of a social contract (Boix, 2001; Stiglitz, 2002: 160–62). Accordingly, the elites in welfare states are more strongly oriented toward the public good, which is reflected in lower corruption among elites: there is a highly significant $r = .69\,(N = 51)$ correlation between elite integrity (i.e., the inverse of elite corruption) and the proportion of the state budget invested in public welfare (i.e., health and education).[3] Similarly, public welfare spending correlates strongly with all of the "good governance" indicators developed by Kaufmann et al. (2003). The emergence of the social contract has helped reduce social inequalities: the Gini coefficient of disparities in family incomes correlates with welfare state expenditures at $r = -.50\,(N = 48)$. As Table 12.1 demonstrates, the more heavily governments invest in social welfare, and the less they invest in traditionally male-dominated coercive forces such as the military, the more gender equality is present. Differences in the scope of the welfare state correlate at $r = .77$ with variation in gender equality.

Another way to analyze variations in the welfare state is Esping-Andersen's (1990) typology of welfare state regimes, which distinguishes between corporatist, liberal, and social-democratic types. The corporatist type exists in continental Western Europe, where strong Christian Democratic parties promoted

---

[3] For details, see the Internet Appendix, #13 under Variables.

a patriarchic welfare state, following a strategy aimed at eroding the working class's loyalty to the Social Democrats. Christian Democratic parties designed the welfare state based on extended social insurance systems that favor the traditional family model in which there is only one income, usually earned by the male breadwinner. This type of welfare state provides the weakest incentives for women to leave their traditional role in the household. Under otherwise equal conditions, one would expect this type of the welfare state to produce the lowest degree of gender equality. The liberal welfare state, by contrast, characterizes most of the Anglo-Saxon world. The size of state budgets in liberal welfare states is relatively small, but it does not include budgetary incentives that support traditional gender roles. Consequently, one would expect this type of welfare state to show an intermediate position in terms of gender equality. Finally, the social-democratic welfare state, which is particularly strong in Scandinavia, is not only the most extensive welfare state but also provides the most extensive public caretaking infrastructure, emancipating women from their traditional ties to the household. Accordingly, one would expect to find the highest degree of gender equality in the social-democratic welfare state.

On a limited basis (only postindustrial societies are classified by Esping-Andersen), the evidence in Table 12.1 confirms these assumptions. Although the range of variation among corporatist welfare states is large, on average they clearly show the lowest degrees of gender equality. By contrast, the liberal Anglo-Saxon welfare states show higher levels of gender equality, whereas the Scandinavian social-democratic welfare states show the highest level of gender equality. Overall, these differences in types of welfare institutions correlate at .60 with cross-national variation in gender equality among advanced Western economies.

The Emerging Knowledge Society

Another argument linked with modernization refers to changes in the nature of socioeconomic activities. As a society's work force shifts from agrarian and industrial activities to the service and knowledge sectors – such as financing, marketing, accounting, counseling, communication, education, and research – the emphasis of economic activities shifts from physical to intellectual work (Bell, 1973; Giddens, 1990). As this happens, the relative advantage that muscular power confers on males vanishes. Other conditions being equal, we would expect gender equality to advance with the emergence of knowledge societies.

A good indication of the emerging knowledge society is the spread of information technology, which can be measured by the number of internet hosts per 1,000 inhabitants.[4] As Table 12.1 demonstrates, gender equality does indeed correlate with the penetration of the internet at r = .67.

[4] See the Internet Appendix, #12 under Variables.

Regime Traditions and Institutional Characteristics

It has been argued that democratic traditions tend to favor gender equality. The argument is straightforward (McDonagh, 2002): democratic institutions provide women with more rights and more channels to make their voices heard than are present in autocracies. But it takes time for these institutional opportunities to act on established gender roles. For this to happen, democratic rules must become part of a society's collective identity. This does not take place overnight; to some extent it is linked with the emergence of a new generation of women who have grown up with democratic opportunities. We hypothesize that as the number of years that countries have spent under democratic institutions rises, gender equality will also rise.[5] As Table 12.1 demonstrates, this is indeed the case, although the correlation is considerably weaker than that with the welfare state (r = .67).

Another institutional factor that has been claimed to be important, is the type of democratic regime, as indicated by Lijphart's (1999) index of majoritarian versus consociational democracy. Variations along the consociational dimension are restricted to formal democracies, excluding all nondemocratic societies, so the index is only available for twenty-three nations of our sample. But Lijphart argues that consociationalism has a major impact on a variety of aspects of societal development. In particular, he argues that consociational democracies are more consensus-oriented in their search for a better balance between opposing societal groups and interests. If what Lijphart describes as the "gentler" outlook of consociational democracies applied to the gender cleavage, we would expect to find greater recognition of female interests, reflected in higher degrees of gender equality, in societies with high levels of consociational democracy.

The evidence does not support this assumption, as Table 12.1 demonstrates. Variation in the degree of consociationalism[6] is uncorrelated with variation in gender equality. Countries scoring as high on consociationalism as Switzerland, Belgium, or the Netherlands show lower degrees of gender equality than countries with low degrees of consociationalism, such as Canada or New Zealand. Consociational democracies are not "gentler" than other democracies with respect to gender equality, but social democratic welfare states *are* "gentler" than other welfare states. Variations in the type of welfare state seem to have more impact on gender equality than variations in the type of democracy.

Religious Heritage: Western versus Non-Western Societies

Another prominent school of thought traces differences in gender equality to cultural traditions linked with a society's religious heritage. Following Max Weber (1958 [1904]), sociologists have argued that religious traditions have

---

[5] For measuring the years under democracy, see the Internet Appendix, #23 under Variables.

[6] We use scores on Lijphart's (1999) first dimension of consociationalism, which he calls the "parties-executive" dimension. His second dimension of consociationalism, the "federalism" dimension, shows also no linkage to gender equality.

a lasting impact on a society's overall makeup. More specifically, it has been argued that the Protestant tradition of decentralized churches and its emphasis on laymen's voluntary engagement in community life have left Protestant societies with a more individualistic, liberal, democratic, and civil-societal imprint. Thus, Protestant societies led the way in introducing women's suffrage. If the Protestant activist-egalitarian ideals also affect women, it would fuel their demands for gender equality. Under otherwise equal conditions, Protestant societies should still have higher degrees of gender equality than non-Protestant societies.

The sharpest division in individualistic and democratic values, according to Huntington (1996: 159), separates Western Protestant societies from Oriental Islamic societies. Islam, it is argued, was historically built on nomadic tribes that gave Islam a strong patriarchic imprint (Jawad, 1998). If this patriarchic tradition persists, one would find the lowest degrees of gender equality in societies with an Islamic heritage. Overall, variations in gender equality might be structured along a polarization between Protestant and Islamic religions.

In order to locate a society's position in the Protestant-versus-Muslim polarity, we calculated a percentage difference index that subtracts the percentage of a society's Islamic population from the percentage that is Protestant, so that a country obtains higher positive scores on this index as its Protestant population exceeds its Muslim population. As Table 12.1 demonstrates, this Protestant-versus-Muslim index correlates at .74 with gender equality.[7]

Rising Self-Expression Values

Why do a society's religious traditions help shape levels of gender equality? The reason, presumably, is because religion shapes value orientations that have an impact on gender equality. If this is true, then value orientations themselves should have a more direct impact on gender equality than does religion. The same should be true for such objective factors as the welfare state and knowledge society, which operate largely through changing mass beliefs. In other words, religious traditions, the welfare state, democracy, and the knowledge society should have an effect on gender equality because these factors tend to shape the emancipative cultural forces that are tapped by self-expression values, bringing changing orientations toward gender roles. As Figure 12.4 demonstrates, self-expression values do indeed have a stronger impact on gender equality than any of the variables we have examined so far, explaining 65 percent of the variance in gender equality.

Table 12.2 introduces our various explanatory factors into a regression analysis (we only included variables that proved significant in the correlation analyses shown in Table 12.1). The analysis demonstrates that self-expression values have the strongest effect on gender equality, regardless of which other explanatory factors are included in the analysis.

---

[7] For details on measuring this percentage difference index, see the Internet Appendix, #14.

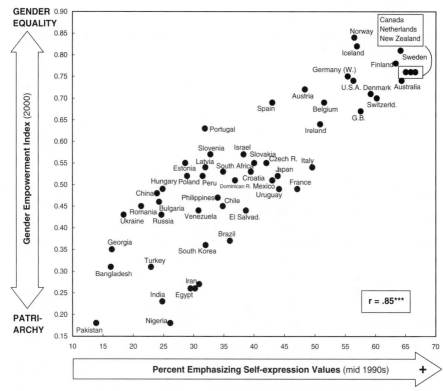

FIGURE 12.4. Self-expression values and the actual scope of gender empowerment in a society.

TABLE 12.2. *Explaining Gender Empowerment (multiple regression)*

Predictors	Dependent Variable: Gender Empowerment Index 2000
Percent emphasizing self-expression values in early 1990s	.45*** (3.64)
Public welfare investment minus military investment, 1990	.33*** (3.51)
Percent Protestants minus Muslims around 1990	.09 (.84)
Internet hosts per 1,000 inhabitants, 1998	.15 (1.61)
Adjusted R^2	.79

Note: Entries are standardized regression coefficients (T-ratios in parentheses). N = 48. Significance levels: *p < .100; **p < .010; ***p < .001.

Conclusion

Along with the spread and deepening of democratic institutions, rising gender equality reflects the humanistic tendency inherent in human development.
Indeed, rising gender equality is an essential aspect in the strengthening of
democratic institutions. Gender equality reflects the degree to which women
have equal opportunity to develop their potential for autonomous choice. In
keeping with our theory, the emancipative social forces tapped by mass emphasis on self-expression values seems to play the most crucial role in giving rise to
gender equality. Only one other factor, the degree to which societal expenditures
emphasize the welfare state rather than the means of coercion, approaches the
importance of self-expression values. Other factors, particularly the number
of years that a society has lived under democratic institutions and its religious
heritage, have a greatly reduced impact on gender equality when we take self-
expression values into account. These variables are mainly relevant to gender
equality insofar as they are linked with self-expression values. The emancipative
social forces reflected in self-expression values promote human development on
many fronts: not only do they increase elite integrity and strengthen effective
democracy; they also promote female empowerment and gender-egalitarian
democracy. This trend is another indication of the central importance of rising
self-expression values in promoting human choice. Rising gender equality is a
major component in the emergence of humanistic societies; it is comparable in
magnitude to the global trend toward democracy and closely linked with it.

Gender equality was not part of the original definition of democracy. In
ancient Athens, the original model of democracy, less than 10 percent of the
population had political rights, and women were excluded from politics (Bollen
and Paxton, 1997). Even today, women are still excluded from politics in some
societies. But democracy is an evolving concept, and it shows a pervasive trend
toward becoming more inclusive and humanistic.

13

The Implications of Human Development

A Humanistic Transformation of Modernization

As the preceding chapters have demonstrated, socioeconomic development, self-expression values, and democratic institutions are so closely correlated that they tap a single underlying dimension. Each of these three components helps develop a society's human potential – that is, people's ability to shape their lives on the basis of their autonomous choices. Accordingly, this dimension reflects human development.

The linkages between socioeconomic development, cultural values, and political institutions that constitute human development were partly foreshadowed by modernization theorists (see Lipset, 1959a; Almond and Coleman, 1960; Pye and Verba, 1963; Apter, 1965; Almond and Powell, 1966; Weiner, 1966; Coleman, 1968; Huntington, 1968; Binder et al., 1971; Pye, 1990). But while many of these social scientists speculated that some set of "modern" values provided the essential link between socioeconomic development and democratic institutions, few examined this linkage empirically, and those who did examined only a handful of nations (see Lerner, 1958; Inkeles and Smith, 1974; Inkeles, 1983). Moreover, they focused on the emergence of secular-rational values as the key cultural manifestation of modernity. This view was accurate enough during the industrialization phase of modernization, but it is outmoded today. In postindustrial society, things have changed in ways that have important political consequences. As long as secularization, rationalization, and bureaucratization were the dominant cultural trends, modernization did not necessarily lead to democracy; it was perfectly compatible with authoritarian and totalitarian regimes, as theorists of "totalitarianism" (Friedrich and Brzezinski, 1965), "mobilization regimes" (Johnson, 1970), and "bureaucratic authoritarianism" (O'Donnell, 1973) correctly noted.

Our data confirm this view, demonstrating that secular-rational values – the hallmark of industrial society – do not show a strong linkage with democracy. For secular-rational values do not question unlimited authority; they simply shift its basis from religion to science and from religious authority to the bureaucratic state. The rise of secular-rational values does indeed bring an important change: it makes the legitimacy of any authority depend increasingly on mass approval and the elites' claims to work for the common good (Meyer et al., 1997). Thus, all modern political systems introduced universal suffrage in order to demonstrate that they rule with the consent of the masses. But fascist and communist regimes were quite adept at devising elite-controlled forms of universal suffrage – indeed, they attained higher levels of participation in elections and referenda than liberal democracies ever did. While secularization and rationalization were the dominant cultural trend, universal suffrage was as likely to result in fascist, communist, and authoritarian regimes as in genuinely democratic ones.

Secular-rational values are perfectly compatible with nondemocratic systems. The processes of secularization and rationalization require that the masses be included in politics, because public consent becomes the only source of legitimacy. But public consent can be mobilized in authoritarian ways that do not necessarily bring mass dissatisfaction and protest, as long as most people give a higher priority to conformist survival values than to civil and political liberties.

Modernization theorists underestimated the importance of emancipative values that question authority and fuel mass pressures for the civil and political rights that constitute liberal democracy. Accordingly, the dimension tapped by self-expression values was almost entirely overlooked by theorists of modernization and political culture. But with the emergence of postindustrial society, it is becoming increasingly clear that emancipative values among the public are essential to democracy. Self-expression values have an inherently anti-authoritarian thrust that undermines autocratic rule and also the "subject orientation" that Almond and Verba (1963) saw as an integral part of a democratic civic culture. Self-expression values (or what other social scientists refer to as "individualism" or "autonomy" values) motivate the crucial social force involved in the rise of effective democracy. The spread of emancipative self-expression values constitutes the key link in the process of human development, linking socioeconomic development with democratic institutions.

This book has presented a revised version of modernization theory that views the growth of human choice as the underlying theme of socioeconomic development, rising self-expression values, and the strengthening of democratic institutions. We build on Sen (1999) and Anand and Sen (2000), who argue that expanding human choice is the essence of societal development. But we broaden Sen's concept of human development to include culture, which provides the essential link between economic development and democratic freedom.

Anand and Sen's account of human development focuses on the objective conditions shaping human choice, such as socioeconomic resources and civil and political rights. But choice is not only a question of such objective factors as resources and rights; it also involves people's values. People may have broad resources and legal rights, but if they live in a culture that emphasizes survival above anything else, it does not give high priority to freedom of choice. In a culture of conformism, people's minds tend to be closed, excluding potentially important options. The range for autonomous choice remains narrow. A society conducive to choice requires a culture that emphasizes human autonomy and self-expression values.

The Human Development Sequence

Chapter 8 documented the linkages between socioeconomic development, self-expression values, and democratic institutions. As we demonstrated, these linkages are remarkably strong – so much so that they tap a single underlying dimension, that of human development. In a factor analysis, socioeconomic development (as measured by Vanhanen's index of socioeconomic resources in the mid-1990s), mass self-expression values in the mid-1990s, and effective democracy in 2000–2 converge in one common factor that explains 91 percent of the total variance among its three components, with loadings of .96 for each of the three components in seventy-three nations. This dimension seems to be generated by a specific causal sequence: our findings indicate that socioeconomic development leads to rising self-expression values, which in turn lead to effective democracy.

Each of the three components of human development is a distinct manifestation of a common underlying theme: autonomous human choice. Socioeconomic development increases people's resources, giving people the objective means that enable them to make autonomous choices. With self-expression values, people give high priority to acting according to their autonomous choices. And democracy provides civil and political liberties, granting people the rights to act according to their autonomous choices.

Thus, the linkages between socioeconomic development, self-expression values, and democratic institutions reflect the linkages between people's existential experience of choice, their subjective emphasis on choice, and their legal entitlements to choice.

People's prevailing value orientations reflect their existential experiences. If people grow up with severely limited resources, this nourishes survival values that restrict self-expression. Growing up with abundant resources, by contrast, leads them to place stronger emphasis on self-expression values. Our finding that emphasis on survival values prevails in poor societies, while emphasis on self-expression values prevails in rich societies, supports the interpretation that one's level of existential security is causally prior to subjective emphasis on choice. In short, socioeconomic development leads to the emergence of self-expression values rather than the other way around.

The relationship between self-expression values and democratic institutions also can be inferred from the principle of autonomous human choice: it reflects the linkage between people's emphasis on choice and their entitlements to choice. When people give high priority to choice, it gives rise to demands for entitlements to choice – in the political realm and everywhere else. If existing institutions do not satisfy this demand, it leads to growing pressure for regime changes toward democracy, bringing stronger entitlements to choice. Conversely, as we have demonstrated, if democratic institutions are in place but emphasis on self-expression values is weak, democracy tends to be ineffective. Because entitlements to choice cannot become effective unless people emphasize choice, self-expression values are causally prior to sustainable and effective democratic institutions.

The expansion of human choice underlies the human development sequence, a sequence that moves from the experience of choice to an emphasis on choice to entitlements to choice – or from socioeconomic development to rising self-expression values to the establishment and strengthening of democratic institutions.

Moral Aspects of Human Development

Our concept of human development is operationalized using variables that can be measured and analyzed empirically. But the selection of these variables is guided by a normative standard that uses the extent of human choice as its developmental criterion (see Anand and Sen, 2000). This perspective underlies the empirical question: to what extent do societies differ in the range of choices they offer their constituents? The capacity to act according to one's autonomous choices is inherent in every human being. It is, indeed, an essential part of what defines human beings as a distinct species (see Marx, 1973 [1858]; Quigley, 1961; Birch and Cobb, 1981; Barkow et al., 1992).

We follow Birch and Cobb (1981) in arguing that the ability to go beyond instinctive behavioral patterns and to base one's actions on free and deliberate choices is the most unique human ability, distinguishing humans as a species from all other creatures (see also Alexander, 1987; Ehrlich, 2000). Hence, basing a theory of human development on the principle of choice does not establish a normative standard that is biased against certain cultures, since the ability to act in accordance with one's autonomous choice is a universal ability of the human species. This ability constitutes the human potential of any society. Societies do not differ in the presence of this human potential; they differ in how much space they offer for this potential to develop. Our concept is designed to measure and analyze this space.

Autonomous human choice is an anthropologically appropriate criterion to conceptualize human development, because acting according to one's autonomous choices is not only a universal human ability but it is also a universal human aspiration. As we demonstrated in Chapter 6, opportunities for making autonomous choices are closely linked with human happiness. This association holds true in a systematic way that operates across cultures: in all cultural zones, societies that offer their people more room for choice produce higher levels of overall life satisfaction and happiness. A society's level of subjective well-being is a strong indicator of the human condition, and it is systematically linked with freedom of choice. Respondents may not be aware of this linkage, but people who feel that they have little choice in shaping their lives systematically report lower levels of subjective well-being. To be sure, the human aspiration for choice is seriously constrained by rigid cultural norms in many places. Thus, cultures succeed to varying degrees in imposing constraints on human choice.

But being "successful" in this respect has human costs: it diminishes human well-being. In the long run, the reduction of human well-being imposes an evolutionary disadvantage on societies that constrain human choice, for they are less able to mobilize people's autonomous motivations, reducing the creativity and productivity of their subjects.

Does our approach propose a uniquely Western standard that cannot be applied to non-Western cultures? In the debate about "Asian values," the former prime minister of Singapore, Lee Kwan Yew, claimed that the Western conception of individual freedom is alien to Asian cultures, which emphasize conformity to the community (Thompson, 2000). Chinese officials were quick to support this view, justifying their country's restrictions on human rights on grounds of cultural diversity. Even in the Western world, this argument found supporters who argue that the diversity of cultures means that the West's emphasis on universal human rights is arrogant (see Orwin and Pangle, 1982; Beitz, 2001).

Are such criticisms morally more firmly grounded than the "ethical universalism" they criticize? We agree with Anand and Sen (2000) that they are not. Arguing that entitling people to choice is a uniquely Western concern that other people neither need nor desire is itself arrogant and patronizing; and it provides a way to justify repression of freedom in the name of cultural diversity. Cultural diversity does indeed exist, as we have emphasized throughout this book. We value it and find it fascinating. But it would be intellectually dishonest to pretend that culture has no bearing on the extent to which a society facilitates freedom of choice. Should it be forbidden to say that one country has a higher level of human development than another? The UN's *Human Development Report* does so every year – and it is harshly criticized by the governments of the low-ranking countries on the grounds that it is methodologically unsound or ethnocentric. Is it really only Western publics that prefer being rich to being poor? To prefer a long life expectancy to a short life? To aspire to being educated instead of ignorant? All the empirical evidence indicates that these are universal human aspirations. Our interpretation of human development holds that the expansion of autonomous human choice is a central component of human development, and the evidence we have presented indicates that autonomous choice is *also* a universal human aspiration. On this point, there is no difference between human societies. What differs is the extent to which their circumstances allow people to emphasize the universal aspiration for choice.

Producing explicit rankings of human development is not just an academic exercise. The *Human Development Report* is anxiously awaited each year by political elites. Those whose countries rank low may criticize the report, but it puts pressure on them to do better – and there is evidence that they actually respond, taking at least modest steps to expand educational access or to improve public health. Similarly, it is a safe assumption that authoritarian elites will resist the suggestion that freedom of expression is a component of human development: the first line of defense is to pin the ethnocentric label on it, as in the "Asian values" debate.

What is true in Lee Kwan Yew's "Asian values" claim is that there *is* a universal polarization between self-expression values emphasizing human emancipation and survival values emphasizing social conformism. But in every culture, one finds a wide spectrum of positions on this continuum, with adherents of both extreme positions. The position of Asian officials who emphasize social conformism is countered by influential dissidents, such as Aung San Suu Kyi or the Dalai Lama, who advocate freedom of expression (Dalai Lama, 1999). Conversely, even Western societies have adherents of conformist values, including Christian fundamentalists, right-wing extremists, and others who condemn excessive individual liberties in Western societies as an indication of decay (see, e.g., Lawler and McConkey, 1998).

Neither emancipative values nor conformist values are unique to specific cultures. McNeill (1990: 337–41), for instance, has pointed out that Judaism, Christianity, Hinduism, Buddhism, and Islam all originally gained mass support because they propagated the idea of salvation for everyone, regardless of social status. In this sense, the idea of salvation is inherently egalitarian, democratic, and individualistic. Like emancipation, salvation is an idea of deliverance; and like the emancipative concept of deliverance, the salvationist concept addresses the inherent uniqueness and dignity of the individual, and it does so for each individual equally (Lal, 1998: 37). There are no social classes in heaven, and the master has to face the same punishment in the afterworld as the servant or slave for misbehavior in this world. The basic ideas of human equality and individual deliverance (which ultimately underlie democracy) are by no means uniquely Western. They are pervasive in all religious ideas of salvation as well as in secular ideas of emancipation. The crucial difference is that salvation defers deliverance to the afterlife, whereas emancipation seeks deliverance in this life – increasingly, through democracy (Dumont, 1986). But the ideas of human equality and individual freedom are central to both.

The appeal of emancipation tends to replace that of salvation as existential constraints on human choice recede, because if freedom can be realized in this world, it need not be postponed to the afterworld. Accordingly, in poor societies emancipative values tend to be linked with religious values. But as societies develop economically, emancipative values become decoupled from religious values and become linked with secular values. In rich countries, emancipative values are linked with secular values: the "modern" poles of the two main dimensions go together, showing individual-level correlations as high as $r = .24$. But in low-income countries, the correlation is reversed, so that in Bangladesh, Pakistan, Egypt, Nigeria, Uganda, Tanzania, Zimbabwe, and other low-income countries, emancipative values go together with religious values, showing correlations as high as $r = .47$.[1] With receding existential constraints on human

---

[1] The United States is exceptional in two respects. It is the only rich society in which strong emphasis on self-expression values coexists with relatively strong traditional religious orientations. And it also shows a relatively low individual-level correlation between self-expression values and secular-rational values ($r = .04$).

choice, the notion of personal deliverance shifts from religious salvation to secular emancipation. Nevertheless, both salvation and emancipation are based on a sense of human autonomy, dignity, and choice. The ideal of freedom is based on a sense of human equality and individual freedom. These ideals are not incompatible with non-Western cultures, and it would be arrogant in the extreme to claim that these ideals are a unique feature of Western society (see Dalai Lama, 1999; Sen, 1999).

The polarization between emancipation and conformism is universal. One can find elements that emphasize either of these poles in any culture. At any given time, certain cultures may place relatively strong emphasis on emancipation or on conformism. Ten centuries ago, Islamic societies provided greater leeway for religious, artistic, and economic freedom than did contemporary Christian societies, which were then characterized by extreme conformity pressures and the Inquisition. This disparity lasted until the advent of an urban market society in the Renaissance, when economic prosperity brought intellectual freedom, a humanistic ethos, and political representation in the urban centers of the Netherlands and northern Italy (see Jones, 1985; Hall, 1989). If Islamic societies place relatively low emphasis on human self-expression today, this is largely because the existential constraints on human autonomy in these societies are relatively severe, and survival values prevail. The desire for individual deliverance is present in every culture. What varies is the relative emphasis on its religious notion or its secular notion, reflecting existential constraints on human choice.

Egocentric versus Humanistic Values?

Flanagan et al. (forthcoming) recently sounded an alarm against the dangers they see in the shift from "authoritarian values to libertarian values." Although Flanagan's libertarian values are not identical to self-expression values, they overlap heavily and his warnings apply to them. Furthermore, they resonate with other admonitions about the erosion of public morale, of the community spirit, and of civil societal life in contemporary societies, reminding one of arguments made earlier by Crozier et al. (1975) about the "crisis of governability," and more recently in Putnam's (2000) thesis of the dissolution of social capital in America.

Flanagan argues that the transition from preindustrial to industrial societies brought a shift from religious authority to secular authority, but this shift did not change the basic fact that authority remained external to the self, enshrined in religious or secular bodies to which the individual was assigned without individual choice. By contrast, the transition from industrial to postindustrial societies brings a sharp break, so that individuals become less willing to subscribe to external authority, whether religious or secular. Accordingly, individuals no longer accept prescribed rules and norms and no longer give their loyalty to the institutions, organizations, and associations that keep civil society and community activities alive. Flanagan argues that the emerging values reflect a

postmodern spirit, in which there are no more absolute rules and moral principles, but everything is socially constructed and relative, so everything must be
tolerated. Moreover, people base any investment in community life on egoistic
cost calculations, engaging themselves only if they see an immediate profit and
if this engagement does not impact too greatly on their individual freedom.
In general, there is an inflation of demands without a corresponding readi-
ness to take on duties and obligations toward the broader community. The
implications are clear: rising self-expression values systematically undermine
democratic communities.

Fears about the corrosive consequences of modernization have a long history,
as is evident in a comment by Inkeles (1983: 48): "No belief is more widespread
among critics of industrialization than the conviction that industrialization dis-
rupts basic social ties, breaks down social controls, and therefore produces a
train . . . which ultimately leads to misery and . . . breakdown." In much the same
vein, Lawler and McConkey (1998: xi) maintain that "community is threatened by individuals who are excessively self-conscious, who relate to others too
exclusively in terms of egoistic calculation. The source of that preoccupation
with calculating selfishness is . . . liberal thought." There is a widespread fear
that self-expression values are inherently egocentric and tend to destroy the
community bonds that democracies need in order to flourish. These fears focus
on the excessive selfishness in some aspects of social life, many examples of
which are indeed present. Flanagan et al. rely on an impressionistic reading of
such examples.

Nevertheless, several points in Flanagan's interpretation are innovative and
insightful. In particular, seeing a fundamental shift in authority from external
institutional bodies to the individual itself is crucial to understanding the logic
of self-expression values. However, we suggest that a *humanistic* reading – interpreting this as reflecting an internalization of authority – is more accurate
than the *ego*centric reading that Flanagan and his associates propose.

In our view, rising self-expression values manifest the trend toward humanistic societies in which the innate human potential for autonomous choice becomes an ultimate norm and a moral authority in itself. It is not true that
everything is tolerated today, in a spirit of postmodern relativism. In fact, many
things that were tolerated in earlier times are no longer considered acceptable
today, particularly if they violate humanistic norms. Such violations are forbidden by an expanding body of legislation designed to prevent discrimination
against ethnic minorities, women, the aged, children, handicapped persons,
and other groups. Affirmative action, children's rights, women's rights, emphasis on the rights of gays and lesbians and racial and ethnic minorities, consumer
protection, environmental protection, and data protection have all become increasingly prominent. Also, growing opposition to violations of human rights
(and the rights of living beings in general); a proliferation of codes of integrity
in education, science, and technology; the intensified screening of public admin-
istration and corporate governance for rules of good conduct; and the spread
of politically correct language all demonstrate that ethical issues continue to

have a widespread prominence in public life. The norms have changed indeed, but ethical concerns are as salient as ever.

Slavery was once accepted in virtually all cultures; only relatively recently has it come to be almost universally viewed as incompatible with human rights. This change took place at different times in different cultures. Britain led the way in outlawing slavery in 1830; in the United States, emancipation became effective throughout the country only in 1865; during the next 140 years, it was abolished throughout the world in various stages. During those decades, a cultural relativist position would have held that condemning slavery reflected narrow Western ethnocentrism, but today slavery is condemned in virtually all societies, persisting only in small isolated pockets (Sowell, 1994).

Castrating males to serve as eunuchs was once practiced in societies around the world; it is now universally considered incompatible with the norms of civilized societies. Genital mutilation of women is still practiced in a number of societies, but it is becoming viewed as unacceptable in most societies, including a majority of Islamic societies. The use of torture is on a similar trajectory. At earlier points in history, the claim that these practices were incompatible with human rights could have been rejected as ethnocentric. The very idea that such a thing as universal human rights exist is relatively recent (Donnelly, 1993).

Old norms such as the prohibition of homosexuality are indeed eroding, as postindustrial societies adopt a more humanistic character, emphasizing the right of individuals to choose their own life-styles. Moral principles are increasingly focused on human emancipation and against violations of personal autonomy. This humanistic trend tends to maximize human well-being, placing elites under increasingly powerful pressures to be responsive to the people. It tends to strengthen civil society and democracy, as is reflected in the close linkage between emphasis on self-expression values and effective democracy. Throughout postindustrial societies, mass publics are becoming more likely than ever before to engage in increasingly effective forms of elite-challenging political action, as we saw in Chapter 4. This evidence contradicts the interpretation that rising self-expression values undermine civil society and democracy.

The trend underlying value changes in developed countries is not simply an erosion of authority but a humanistic shift in the prevailing concept of authority. External authority that does not serve human well-being tends to be rejected, as self-expression values become more widespread. This is consistent with the core goal of democracy: empowering people in ways that make community life reflect people's autonomous choices.

Human Development and Social Capital

Self-expression values are not uncivic. For the goal of human emancipation, on which these values focus, involves an inherently antidiscriminatory orientation, which provides people with a strong motivation to engage in social movements, fighting for improvements in many areas from fair trade to environmental protection to gender equality.

Rising self-expression values have not brought a decline in all civic activities. The bureaucratic organizations that once controlled the masses, such as political machines, labor unions, and churches, are losing their grip, but more spontaneous, expressive, and issue-oriented forms of participation, such as joining in petitions and demonstrations, are becoming more widespread. The rise of self-expression values is linked with higher levels of political action, focused on making elites more responsive to popular demands. On this point, we disagree with Putnam (2000), who views with alarm the decline in various kinds of "bonding" activities, such as bowling leagues and card-playing clubs. Postindustrial societies diminish people's exposure to social controls, making them less dependent on closely knit groups to which people are assigned without choice, such as one's relatives or neighbors. Today, to an increasing extent, when people interact with family members, neighbors, or colleagues, these are relationships that people have chosen autonomously. This shift away from "bonding ties" makes people more open to "bridging ties" that connect people across the boundaries of predefined groupings (Simmel, 1984 [1908]; Mutz, 2002). Bridging ties lack the element of necessity that underlies bonding ties. People can loosen and tighten bridging ties as they choose. And as Granovetter (1973) argues persuasively, bridging ties produce social capital with a wider reach than that of bonding ties, improving a society's self-organizing capacity (Wessels, 1997).

These changes were foreseen by classical sociologists. Durkheim (1988 [1893]) emphasized the transition from "mechanical solidarity" to "organic solidarity." Mechanical solidarity occurs automatically among the members of closely knit groups to which one belongs by birth or external ascription. Organic solidarity evolves among people who choose to coordinate their activities because they agree on common interests. Accordingly, mechanical solidarity is based on bonding ties and organic solidarity is based on bridging ties. In the same vein, Tönnies (1955 [1887]) differentiated between the traditional community (*Gemeinschaft*) held together by bonding ties and the modern association (*Gesellschaft*) held together by bridging ties. It is a shift from "communities of necessity" to "elective affinities" (U. Beck, 2002).

People's increased openness to bridging ties vastly extends the possibilities to initiate public campaigns, to mobilize large numbers of people for collective action, and to generate social movements that cross closely knit social circles and national boundaries. In an era in which the internet operates as a virtual mobilizing agency, people do not have to sustain deep personal bonds in order to participate in collective actions (Walgrave and Manssens, 2000). If one defines social capital as any societal resource that makes it possible to coordinate people's actions, then the symbolic identities sustained by organizations such as Greenpeace create more social capital than the personal bonds created by card-playing clubs or bowling leagues. Greenpeace is able to coordinate the actions of thousands of people in consumer boycotts and public demonstrations, despite the fact that they do not have personal bonds with each other (see Boggs, 2001). The bridging ties created by symbolic identities are a more powerful ingredient of social capital than the bonding ties created within closely knit, inward-looking personal networks.

In *The Rise of the Creative Class*, Florida (2002) shows that virtually all of the cities that Putnam ranks high on social capital rank low on Florida's "creativity index" – that is, they show low rates of ethnic diversity, few gays, relatively few creative people, and low rates of economic growth. The places that rank highest on Putnam's measure of social capital are stagnant towns with very little in-migration, like Bismarck, North Dakota. The places that rank low on Putnam's measure of social capital are places like Silicon Valley; Austin, Texas; Boulder, Colorado; and Ann Arbor, Michigan. As we have pointed out, what Putnam defines as social capital is the traditional, tight-exclusive-conformist type of social capital – which is indeed declining. But this is giving way to a new, more open kind of social capital that is much more conducive to the kinds of cooperation that are central to the knowledge society. Furthermore, Putnam finds that, although television and urban sprawl contribute to what he sees as the decline of social capital, the biggest factor – by far – is a mysterious "generational change." He never quite explains why this generational change has taken place. We have an explanation: it is the generational shift from inward-looking survival values to more open self-expression values, which Florida correctly links with the rise of the creative class.

As Bourdieu (1986) and Coleman (1990) have argued, any form of social interaction and relationship reflects social capital. Even corruption, nepotism, and favoritism constitute social capital. But these forms of social capital are not "civic"; they aim at group-selective and discriminatory versions of human well-being (see the discussion of "social" and "unsocial" capital by Levi, 1996; Rose, 2000). Thus, not all social capital is conducive to democracy. Uncivic social capital, such as corruption and nepotism, is detrimental to democracy. Whether social capital is civic or uncivic depends on its underlying values, which shape how it is used. Self-expression values are particularly relevant in this respect: they create *civic* social capital because they direct its use toward antidiscriminatory, humanistic goals.

Human Development in Historical Perspective

The emergence of even very limited forms of democracy is a rare event in recorded human history,[2] and whenever people struggled for civil and political liberties, their efforts were built on a relatively strong sense of existential autonomy. For example, freeholders in ancient Athens struggled successfully for "hoplite suffrage" in the sixth century B.C. Freeholders again struggled successfully for "plebeian suffrage" in the early Roman Republic. Similarly,

---

[2] This interpretation is based on our reading of the following literature: Moore (1966), Dahl (1973: 33–47), North (1981: chap. 10), Jones (1985: 225–38), McNeill (1990: 189–205, 578–98), Downing (1992: 18–55), Tilly (1997: 38–66), Lal (1998: 69–98), Landes (1998: chap. 2), Finer (1999: 38–78, 341–68, 395–420, 1024–51), Midlarski (1999).

shopkeepers, craftsmen, and free merchants established city republics in late medieval times, invoking the principle of "no taxation without representation." Later on, this principle was successfully established by freeholders and urban burghers on a national scale in the liberal revolutions of the seventeenth and eighteenth centuries. In a similar vein, it is argued that a form of "protodemocracy" was established by townsmen in the Sumerian city-states (McNeill, 1990; Finer, 1999; Midlarski, 1999) and by freeholders in the ancient republics of northern India (McNeill, 1990; Lal, 1998). In each case, establishing these limited preindustrial versions of democracy was driven by the liberty aspirations of people who had a considerable degree of existential autonomy. There is an inherent linkage between existential autonomy, emancipative values, and civil and political freedom.

During most of preindustrial history, the lack of existential autonomy hampered the rise of emancipative values, resulting in the absence of a struggle for democratic freedom. Agrarian empires, from the Middle East to China, lacked property rights and had labor-repressive regimes that reduced most people's resources and autonomy to a minimum (Jones, 1985; McNeill, 1990; J. Diamond, 1997). Emancipative values were unlikely to take high priority in such societies, and demands for civil and political rights were largely absent. To be sure, the history of imperial China is full of peasant revolts, but they were spontaneous outbreaks of collective frustration among the exploited – and they never gave rise to claims for even a limited version of democracy.

Industrialization brought a decisive change in human history, mobilizing the masses into politics based on universal (male) suffrage. But universal suffrage did not necessarily mean liberal democracy. It was equally likely to bring authoritarian, fascist, or communist regimes with weak or nonexistent civil liberties. What Lipset (1959b) described as "working class authoritarianism" illustrates the fact that industrialization was not necessarily linked with an emancipative ethos and did not necessarily bring genuinely effective democracy. Even in the traditional Western democracies, industrialization favored an elite-centered model in which elected authorities could reliably count on the loyalty of uniform camps of voters.

The major change came only recently, with postindustrial society, pushing elite-centered societies toward a people-centered model in which authorities can no longer take mass loyalty for granted and are forced to become increasingly responsive to mass demands. Elite-led democracies become increasingly humanistic. Moreover, with postindustrialization, democracy expanded its reach well beyond the West. The same social force underlies both the humanistic transformation of traditional democracies and the spread of democracy – the rise of an emancipative ethos based on rising self-expression values. Postindustrialization moves beyond the regimented ways in which industrial society dominated people's lives, giving them a new sense of existential autonomy in shaping their lives.

Today, we are witnessing a new stage of history, in which an emancipative ethos is becoming a broadly based mass phenomenon in scores of societies. This process manifests itself in the rise of self-expression values among postindustrial societies, within and beyond the West. It reflects the universal sequence of human development: (1) a growing sense of existential security and autonomy (2) gives rise to an emancipative ethos based on self-expression values (3), which are conducive to the emergence and strengthening of effective democracy.

Foreign Policy Implications

We have presented evidence that socioeconomic development brings a shift from the xenophobic and authoritarian outlook linked with survival values toward the increasingly tolerant and democratic outlook linked with self-expression values. If this is true, it has important foreign policy implications.

Current U.S. policy gives central importance to the war on terrorism. Halting terrorism is a goal shared by most civilized people. The question is, How?

It has often been observed that even in social revolutions precipitated by economic deprivation, the revolutionary activists themselves rarely come from the most deprived strata. Like other kinds of activists, they generally come from relatively prosperous families who provided them with the education and resources that enabled them to play activist roles. Terrorists, too, often emerge from relatively prosperous backgrounds, which has sometimes been interpreted as proving that economic deprivation has nothing to do with terrorism. To be sure, there is no one-to-one relationship, but the evidence examined here shows that there is a strong relationship between existential insecurity and the prevalence of xenophobia, intolerance, and extremism in a society (the societal-level correlation between real GNP per capita and survival values being .81). Xenophobic terrorists *themselves* are usually not destitute, but they tend to emerge in societies shaped by existential insecurity.

If this is true, then the U.S. government's current war on terrorism is too narrowly conceived to have much chance of success. Without question, it is sometimes necessary to use force against terrorists, but killing individual terrorists is merely treating the symptoms while ignoring the causes. Military victory over countries that harbor terrorists, such as Afghanistan, or were believed to harbor terrorists, such as Iraq, was relatively easy – the problem was what came next. Merely overthrowing the government and then withdrawing would solve nothing. Establishing stable democratic societies was seen as the next step, but this proved to be much more difficult. The facile assumption that democracy is really pretty easy to establish provided a feel-good ideology, but it collided with reality. All the evidence examined here indicates that, although holding elections *is* relatively easy, it is not at all easy to establish stable democracy under conditions of severe existential insecurity. Stable and effective democracy generally emerges through a process of human development that starts with economic development, which leads to a culture of tolerance, trust, and emphasis on human autonomy. As long as a large share of the public feels that physical survival is insecure, democracy is not likely to flourish.

The war on terrorism will not be won in any lasting fashion as long as the lives of a large share of the world's population are shaped by a sense of desperation and an awareness that much of the world is incomparably more prosperous, feeding feelings that the world is unjust and creating conditions under which extremist demagogues can manipulate people into accepting xenophobic ideologies. The indiscriminant slaughter of innocent people espoused by terrorists like bin Laden is a twisted ideology that runs counter to mainstream Islamic traditions, which inculcate tolerance, generosity, and humanitarian conduct. But conditions of frustration and desperation provide fertile ground for extremist ideologies like those of Hitler and bin Laden.

Although the United States has allocated billions of dollars to military expenditures, it has given low priority to global economic development. Rich countries have set a target of allocating 0.7 percent of their gross national incomes to development aid; there is widespread agreement among developmental economists that if they met this target, the UN Millennium Goals to eradicate extreme poverty, achieve universal primary education, promote gender equality, and other important steps forward could be met within the next fifteen years. But, in practice, the developed countries have fallen far short of meeting this goal, and the United States has been a striking underachiever in comparison with other developed countries, providing only 0.15 percent of the U.S. gross national income, far lower than the percentage spent by other OECD countries, which ranges from almost 1 percent provided by Norway, to the one-seventh of 1 percent provided by the United States in 2003.

Conquering global poverty is an attainable goal. China and India, which together contain almost 40 percent of the world's population, are now moving from subsistence-level poverty to conditions of reasonable security. Other impoverished countries can do the same. The necessary resources are available: sums that seem relatively minor to the economies of rich nations can make a large difference in low-income countries. The United States currently spends $405 billion annually on defense and $60 billion on alcoholic drinks; it spends $3 billion on official development assistance to less-developed countries. The European Union alone annually spend $350 billion on domestic agricultural subsidies, most of which benefit large and politically well-connected agrobusinesses. Simply ending these subsidies would make an important contribution, enabling low-income agrarian societies to earn badly needed foreign exchange.

The sad truth is that a large share of past development aid has been wasted on meaningless prestige projects that served only to prop up whoever was in power. The UN Millennium Goals provide a promising alternative approach. They are realistic and focus on solving urgent problems that are crucial to effective development, that is, empowering ordinary people to help shape their own lives.

There is no quick and easy solution to world poverty, but if the UN Millennium Goals were met by the target date of 2015, it would constitute impressive progress. Moreover, it would demonstrate that progress is possible and that the world is not malevolent. There would be hope for the future.

Conclusion

An Emancipative Theory of Democracy

Socioeconomic development brings increasingly favorable existential conditions and diminishes external constraints on intrinsic human choice. Favorable existential conditions contribute to emerging self-expression values that give individual liberty priority over collective discipline, human diversity over group conformity, and civic autonomy over state authority. The emergence of these values transforms modernization into a process of human development in which the underlying theme is the growth of autonomous human choice, giving rise to a new type of humanistic society that has never existed before. Rising self-expression values provide a social force that operates in favor of democracy, helping to establish democracy where it does not yet exist, and strengthening democracy where it is already in place, improving the effectiveness of democratic institutions.

Mere formal democracy is linked with the emancipative thrust of rising self-expression values, but genuinely effective democracy is even more strongly tied to it. Elite integrity makes the difference between formal democracy and effective democracy – between democracy in name only, where elections are held and where civil and political liberties exist on paper but the governing elites feel free to ignore people's rights and govern on their own behalf; and democracy that is genuinely responsive to mass preferences and respects people's civil and political liberties. For elite corruption can make the best democratic constitution meaningless, rendering people's civil and political liberties ineffective. And elite integrity, itself, is largely determined by the strength of self-expression values in the society. For a public that emphasizes self-expression values tends to put its elites under pressure to govern according to the rule of law, and a society that emphasizes these values tends to produce new generations of elites that are themselves likely to have internalized emancipative ideals.

The emergence of genuine effective democracy largely reflects the human development sequence of socioeconomic development, rising self-expression values, and democratic institutions. Democracy is the institutional reflection of the emancipative forces inherent in human development, and self-expression values are the best available indicator of these forces. In light of this finding, it is surprising how little attention the recent democratization literature has paid to these values (see the overviews of Geddes, 1999; Bunce, 2000). A massive literature has largely overlooked democracy's most fundamental aspect: human emancipation.

Democracy is not simply the result of clever elite bargaining and constitutional engineering. It depends on deep-rooted orientations among the people themselves. These orientations motivate them to press for freedom, effective civil and political rights, and genuinely responsive government – and to exert continual vigilance to ensure that the governing elites remain responsive to them. Genuine democracy is not simply a machine that, once set up, will function effectively by itself. It depends on the people.

Human development on a mass scale is a recent phenomenon, but self-expression values have always existed. Until recently, they were largely limited to privileged elite circles, but in the past several decades they have transformed mass belief systems. During the second half of the nineteenth century, it was widely believed that progress was inevitable: technological and socioeconomic development would automatically bring a better life to people around the world.

The mass slaughter of World War I and the suffering of the Great Depression made the idea of progress seem hopelessly naive, and World War II discredited it completely: technological development only made it possible to fight increasingly disastrous wars. The rise of cultural relativism completed the process, making the idea of progress anathema because it implied that some societies were more advanced than others. This ideology stems from good intentions, but it has a deeply pernicious aspect: it justifies all patterns of social relations, no matter how repressive or damaging to human dignity. Slavery and genocide were once accepted in virtually all cultures; torturing prisoners and treating women as second-class humans is still widespread. Consistent cultural relativism would reject the claim that these practices are incompatible with human rights, branding such claims as ethnocentric. The concept of universal human rights is relatively recent. But it is linked with deep-rooted historic trends that are advancing globally because they reflect universal human aspirations. As long as survival seems uncertain, these aspirations tend to be overshadowed by survival concerns; but as external constraints on intrinsic human choice recede, they become increasingly salient.

In this sense, human development constitutes progress. As we have argued, the rise of democracy is inherent in high levels of human development. As we saw in Chapter 7, effective democracy is very likely to emerge when more than 45 percent of a society's public ranks high on self-expression values. This is a probabilistic relationship, not a deterministic one, but the statistical relationship is very strong. Economic development is conducive to cultural changes that make democracy increasingly probable. And there is widespread evidence that democracies almost never fight other democracies. If so, the idea that technological advances only bring increasingly destructive wars may prove to be untrue. It is painfully evident that progress and human development are not inevitable. But they are possible, and they are worth striving for.

Bibliography

Abramson, Paul. 1989. "Generations and Political Change in the United States." *Research in Political Sociology* 4: 235–80.

Abramson, Paul, and Ronald Inglehart. 1995. *Value Change in Global Perspective.* Ann Arbor: University of Michigan Press.

Alesina, Alberto, and Arnaud Devleeschauwer. 2002. "Fractionalization." Harvard University: http://www.wcfia.harvard.edu/papers/548_fractjune20.pdf.

Alexander, Richard D. 1987. *The Biology of Moral Systems.* New York: de Gruyter.

Alker, Hayward R., Jr. 1969. "A Typology of Ecological Fallacies." In Mattei Dogan and Stein Rokkan (eds.), *Quantitative Ecological Analysis in the Social Sciences.* Cambridge, MA: MIT Press, pp. 69–86.

Almond, Gabriel A., and James S. Coleman (eds.). 1960. *The Politics of the Developing Areas.* Princeton: Princeton University Press.

Almond, Gabriel A., and G. Bingham Powell. 1966. *Comparative Politics: A Developmental Approach.* Princeton: Princeton University Press.

Almond, Gabriel A., and Sidney Verba. 1963. *The Civic Culture: Political Attitudes in Five Western Democracies.* Princeton: Princeton University Press.

(eds.). 1980. *The Civic Culture Revisited.* Boston: Little, Brown.

Anand, Sudhir, and Amartya Sen. 2000. "Human Development and Economic Sustainability." *World Development* 28: 2029–49.

Anderson, Christopher J., and Yuliya V. Tverdova. 2001. "Winners, Losers, and Attitudes about Government in Contemporary Democracies." *International Political Science Review* 22: 321–38.

Anheier, Helmut K., Marlies Glasius, and Mary Kaldor. 2001. *Global Civil Society, 2001.* Oxford: Oxford University Press.

2004. *Global Civil Society Yearbook.* Oxford: Oxford University Press.

Apter, David E. 1965. *The Politics of Modernization.* Chicago: University of Chicago Press.

Arat, Zehra F. 1991. *Democracy and Human Rights in Developing Countries.* Boulder, CO: Lynne Rienner.

Arrighi, Giovanni. 1994. *The Long Twentieth Century: Money, Power, and the Origins of Our Times.* London: Verso.

Arrighi, Giovanni, and Jessica Drangel. 1986. "The Stratification of the World-Economy: An Exploration of the Semiperipheral Zone." *Review* 10: 9–74.

Axelrod, Robert. 1984. *The Evolution of Cooperation*. London: Penguin Books.

Baechler, Jean, John A. Hall, and Michael Mann (eds.). 1989. *Europe and the Rise of Capitalism*. Oxford: Basil Blackwell.

Baker, Kendall L., Russell J. Dalton, and Kai Hildebrandt. 1981. *Germany Transformed*. Cambridge, MA: Harvard University Press.

Baker, Wayne E. 2005. *America's Crisis of Values: Reality and Perception*. Princeton: Princeton University Press.

Baker, Wayne E., and David Obstfeld. 1999. "Social Capital by Design: Structures, Strategies, and Institutional Context." In R. T. A. J. Leenders and Shaul Gabbay (eds.), *Corporate Social Capital and Liability*. Norwell, MA: Kluwer Academic, pp. 31–58.

Banfield, Edward. 1958. *The Moral Basis of Backwardness*. New York: Free Press.

Barkow, Jerome, Leda Cosmides, and John Tooby. 1992. *The Adapted Mind: Evolutionary Psychology and the Generation of Culture*. Oxford: Oxford University Press.

Barnes, Samuel H., Max Kaase, et al. 1979. *Political Action: Mass Participation in Five Western Democracies*. Beverly Hills, CA: Sage.

Barnet, Richard, and John Cavanagh. 1994. *Global Dreams: Imperial Corporations and the New World Order*. New York: Simon and Schuster.

Barro, Robert J. 1997. *Determinants of Economic Growth: A Cross-Country Empirical Study*. Cambridge, MA: MIT Press.

Beck, Nathaniel, and Jonathan N. Katz. 1995. "What to Do (and Not to Do) with Time-Series Cross-Section Data." *American Political Science Review* 89 (September): 634–47.

Beck, Ulrich. 1992. *Risk Society*. London: Sage.

    2002. "Losing the Traditional: Individualization and 'Precarious Freedoms.'" In Ulrich Beck and Elisabeth Beck-Gernsheim (eds.), *Individualization*. London: Sage, pp. 1–21.

Beitz, Charles. 2001. "Human Rights as a Common Concern." *American Political Science Review* 95: 269–81.

Bell, Daniel. 1973. *The Coming of Postindustrial Society*. New York: Basic Books.

    1976. *The Cultural Contradictions of Capitalism*. New York: Basic Books.

    1993. *Communitarianism and Its Critics*. Oxford: Clarendon Press.

Benford, Robert D., and David A. Snow. 1988. "Ideology, Frame Resonance, and Participant Mobilization." In Bert Klandermans, Hanspeter Kriesi, and Sidney Tarrow (eds.), *From Structure to Action*. Greenwich, CT: JAI, pp. 197–218.

Berg-Schlosser, Dirk. 2003. "Comment on Welzel, Inglehart & Klingemann's Theory of Human Development." *European Journal for Political Research* 42: 381–86.

Berg-Schlosser, Dirk, and Jeremy Mitchell. 2000. *Conditions of Democracy in Europe, 1919–1939*. London: Macmillan.

Berlin, Isaiah. 1969. *Four Essays on Liberty*. Oxford: Oxford University Press.

Bernhard, Michael. 1993. "Civil Society and Democratic Transitions in East Central Europe." *Political Science Quarterly* 108: 307–26.

Bernstein, Mary. 1997. "Celebration and Suppression: The Strategic Uses of Identity by the Lesbian and Gay Movement." *American Journal of Sociology* 103: 531–65.

Bernstein, William J. 2004. *The Birth of Plenty*. New York: McGraw Hill.

Binder, Leonard, et al. (eds.). 1971. *Crises and Sequences in Political Development*. Princeton: Princeton University Press.

Birch, Charles, and John B. Cobb Jr. 1981. *The Liberation of Life: From the Cell to the Community*. Cambridge: Cambridge University Press.

Blalock, Hubert M., Jr. 1964. *Causal Inferences in Nonexperimental Research*. New York: Seminar Press.

Blau, Peter M. 1994. *Structural Contexts of Opportunity*. Chicago: University of Chicago Press.

Boggs, Carl. 2001. "Social Capital and Political Fantasy." *Theory and Society* 30: 281–97.

Boix, Carles. 2001. "Democracy, Development and the Public Sector." *American Journal of Political Science* 45: 1–17.

Boix, Carles, and Susan L. Stokes. 2003. "Endogenous Democratization." *World Politics* 55: 517–49.

Bollen, Kenneth A., and Robert W. Jackman. 1985. "Political Democracy and the Size Distribution of Income." *American Sociological Review* 50: 438–57.

Bollen, Kenneth A., and Pamela M. Paxton. 1997. "Democracy before Athens." In Manus Midlarski (ed.), *Inequality, Democracy and Economic Development*. Cambridge: Cambridge University Press, pp. 13–44.

2000. "Subjective Measures of Liberal Democracy." *Comparative Political Studies* 33: 58–86.

Borgatti, Stephen P., Candace Jones, and Martin G. Everett. 1998. "Network Measures of Social Capital." *Connections* 21: 27–36.

Borre, Ole, and Elinor Scarbrough (eds.). 1995. *The Scope of Government* (*Beliefs in Government*, vol. 3). Oxford: Oxford University Press.

Bourdieu, Pierre. 1986. "The Forms of Capital." In J. G. Richardson (ed.), *Handbook of Theory and Research for the Sociology of Education*. New York: Greenwood.

Boynton, Robert, and Gerhard Loewenberg. 1973. "The Development of Public Support for Parliament in Germany, 1951–1959." *British Journal of Political Science* 3: 169–89.

Bracher, Karl Dietrich. 1971 [1955]. *Die Auflösung der Weimarer Republik* [The Dissolution of the Weimar Republic] (5th ed.). Königstein, Germany: Deutsche Verlagsanstalt.

Bradshaw, York W., Rita Noonan, Laura Gash, and Claudia Buchmann. 1993. "Borrowing against the Future: Children and Third World Indebtedness." *Social Forces* 71: 629–56.

Bradshaw, York W., and Michael Wallace. 1996. *Global Inequalities*. Thousand Oaks, CA: Pine Forge.

Bratton, Michael, and Robert Mattes. 2001. "Support for Democracy in Africa: Intrinsic or Instrumental?" *British Journal of Political Science* 31: 447–74.

Brint, Steven. 1984. "New Class and Cumulative Trend Explanations of the Liberal Political Attitudes of Professionals." *American Journal of Sociology* 90: 30–71.

Brown, Archie. 2001. "From Democratization to 'Guided Democracy.'" *Journal of Democracy* 12: 35–41.

Brzezinski, Zbigniew. 2001. "The Primacy of History and Culture." *Journal of Democracy* 12: 20–26.

Bunce, Valerie. 2000. "Comparative Democratization: Big and Bounded Generalizations." *Comparative Political Studies* 33: 703–34.

Burke, Edmund. 1999 [1790]. *Reflections on the Revolution in France*. Oxford: Oxford University Press.

Burkhart, Ross E., and Michael S. Lewis-Beck. 1994. "Comparative Democracy: The Economic Development Thesis." *American Political Science Review* 88 (December): 903–10.

Burt, Ronald S. 1992. *Structural Holes*. Cambridge, MA: Harvard University Press.

Cain, Bruce E., Russell J. Dalton, and Susan E. Scarrow. 2003. *Democracy Transformed? Expanding Political Opportunities in Advanced Industrial Democracies*. Oxford: Oxford University Press.

Cardoso, Fernando Henrique, and Enzo Faletto. 1979. *Dependency and Development in Latin America*. Berkeley: University of California Press.

Carneiro, Robert. 1988. "The Circumscription Theory: Challenge and Response." *American Behavioral Scientist* 31: 497–511.

2003. *Evolutionism in Cultural Anthropology*. Boulder, CO: Westview Press.

Casper, Gretchen, and Michelle M. Taylor. 1996. *Negotiating Democracy: Transitions from Authoritarian Rule*. Pittsburgh: University of Pittsburgh Press.

Castles, Francis G. (ed.). 1993. *Families of Nations: Patterns of Public Policy in Western Democracies*. Aldershot: Dartmouth.

Cavalli-Sforza, Luigi Luca. 1996. *Gene, Völker und Sprachen: Die biologischen Grundlagen unserer Zivilisation* [Genes, Peoples, and Languages: The Biological Foundations of Civilization]. Munich: Carl Hanser.

Chanley, Virginia A., Thomas J. Rudolph, and Wendy M. Rahn. 2000. "The Origins and Consequences of Public Trust in Government: A Time Series Analysis." *Public Opinion Quarterly* 64: 239–56.

Chase-Dunn, Christopher. 1989. *Global Formations: Structures of the World-Economy*. Cambridge, MA: Basil Blackwell.

Chase-Dunn, Christopher, and Thomas D. Hall. 1997. *Rise and Demise: Comparing World-Systems*. Boulder, CO: Westview Press.

Chirkov, V. I., R. M. Ryan, Y. Kim, and U. Kaplan. 2003. "Differentiating Autonomy from Individualism and Independence: A Self-Determination Theory Perspective on Internalization of Cultural Orientations and Well-Being." *Journal of Personality and Social Psychology* 84: 97–110.

Chirot, Daniel. 1977. *Social Change in the Twentieth Century*. New York: Harcourt Brace Jovanovich.

1994. *How Societies Change*. Thousand Oaks, CA: Pine Forge.

Cingranelli, David Louis (ed.). 1996. *Human Rights and Development*. Greenwich, CT: JAI Press.

Coleman, James S. 1968. "Modernization: Political Aspects." In David L. Sills (ed.), *International Encyclopedia of the Social Sciences* (vol. 10). Washington, DC: Free Press, pp. 395–402.

1988. "Social Capital in the Creation of Human Capital." *American Journal of Sociology* 94: 95–121.

1990. *Foundations of Social Theory*. Cambridge, MA: Harvard University Press.

Collier, David, and Robert Adcock. 1999. "Democracy and Dichotomies." *Annual Review of Political Science* 2: 537–65.

Collier, Ruth B. 1999. *Paths toward Democracy*. Cambridge: Cambridge University Press.

Condorcet, Jean-Antoine-Nicolas de Caritat. 1979 [1795]. *Sketch for a Historical Picture of the Progress of Human Mind*. Westport, CT: Hyperion Press.

Conradt, David. 1980. "Changing German Political Culture." In Gabriel A. Almond and Sidney Verba (eds.), *The Civic Culture Revisited*. Boston: Little, Brown, pp. 212–72.

Converse, Philip E. 1964. "The Nature of Belief Systems among Mass Publics." In David E. Apter (ed.), *Ideology and Discontent*. New York: Free Press, pp. 206–61.

1970. "Attitudes and Non-Attitudes." In E. R. Tufte (ed.), *The Quantitative Analysis of Social Problems*. Reading, MA: Addison-Wesley, pp. 168–89.

Costa, Paul T., Robert R. McCrae, and Alan B. Zonderman. 1987. "Environmental and Dispositional Influences on Well-Being." *British Journal of Psychology* 78: 299–306.

Cox, David R., and Nanny Wermuth. 2001. "Some Statistical Aspects of Causality." *European Sociological Review* 17: 65–74.

Crenshaw, Edward. 1997. "Democracy and Proto-Modernity: Technoecological Influences on the Growth of Political and Civil Rights." In Manus Midlarski (ed.), *Inequality, Democracy and Economic Development*. Cambridge: Cambridge University Press, pp. 80–109.

Crothers, Lane, and Charles Lockhard (eds.). 2000. *Culture and Politics: A Reader*. New York: St. Martin's Press.

Crozier, Michel, Samuel H. Huntington, and Joji Watanuki. 1975. *The Crisis of Democracy*. New York: New York University Press.

Cummins, Robert A. 2000. "Objective and Subjective Quality of Life: An Interactive Model." *Social Indicators Research* 52: 55–72.

Dahl, Robert A. 1973. *Polyarchy: Participation and Opposition* (1st ed., 1971). New Haven: Yale University Press.

1989. *Democracy and Its Critics*. New Haven: Yale University Press.

1998. "Development and Democratic Culture." *Journal of Democracy* 9: 34–39.

2003. *How Democratic Is the American Constitution?* New Haven: Yale University Press.

Dalai Lama. 1999. "Buddhism, Asian Values, and Democracy." *Journal of Democracy* 10: 3–7.

Dalton, Russell J. 1985. "Political Parties and Political Representation: Party Supporters and Party Elites in Nine Nations." *Comparative Political Studies* 18: 267–99.

1988. *Politics and Culture in West Germany*. Samuel Barnes (ed.), Politics and Culture Series (No. 10). Ann Arbor: University of Michigan.

1994. *The Green Rainbow: Environmental Groups in Western Europe*. New Haven: Yale University Press.

1999. "Political Support in Advanced Industrial Democracies." In Pippa Norris (ed.), *Critical Citizens*. Oxford: Oxford University Press, pp. 57–77.

2000. "Value Change and Democracy." In Susan J. Pharr and Robert D. Putnam (eds.), *Disaffected Democracies: What's Troubling the Trilateral Countries?* Princeton: Princeton University Press, pp. 252–69.

2001. *Citizen Politics: Public Opinion and Political Parties in Advanced Western Democracies* (3rd ed.). Chatham, NJ: Chatham House.

Dalton, Russell J., and Martin P. Wattenberg (eds.). 2000. *Parties without Partisans: Political Change in Advanced Industrial Democracies*. Oxford: Oxford University Press.

Daly, Mary. 1978. *Gyn/Ecology: The Metaethics of Radical Feminism*. London: Women's Press.

Davenport, Christian, and David A. Armstrong. 2004. "Democracy and the Violation of Human Rights: A Statistical Analysis from 1976 to 1996." *American Journal of Political Science* 48: 538–54.

Deutsch, Karl. 1963. *The Nerves of Government*. New York: Free Press.

Diamond, Jared. 1997. *Guns, Germs, and Steel: The Fate of Human Societies.* New York: W. W. Norton.

Diamond, Larry. 1992. "Economic Development and Democracy Reconsidered." In Larry Diamond and Gary Marks (eds.), *Reexaming Democracy.* London: Sage, pp. 93–139.

1993a. "The Globalization of Democracy." In Robert O. Slater, Barry M. Schutz, and Steven R. Dorr (eds.), *Global Transformation and the Third World.* Boulder, CO: Lynne Rienner, pp. 31–69.

1993b. "Causes and Effects." In Larry Diamond (ed.), *Political Culture and Democracy in Developing Countries.* Boulder, CO: Lynne Rienner, pp. 411–35.

(ed.). 1993c. *Political Culture and Democracy in Developing Countries.* Boulder, CO: Lynne Rienner.

2003. "How People View Democracy: Findings from Public Opinion Surveys in Four Regions." Paper presented to the Stanford Seminar on Democratization, January 2003.

Diamond, Larry, Juan J. Linz, and Seymour M. Lipset (eds.). 1995. *Politics in Developing Countries: Experiences with Democracy* (2nd ed.). Boulder, CO: Lynne Rienner.

Diamond, Larry, and Gary Marks (eds.). 1992. *Reexamining Democracy* (Essays in Honor of Seymour Martin Lipset). London: Sage.

Diamond, Larry, and Marc F. Plattner (eds.). 1993. *The Global Resurgence of Democracy.* Baltimore: Johns Hopkins University Press.

Diener, Ed, M. Diener, and C. Diener. 1995. "Factors Predicting the Subjective Well-Being of Nations." *Journal of Personality and Social Psychology* 69: 851–64.

DiMaggio, Paul. 1994. "Culture and Economy." In Neil J. Smelser and Richard Swedberg (eds.), *The Handbook of Economic Sociology.* Princeton: Princeton University Press, pp. 27–57.

DiMaggio, Paul, John Evans, and Bethany Bryson. 1996. "Have Americans' Social Attitudes Become More Polarized?" *American Journal of Sociology* 102: 690–755.

DiPalma, Guiseppe. 1990. *To Craft Democracies: An Essay on Democratic Transitions.* Berkeley: University of California Press.

Dogan, Mattei, and Dominique Pelassy. 1984. *How to Compare Nations: Strategies in Comparative Politics.* Chatham, NJ: Chatham House.

Dollar, David. 1992. "Outward-Oriented Developing Economies Really Do Grow More Rapidly: Evidence from 95 LDCs, 1976–1985." *Economic Development and Cultural Change* 13: 523–44.

Domes, Jürgen. 1990. *After Tiananmen Square.* Washington, DC: Brassey's.

Donnelly, Jack. 1993. *Human Rights and World Politics.* Boulder, CO: Westview Press.

Doorenspleet, Renske. 2000. "Reassessing the Three Waves of Democratization." *World Politics* 52: 384–406.

2004. "The Structural Context of Recent Transitions to Democracy." *European Journal of Political Research* 43: 309–36.

Downing, Brian M. 1992. *The Military Revolution and Political Change: Origins of Democracy and Autocracy in Early Modern Europe.* Princeton: Princeton University Press.

Dumont, Louis. 1986. *Essays on Individualism.* Chicago: University of Chicago Press.

Durham, William H. 1991. *Coevolution: Genes, Culture, and Human Diversity.* Stanford: Stanford University Press.

Durkheim, Émile. 1988 [1893]. *Über soziale Arbeitsteilung* [On Social Division of Labor]. Frankfurt am Main: Suhrkamp.

Dworkin, Ronald. 1988. *The Theory and Practice of Autonomy.* Cambridge: Cambridge University Press.

Easton, David. 1965. *A Systems Analysis of Political Life.* New York: Wiley.

Eckersley, Richard. 2000. "The State and Fate of Nations: Implications of Subjective Measures of Personal and Social Quality of Life." *Social Indicators Research* 52: 3–27.

Eckstein, Harry. 1966. *A Theory of Stable Democracy.* Princeton: Princeton University Press.

Eckstein, Harry, Frederic J. Fleron Jr., Erik P. Hoffmann, and William M. Reisinger (eds.). 1996. *Can Democracy Take Root in Post-Soviet Russia? Explorations in State-Society Relations.* Lanham, MD: Rowman and Littlefield.

Eckstein, Harry, and Ted R. Gurr. 1975. *Patterns of Authority: A Structural Basis for Political Inquiry.* New York: Wiley-Interscience.

Ehrlich, Paul R. 2000. *Human Natures: Genes, Cultures, and the Human Prospect.* Covelo, CA: Island Press.

Elkins, Zachary. 2000. "Gradations of Democracy? Empirical Tests of Alternative Conceptualizations." *American Journal of Political Science* 44: 293–300.

Ember, Carol R., and Melvin Ember. 1996. *Cultural Anthropology.* London: Prentice-Hall.

Ember, Melvin, Carol R. Ember, and Bruce M. Russett. 1997. "Inequality and Democracy in the Anthropological Record." In Manus Midlarski (ed.), *Inequality, Democracy and Economic Development.* Cambridge: Cambridge University Press, pp. 110–30.

Erikson, Robert S., Michael B. MacKuen, and James A. Stimson. 2002. *The Macro Polity.* Cambridge: Cambridge University Press.

Esping-Andersen, Gøsta. 1990. *The Three Worlds of Welfare Capitalism.* Princeton: Princeton University Press.

Esposito, John L., and John O. Voll. 1996. *Islam and Democracy.* New York: Oxford University Press.

Estes, Richard J. 1984. *The Social Progress of Nations.* New York: Praeger.

  1998. "Trends in World Social Development, 1970–1995: Development Challenges for a New Century." *Journal of Developing Societies* 14: 11–39.

Etzioni, Amitai. 1996. *The New Golden Rule: Community and Morality in a Democratic Society.* New York: Basic Books.

Evans, Peter. 1995. *Embedded Autonomy: States and Industrial Transformation.* Princeton: Princeton University Press.

Fairbanks, Charles H. 2001. "Disillusionment in the Caucasus and Central Asia." *Journal of Democracy* 12: 49–56.

Falter, Jürgen. 1991. *Hitlers Wähler* [Hitler's Voters]. Munich: C. H. Beck.

Fedigan, Linda Marie. 1991. *Sex Roles and Social Bonds.* Chicago: University of Chicago Press.

Finer, Samuel E. 1999. *The History of Government* (3 vols.). Oxford: Oxford University Press.

Finke, Roger, and Rodney Stark. 1989. "Evaluating the Evidence: Religious Economies and Sacred Canopies." *American Sociological Review* 53: 41–49.

  1992. *The Churching of America, 1776–1990: Winners and Losers in Our Religious Economy.* New Brunswick, NJ: Rutgers University Press.

Firebaugh, Glenn. 1992. "Growth Effects of Foreign and Domestic Investment." *American Journal of Sociology* 98: 105–30.

1996. "Does Foreign Capital Harm Poor Nations?" *American Journal of Sociology* 102: 563–75.

Firebaugh, Glenn, and Frank Beck. 1994. "Does Economic Growth Benefit the Masses? Growth, Dependence, and Welfare in the Third World." *American Sociological Review* 59: 631–53.

Flanagan, Scott. 1987. "Value Change in Industrial Society." *American Political Science Review* 81: 1303–19.

Flanagan, Scott, et al. Forthcoming. "Shifting Worldviews and the Authoritarian-Libertarian Value Change in Advanced Industrial Democracies."

Flannery, Kent V. 1972. "The Cultural Evolution of Civilizations." *Annual Review of Ecology and Systematics* 3: 399–426.

Fleron, Frederick, and Richard Ahl. 1998. "Does Public Opinion Matter for Democratization in Russia?" In Harry Eckstein (ed.), *Can Democracy Take Root in Post-Soviet Russia?* Lanham, MD: Rowman and Littlefield, pp. 249–85.

Florida, Richard. 2002. *The Rise of the Creative Class*. New York: Basic Books.

Förster, Jens, E. T. Higgins, and L. C. Idson. 1998. "Approach and Avoidance Strength during Goal Attainment: Regulatory Focus and the 'Goal Looms Larger' Effect." *Journal of Personality and Social Psychology* 75: 1115–31.

Foweraker, John, and Todd Landman. 1997. *Citizenship Rights and Social Movements: A Comparative Statistical Analysis*. Oxford: Oxford University Press.

Frank, Andre Gunder. 1966. "The Development of Underdevelopment." *Monthly Review* 18: 17–30.

Freedom House (ed.). Annual. *Freedom in the World*. Lanham, MD: University Press of America.

Friedheim, Daniel K. 1993. "Regime Collapse in Democratic Transition: The East German Revolution of 1989." *German Politics* 2: 97–112.

Friedrich, Carl Joachim, and Zbigniew Brzezinski. 1965. *Totalitarian Dictatorship and Autocracy* (2nd ed.). Cambridge: Cambridge University Press.

Fukuyama, Francis. 1967. *Capitalism and Underdevelopment in Latin America*. New York: Monthly Review Press.

1992. *The End of History and the Last Man*. New York: Free Press.

1995. *Trust: Social Virtues and the Creation of Prosperity*. New York: Free Press.

2000. "Social Capital." In Lawrence E. Harrison and Samuel P. Huntington (eds.), *Culture Matters: How Values Shape Human Progress*. New York: Basic Books, pp. 99–111.

Fulcher, James, and John Scott. 2003. *Sociology*. Oxford: Oxford University Press.

Galston, William A. 2001. "Political Knowledge, Political Engagement, and Civic Education." *Annual Review of Political Science* 4: 217–34.

Gasiorowski, Mark J., and Timothy J. Power. 1998. "The Structural Determinants of Democratic Consolidation: Evidence from the Third World." *Comparative Political Studies* 31: 740–71.

Gaskell, George, and Martin Bauer. 2001. *Biotechnology: The Making of Global Controversy*. Cambridge: Cambridge University Press.

Geddes, Barbara. 1999. "What Do We Know about Democratization after Twenty Years?" *Annual Review of Political Science* 2: 115–44.

Geertz, Clifford. 1973. *The Interpretation of Cultures*. New York: Basic Books.

Gereffi, Gary. 1994. "The International Economy and Economic Development." In Neil J. Smelser and Richard Swedberg (eds.), *The Handbook of Economic Sociology*. Princeton: Princeton University Press, pp. 206–33.

Gibson, James L. 1996. "'A Mile Wide but an Inch Deep'? The Structure of Democratic Commitments in the Former USSR." *American Journal of Political Science* 40: 396–420.

1997. "Mass Opposition to the Soviet Putsch of August 1991: Collective Action, Rational Choice, and Democratic Values." *American Political Science Review* 91: 671–84.

2001. "Social Networks, Civil Society, and the Prospects for Consolidating Russia's Democratic Transition." *American Journal of Political Science* 45: 51–69.

Gibson, James L., and Raymond M. Duch. 1992. "The Origins of a Democratic Culture in the Soviet Union: The Acquisition of Democratic Values." Paper presented at the 1992 annual meeting of the Midwest Political Science Association, Chicago, September.

1994. "Postmaterialism and the Emerging Soviet Democracy." *Political Research Quarterly* 47: 5–39.

Gibson, James L., Raymond M. Duch, and Kent L. Tedin. 1992. "Democratic Values and the Transformation of the Soviet Union." *Journal of Politics* 54: 329–71.

Giddens, Anthony. 1990. *The Consequences of Modernity.* Cambridge: Polity Press.

1991. *Modernity and Self-Identity: Self and Society in the Late Modern Age.* Cambridge: Polity Press.

Gills, B., and J. Rocamora. 1992. "Low Intensity Democracy." *Third World Quarterly* 13: 501–24.

Goesling, Brian. 2001. "Changing Income Inequalities within and between Nations: New Evidence." *American Sociological Review* 66: 745–61.

Granger, C. W. J. 1969. "Investing Causal Relations by Econometric Methods and Spectral Methods." *Econometrica* 34: 424–38.

Granovetter, Mark S. 1973. "The Strength of Weak Ties." *American Journal of Sociology* 78: 1360–80.

Greenfield, P. M. 2000. "Three Approaches to the Psychology of Culture: Where Do They Come From? Where Can They Go?" *Asian Journal of Social Psychology* 3: 223–40.

Guillén, Mauro. 1994. *Models of Management: Work, Authority, and Organization in a Comparative Perspective.* Chicago: University of Chicago Press.

Guo, Guang, and Elizabeth Stearns. 2002. "The Social Influences on the Realization of Genetic Potential for Intellectual Development." *Social Forces* 80 (3): 881–910.

Gurr, Ted R. 1974. "Persistence and Change in Political Systems, 1800–1971." *American Political Science Review* 68: 1482–1504.

Gurr, Ted R., and Keith Jaggers. 1995. "Tracking Democracy's Third Wave with the Polity III Data." *Journal of Peace Research* 32: 469–82.

Habermas, Jürgen. 1975. *Legitimation Crisis.* Boston: Beacon Press.

Hadenius, Axel. 1992. *Democracy and Development.* Cambridge: Cambridge University Press.

Hadenius, Axel, and Jan Teorell. 2004. "Cultural and Economic Prerequisites of Democracy: Reassessing Recent Evidence." *Studies in Comparative International Development* 39: 89–111.

Haggard, Stephan, and Robert R. Kaufman. 1995. *The Political Economy of Democratic Transitions.* Princeton: Princeton University Press.

Hajnal, John. 1982. "Two Kinds of Pre-Industrial Household Formation Systems." In Richard Wall, Jean Robin, and Peter Laslett (eds.), *Family Forms in Historic Europe.* Cambridge: Cambridge University Press, pp. 65–104.

Hall, John A. 1989. "States and Societies: The Miracle in Comparative Perspective." In Jean Baechler, John Hall, and Michael Mann (eds.), *Europe and the Rise of Capitalism*. Oxford: Basil Blackwell, pp. 20–38.

Hamilton, Gary G. 1994. "Civilizations and Organization of Economies." In Neil J. Smelser and Richard Swedberg (eds.), *The Handbook of Economic Sociology*. Princeton: Princeton University Press, pp. 183–205.

Hampden-Turner, Charles, and Alfons Trompenaars. 1993. *The Seven Cultures of Capitalism*. New York: Currency/Doubleday.

Hannan, Michael T., and Glenn R. Carroll. 1981. "Dynamics of Formal Political Structure: An Event-History Analysis." *American Sociological Review* 46: 19–35.

Hein, Simon. 1992. "Trade Strategy and the Dependency Hypothesis: A Comparison of Policy, Foreign Investment and Economic Growth in Latin America and East Asia." *Economic Development and Cultural Change* 13: 495–521.

Held, David, Anthony G. McGrew, David Goldblatt, and Jonathan Perraton. 2003. *Global Transformations: Politics, Economics and Culture*. London: Polity.

Heller, Patrick. 2000. "Degrees of Democracy: Some Comparative Lessons from India." *World Politics* 52: 484–519.

Helliwell, John F. 1993. "Empirical Linkages between Democracy and Economic Growth." *British Journal of Political Science* 24: 225–48.

Henrich, Joe, and Robert Boyd. 1998. "The Evolution of Conformist Transmission and the Emergence of Between-Group Differences." *Evolution and Human Behavior* 19: 215–41.

Higgins, E. T. 1998. "Promotion and Prevention: Regulatory Focus as a Motivational Principle." *Advances in Experimental Social Psychology* 46: 1–46.

Higley, John, and Michael G. Burton. 1989. "The Elite Variable in Democratic Transitions and Breakdowns." *American Sociological Review* 54: 17–32.

Higley, John, and Richard Gunther (eds.). 1992. *Elites and Democratic Consolidation in Latin America and Southern Europe*. Cambridge: Cambridge University Press.

Hirschman, Albert O. 1970. *Exit, Voice, and Loyalty: Responses to Decline in Firms, Organizations, and States*. Cambridge, MA: Harvard University Press.

Hirschmann, Nancy. 2001. "A Question of Freedom: A Question of Rights? Women and Welfare." In Nancy Hirschmann and Ulrike Liebert (eds.), *Women and Welfare*. New Brunswick, NJ: Rutgers University Press, pp. 84–110.

Hofferbert, Richard I., and Hans-Dieter Klingemann. 1999. "Remembering the Bad Old Days: Human Rights, Economic Conditions, and Democratic Performance in Transitional Regimes." *European Journal of Political Research* 36: 155–74.

Hofstede, Geert. 1980. *Culture's Consequences: Intentional Differences in Work-Related Values*. Beverly Hills, CA: Sage.

Hughes, Barry B. 1999. *International Futures: Choices in the Face of Uncertainty* (3rd ed.). Boulder, CO: Westview Press.

Humana, Charles. 1992. *World Human Rights Guide* (3rd ed.). New York: Oxford University Press.

Humphrey, Nicholas. 1984. *Consciousness Regained: Chapters in the Development of Mind*. New York: Oxford University Press.

Hunter, Allen. 1995. "Globalization from Below? Promises and Perils of the New Internationalism." *Social Policy* 25: 6–14.

Hunter, Shireen T. 1998. *The Future of Islam and the West*. Westport, CT: Praeger.

Huntington, Samuel P. 1968. *Political Order in Changing Societies*. New Haven: Yale University Press.

1984. "Will More Countries Become Democratic?" *Political Science Quarterly* 99: 193–218.

1991. *The Third Wave: Democratization in the Late Twentieth Century.* Norman: University of Oklahoma Press.

1996. *The Clash of Civilizations and the Remaking of the World Order.* New York: Simon and Schuster.

Inglehart, Ronald. 1977. *The Silent Revolution.* Princeton: Princeton University Press.

1990. *Culture Shift in Advanced Industrial Societies.* Princeton: Princeton University Press.

1997. *Modernization and Postmodernization: Cultural, Economic and Political Change in 43 Societies.* Princeton: Princeton University Press.

Inglehart, Ronald, and Paul Abramson. 1999. "Measuring Postmaterialism." *American Political Science Review* 93: 665–77.

Inglehart, Ronald, and Wayne E. Baker. 2000. "Modernization, Cultural Change, and the Persistence of Traditional Values." *American Sociological Review* 65: 19–51.

Inglehart, Ronald, and Gabriela Catterberg. 2003. "Trends in Political Action: The Development Trend and the Post-Honeymoon Decline." In Ronald Inglehart (ed.), *Islam, Gender, Culture, and Democracy.* Willowdale, Canada: de Sitter, pp. 77–93.

Inglehart, Ronald, and Pippa Norris. 2002. "Islamic Culture and Democracy: Testing the Clash of Civilization Thesis." *Comparative Sociology* 1: 235–64.

2003. *Rising Tide: Gender Equality and Cultural Change around the World.* Cambridge: Cambridge University Press.

Inglehart, Ronald, Pippa Norris, and Christian Welzel. 2002. "Gender Equality and Democracy." *Comparative Sociology* 1: 321–46.

Inglehart, Ronald, and Christian Welzel. 2002. "Political Culture and Democracy." In Howard Wiarda (ed.), *New Directions in Comparative Politics.* New York: Westview Press, pp. 141–64.

2003. "Political Culture and Democracy: Analyzing the Cross-Level Linkages." *Comparative Politics* 36: 61–79.

Inkeles, Alex. 1983. *Exploring Individual Modernity.* New York: Columbia University Press.

(ed.). 1993. *On Measuring Democracy: Its Consequences and Concomitants.* New Brunswick, NJ: Transaction.

Inkeles, Alex, and David Smith. 1974. *Becoming Modern: Individual Changes in Six Developing Societies.* Cambridge, MA: Harvard University Press.

Iversen, Torben. 1994. "Political Leadership and Representation in Western European Democracies." *American Journal of Political Science* 38: 46–74.

Jackman, Robert W., and Ross A. Miller. 1998. "Social Capital and Politics." *Annual Review of Political Science* 1: 47–73.

James, Harold. 1986. *The German Slump.* Oxford: Oxford University Press.

Jawad, Haifaa. 1998. *The Rights of Women in Islam: An Authentic Approach.* London: Macmillan.

Jennings, M. Kent, and Jan van Deth (eds.). 1989. *Continuities in Political Action.* Berlin: de Gruyter.

Johnson, Chalmers (ed.). 1970. *Change in Communist Systems.* Stanford: Stanford University Press.

Jones, Eric L. 1985. *The European Miracle: Environments, Economies and Geopolities in the History of Europe and Asia* (3rd ed.). Cambridge: Cambridge University Press.

Joppke, Christian. 1994. "Revisionism, Dissidence, Nationalism: Opposition in Leninist Regimes." *British Journal of Sociology* 45: 543–61.

Kaase, Max, and Kenneth Newton (eds.). 1995. *Beliefs in Government* (4 vols.). Oxford: Oxford University Press.

Karklins, Rasma, and Roger Petersen. 1993. "Decision Calculus of Protestors and Regimes." *Journal of Politics* 55: 588–614.

Karl, Terry Lynn, and Philippe C. Schmitter. 1991. "Modes of Transition in Latin America, Southern and Eastern Europe." *International Social Science Journal* 128: 269–84.

Katznelson, Ira, and Aristide Zolberg (eds.). 1986. *Working Class Formation: Nineteenth Century Patterns in Western Europe and the United States*. Princeton: Princeton University Press.

Kaufmann, Daniel, Aart Kraay, and Massimo Mastruzzi. 2003. "Governance Matters III: Governance Indicators for 1996–2002." *World Bank Policy Research Department Working Paper*, No. 2195. Washington, DC: World Bank.

Kennedy, Paul. 1996. "Globalization and Its Discontents: The Triumph of Capitalism Revisited." *New Perspectives Quarterly* 13: 31–33.

Kittel, Bernhard. 1999. "Sense and Sensitivity in Pooled Analyses of Political Data." *European Journal of Political Research* 35: 225–53.

Klandermans, Bert. 1984. "Mobilization and Participation." *American Sociological Review* 49: 583–600.

Klingemann, Hans-Dieter. 1999. "Mapping Political Support in the 1990s: A Global Analysis." In Pippa Norris (ed.), *Critical Citizens: Global Support for Democratic Governance*. New York: Oxford University Press, pp. 31–56.

Klingemann, Hans-Dieter, and Dieter Fuchs (eds.). 1995. *Citizens and the State* (*Beliefs in Government*, vol. 1). Oxford: Oxford University Press.

Kmenta, Jan, and J. B. Ramsey (eds.). 1980. *Evaluation of Econometric Models*. New York: Academic Press.

Konrad, György, and Ivan Szelenyi. 1991. "Intellectuals and Domination in Post-Communist Societies." In Pierre Bourdieu and James S. Coleman (eds.), *Social Theory for a Changing Society*. Boulder, CO: Westview Press, pp. 337–61.

Kopstein, Jeffrey S., and David A. Reilly. 2000. "Geographic Diffusion and the Transformation of the Postcommunist World." *World Politics* 53 (October): 1–37.

Korten, David C. 1996. *When Corporations Rule the World*. San Francisco: Berrett-Koehler.

Kühnen, Ulrich, and Daphna Oyserman. 2002. "Thinking about the Self Influences Thinking in General: Cognitive Consequences of Salient Self-Concept." *Journal of Experimental Social Psychology* 38: 492–99.

Kuran, Timur. 1991. "Now Out of Never: The Element of Surprise in the East European Revolution of 1989." *World Politics* 44: 7–48.

Kurzman, Charles. 1998. "Waves of Democratization." *Studies in Comparative International Development* 33: 42–64.

Lal, Deepak. 1998. *Unintended Consequences: The Impact of Factor Endowments, Culture, and Politics on Long Run Economic Performance*. Cambridge, MA: MIT Press.

Landes, David S. 1998. *The Wealth and Poverty of Nations: Why Some Are So Rich and Some So Poor*. New York: W. W. Norton.

Laslett, Peter. 1989. "The European Family and Early Industrialization." In Jean Baechler, John Hall, and Michael Mann (eds.), *Europe and the Rise of Capitalism*. Oxford: Basil Blackwell, pp. 234–42.

Lasswell, Harold D. (ed.). 1958a. *The Political Writings*. Glencoe, IL: Free Press.
1958b. *Politics: Who Gets What, When, and How*. New York: Meridian Books.
Lawler, P. A., and D. McConkey (eds.). 1998. *Community and Political Thought Today*. Westport, CT: Praeger.
Lee Kuan Yew, and Fareed Zakaria. 1994. "Culture Is Destiny: A Conversation with Lee Kuan Yew." *Foreign Affairs* 73: 109–26.
Lerner, Daniel. 1958. *The Passing of Traditional Society: Modernizing the Middle East*. New York: Free Press.
1968. "Modernization: Social Aspects." In David L. Sills (ed.), *The International Encyclopedia of the Social Sciences* (vol. 10). New York: Free Press, pp. 386–95.
Levi, Margaret. 1996. "Social and Unsocial Capital." *Politics & Society* 24 (1): 45–55.
Levi, Margaret, and Laura Stoker. 2000. "Political Trust and Trustworthiness." *Annual Review of Political Science* 3: 475–507.
Levitt, Theodore. 1983. "The Globalization of Markets." *Harvard Business Review* 61: 92–102.
Lewis, W. A. 1955. *The Theory of Economic Growth*. Homewood, IL: Richard D. Irvin.
Lieberman, Benjamin. 1998. *From Recovery to Catastrophe: Municipal Stabilization and Political Crisis in Weimar*. New York: Berghahn.
Liebert, Ulrike. 1999. "Gender Politics in the European Union: The Return of the Public." *European Societies* 1: 201–38.
Lijphart, Arend. 1999. *Patterns of Democracy*. New Haven: Yale University Press.
Lijphart, Arend, and Carlos H. Waisman (eds.). 1996. *Institutional Design in New Democracies: Eastern Europe and Latin America*. Boulder, CO: Westview Press.
Linz, Juan J., and Alfred Stepan. 1996. *Problems of Democratic Transition and Consolidation: Southern Europe, South America, and Post-Communist Europe*. Baltimore: Johns Hopkins University Press.
Linz, Juan J., and Arturo A. Valenzuela (eds.). 1994. *The Failure of Presidential Democracy*. Baltimore: Johns Hopkins University Press.
Lipset, Seymour Martin. 1959a. "Some Social Requisites of Democracy: Economic Development and Political Legitimacy." *American Political Science Review* 53: 69–105.
1959b. "Democracy and Working-Class Authoritarianism." *American Sociological Review* 24: 482–501.
1960. *Political Man: The Social Bases of Politics*. Garden City, NY: Doubleday.
1991. "American Exceptionalism Reaffirmed." In Byron Shafer (ed.), *Is America Different?* Oxford: Oxford University Press, pp. 1–45.
1996. *American Exceptionalism*. New York: W. W. Norton.
Lipset, Seymour Martin, and Gabriel S. Lenz. 2000. "Corruption, Culture and Markets." In Lawrence E. Harrison and Samuel P. Huntington (eds.), *Culture Matters: How Values Shape Human Progress*. New York: Basic Books, pp. 112–24.
Lipset, Seymour Martin, Kyoung-Ryung Seong, and John C. Torres. 1993. "A Comparative Analysis of the Social Requisites of Democracy." *International Social Science Journal* 45: 155–75.
Macpherson, Crawford B. 1977. *The Life and Times of Liberal Democracy*. Oxford: Oxford University Press.
Mainwaring, Scott, Guillermo O'Donnell, and Arturo Valenzuela (eds.). 1992. *Issues in Democratic Consolidation: The New South American Democracies in Comparative Perspective*. Notre Dame: University of Notre Dame Press.
Mainwaring, Scott, and Matthew Soberg Shugart (eds.). 1997. *Presidentialism and Democracy in Latin America*. Cambridge: Cambridge University Press.

Malthus, Thomas R. 1970 [1798]. *An Essay on the Principle of Population.* Harmondsworth: Penguin.

Mark, Noah P. 2002. "Cultural Transmission, Disproportionate Prior Exposure, and the Evolution of Cooperation." *American Sociological Review* 67: 323–44.

Markoff, John. 1996. *Waves of Democracy: Social Movements and Political Change.* Thousand Oaks, CA: Pine Forge.

Marks, Gary. 1992. "Rational Sources of Chaos in Democratic Transitions." In Gary Marks and Larry Diamond (eds.), *Reexamining Democracy: Essays in Honor of Seymour Martin Lipset.* London: Sage, pp. 47–69.

Marks, Gary, and Larry Diamond (eds.). 1992. *Reexamining Democracy: Essays in Honor of Seymour Martin Lipset.* London: Sage.

Marshall, Monty G., and Keith Jaggers. 2000. *Polity IV Project.* Data Users Manual. University of Maryland.

Marx, Karl. 1973 [1858]. *Grundrisse.* Harmondsworth: Penguin.

Maslow, Abraham. 1988 [1954]. *Motivation and Personality* (3rd ed.). New York: Harper and Row.

Mayer, Lawrence G. 2001. *Comparative Politics: Nations and Theories in a Changing World.* London: Prentice-Hall.

McAdam, Douglas. 1986. "Recruitment to High-Risk Activism: The Case of Freedom Summer." *American Journal of Sociology* 92: 64–90.

McAdam, Douglas, Sidney Tarrow, and Charles Tilly. 2001. *Dynamics of Contention.* Cambridge: Cambridge University Press.

McDonagh, Eileen. 2002. "Political Citizenship and Democratization: The Gender Paradox." *American Political Science Review* 96: 535–52.

McMichael, Philip. 1996. "Globalization: Myths and Realities." *Rural Sociology* 61: 25–56.

McNeill, William. 1990. *The Rise of the West: A History of the Human Community.* Chicago: University of Chicago Press.

Meadows, Donella H., et al. 1972. *The Limits to Growth.* New York: Universe Books.

Merkel, Wolfgang, Hans-Jürgen Puhle, Aurel Croissant, Claudia Eicher, and Peter Thierry. 2003. *Defekte Demokratien: Theorien und Probleme* [Deficient Democracies: Theories and Problems]. Opladen: Leske and Budrich.

Meyer, John W., John Boli, George M. Thomas, and Francisco O. Ramirez. 1997. "World Society and the Nation-State." *American Journal of Sociology* 103: 144–81.

Michels, Robert. 1962 [1912]. *Political Parties.* London: Collins Books.

Midlarski, Manus I. (ed.). 1997. *Inequality, Democracy and Economic Development.* Cambridge: Cambridge University Press.

    1999. *The Evolution of Inequality: War, State Survival, and Democracy in Comparative Perspective.* Stanford: Stanford University Press.

Miller, Arthur H., Vicki L. Hesli, and William Reisinger. 1994. "Reassessing Mass Support for Political and Economic Change in the Former USSR." *American Political Science Review* 88: 399–411.

Mishler, William, and Richard Rose. 2001. "Political Support for Incomplete Democracies: Realist vs. Idealist Theories and Measures." *International Political Science Review* 22: 303–20.

Monroe, Kristen R. 1996. *The Heart of Altruism.* Princeton: Princeton University Press.

    2003. "How Identity and Perspective Constrain Moral Choice." *International Political Science Review* 24: 405–26.

Monroe, Kristen R., J. Hankin, and R. van Vechten. 2000. "The Psychological Foundations of Identity Politics." *Annual Review of Political Science* 3: 419–47.

Montesquieu, Charles de. 1989 [1748]. *The Spirit of the Laws.* Cambridge: Cambridge University Press.

Moore, Barrington. 1966. *The Social Origins of Democracy and Dictatorship: Lord and Peasant in the Making of the Modern World.* Boston: Beacon Press.

Mouzelis, Nicos. 1999. "Modernity: A Non-European Conceptualization." *British Journal of Sociology* 50: 141–59.

Muller, Edward N. 1997. "Economic Determinants of Democracy." In Manus I. Midlarski (ed.), *Inequality, Democracy and Economic Development.* Cambridge: Cambridge University Press, pp. 133–55.

Muller, Edward N., and Mitchell A. Seligson. 1994. "Civic Culture and Democracy: The Question of Causal Relationships." *American Political Science Review* 88: 635–52.

Mutz, Diana C. 2002. "Cross-Cutting Social Networks: Testing Democratic Theory in Practice." *American Political Science Review* 96 (March): 111–26.

Nagle, John D., and Alison Mahr. 1999. *Democracy and Democratization.* London: Sage.

Nevitte, Neil. 1996. *The Decline of Deference.* Petersborough, Ontario: Broadview Press.

Newton, Kenneth. 2001. "Trust, Social Capital, Civil Society, and Democracy." *International Political Science Review* 22: 201–14.

Newton, Kenneth, and Pippa Norris. 2000. "Confidence in Public Institutions: Faith, Culture, or Performance?" In Susan J. Pharr and Robert D. Putnam (eds.), *Disaffected Democracies: What's Troubling the Trilateral Countries?* Princeton: Princeton University Press, pp. 52–73.

Nolan, Patrick, and Gerhard Lenski. 1999. *Human Societies: An Introduction to Macrosociology* (8th ed.). New York: McGraw-Hill.

Norris, Pippa (ed.). 1999. *Critical Citizens: Global Support for Democratic Governance.* New York: Oxford University Press.

2002. *Democratic Phoenix: Political Activism Worldwide.* Cambridge: Cambridge University Press.

Norris, Pippa, and Ronald Inglehart. 2004. *Sacred and Secular: Religion and Politics Worldwide.* Cambridge: Cambridge University Press.

North, Douglas C. 1981. *Structure and Change in Economic History.* New York: W. W. Norton.

Nye, Joseph S., Philip D. Zelikow, and David King (eds.). 1997. *Why People Don't Trust Government.* Cambridge, MA: Harvard University Press.

O'Donnell, Guillermo. 1973. *Modernization and Bureaucratic Authoritarianism: Studies in South American Politics.* Berkeley: University of California Press.

1996. "Illusions about Consolidation." *Journal of Democracy* 7: 34–51.

O'Donnell, Guillermo, and Philippe C. Schmitter. 1986. "Tentative Conclusions about Uncertain Democracies." In Guillermo O'Donnell, Philippe C. Schmitter, and Laurence Whitehead (eds.), *Transitions from Authoritarian Rule* (vol. 4). Baltimore: Johns Hopkins University Press, pp. 1–78.

O'Donnell, Guillermo, Jorge Vargas Cullel, and Osvaldo Miguel Iazzetta (eds.). 2004. *The Quality of Democracy: Theory and Applications.* Notre Dame: University of Notre Dame Press.

Orwin, Clifford, and Thomas Pangle. 1982. "The Philosophical Foundation of Human Rights." *This World* 4: 1–22.

Ottaway, Marina. 2003. *Democracy Challenged: The Rise of Semi-Authoritarianism.* Washington, DC: Carnegie Endowment for International Peace.

Oyserman, Daphna. 2001. "Self-Concept and Identity." In A. Tesser and N. Schwarz (eds.), *The Blackwell Handbook of Social Psychology* (vol. 1). Malden, MA: Blackwell, pp. 402–15.

Oyserman, Daphna, Heather McCoon, and Markus Kemmelmeier. 2002. "Rethinking Individualism and Collectivism." *Psychological Bulletin* 128: 3–72.

Page, Benjamin, and Robert Y. Shapiro. 1992. *The Rational Public: Fifty Years of Trends in Americans' Policy Preferences.* Chicago: University of Chicago Press.

    1993. "The Rational Public and Democracy." In G. E. Marcus and R. L. Hanson (eds.), *Reconsidering the Democratic Public.* University Park: Pennsylvania State University Press, pp. 35–64.

Paxton, Pamela. 2002. "Social Capital and Democracy: An Interdependent Relationship." *American Sociological Review* 67: 254–77.

Peterson, Dale, and Richard Wrangham. 1996. *Demonic Males: Apes and the Origin of Human Violence.* Boston: Houghton Mifflin.

Pettigrew, Thomas F. 1998. "Reactions towards the New Minorities of Western Europe." *Annual Review of Sociology* 24: 77–103.

Pharr, Susan, and Robert D. Putnam (eds.). 2000. *Disaffected Democracies.* Princeton: Princeton University Press.

Pharr, Susan, Robert D. Putnam, and Russell J. Dalton. 2000. "Trouble in Advanced Democracies? A Quarter Century of Declining Confidence." *Journal of Democracy* 11: 6–25.

Poggi, Gianfranco. 1978. *The Development of the Modern State: A Sociological Introduction.* London: Hutchinson.

Popper, Karl Raimund. 1966 [1945]. *The Open Society and Its Enemies* (2 vols.). Princeton: Princeton University Press.

    1992 [1959]. *The Logic of Scientific Discovery.* New York: Routledge.

Porter, Michael E. (ed.). 1986. *Competition in Global Industries.* Boston: Harvard Business School Press.

Pridham, Geoffrey (ed.). 1991. *Encouraging Democracy: The International Context of Regime Transition in Southern Europe.* Leicester: Leicester University Press.

Pridham, Geoffrey, and Tatu Vanhanen (eds.). 1995. *Democratization in Eastern Europe: Domestic and International Perspectives.* London: Routledge.

Przeworski, Adam. 1992. "The Games of Transition." In Scott Mainwaring, Guillermo O'Donnell, and Arturo Valenzuela (eds.), *Issues in Democratic Consolidation: The New South American Democracies in Comparative Perspective.* Notre Dame: University of Notre Dame Press, pp. 105–52.

Przeworski, Adam, and Fernando Limongi. 1997. "Modernization: Theories and Facts." *World Politics* 49: 155–83.

Przeworski, Adam, and Henry Teune. 1970. *The Logic of Comparative Social Inquiry.* New York: John Wiley.

Putnam, Robert D. 1993. *Making Democracy Work: Civic Traditions in Modern Italy.* Princeton: Princeton University Press.

    2000. *Bowling Alone: The Collapse and Revival of American Community.* New York: Simon and Schuster.

Putnam, Robert D., and Kristin A. Goss. 2002. Introduction. In Robert D. Putnam (ed.), *Democracies in Flux: The Evolution of Social Capital in Contemporary Society.* Oxford: Oxford University Press, pp. 3–20.

Pye, Lucian W. 1990. "Political Science and the Crisis of Authoritarianism." *American Political Science Review* 84: 3–19.

Pye, Lucian W., and Sidney Verba (eds.). 1963. *Political Culture and Political Development.* Princeton: Princeton University Press.

Quigley, Carroll. 1961. *The Evolution of Civilizations: An Introduction to Historical Analysis.* New York: Harper.

Randall, Vicky, and Robin Theobald. 1998. *Political Change and Underdevelopment* (2nd ed.). Durham: Duke University Press.

Reisinger, William, Arthur H. Miller, Vicki L. Hesli, and Kristen Maher. 1994. "Political Values in Russia, Ukraine and Lithuania: Sources and Implications for Democracy." *British Journal of Political Science* 45: 183–223.

Rice, Tom W., and Jan L. Feldman. 1997. "Civic Culture and Democracy from Europe to America." *Journal of Politics* 59: 1143–72.

Ritzer, George. 1996. "Cultures and Consumers: The McDonaldization Thesis: Is Expansion Inevitable?" *International Sociology* 11: 291–308.

Robertson, Hector M. 1973 [1933]. *Aspects of the Rise of Economic Individualism: A Criticism of Max Weber and His School.* London: Kelley Publishers.

Robinson, William I. 1996. *Promoting Polyarchy: Globalization, US Intervention, and Hegemony.* Cambridge: Cambridge University Press.

Robinson, William S. 1950. "Ecological Correlations and the Behavior of Individuals." *American Sociological Review* 15: 351–57.

Roeder, Philip G. 2001. "Ethnolinguistic Fractionalization Indices. 1961 and 1985." http://www.ucsd.edu/~proeder/elf.htm.

Rohrschneider, Robert. 1999. *Learning Democracy: Democratic and Economic Values in Unified Germany.* Oxford: Oxford University Press.

Rokeach, Milton. 1960. *The Open and Closed Mind: Investigations into the Nature of Belief Systems and Personality Systems.* New York: Basic Books.

1968. *Beliefs, Attitudes and Values.* San Francisco: Jossey-Bass.

1973. *The Nature of Human Values.* New York: Free Press.

Rokkan, Stein. 1970. "Nation-Building, Cleavage Formation and the Structuring of Mass Politics." In Angus Campbell et al. (eds.), *Citizens, Elections, Parties: Approaches to the Comparative Study of the Processes of Development.* Oslo: Universitetsforlaget, pp. 72–144.

1980. "Territories, Centers and Peripheries: Toward a Geo-Ethnic-Economic-Political Model of Differentiation within Western Europe." In J. Gottmann (ed.), *Center and Periphery: Spatial Variation in Politics.* Beverly Hills, CA: Sage, pp. 163–204.

1983. "The Territorial Structuring of Western Europe." In Stein Rokkan and D. Urwin (eds.), *Economy, Territory, Identity: Politics of Western European Peripheries.* London: Sage, pp. 19–65.

Rose, Richard. 1995. "Freedom as a Fundamental Value." *International Social Science Journal* 145: 457–71.

2000. "Uses of Social Capital in Russia: Modern, Pre-modern, and Anti-modern." *Post-Soviet Affairs* 16: 33–57.

2001. "A Divergent Europe." *Journal of Democracy* 12: 93–106.

Rose-Ackerman, S. 2001. "Trust and Honesty in Post-Socialist Societies." *Kyklos* 54: 415–44.

Rosenberg, Morris, and Timothy J. Owens. 2001. "Low Self-Esteem People: A Collective Portrait." In Timothy J. Owens, Sheldon Stryker, and Norman Goodman (eds.), *Extending Self-Esteem Theory and Research: Social and Psychological Currents.* Cambridge: Cambridge University Press, pp. 400–36.

Ross, Michael L. 2001. "Does Oil Hinder Democracy?" *World Politics* 53: 325–61.

Ross, Robert J. S., and Kent C. Trachte. 1990. *Global Capitalism: The New Leviathan.* Albany: State University of New York Press.

Rössel, Jörg. 2000. "Mobilisierung, Staat und Demokratie [Modernization, the State and Democracy]." *Kölner Zeitschrift für Soziologie und Sozialpsychologie* 52: 609–35.

Rothstein, Bo. 1998. *Just Institutions Matter: The Moral and Political Logic of the Universal Welfare State.* Cambridge: Cambridge University Press.

    2000. "Trust, Social Dilemmas and Collective Memories." *Journal of Theoretical Politics* 12: 477–501.

Rowen, Henry S. 1996. "World Wealth Expanding: Why a Rich, Democratic, and (Perhaps) Peaceful Era Is Ahead." In Ralph Landau, Timothy Taylor, and Gavin Wright (eds.), *The Mosaic of Economic Growth.* Stanford: Stanford University Press, pp. 93–125.

Rueschemeyer, Dietrich, Marilyn Rueschemeyer, and Bjorn Wittrock. 1998. *Participation and Democracy, East and West: Comparisons and Interpretations.* Armonk, NY: M. E. Sharpe.

Rueschemeyer, Dietrich, Evelyn Huber Stephens, and John D. Stephens. 1992. *Capitalist Development and Democracy.* Chicago: University of Chicago Press.

Rustow, Dankwart A. 1970. "Transitions to Democracy: Toward a Dynamic Model." *Comparative Politics* 2: 337–63.

Sainsbury, Diane. 1996. *Gender Equality and Welfare States.* Cambridge: Cambridge University Press.

Sandholtz, Wayne, and Rein Taagepera. 2005. "Corruption, Culture, and Communism." *International Review of Sociology.*

Scarbrough, Elinor. 1995. "Materialist-Postmaterialist Value Orientations." In Jan van Deth and Elinor Scarbrough (eds.), *The Impact of Values* (*Beliefs in Government*, vol. 4). Oxford: Oxford University Press, pp. 123–59.

Schmuck, Peter, Tim Kasser, and Richard M. Ryan. 2000. "Intrinsic and Extrinsic Goals." *Social Indicators Research* 50: 225–41.

Scholz, J. T., and M. Lubell. 1998. "Trust and Taxpaying." *American Journal of Political Science* 42: 398–417.

Schwartz, Shalom H. 1992. "Universals in the Content and Structure of Values: Theoretical Advances and Empirical Tests in 20 Countries." In Mark P. Zanna (ed.), *Advances in Social Psychology.* New York: Academic Press, pp. 1–65.

    1994. "Beyond Individualism/Collectivism: New Cultural Dimensions of Values." In U. Kim, H. C. Triandis, C. Kagitcibasi, S.-C. Choi, and G. Yoon (eds.), *Individualism and Collectivism: Theory, Method and Applications.* Newbury Park, CA: Sage, pp. 85–119.

    2003. "Mapping and Interpreting Cultural Differences around the World." In Henk Vinken, Joseph Soeters, and Peter Ester (eds.), *Comparing Cultures, Dimensions of Culture in a Comparative Perspective.* Leiden: Brill, pp. 43–73.

Sekhon, Jasjeet S. 2004. "Quality Meets Quantity: Case Studies, Conditional Probability, and Counterfactuals." *Perspectives on Politics* 2: 281–93.

Seligson, Mitchell. 2002. "The Renaissance of Political Culture or the Renaissance of the Ecological Fallacy." *Comparative Politics* 34: 273–92.

Sen, Amartya. 1999. *Development as Freedom.* New York: Knopf.

Service, Elman. 1962. *Origins of the State and Civilization.* New York: W. W. Norton.

Shapiro, Ian. 2003. *The State of Democratic Theory.* Princeton: Princeton University Press.

Shevtsova, Lilia. 2001. "Russia's Hybrid Regime." *Journal of Politics* 12: 65–70.

Shugart, Matthew Soberg, and John M. Carey. 1992. *Presidents and Assemblies: Constitutional Design and Electoral Dynamics.* Cambridge: Cambridge University Press.

Shuman, Howard, and Jacqueline Scott. 1989. "Generations and Collective Memories." *American Sociological Review* 54: 359–81.

Simmel, Georg. 1984 [1908]. *Das Individuum und die Freiheit* [The Individual and Freedom]. Berlin: Duncker & Humblodt.

Slater, Robert O., Barry M. Schutz, and Steven R. Dorr (eds.). 1993. *Global Transformation and the Third World.* Boulder, CO: Lynne Rienner.

Smith, Adam. 1976 [1776]. *An Inquirey into the Nature and Causes of the Wealth of Nations.* Chicago: University of Chicago Press.

Sniderman, Paul. 1975. *Personality and Democratic Politics.* Berkeley: University of California Press.

Sorensen, Georg. 1993. *Democracy and Democratization: Processes and Prospects in a Changing World.* Boulder, CO: Westview Press.

Sowell, Thomas. 1994. *Race and Culture: A World View.* New York: Basic Books.

Spier, Fred. 1996. *The Structure of Big History: From the Big Bang until Today.* Amsterdam: Amsterdam University Press.

Starr, Harvey. 1991. "Diffusion Approaches to the Spread of Democracy in the International System." *Journal of Conflict Resolution* 35: 356–81.

Stevenson, Mark. 1997. "Globalization, National Cultures, and Cultural Citizenship." *Sociological Quarterly* 38: 41–67.

Stiglitz, Joseph. 2002. *Globalization and Its Discontents.* New York: W. W. Norton.

Stinchcomb, Arthur L. 1965. "Social Structure and Organization." In J. G. March (ed.), *Handbook of Organizations.* Chicago: Rand McNally, pp. 142–93.

Stokes, Randall G., and Anthony Harris. 1978. "Modernization from the Center: Racial Particularism in South Africa." *Economic Development and Cultural Change* 26: 245–69.

Stokes, Randall G., and Susan Marshall. 1981. "Tradition and the Veil: Female Status in Tunisia and Algeria." *Journal of Modern African Studies* 19: 625–46.

Sullivan, J. L., and J. E. Transue. 1999. "The Psychological Underpinnings of Democracy: A Selective Review of Research on Political Tolerance, Interpersonal Trust, and Social Capital." *Annual Review of Psychology* 50: 625–50.

Swindler, Ann, and Jorge Arditti. 1994. "The New Sociology of Knowledge." *Annual Review of Sociology* 20: 305–29.

Tarrow, Sidney. 1998. *Power in Movement: Social Movements and Contentious Politics.* Cambridge: Cambridge University Press.

Thompson, John B. 2000. "The Survival of Asian Values as 'Zivilisationskritik.'" *Theory and Society* 29: 651–86.

Tilly, Charles. 1978. *From Mobilization to Revolution.* Reading, MA: Addison-Wesley.

    1984. *Big Structures, Large Processes, Huge Comparisons.* New York: Russell Sage Foundation.

    1997. *Coercion, Capital, and European States, AD 990–1992.* Oxford: Blackwell.

Tocqueville, Alexis de. 1994 [1837]. *Democracy in America.* London: Fontana Press.

Toffler, Alvin. 1970. *Future Shock.* New York: Random House.

Tönnies, Ferdinand. 1955 [1887]. *Community and Association.* London: Routledge and Kegan Paul.

Triandis, Harry C. 1989. "The Self and Social Behavior in Differing Cultural Contexts." *Psychological Review* 96: 506–20.

1995. *Individualism and Collectivism*. Boulder, CO: Westview Press.

2001. "Individualism and Collectivism." In D. Matsumoto (ed.), *Handbook of Cross-Cultural Psychology*. New York: Oxford University Press, pp. 406–20.

2003. "Dimensions of Culture beyond Hofstede." In Henk Vinken, Joseph Soeters, and Peter Ester (eds.), *Comparing Cultures: Dimensions of Culture in a Comparative Perspective*. Leiden: Brill, pp. 28–42.

Tronto, Joan. 2001. "Who Cares? Public and Private Caring and the Rethinking of Citizenship." In Nancy J. Hirschmann and Ulrike Liebert (eds.), *Women and Welfare*. New Brunswick, NJ: Rutgers University Press, pp. 65–83.

Tyler, T. R. 1998. "Trust and Democratic Governance." In V. Braithwaite and Margaret Levi (eds.), *Trust and Government*. New York: Russell Sage Foundation, pp. 175–201.

United Nations (ed.). Annual. *United Nations Statistical Yearbook*. New York: United Nations Publication.

United Nations Development Program (ed.). Annual. *Human Development Report*. New York: Oxford University Press.

U.S. Bureau of the Census (ed.). 1996. *World Population Profile: 1996*. Washington, DC.

Uslaner, Eric M. 1999. *The Moral Foundations of Trust*. Cambridge: Cambridge University Press.

Vago, Steven. 1999. *Social Change* (4th ed.). Upper Saddle River, NJ: Prentice-Hall.

van Deth, Jan, and Elinor Scarbrough (eds.). 1995. *The Impact of Values (Beliefs in Government*, vol. 4). Oxford: Oxford University Press.

Vanhanen, Tatu (ed.). 1997. *Prospects of Democracy: A Study of 172 Countries*. London: Routledge.

2003. *Democratization: A Comparative Analysis of 170 Countries*. London: Routledge.

Verba, Sidney, Norman H. Nie, and Jae-On Kim. 1978. *Participation and Political Equality: A Seven Nation Comparison*. Cambridge: Cambridge University Press.

Verba, Sidney, Kay L. Schlozman, and Henry E. Brady. 1995. *Voice and Equality*. Cambridge, MA: Harvard University Press.

Vermeil, Edmond. 1956. *Germany in the Twentieth Century: A Political and Cultural History of Weimar and the Third Reich*. New York: Praeger.

von Barloewen, Wolf D., and Constantin von Barloewen. 1988. *Die Gesetzmäßigkeit der Geschichte* [The Regularity of History]. Frankfurt am Main: Athenäum.

Walgrave, Stefan, and Jan Manssens. 2000. "The Making of the White March: The Mass Media as a Mobilizing Alternative to Movement Organizations." *Mobilization* 5: 217–39.

Wallerstein, Immanuel. 1974. *The Modern World System I*. New York: Academic Press.

1976. "Modernization: Requiescat in Pace." In Lewis A. Coser and Otto N. Larsen (eds.), *The Uses of Controversy in Sociology*. New York: Free Press, pp. 131–35.

Watson, James (ed.). 1998. *Golden Arches East: McDonald's in East Asia*. Stanford: Stanford University Press.

Wattenberg, Martin. 1996. *The Decline of American Political Parties*. Cambridge, MA: Harvard University Press.

Weber, Max. 1958 [1904]. *The Protestant Ethic and the Spirit of Capitalism*. New York: Charles Scribner's Sons.

Weil, Frederick D., and Mary Gautier (eds.). 1994. *Political Culture and Political Structure: Theoretical and Empirical Studies*. Greenwich, CT: JAI Press.

Weiner, Myron (ed.). 1966. *Modernization: The Dynamics of Growth*. New York: Basic Books.

1992. "The Indian Paradox: Violent Social Conflict and Democratic Politics." In Shmuel N. Eisenstadt (ed.), *Democracy and Modernity*. Leiden: Brill, pp. 67–85.

Welzel, Christian. 1999. "Elite Change and Democracy's Instant Success in Eastern Germany." In John Higley and Gyorgy Lengyel (eds.), *Elites after State Socialism: Theories and Analyses*. Lanham, MD: Rowman and Littlefield, pp. 103–22.

2002. *Fluchtpunkt Humanentwicklung: Über die Grundlagen der Demokratie und die Ursachen ihrer Ausbreitung* [Focal Point Human Development: On the Foundations of Democracy and the Causes of its Spread]. Opladen: Westdeutscher Verlag.

2003. "Effective Democracy, Mass Culture, and the Quality of Elites: The Human Development Perspective." *International Journal of Comparative Sociology* 43: 269–98.

Welzel, Christian, and Ronald Inglehart. 2001. "Human Development and the 'Explosion' of Democracy: Variations of Regime Change across 60 Societies." *WZB-Discussion Paper Series, FS III 01-202*. Berlin.

2005. "Liberalism, Postmaterialism, and the Growth of Freedom: The Human Development Perspective." *International Review of Sociology*.

Welzel, Christian, Ronald Inglehart, and Franziska Deutsch. 2005. "Civil Society, Social Capital and Collective Action: Which Type of Civic Activity Is Most Democratic?" Paper presented at the HPSA annual meeting, Chicago, 11 April.

Welzel, Christian, Ronald Inglehart, and Hans-Dieter Klingemann. 2003. "The Theory of Human Development: A Cross-Cultural Analysis." *European Journal of Political Research* 42: 341–80.

Wessels, Bernhard. 1997. "Organizing Capacity of Societies and Modernity." In Jan van Deth (ed.), *Private Groups and Public Life*. London: Routledge, pp. 198–219.

Whitehead, Laurence. 1996. "Three International Dimensions of Democratization." In Laurence Whitehead (ed.), *The International Dimensions of Democratizations*. Oxford: Oxford University Press, pp. 3–25.

Whyte, William H., Jr. 1956. *The Organization Man*. New York: Simon and Schuster.

Wittfogel, Karl. 1957. *Oriental Despotism*. New Haven: Yale University Press.

World Bank (ed.) Annual. *World Development Indicators*. Washington, DC: World Bank.

(ed.). Annual. *World Development Report*. New York: Oxford University Press.

Yule, G. U., and M. G. Kendall. 1950. *An Introduction to the Theory of Statistics*. London: Charles Griffin.

Zaller, John. 1992. *The Nature and Origins of Mass Opinion*. Cambridge: Cambridge University Press.

Index

abortion, 7, 52, 126
Abramson, Paul, 19, 104, 244
absolute rules, 292
activist roles, 297
activities in associations, 248, 254, 255, 259
actor-centered approach, 224
Adcock, Robert, 149, 174, 175
advanced industrial democracies, 108
affirmative action, 292
Afghanistan, 297
African cultural zones, 63
Afrobarometer, 253, 263
aggregate-level analysis, 49
aging effects, 100
agrarian societies, 23, 26, 296
agricultural sector, 58, 75
Ahl, Richard, 19, 263
Albania, 128
Alexander, Richard, 288
Algeria, 85, 86, 128
Almond, Gabriel, 17, 71, 157, 162, 186, 245, 248, 285, 286
altruism, 144
American culture, 91
American exceptionalism, 65
Americanization, 47, 65
amoral familism, 143, 163
Anand, Sudhir, 272, 286, 288, 289
Anderson, Christopher, 247
Anheier, Helmut, 227
anticorruption scores, 154
Apter, David, 285
Armstrong, David, 192
Asian countries, 156
Asian cultures, 289
Asian values, 156, 159, 289
aspiration suppression, 158
association, 24, 294
associational activity, 249

atheists, 27
Athens, 284, 295
attitudinal affinities, 212
Australia, 50, 65
Austria, 121
authoritarianism/authoritarian, 144, 229
    culture, 161
    democracies, 216
    elites, 190, 218
    rule, 158
    societies, 43, 158, 171, 220, 286
    values, 291
authority, 5, 26, 27, 29, 43, 52, 59, 292, 293
autocorrelation, 159, 178, 179, 184, 185, 191
autocracy, 168
autonomy/autonomous, 2, 8, 20, 27, 31, 33, 37, 45, 135, 136–38, 144, 162, 271, 286
    choice, 136, 137, 140, 149, 285, 287, 288, 299
    judgment, 28, 289
autonomy/embeddedness, 136
Azerbaijan, 128

Baker, Kendall, 99, 162
Baker, Wayne, 19, 49, 63, 65, 67, 159, 245
Baltic states, 108, 216
Banfield, Edwin, 143, 163, 260
Bangladesh, 128
bargaining processes, 211
Barkow, Jerome, 23, 288
Barnes, Samuel, 116, 117, 164, 245
Barro, Robert, 16, 18, 45
Bauer, Martin, 32
Beck, Ulrich, 18, 29, 32, 45, 118, 142, 290, 294
behavioral patterns, 288
Beitz, Charles, 289
Belarus, 215

Belgium, 101, 104, 120
Bell, Daniel, 19, 24, 26, 28, 58, 247, 280
Benford, Robert, 212
Berg-Scholosser, Dirk, 204
Berlin, Isaiah, 175
Bernhard, Michael, 119, 175, 211, 225, 257
Bin Laden, Osama, 298
Binder, Leonard, 285
Birch, Charles, 22, 137, 272, 288
birth cohorts, 97, 101, 102, 105, 107, 112
birth control technology, 277
birthrates, 39
Boggs, Carl, 116, 294
Boix, Carles, 157, 160, 169, 205, 213, 279
Boli, John, 19, 286
Bollen, Kenneth, 149, 175, 204, 205, 284
bonding
    activities, 294
    social capital, 142
    ties, 143, 294, 295
Bonn
    constitution, 162
    republic, 162
Bourdieu, Pierre, 262, 295
bowling leagues, 294
boycotts, 123, 261, 262
Boynton, Robert, 162
Bracher, Karl Dietrich, 161, 245
Bradshaw, York, 17
Bratton, Michael, 245, 268
break variables, 213, 214
Brezhnev doctrine, 210, 215–16
bridging
    social capital, 142
    ties, 143, 294
Brint, Steven, 164
Brown, Archie, 193
Brzezinski, Zbigniew, 193, 263, 285
Bunce, Valerie, 149, 196, 300
bureaucracies/bureaucratic, 1, 71, 285
    associations, 262
    authoritarianism, 285
    organizations, 271, 294
    state, 286
Burke, Edmund, 16
Burkhart, Ross, 157, 167
Burton, Michael, 165

Cain, Bruce, 44
Canada, 40
Cardoso, Fernando, 18
card-playing clubs, 294
Carneiro, Robert, 15, 22, 277, 278
Carrol, Glenn, 167
Casper, Gretchen, 165, 175, 211, 217, 224,
    226, 227
Catholics/Catholic, 69
    cultural zone, 65–68
    societies, 71, 135

Catterberg, Gabriela, 119
causal direction, 156, 159, 173, 178, 179, 287
causal impact, 185
causal relationships, 213
certainty, 27
changes, 1, 132
Chanley, Virginia, 247
Chase-Dunn, Christopher, 17
children's rights, 292
Chile, 156, 215
China, 42, 64, 113, 155, 190, 195, 211, 218,
    219, 222, 225, 296, 298
    elites, 219
Chirkov, V. I., 139
Chirot, Daniel, 17
choice, 139, 140
Christian Democratic parties, 279
Christian societies, 291
churches, 31, 118, 262, 294
citizenry, critical, 261
civic action, 123
civic autonomy, 299
civic culture, 11, 157, 245, 247, 286
civic disengagement, 117, 120, 121
civic values, 157, 247, 255
civil and political rights, 153, 176
civil liberties, 9
civil rights initiative, 118
civil society, 21, 76, 225, 227, 293
Civil Society Index, 151
civilian power, 218
civilizational diversity, 21
class, 104, 204
classless societies, 17
clientelistic relations, 163
closed mind, 143
Cobb, John, 22, 137, 272, 288
codes of integrity, 292
coercive capacities, 205
coercive state, 218
cognitive mobilization, 24, 28, 116
cognitive resources, 28, 151
cohort
    analysis, 111, 113
    differences, 102
Cold War, 170
Coleman, James, 17, 71, 144, 163, 255, 262,
    285, 295
collectivism/collective, 136, 144
    actions, 10, 211, 212, 217, 224–29, 262, 294
    discipline, 143, 271, 299
    memories, 99
collectivist cultures, 139
Collier, David, 174, 175
colonial heritage, 66
common good, 286
communal values, 248
communism/communist, 1, 38, 112
    heritage, 66

regimes, 286
rule, 76, 78, 92
societies, 64, 109
communitarian approach, 247, 249, 254
communities of necessity, 29, 118, 294
community, sense of, 24, 291–92
competition for survival, 22
Condorcet, Jean-Antoine, 16
confidence
  in institutions, 243, 250–54, 259, 260,
    261
  in technology, 137
conformism/conformist, 142, 259, 286, 289
  norms, 160, 247–49, 255, 256, 288
  values, 290
Confucian societies, 22, 64, 66, 75, 156
congruence thesis, 9, 174, 186
Conradt, David, 161, 162
constitution/constitutional, 160
  arrangements, 160
  democracy, 151, 152, 153
  engineering, 2, 300
consumer boycotts, 294
consumer protection, 292
consumerism, 33
contractual relations, 163
convergence, 19
Converse, Philip, 237
Coon, Heather, 135
corruption/corrupt, 192, 193, 208, 220, 295
  control of, 193, 196
  elites, 195
Cosmides, Leda, 23, 288
counterelite, 217, 225
Cox, D. R., 178
creativity/creative, 20, 28
  class, 28
crisis
  of democracy, 117, 121
  of governability, 291
Croatia, 167
cross-cultural comparability, 239
cross-cultural variations, 49, 50
cross-level analysis, 10
cross-level linkages, 231, 232
Crothers, Lane, 19
Crozier, Michel, 117, 247, 250, 291
cultural changes, 18, 19, 25, 43, 46, 52, 54,
    95, 96, 97, 104, 134, 171, 215, 285,
    289
cultural determinism, 42
cultural explanations, 173, 209
cultural heritage, 46, 76, 80, 92
cultural map, 6, 66, 89
cultural modernization, 38, 46, 58
  model, 77
cultural norms, 22, 33, 221, 288
cultural relativism, 300
cultural traditions, 76, 99

cultural zones, 62, 65–69, 72, 74, 82, 86, 92,
    197, 198, 288
deviation factor, 73, 76, 78, 80, 82, 86, 88
cumulating variables, 213, 214
cumulative changes, 41
Czech Republic, 126, 215, 216
Czechoslovakia, 216, 218, 219, 222, 225

Dahl, Robert, 36, 149, 157, 163, 205, 218,
    272
Dalai Lama, 290, 291
Dalton, Russell, 19, 44, 99, 117, 157, 161,
    162, 164, 219, 245, 252, 262
Daly, Mary, 272, 277
data protection, 292
Davenport, Christian, 192
defender-challenger games, 217
deliberate choices, 288
demand for freedom, 189
democracy/democratic, 1–2, 59, 139, 145, 149,
    167, 168, 174, 188, 216, 224, 249, 299
  consociational, 281
  effective, 10, 12, 149, 151, 154, 158, 161,
    165, 167, 174, 192, 193, 194, 196, 197,
    198, 200, 201, 202, 207, 208, 209, 212,
    222, 223, 250, 256, 258, 259, 265, 284,
    286, 287, 296, 297, 299
  electoral, 149, 151, 153, 175, 263
  formal, 10, 149, 153, 158, 161, 167, 191,
    193, 194, 196, 207, 208, 209, 222, 250,
    299
  illiberal, 149
  institutions, 134, 151, 156, 171, 229, 285,
    286
  liberal, 9, 151, 153, 158, 161, 173, 174, 175,
    176, 180, 185, 286, 296
  low-intensity, 149
  mid-transition to, 179
  movement, 190, 219
  opposition, 226
  peace thesis, 300
  post-transition, 179, 180, 185
  pre-transition, 179, 180, 185
  support, 119, 120, 231, 233, 247, 249, 253,
    263, 264, 268, 270
  tradition, 196, 197, 202, 203, 250
  transitions to, 119, 120, 121, 125, 167, 198,
    201, 211, 217
democratization, 6, 42, 43, 166, 177, 190,
    210, 211, 212, 225, 229
demonstrations, 123, 261, 262, 294
Denmark, 103, 104, 298
dependency theory, 18
Deutsch, Karl, 19, 44, 257, 262
Diamond, Larry, 18, 19, 35, 119, 160, 167,
    197, 215, 218, 225, 226, 245, 257, 279,
    296
diffusion processes, 197
DiMaggio, Paul, 19, 21

DiPalma, Giuseppe, 165
discrimination, 142, 292
dissident networks, 225
divorce, 39, 52, 126
Dollar, David, 18
Domes, Jurgen, 226
Donnelly, Jack, 271, 293
Doorenspleet, Renske, 42, 177, 204
Downing, Brian, 36, 166
Duch, Raymond, 19, 263
Dumont, Louis, 290
Durham, William, 23, 33
Durkheim, Emile, 24, 29, 135, 163, 294
Dutch, 65, 245

East Asia, 18
East Germany, 43, 126, 225
Easton, David, 247
Eckstein, Harry, 157, 186, 245
ecological fallacy, 231, 232, 233
ecology parties, 39
economic change, 25, 134
economic disaster, 161
economic history, 128
economic prosperity, 162
economic resources, 151
education, 37
    primary, 298
effective choice, 153
egoistic cost calculations, 292
Egypt, 85, 86, 128
Ehrlich, Paul, 286–88
Eichmann, Adolf, 256
elective affinities, 29, 118, 294
elite-centered determinism, 165
elite-centered societies, 296
elite-challenging activities, 115, 117, 118,
    120, 121, 123, 223, 243, 257, 259, 261,
    262
elite-challenging political action, 116, 117,
    126, 130, 142, 293
elite-directed organizations, 117
elite-directed participation, 118
elite-directed political action, 115
elites/elite, 219
    action, 211
    authority, 191, 223
    bargaining, 211, 300
    behavior, 165, 217, 218
    cohorts, 219
    corruption, 192, 196, 279, 299
    culture, 220, 221
    integrity, 9, 151, 154, 192, 194, 207–9, 222,
    223, 279, 284, 299
Elkins, Zachary, 175
emancipation, 25, 29, 60, 290
    from authority, 76
emancipative values, 166, 284, 286, 290, 296
embeddedness, 144

Ember and Ember, 35, 272
end of history, 264
Engels, Friedrich, 16
English-speaking societies, 63, 64, 65, 73, 79,
    80
entitlements, 152, 287
environmental protection, 12, 25, 52, 104,
    292, 293
environmentalist movements, 39, 118
equivalence of mass values, 239
Erikson, Robert, 237
Esping-Andersen, Gøsta, 44, 279, 280
Estes, Richard, 16
ethical issues, 289, 292, 293
ethnic diversity, 52, 205
ethnic fractionalization, 205
Etzioni, Amitai, 247
eunuchs, 293
Eurobarometer surveys, 97, 103
euthanasia, 52
Evans, Peter, 18
ex-communist societies, 82, 96, 108, 109, 110,
    128, 131, 133, 156
existential autonomy, 141, 296
existential experiences, 161, 287
existential insecurity, 104, 138, 139, 143, 161,
    163, 297
existential security, 2, 22, 29, 30, 31, 33, 34,
    37, 38, 45, 56, 96, 108, 114, 126, 134,
    143, 162, 221, 254, 287, 299
external authority, 291, 293
external conditions, 215, 216, 217
extramarital affairs, 126
extremism, 297–98

factor analysis, 50
factories, 27
fair trade, 293
Fairbanks, Charles, 193
Fajnzylber, Pablo, 277
Faletto, Enzo, 18
family, 34, 52, 294
fascism, 1, 264
fatherland, 52
Fedigan, Linda, 277
Feldman, Jan, 64
female empowerment, 273, 284
fertility rates, 39, 109
Finer, Samuel, 166, 192, 296
Finland, 86, 121
Firebaugh, Glenn, 18
Flanagan, Scott, 121, 144, 291, 292
Flannery, Kent, 277
Fleron, Frederick, 19, 263
Florida, Richard, 25, 27, 28, 33, 142,
    262
foreigners, 54, 137
formative years, 99, 113, 126, 132
Forster, Jens, 143

Foweraker, John, 119, 165, 166, 175, 211, 224, 225, 257
France, 88, 101, 104, 113, 232
Frank, Andre Gunder, 17
free election, 208
freedom campaigns, 218
Freedom House, 9, 153, 175, 192, 193, 195
freedom of choice, 174, 271
freedom of speech, 265
Friedheim, Daniel, 225
Friedrich, Carl, 285
Front Nationale, 232
Fuchs, Dieter, 245
Fukuyama, Francis, 18, 19, 21, 71, 142, 149, 260, 264
Fulcher, John, 272
fundamentalists, 45, 290

Galston, William, 144
Gasiorowski, Mark, 19, 165, 197, 204
Gaskell, George, 32
gays and lesbians, 12, 52, 54, 137, 292
Geddes, Barbara, 169, 300
Geertz, Clifford, 141
Gemeinschaft, 135, 294
gender empowerment, 151, 278–80, 282–83
gender equality, 11, 54, 91, 129, 130, 244, 272, 273, 275, 277, 278, 280, 282, 284, 293, 298
gender roles, 52, 54, 126, 278, 281
generations/generational
   change, 100, 132
   comparisons, 95, 96
   differences, 94, 95, 102
generosity, 298
genetic engineering, 32
genital mutilation, 293
genocide, 142, 300
Germany, 113, 161, 166, 195
Gesellschaft, 135, 294
Gibson, James, 19, 157, 218, 245, 247, 263
Giddens, Anthony, 32, 280
Gills, B., 149, 215
Glasius, Marlies, 227
globalization/global, 4, 19, 22, 45
   capitalism, 18
   civil society project, 227
   communication, 20
   cultural map, 56, 61, 66, 69, 81, 87
   of culture, 69
   economic development, 298
God, 15, 37, 52
good governance, 279
Gorbachev, Mikhail, 42, 43, 210, 215
Gosling, Brian, 45
Goss, Kristin, 117
Granger causality, 157, 178, 196, 200, 205
Granger, C. W., 178

Granovetter, Mark, 163, 261, 290, 294
Great Britain, 101, 104, 113, 121, 160, 195
Great Depression, 102, 113, 161, 162
Greece, 85, 86, 298
Green parties, 39
Greenfield, P. M., 135
Greenpeace, 294
group
   conformity, 143, 271, 294, 299
   discipline, 161
Guillén, Mauro, 21
Gunther, Richard, 165, 211, 217
Gurr, Ted, 152

Habermas, Jürgen, 117
habituation, 159, 165, 246
habituation theory, 223
Hall, John, 15, 35, 291
Hamilton, Gary, 21
handicapped people, 47, 292
Hankin, J., 142
Hannan, Michael, 167
happiness, 130
Hein, Simon, 18
Held, David, 133
Heller, Patrick, 149, 161, 193
Helliwell, John, 157
Hesli, Vicki, 19
hierarchy, 71
Higgins, E. T., 143
high-income societies, 57, 106, 128, 129, 131, 167
higher power, 27
Higley, John, 165, 211, 217
Hildebrandt, Kai, 99, 162, 245
Hirschmann, Albert, 279
historical breakthroughs, 214
historical heritage, 80, 81, 82, 92
Hitler, Adolf, 162, 298
Hofferbert, Richard, 119, 245
Hofstede, Geert, 135, 136, 137, 143
homosexuality, 7, 40, 41, 43, 47, 126, 127, 128, 273, 293
Honnecker, Erich, 225
hoplite suffrage, 295
horizontal ties, 72
horizontal trust, 260, 261
Hughes, Barry, 16
human autonomy, 54, 56, 287
human capital, 45
human choice, 2, 20, 139, 141, 152, 248, 268, 286, 288
human development, 1–4, 12, 47, 76, 134, 135, 141, 145, 149, 152, 173, 174, 191, 247, 272, 273, 284, 286–89, 293, 297, 299, 300
human development approach, 139, 249, 256
Human Development Index, 150
human development sequence, 287, 299

human diversity, 143, 271, 299
human emancipation, 12, 290, 293, 300
human equality, 290, 291
human potential, 285, 288
human rights, 142, 143, 192, 289, 292, 293, 300
humanism/humanistic, 144
  culture, 3
  ethos, 291
  norms, 126, 292, 293
  orientation, 137
  shift, 273
  societies, 4, 292
  values, 17, 291
humanitarian conduct, 298
Hungary, 126, 215, 216, 226
Huntington, Samuel, 18, 19, 36, 61, 64, 117, 163, 167, 177, 197, 216, 218, 247, 250, 263, 282, 285, 291
hydraulic state, 35
hyperinflation, 161

Idson, L. C., 143
import substitution, 18
income groups, 69
incongruence scale, 188, 189
India, 113, 160, 161, 195, 296, 298
individualism/collectivism, 136, 138
individualism/individual, 8, 135, 136, 137, 144, 286
  deliverance, 291
  freedom, 290, 291
  judgment, 29
  liberty, 143, 271, 290, 299
  self-expression, 22
individualization, 29, 45, 142
individual-level analysis, 51
individual-level attitudes, 232, 246
individual-level correlation, 234, 236
individual-level data, 51, 232
individual-level values, 61, 149, 164, 233, 234
Indonesia, 85, 86, 128
industrialization/industrial, 1, 26, 27, 30, 59, 285
  sector, 58, 75, 78
  society, 23, 26, 31, 285, 296
  workers, 82
infant mortality, 34, 277
inflation, 102, 104
information, 28
Inglehart, Ronald, 8, 19, 24, 26, 39, 44, 45, 48, 49, 50, 52, 63, 67, 99, 100, 104, 116, 119, 134, 137, 138, 155, 157, 159, 164, 165, 168, 170, 231, 232, 235, 237, 244, 245, 246, 257, 262, 272, 273, 276, 277, 278
in-groups, 136, 143
initiative, 144
Inkeles, Alex, 17, 24, 37, 163, 285, 292
innovation, 28

insecurity, 31, 102, 143
institution-centered determinism, 165
institutions/institutional, 271
  changes, 43, 210
  explanations, 173, 200, 209
  learning, 159
intellectual freedom, 291
intergenerational changes, 94, 96, 97, 111, 223
  comparisons, 114
  differences, 102, 110, 113, 115, 128
intergenerational population replacement, 99, 132, 133
intergenerational value changes, 95, 106, 107, 113, 114
internal conditions, 216, 217
international events, 212
internet, 70
Internet Appendix, 7, 50, 92
intolerance, 128, 297
Iran, 85, 86, 128, 156, 159, 210
Iraq, 44, 297
Ireland, 39, 65, 103, 104
Iron Law of Oligarchy, 44, 262
Islamic cultural zone, 22, 73
Islamic societies, 64, 68, 73, 81, 128, 129, 156, 159, 205, 263, 291, 293
Islamic traditions, 298
Italy, 39, 101, 104, 121
Iversen, Torben, 219

Jackman, Robert, 159, 165, 204, 205, 246
Jaggers, Keith, 152, 176
James, Harold, 161
Japan, 66, 156, 166
Jawad, Haifaa, 282
Johnson, Chalmers, 285
Jones, Eric, 15, 23, 35, 36, 144, 279, 291, 296
Joppke, Christian, 225
Jordan, 85, 86, 128

Kaase, Max, 116, 117, 164, 245
Kaldor, Mary, 227
Karklins, Rasma, 218
Karl, Terry, 159, 165, 211, 217, 224
Kasser, Tim, 139
Kaufmann, Daniel, 154, 193, 279
Kemmelman, Markus, 135
key dimensions, 48, 62
Kim, Jae-on, 164
King, David, 117
Klingemann, Hans-Dieter, 119, 245, 247, 253, 254, 272
knowledge society, 1, 16, 28, 31, 44, 45, 280
Konrad, György, 226
Kopstein, Jeffrey, 196, 197
Kraay, Aart, 154, 193, 279
Kühnen, Ulrich, 136, 143

Kuran, Timur, 158
Kurzman, Charles, 177
Kuwait, 164

labor unions, 44, 262, 294
labor-repressive regimes, 36, 296
Lal, Deepak, 15, 36, 222, 290, 296
Landes, David, 16, 26, 35, 36, 204
Landman, Todd, 119, 165, 166, 175, 211, 224, 225, 257
Lasswell, Harold, 157
Latin American cluster, 67
Latin American countries, 63, 65
Latinobarometer, 253, 263
Latvia, 195
Lawler, P. A., 121, 144, 290, 292
Lederman, Daniel, 277
Lee, Kuan Yew, 156
legitimacy, 164, 247, 249, 250, 259, 286
Lenski, Gerhard, 22, 35, 272, 277
Lenz, Gabriel, 19
Lerner, Daniel, 17, 24, 37, 163, 245, 285
lesbians, 12, 52, 54, 137
Levi, Margaret, 247, 255, 295
Lewis-Beck, Michael, 157, 167
liberalism/liberal, 144
    reforms, 226
    revolutions, 166, 296
    welfare state, 280
liberation campaigns, 211
libertarian values, 291
liberty aspirations, 223, 239, 241, 249, 257–62, 265, 296
Lieberman, Benjamin, 161
life-cycle effects, 94–101, 105
life expectancy, 24, 28, 108, 277
life satisfaction, 139, 140, 238, 257
Lijphart, Arend, 165, 281
Limongi, Fernando, 157, 168, 169, 171, 175, 218, 224
Linz, Juan, 165, 192, 196, 217
Lipset, Seymour Martin, 18, 19, 65, 160, 163, 285, 296
Lithuania, 87
Loayza, Norman, 277
Lockhart, Charles, 19
Loewenberg, Gerhard, 162
long-term trends, 115, 119
low-income societies, 57, 108, 111, 167, 213, 290
Lubell, M., 255
Luxembourg, 41, 85, 86

MacKuen, Michael, 237
Macpherson, Crawford, 175, 271
Mainwaring, Scott, 165
majority rule, 232
male monopoly of politics, 276, 278
Malthus, Thomas, 16

Manssens, Jan, 121, 294
Mark, Noah, 33, 38
Markoff, John, 166, 175, 218, 225
Marks, Gary, 165, 217, 218, 225, 226
Marshall, Monty, 152, 176
Marx, Karl, 1, 16, 19, 20, 288
Maslow, Abraham, 33, 139
mass approval, 286
mass culture, 165, 217, 220, 221
mass demonstrations, 123, 211, 218, 219
mass influences, 165
mass media, 226
mass movements, 121, 211, 217, 218
mass production, 34
mass values, 164, 165, 218, 300
Mastruzzi, Massimo, 154, 193, 279
materialists/materialist, 99, 103
    goals, 97
    values, 33, 54, 97, 101
materialist/postmaterialist values, 100
Mattes, Robert, 245, 268
McAdam, Douglas, 175, 211
McConkey, D., 121, 144, 290, 292
McDonagh, Eileen, 272, 281
McNeill, William, 15, 35, 204, 290, 296
measurement errors, 237
mechanical solidarity, 24, 135, 294
Merkel, Wolfgang, 149
Michels, Robert, 44, 262
middle class, 163, 166
middle-income societies, 57, 167, 213
Midlarski, Manus, 296
Miller, Arthur, 19, 263
Mishler, William, 245, 247
Mitchell, Jeremy, 204
mobilization regimes, 285
modernization, 1, 12, 76, 160, 171, 191, 211, 273, 280, 285, 286, 292, 299
modernization theory, 1–6, 15–18, 37–38, 160, 165, 167, 168, 285, 286
monocausality, 157
Monroe, Kristen, 142, 143
Montesquieu, Charles de, 245
Moore, Barrington, 17, 21, 36
Morocco, 85, 86
Muller, Edward, 159, 165, 167, 205, 246
multi-item index, 264
multinational corporations, 18
muscular strength, 277, 280
Mutz, Diana, 294

national culture, 52, 68
national-level values, 61
nationality, 70
Nazi Party, 162
Nazi support, 235
needs, nonmaterial, 98, 289, 291
neighbors, 294
nepotism, 192, 295

Netherlands, 40, 41, 101, 104, 121, 291
Nevitte, Neil, 157, 164, 261
New Democracies Barometer, 253, 263
New Russia Barometer, 263
Newton, Kenneth, 157, 245, 246, 247, 254
Nie, Norman, 164
Nigeria, 41, 129
Nolan, Patrick, 22, 35, 272, 277
Norris, Pippa, 8, 39, 44, 45, 117, 134, 157,
    164, 245, 247, 254, 262, 272, 273, 276,
    277, 278
North Korea, 175
North, Douglas, 15
Northern Italy, 163, 291
Nye, Joseph, 117

objective capabilities, 152
observed score, 83
occupied buildings, 123
O'Donnell, Guillermo, 18, 149, 154, 165, 168,
    211, 217, 224
oil-exporting countries, 45, 160
open-mindedness, 261
organic solidarity, 24, 135, 294
organizational machines, 262
Orthodox societies, 64, 109
Orwell, George, 21
Orwin, Clifford, 289
Ottaway, Marina, 149, 154
outgroups, 54, 136
    discrimination, 143
Owens, Timothy, 261
Oyserman, Daphna, 135, 136, 143

Page, Benjamin, 237
Pakistan, 113, 128, 210, 264
Pangle, Thomas, 289
participant orientations, 245
participation, 43, 44, 52, 56, 59, 116, 163,
    286
path analysis, 222
path dependence, 19, 20
patriarchic cultures, 275
Paxton, Pamela, 119, 149, 158, 175, 218, 225,
    246, 257, 284
peasant revolts, 296
people power, 119, 166, 175, 193, 227, 262
performance evaluations, 268
period effects, 38, 97, 101, 102, 111, 119, 132,
    294
personal deliverance, 291
Peru, 190
Petersen, Roger, 218, 277
petitions, 122, 124, 125, 261, 262, 294
Pettigrew, Thomas, 98, 157
Pharr, Susan, 117, 245, 252
Philippines, 64, 156, 210, 225
Poland, 126, 156, 166, 210, 215, 216
political action surveys, 117, 118, 121

politically correct language, 292
politics/political, 156, 157, 160, 209, 245, 246,
    258, 259, 286
    action, 116, 123, 294
    activism, 117
    change, 134
    leaders, 129
    liberties, 76, 159, 191, 194, 248, 287
    machines, 294
    participation, 164
    parties, 262
    protest, 98, 104, 116, 120, 161, 235
    rights, 192, 195, 225
    skills, 116
polity scores, 153, 176
Popper, Karl, 6, 143
postindustrial society, 20, 60, 118, 286, 296
postindustrialization, 27, 29, 30, 44
postmaterialism/postmaterialist, 104, 126, 248
    goals, 97
    issues, 104
    liberty aspirations, 159, 257, 258
    values, 33, 52, 97–106, 130, 239, 244
postmaterialists, 99, 101, 115, 116, 126
postmodern relativism, 292
postmodern spirit, 291
poverty, 107, 287, 298
Powell, G. Bingham, 17, 285
power, 19, 165, 197, 204
prayer, 26
preconditions, 224
predetermined behavior, 137
predicted score, 83
predictions, 6–7, 77–79, 81–92, 93
predictive formulas, 81
predictive model, 77
prevention focus, 143, 144
Pridham, Geoffrey, 210, 215
probabilistic relationship, 161
prodemocracy movements, 210
prodemocratic civic culture, 254
prodemocratic values, 159
progress, 300
promotion focus, 144
prostitution, 126
protest activities, 120, 218, 248
Protestantism/Protestant, 22, 36, 68, 205
    ethic, 71
    Europe, 65, 66, 80
    societies, 64, 69, 71, 135, 282
    tradition, 282
proximate cause, 218
Przeworski, Adam, 157, 165, 168, 169, 171,
    175, 217, 218, 224, 226, 233
public campaigns, 218
public consent, 223, 286
public morale, erosion of, 291
public welfare, 279
Puerto Rico, 87

Putnam, Robert D., 18, 21, 71, 116, 117, 121, 142, 143, 157, 163, 165, 245, 246, 247, 252, 254, 260, 262, 291, 294
Pye, Lucian, 17, 18, 19, 149, 285

quality of life, 31, 33, 97, 104
Quigley, Carroll, 288

Rahn, Wendy, 247
Ramirez, Francisco, 19, 286
Randall, Vicky, 17, 18, 215
random predictions, 84
rational risk calculations, 221
rationalization, 1, 76, 285, 286
reciprocal effects, 173
Red Army, 42, 170, 215
regime change, 169, 191, 213, 214, 215, 217, 225
regime stability, 217
regulatory focus theory, 143
Reilly, David, 196, 197
Reisinger, William, 19
religion/religious, 31, 46, 91, 285
  authority, 285
  dogmas, 27
  heritage, 281
  salvation, 291
  traditions, 64
  values, 21, 290
Renaissance, 291
rentier economies, 45
resource-mobilization theory, 211
revolutions, 16
revolutionary activists, 297
Rice, Tom, 64
rich countries, 287, 290
rights
  of gays and lesbians, 292
  to a job, 91
  of living beings, 292
risk, 32, 33
Robinson, William, 215, 231
Rocamora, J., 149, 215
Rohrschneider, Robert, 19
Rokeach, Milton, 23, 99, 143, 163, 261
Roman Catholic societies, 64
Roman Republic, 295
Romania, 113, 210
Rose, Richard, 111, 149, 174, 175, 193, 195, 245, 247, 253, 263, 272, 295
Rose-Ackerman, S., 255
Rosenberg, Morris, 261
Ross, Michael, 45, 170
Rössel, Jörg, 224
Rothstein, Bo, 247, 255
Rudolph, Thomas, 247
Rueschemeyer, Dietrich, 17, 36, 120, 224
rule of law, 193, 299
Russett, Bruce, 35

Russia, 113, 120, 159, 215, 216, 263
Russian public, 159, 165, 196, 246, 264
Ryan, Richard, 139

Sainsbury, Diane, 279
salvation, 36, 290
same-sex marriage, 40, 43, 214
Sandholtz, Wayne, 192, 195
Saudi Arabia, 211, 215
Scarbrough, Elinor, 164, 245
scarcity hypotheses, 97, 98, 99
Scarrow, Susan, 44
Schmitter, Phillippe, 159, 165, 168, 211, 217, 224
Schmuck, Peter, 139
Scholz, J. T., 255
Schwartz, Shalom, 136, 137, 138
science/scientific, 285
  knowledge, 38
  socialism, 20
  thought, 38
Scott, Jacqueline, 99, 272
secularism/secular, 75
  emancipation, 291
  ideologies, 29
  values, 69, 290
secularization thesis, 1, 5, 22, 25, 26, 58, 75, 285, 286
secular-rational values, 6, 20, 26, 27, 30, 37, 49, 57, 58, 76
security, 33, 98
segregationists, 232
Sekhon, Jasjeet, 235
self-expression, 23, 33, 43, 97, 137, 144, 254, 265
self-expression values, 1–3, 6–8, 12, 20, 26, 27–30, 37, 43, 45, 49, 54–61, 69, 76, 95, 105, 111, 121, 123, 129, 133, 134, 136–38, 143, 144, 149–56, 157, 158, 162, 163, 164–67, 170, 178, 185, 191, 196–203, 207, 208, 211, 212, 214, 219–29, 237, 248, 257, 265, 273, 282, 284, 285–87, 293, 295, 296, 299
self-expression values syndrome, 256, 259
self-fulfillment, 135
Seligson, Mitchell, 159, 165, 167, 205, 231, 233, 246, 247
Sen, Amartya, 22, 149, 175, 272, 286, 288, 289, 291
Seong, Kyoung-Ryung, 18
Serbia, 167, 216
Service, Elman, 277
service sector, 16, 58, 61, 67, 78
sexual division of labor, 277
sexual norms, 54, 126
Shapiro, Ian, 175, 237
Shuman, Howard, 99
Simmel, Georg, 24, 29, 163, 294
Singapore, 160, 175

skill levels, 116
slavery, 273, 293, 300
Slovakia, 126, 195
Slovenia, 126, 156, 167, 215, 216
Smith, Adam, 16
Smith, David, 17, 24, 37, 285
Sniderman, Paul, 157
Snow, David, 212
social capital, 116–18, 141, 142, 247–49, 254,
    262, 291–95
social-class voting, 104
social collapse, 96
social conformity, 52, 139, 271, 290
social-democratic welfare state, 280
social determinism, 165
social forces, 10, 211, 212, 224
social inequality, 205
social insurance, 138
social mobility, 36
social movements, 211, 218, 293, 294
social polarization, 204
socialization effects, 99, 102
socialization hypothesis, 98, 99
societal level, 10, 149, 164
societal-level linkages, 233, 234
societies, 1–6, 108, 110, 135
socioeconomic development, 25, 82, 151, 164,
    170, 171, 204, 213, 285, 287
socioeconomic resources, 182, 197, 203
solid democrats, 267
South Africa, 87, 156
South Korea, 18, 113, 156, 210, 215, 225
southern Italy, 163
Soviet empire, 66, 79
Soviet successor states, 38, 96, 109, 111, 120,
    159, 186
Soviet Union, 42, 96, 210, 215
Sowell, Thomas, 293
Spain, 39, 113
Spier, Fred, 26
spirituality/spiritual, 31, 32
    concerns, 30, 32
    life, 22
spuriousness, 178, 185
Starr, Harvey, 167, 197
state authority, 299
Stepan, Alfred, 193, 196, 217
Stephens, John, 17, 36, 224
Stevenson, Mark, 19
Stiglitz, Joseph, 192, 279
Stimson, James, 237
Stinchcomb, Arthur, 19
Stoker, Laura, 247, 255
Stokes, Randall, 157, 160, 169, 213
Stokes, Susan, 157, 160, 169, 213
subject orientations, 245, 286
subjective motivations, 152
sub-Saharan Africa, 80, 81
subsistence societies, 27

successor generations, 226
sudden breakthroughs, 41
suffrage, 59, 286, 295, 296
suicide, 52
Sullivan, J. L., 144, 157
suppression costs, 218
survival, 23, 28, 37, 49, 54, 98, 142, 286, 297
    concerns, 300
    values, 6, 54, 56, 57, 105, 107, 123, 133,
        142, 143, 161, 208
survival/self-expression dimension, 50, 52, 79,
    115, 131
survival/self-expression values, 73, 81, 83, 86,
    110, 136, 144
Sweden, 65, 87, 113, 221
Switzerland, 121
system support, 247, 249
system-level effects, 246
Szelenyi, Ivan, 226

Taagepera, Rein, 192, 195
Taiwan, 18, 166, 226
Tanzania, 85, 86, 113, 221
Tarrow, Sidney, 175
taxation without representation, 296
Taylor, Michelle, 165, 175, 211, 217, 224, 226,
    227
Tedin, Kent, 19, 245
temporal order, 178, 185
terrorism, 297
Teune, Henry, 233
Theobald, Robin, 17, 18, 215
theocratic rule, 156
theological questions, 31
Third Wave of democratization, 9, 121, 149,
    165–67, 174, 176, 185, 190, 213, 217,
    225
Thompson, John, 156, 289
Tiananmen Square, 190, 225
Tilly, Charles, 36, 166, 175, 210, 211, 218,
    279
time-series analysis, 213, 214
time-series evidence, 95
Tocqueville, Alexis de, 254
Toffler, Alvin, 19
tolerance, 56, 223, 238, 242, 248
    of homosexuality, 129, 130, 257, 273
    of outgroups, 258, 273
Tönnies, Ferdinand, 24, 29, 135, 163, 294
Tooby, John, 23, 288
Torres, John, 18
torture, 293, 300
totalitarianism, 285
trade-union membership, 118
tradition/traditional, 4, 15–18, 76
    community, 294
    religious beliefs, 27
    role limitations, 273
    values, 6, 19, 49, 57

traditional vs. secular-rational dimensions, 50
traditional vs. secular-rational values, 8, 52, 73, 79, 80, 81, 83, 86
Transue, J. E., 144, 157
Triandis, Harry, 135, 136
Tronto, Joan, 279
trust, 21, 131, 143, 223, 247
  interpersonal, 71, 130, 247–49, 256, 257, 260
  intimate, 143
trustworthiness, 247, 255
Turkey, 128, 156, 159
Tverdova, Yulia, 247
Tyler, T. R., 255

Uganda, 85, 86, 87
UN Human Development Report, 289
UN Millennium Goals, 298
United States, 47, 50, 65, 89, 91, 103, 113, 121, 161, 210, 215, 264, 298
universal aspirations, 288, 289
university education, 221
unofficial strikes, 123
Uruguay, 156
Uslaner, Eric, 255

Valenzuela, Arturo, 165
value change, 33, 34, 99
value priorities, 99, 221, 285
values surveys, 6–7, 31, 40, 48–50, 62, 63, 77, 81, 86, 88, 103, 117, 118, 121, 158, 263
van Deth, Jan, 245
Van Vechten, R., 142
Vanhanen, Tatu, 180, 215
Vanhanen index, 153
Vargas Cullel, Jorge, 149, 154
Venezuela, 190
Verba, Sidney, 17, 19, 71, 157, 162, 164, 186, 245, 248, 285, 286
Vermeil, Edmond, 161
vertical ties, 72
vertical trust, 260, 261
Vietnam, 85, 86, 155, 211
voluntary associations, 247, 254
Von Barloewen, Wolf, 288
voting, 118

Walgrave, Stefan, 121, 294
Wallace, Michael, 17
Wallerstein, Immanuel, 17, 204
war on terrorism, 297
Washington consensus, 210
Watanuki, Joji, 117, 247, 250, 291
Wattenberg, Martin, 44, 117
wealth, distribution of, 205
Weber, Max, 1, 19, 21, 37, 64, 76, 135, 281
Weimar Germany, 161, 162, 166
Weiner, Myron, 17, 285
welfare state, 28, 29, 98, 102, 278–80, 284
well-being
  maximization of, 295
  subjective, 54, 111, 139, 141, 223, 248, 259, 265, 288
Welzel, Christian, 2, 44, 149, 155, 158, 164, 168, 232, 235, 257, 262, 272, 273, 276, 277
Wermuth, Nanny, 178
Wessels, Bernhard, 249, 294
West Germany, 39, 87, 101, 104, 112, 121
Western cultural standards, 273, 289
Western ethnocentrism, 293
Western societies, 133, 140
Westernization, 47
Whitehead, Laurence, 197, 215
Whyte, William, 27, 34
will of the people, 232
Wittfogel, Karl, 35
women in parliament, 277
women's movement, 52
women's rights, 282, 292
working-class authoritarianism, 296
World Bank, 154, 193
world systems, 18
World Values Survey, 7, 83, 92
World War I, 161
World War II, 102, 113, 162
worship, 27
Wrangham, Richard, 277

xenophobia, 4, 142, 144, 162, 297

Yugoslavia, 128, 167

Zelikow, Phillip, 117
Zimbabwe, 85, 86, 113